D1156620

An illustrated Dictionary of

# Chess

Edward R. Brace

Introduction by

**Svetozar Gligorić**

*International Grandmaster*

HAMLYN

First published in 1977 by
The Hamlyn Publishing Group Limited
a division of
The Octopus Publishing Group
Michelin House
81 Fulham Road
London SW3 6RB
and distributed for them by
Octopus Distribution Services
Rushden
Northamptonshire NN10 9RZ

Reprinted 1989



ISBN 0 600 32920 8

Printed in Czechoslovakia
**50413**

# Author's Preface

*An Illustrated Dictionary of Chess* contains well over 2,000 separate entries, covering all aspects of the game. Here in one continuous alphabetical listing are clear definitions of all chess terms, phrases, openings, defences, variations, systems and about 600 biographical entries – including International Grandmasters, International Masters, and a generous selection of other players and writers who have contributed significantly to our enjoyment and understanding of chess. Definitions are given for all terms used in Fairy Chess (and other variants), chess problems and endgame studies. All major tournaments are listed under the venue and year of play – e.g., 'New York (1924)'. A representative sample of the more interesting and useful books about chess and chess players is included, as well as films and novels with a chess motif.

In its treatment of major entries, such as all the world chess champions and other outstanding players, *An Illustrated Dictionary of Chess* is truly encyclopedic. Every player who in 1976 held the title International Grandmaster or International Master is listed, together with the dates they received their titles, details of their major tournament successes, and years of entry in the various chess olympiads. One of the most useful features of the dictionary is the extensive use of cross-references, which are invaluable in locating a major or minor associated entry or in gaining ancillary information.

Where appropriate, the characteristic or defining move or moves of an opening or defence or variation are indicated in italics in the text of an entry. A few entries have been included merely because they are amusing or curious ('Frankenstein-Dracula Variation' is a good example) or because they have been coined by a chess expert, although rarely, if ever, used. The vast majority of the terms defined, however, have been or currently are in regular use and form an important part of the specialized chess terminology that this dictionary attempts to define and clarify for readers of all ages and playing strengths.

As author of this work, I must assume total responsibility for the choice and content of all entries. This project would have been impossible, however, without the research and editorial contributions of Glyn Thomas and William R. Hartston (a well-known chess author and International Master, who kindly agreed to act as the advisory editor). In addition, I must acknowledge the helpful cooperation and assistance provided by the British Chess Federation and the United States Chess Federation (particular thanks go to Martin E. Morrison, Technical Director of the U.S.C.F.).

*An Illustrated Dictionary of Chess* was designed to be an indispensable reference work as well as providing endless hours of enjoyable browsing. We believe you will find that nothing quite like it exists in such a handy lexicographic format, or can compete with its general coverage of chess.

**Edward R. Brace**

# Introduction

Since the middle of the 19th century chess has become a matter of personal challenge and international competition. Long before then, however, leading chess players had tried to accumulate knowledge about the game and to discover the specific laws of logic which govern chess. Comprising elements of science, art and sports, the game of chess has intrigued many a great mind. A vast amount of experience and theory has been gathered; this shows no signs of becoming exhausted and the game continues to attract the attention of millions of people throughout the world.

Nowadays we have hundreds of chess books about different systems, about openings and variations or other phases of the game (middle game and endgame); about individuals who, by their way of thinking in chess, have influenced generations; about champions and players with international titles; about matches and tournaments, different kinds of competitions, chess compositions, studies and problems, the history of chess, schools of thought, etc.

All these books are available on the various aspects of the game. But because of the scope of chess, few individual books exist that provide access to a wide variety of topics. One would normally have to go to the library, spend much time, and look in many different books to find information on specific items of interest. As a matter of fact, there is virtually no other book available which gives comprehensive information in concise form about every topic that might interest the player, referee, organizer, instructor, journalist, lecturer, writer or other chess devotee.

The only solution is *An Illustrated Dictionary of Chess*. Here in one book we have entries on chess history, biographies of all important past and present players, entries on F.I.D.E. and other tournaments, grading systems, the theory of openings with names of lines in current and past use, chess composition, major venues of important international events, expressions used in chess, strategy and tactics, initials, abbreviations, etc. – all in alphabetical order.

Such a book could also be useful as a general guide to chess, but it is more than that. It is, in fact, a guide to chess culture, embracing the wide range and variety of knowledge that this term implies.

A chess dictionary cannot replace a monograph or a chess book dealing with specific and important subjects. Any one such subject would need several books by itself. *An Illustrated Dictionary of Chess* is an attempt to diminish the existing gap between the huge amount of literature published about chess and the lack of books giving general information about the game and all its aspects.

**Svetozar Gligorić**

# A

**Aaron, Manuel** (b. 1935) Indian chess player; awarded the title International Master in 1961, which he gained by qualifying for the 1962 interzonal tournament. (1976 Elo rating: 2295)

**Aben-Ezra** (1119–1174) twelfth-century Jewish rabbi, writer and chess player, also known as Abraham, son of Mayer-Ezra. His many writings (mainly on religion, poetry, grammar, astronomy and medicine) included *Charusim al sechok Shahmath* (Verses on the Game of Chess). He was born in Spain and died on the island of Rhodes, but his remains were later removed to Palestine.

**Abonyi Gambit** another name for the **Zukertort Gambit.**

**Abrahams, Gerald** (b. 15 April 1907) British author and barrister, born in Liverpool. Among his books on chess are *Teach Yourself Chess, Technique in Chess, The Chess Mind* and *Not Only Chess*. He has also written a book on bridge and several books on law and politics.

**Absolute Champion** a chess title awarded in the U.S.S.R. in 1941 to the victor in a special match-tournament designed to incorporate the best features of both match and tournament play. The title was won by Mikhail Botvinnik, who finished ahead of the Soviet Masters Boleslavsky, Bondarevsky, Keres, Lilienthal and Smyslov. See **match-tournament.**

**Accelerated Fianchetto 1.** a variation of the Sicilian Defence which arises either by: 1. P–K4, P–QB4 2. N–KB3, *P–KN3* or by: 1. P–K4, P–QB4 2. N–KB3, N–QB3 3. P–Q4, P×P 4. N×P, *P–KN3.*

**2.** an uncommon name for a variation of the Queen's Gambit Accepted: 1. P–Q4, P–Q4 2. P–QB4, P×P 3. N–KB3, N–KB3 4. P–K3, P–K3 5. B×P, P–B4 6. O–O, P–QR3 7. Q–K2, *P–QN4* 8. B–N3, *B–N2*.

**Accelerated Meran** an opening sequence arising out of the Slav Defence to the Queen's Gambit Declined: 1. P–Q4, P–Q4 2. P–QB4, P–QB3 3. N–KB3, N–B3 4. N–B3, P–K3 5. P–K3, *P–QR3*. Black delays developing his Queen Knight in favour of a swifter Queen-side pawn advance than normal. Common continuations are: 6. B–Q3, and 6. P–B5. See **Meran Defence.**

**accelerated pairing system** a modification of the Swiss System by which the number of tournament frontrunners is reduced in as few rounds as possible. A typical example occurs when low-scoring players with high ratings are matched against high-scoring players with low ratings; in this way, ties are eliminated even more quickly than is usual under the Swiss System.

**accumulation, theory of** a policy advocating moves that seize and retain advantages, no matter how small, in preference to moves made with more ambitious motives. It was first propounded by Steinitz.

Chernev has written, 'It is more consistent with a common-sense approach to win by accumulating little advantages to strengthen one's own position gradually while undermining that of the opponent than to seek to overwhelm him with bewildering combinations and venturesome sacrificial attacks'.

**active** **1.** relating to a move that is more aggressive than any alternative. **2.** relating to a piece that is more mobile than its counterpart on the other side. An active Bishop is unimpeded by pawns. Compare **passive.**

**Adams Gambit** an opening sequence arising out of the Vienna Game: 1. P–K4, P–K4 2. N–QB3, N–KB3 3. B–B4, N×P 4. Q–R5, N–Q3 5. B–N3, N–B3 6. *P–Q4*. The most common continuation is: 6 . . ., N×P, accepting the gambit in the belief that it is unsound. This variation was invented by the American player Weaver Adams. Compare **Frankenstein-Dracula Variation.**

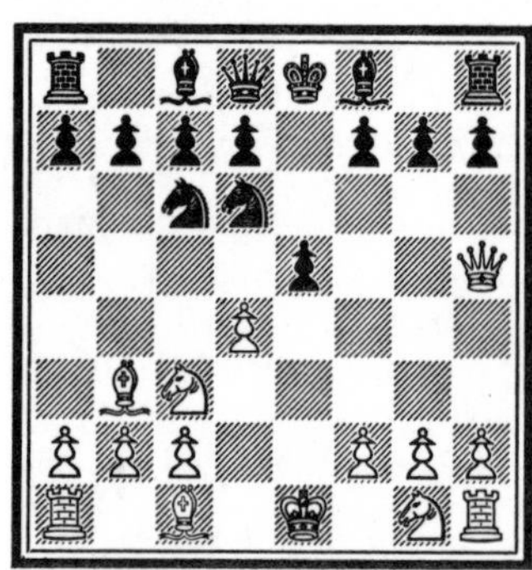

Position after 6. P–Q4

**Adamski, Jan** (b. 11 November 1943) Polish chess player; awarded the title International Master in 1976. (1976 Elo rating: 2415)

**adjourn** to postpone an unfinished game allowing time for the analysis of the position by each player.

**adjournment** the postponement of an unfinished game allowing the players time to rest and analyse the position. In international chess, games are adjourned after five hours of play (usually after playing at sixteen moves per hour). At the adjournment the player with the move will seal it and hand it to the tournament official. In this way, neither player can be absolutely certain what the position will be when it is his turn to move again. This uncertainty can badly affect a player's form in other games, since adjournments are normally allowed to continue while other rounds are played. It was called 'the agony that accompanies an adjourned game' by the Soviet Grandmaster, Paul Keres, who eloquently described how any adjournment, in no matter what position, affects the player's temperament and forces him to devote precious time in analysis that might ultimately be useless. These are some of the reasons why it has occasionally been suggested that adjournments should be abolished at this level. Another important reason is that the outcome of the game would be less likely to be decided by the analyses of colleagues. Capablanca proposed that games should begin in the morning rather than the afternoon so allowing any adjournment to last only for the lunch-break, but this would find favour with few modern masters.

**adjudicate** to determine the nominal winner of an unfinished chess game by judging the probable result given best play on both sides.

**adjudication** the determination of the nominal winner of an unfinished chess game by a qualified judge, tournament official, etc., based on the probable result, given best play on both sides. It occurs mainly in situations such as club play, where limited time prohibits completion of a game. It occurs only rarely in serious international competition.

**adjust** to touch or move a chessman without the intention of making an official move. This intention must be stated by the player before he touches the piece or pawn. See **j'adoube, touch-move**.

**adjustment** the touching or moving of a chessman without the intention of making an official move, or the state or condition of the adjusted piece or pawn.

**advanced pawn** any pawn in the opponent's half of the board. Such a pawn can disrupt the opponent's defence by driving pieces from their best squares, hamper movement from one wing to another of the defender's pieces (increasing the likelihood of success of a flank attack), and can control important squares to act as support-points for the attacker's pieces. If the advanced pawn is also a passed pawn it can become very threatening indeed.

**Advance Variation** **1.** a line in the French Defence in which White advances his King pawn at move three instead of developing a piece to defend it: 1. P–K4, P–K3 2. P–Q4, P–Q4 3. *P–K5*.

**2.** an unusual line against the Caro-Kann characterized by the moves: 1. P–K4, P–QB3 2. P–Q4, P–Q4 3. *P–K5*. This was played by Tal against Botvinnik on several occasions in their 1961 world title match, but without conspicuous success.

***Adventure of Chess, The*** a book by the U.S. International Master Edward Lasker on the history and development of the game, together with articles on topics such as chess and the arts and the prospects for computer chess. There are also reminiscences on some of the great players that Lasker has met (including his namesake). It was first published in 1949 and uses descriptive notation.

**aesthetic effect in chess** the pleasure or delight derived from a chess game, especially one in which economy of moves is coupled with one or more brilliant moves (such as the unexpected sacrifice of a major piece to gain a deciding positional advantage or render checkmate in the following move or forced series of moves).

**Ahues, Carl Oscar** (1883–1968) West German chess player; born on 26 December 1883 and died on 31 December 1968. He was awarded the title International Master in 1950. Ahues was German Champion in 1929 and represented Germany in the 1930 and 1931 Chess Olympiads.

**Ajeeb** ostensibly a chessplaying automaton, constructed by Charles Arthur Hopper, an Englishman, in 1868. It was a larger than life-size figure of an Egyptian, operated by a player of small physique concealed inside it. The mechanism was much less ingenious than that of the **Turk**. For instance, the hidden player would watch the game through a peephole near Ajeeb's naval, while the player hidden inside the Turk had no direct view of the game at all. Nevertheless Ajeeb was outstandingly successful. It toured throughout the United Kingdom and Europe, drawing large crowds: over 100,000 people visited Ajeeb when it was exhibited at Castan's Panopticum in Berlin. In 1885 it was taken to the United States where it was equally successful. Ensconced at the Eden Musée, a New York amusement arcade and waxworks, it took on all comers including O. Henry and Sarah Bernhardt. It was almost always victorious, which is not surprising since its operators were strong players such as Albert B. Hodges and Harry Nelson Pillsbury. Indeed, Marshall's first game against Pillsbury was played when the latter was manipulating Ajeeb. In 1915 the Eden Musée closed down and Ajeeb was transferred to Coney Island where it stayed until its retirement in 1925. After this it was seen only infrequently, although it toured the United States again in 1936, promoting Radio Corporation of America. Compare **Mephisto, Turk.**

**Alapin, Semyon Zonovyevich** (1856–1923) Russian chess player and theorist; born in Vilna on 7 November 1856. While studying at St Petersburg Engineering Institute he tied with Tchigorin for first place at the tournament of 1878, but lost the playoff. Later results included sixth place at Berlin (1897) and fifth place at Monte Carlo (1901). He won a match against Von Bardeleben in 1893 (+3 −1 =1), and drew another against Schlechter in 1899 (+1 −1 =4). Alapin was a noted analyst of the openings.

**Alapin's Opening** the opening: 1. P–K4, P–K4 2. *N–K2*. The Knight blocks lines of the Bishop and Queen and is itself awkwardly placed. Black should equalize easily.

**Alatortsev, Vladimir** (b. 14 May 1909) Soviet chess player; awarded the titles International Master in 1950 and International Judge in 1953. He came second in the 1933 Soviet Championship, was Champion of Leningrad in 1934 and was Champion of Moscow in 1936 and 1937. In 1938 he won the Soviet Trade Union Championship.

**Albin, Adolph** (1848–1920) Austrian chess writer and player. Noted mainly for his sharp defence to the Queen's Gambit. See **Albin Counter Gambit.**

**Albin Counter Gambit** an opening sequence in which Black

immediately declines the pawn offered by White in the Queen's Gambit. In this version of the Queen's Gambit Declined, Black counters White's move by offering his King's pawn: 1. P–Q4, P–Q4  2. P–QB4, *P–K4*. It was named after Adolph Albin, the Austrian chess player who invented it.

**Alburt, Lev** (b. 21 August 1946) Soviet chess player; awarded the title International Master in 1976. (1976 Elo rating: 2520)

**Alcoholic Chess** an absurd game played on a large board, with glasses or bottles of alcoholic drink replacing the chessmen. If the opponent's 'man' is captured, the drink it represents must be consumed by the capturer before play proceeds. B. H. Wood (in *A History of Chess*, for which he edited the English translation) relates the story that Lasker is said to have won such a game 'by sacrificing his queen in ridiculous fashion at the very outset of the game. The queen contained about a quarter litre of cognac; quaffing this seriously incapacitated his opponent in the ensuing complications.'

**Alekhine, Alexander** (1892–1946) World Champion 1927–1935 and from 1937 to his death; born in Moscow, the son of an aristocratic family (Russian name: **Aleksandr Aleksandrovich Alekhin**). He moved to Paris in 1921 and became a naturalized French citizen in 1925, the same year that he received a doctorate in law from the Sorbonne. He never practiced law, however, because of his passion for chess.

In his first international tournament (Hamburg, 1910) he tied for seventh place, although he was first in the Stockholm tournament of 1912 and two years later tied with Nimzovitch for the Russian Championship and came fourth in the St Petersburg tournament. In 1920 he won the Russian Championship. Alekhine was slow to develop as a master player, but from 1921 his successes in many great tournaments made him the logical choice to meet Capablanca in a match for the World Championship in 1927. By that time he had played 406 games in a total of 31 major tournaments, winning 235, drawing 119 and losing only 51. He took first prize 14 times and equal first on four of these occasions.

The match with Capablanca (1927) went to 34 games. At that time it was generally considered that Capablanca was virtually invincible; however, much to the surprise of the chess world, Alekhine won by a margin of three games (+6 −3 =25). Several promises were made to permit Capablanca a chance to regain the title, but to Alekhine's discredit these promises were never honoured.

There is no doubt that Alekhine was one of the greatest chess players of all time. Unlike the cool and calculating Capablanca, who sought to simplify by exchanging pieces early in the game, the new World Champion thrived on complicated positions and the beauty involved in working out potential or actual combinations in unlikely situations. To him chess was truly an art and he enriched the game by being one of its most profound artists.

From 1927 until 1939, Alekhine played in 33 major tournaments and took first (or equal first) prize 20 times. His loss of the World

Championship in 1935 to Dr Max Euwe (+8 −9 =13) was blamed by many, including Alekhine, on his alcoholic excesses. The shock of losing the chess crown determined him to control his drinking habits and go into intensive training, devouring and memorizing every important game Dr Euwe had ever played. In the rematch of 1937, Alekhine became the first man ever to regain the World Championship title which he then held until his death. The score was impressive (+10 −4 =11).

Alekhine had very few, if any, close friends and a black cloud hangs over much of his personal life. The details are somewhat confused but it seems that he collaborated with the Nazis during World War II by writing two articles for German publications that were violently anti-Jewish. After the war he at first disclaimed authorship, later claiming that he was forced to write the articles because he feared for the safety of his wife, who was in the hands of the Germans in occupied France.

In summing up the dazzling chess career of Alekhine, Hugh Alexander has stated, 'Whether or not Alekhine at his best was better than Capablanca, Lasker or Morphy at their respective bests no one knows or can ever know, and it does not matter; what does matter, and is undeniable, is that Alekhine was one of the very greatest players who has ever lived, and that his games have a beauty and fascination entirely of their own.'

Alekhine's life was dominated by chess and he spent every spare moment analyzing games on a pocket set. It is claimed that one was found in his lap when he died (near Lisbon, 23 March 1946) alone, friendless, and without enough money even to buy cigarettes.

**Alekhine-Chatard Attack** an opening sequence arising out of the French Defence: 1. P–K4, P–K3 2. P–Q4, P–Q4 3. N–QB3, N–KB3 4. B–KN5, B–K2 5. P–K5, KN–Q2 6. *P–KR4*. Black can

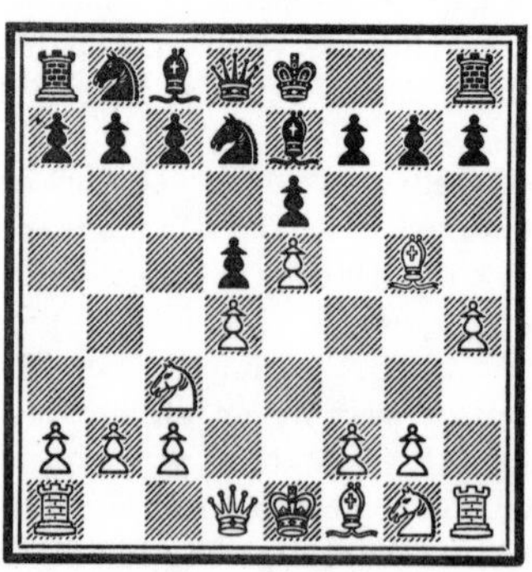

Position after 6. P–KR4

accept the offer of the pawn by: 6 . . ., B×B 7. P×B, Q×P, but in return White obtains a fierce attack and can develop with a gain of tempo by attacking the Black Queen. The most common continuation is: 6 . . ., P–QB4. This variation was introduced by Albin in a game against Czank (1897) and was revived in the early years of the century by Eugène Chatard (1850–1924), a Parisian amateur player who used it regularly in games in the Café de la Régence. It came to prominence when adopted by Alekhine at Mannheim (1914).

**Alekhine Memorial Tournament** a tournament in memory of Alexander Alekhine which has been held at irregular intervals in Moscow. The first, in 1956, was jointly won by Mikhail Botvinnik and Vassily Smyslov, with 11 points out of 16. The second, in 1971, was won by Anatoly Karpov and Leonid Stein, with 11 points out of 17. The third, in 1975, was won by Efim Geller with 10½ points out of 15, followed by Boris Spassky with 10 points.

***Alekhine's Best Games of Chess 1938–45*** a collection of 42 of Alekhine's best games compiled by C. H. O'D. Alexander. It covers the period immediately before the Second World War and the years Alekhine spent in Europe during the war. It was first published in 1949 and uses descriptive notation. See ***My Best Games of Chess 1908–23, My Best Games of Chess 1924–37, 100 Instructive Games of Alekhine***.

**Alekhine's Defence** a defence to the King's pawn opening: 1. P–K4, *N–KB3*. Black's basic idea is to encourage a wholesale advance of White's pawns in driving away the Knight, after which the pawns are often made targets for attack. Although this defence was made popular by a World Champion, Alexander Alekhine, in less experienced hands it often leads to a favourable position for White. White's usual immediate reply: 2. P–K5.

**Alekhine Variation** a variation occurring in the Queen's Gambit Declined, arising out of the Orthodox Defence: 1. P–Q4, P–Q4 2. P–QB4, P–K3 3. N–QB3, N–KB3 4. B–N5, B–K2 5. P–K3, O–O; 6. N–B3, QN–Q2 7. R–B1, P–B3 8. B–Q3, P×P 9. B×P, N–Q4 10. B×B, Q×B 11. *N–K4*. It was named after Alexander Alekhine, who first played this line in 1927 during a match with Capablanca.

**Aleppo Gambit** an older name for the **Queen's Gambit**. According to Staunton (*Handbook of Chess*), this name is derived 'from its having been the favourite game of Stamma, of Aleppo.' (Aleppo is a town in NW Syria.)

**Alexander, Conel Hugh O'Donel** (1909–74) British chess player and writer; awarded the title International Master in 1950. Former British Champion (1938, 1956). His books include *Alekhine's Best Games of Chess 1938–45, Chess, Learn Chess* (co-author), *Fischer-Spassky – Reykjavik 1972*, and *A Book of Chess*.

**Alexander Memorial Tournament** a tournament in memory of C. H. O'D. Alexander that was held in Middlesbrough, Cleveland in September 1975. It was the strongest tournament to be held in the United Kingdom since Nottingham (1936) and was graded by FIDE as being category 12. The tournament was won by Geller with 9½ points out of 14 followed by Smyslov with 8½ points. The brilliancy prize was won by Bronstein for his win against Keene. The high proportion of draws (68%) was the most disappointing feature of the event. A more pleasing result was the attainment of a second *norm* by Michael Stean, so qualifying him as an International Master.

**Alexandria, Nana** (b. 13 December 1949) Soviet female chess player; awarded the title International Woman Grandmaster in 1976. She was Soviet reserve at the 1969 Women's Olympiad and in 1975 defeated Levitina in the final of the Candidates' matches (+4 −3 =10), but was defeated by Gaprindashvili in the World Championship match (+2 −8 =1). (1976 Elo rating: 2340)

**al-fil** *Arabic for* elephant. English equivalent: Bishop. See **Bishop**.

**Alfonso manuscript** a manuscript written for Alfonso X of Castile that was completed in 1283. It describes the chess of that time and gives 103 problems mainly drawn from older Muslim sources. There are also other sections on backgammon games, dice games, variants of chess, and miscellaneous games. An archaic form of descriptive notation is used. The manuscript is now at the Monastery of St Lorenzo del Escorial near Madrid. The Spanish text on chess is given in H. J. R. Murray's *History of Chess*.

**Alfred Wolf Gambit** an opening sequence arising out of the Réti Opening: 1. N–KB3, P–Q4 *2. P–B4*. With this offer of a pawn, which can be won back immediately, White attempts to destroy Black's centre. Black has several satisfactory replies.

This opening was devised by the Viennese master after whom it is named. Also called **Landstrasse Gambit**.

**algebraic notation** a system of notation in which each square on the board is identified by a grid system. Each file is assigned a letter and each rank is assigned a number. In this way every square is uniquely

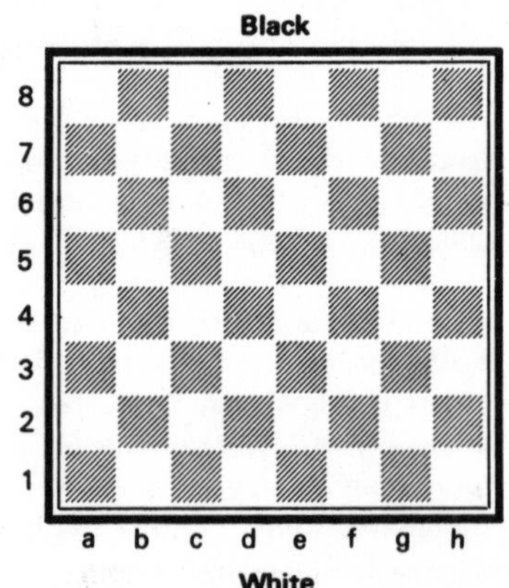


Alphanumeric coordinates for algebraic notation

identified by a combination of letter and number. Viewed from White's side of the board, the files from left to right are lettered from a to h and the ranks numbered 1 to 8 working from bottom to top.

In full algebraic a move is written down by giving the sign or symbol of the piece, its initial square and its final square. The pawns are not represented by any signs or symbols and a pawn move is shown by writing down the two squares on which the pawn begins and ends its move, e.g. e2–e4 is the notation for P–K4. Captures are indicated by either : or x. A check is shown by +, double check is shown by ++ and checkmate is shown by # or mate. The symbols for castling are O–O and O–O–O as in descriptive notation. Thus the opening: 1. P–K4, P–Q4 2. P×P, Q×P 3. N–QB3, Q–QR4 would be shown by: 1. e2–e4, d7–d5 2. e4×d5, Qd8×d5 3. Nb1–c3, Qd5–a5.

Condensed algebraic differs only in that the starting square is omitted unless this is ambiguous. The above opening would be noted: 1. e4, d5 2. exd5, Qxd5 3. Nc3, Qa5.

Algebraic notation has several advantages over descriptive notation. It is more concise, less open to ambiguity and internationally understood. Its superiority is so great that from 1980 it will be the only system of notation officially recognized by FIDE. However, it has not been used in this book, as descriptive notation is still the prevalent system among most players in the United Kingdom and the United States.

**Algemeene Vereeniging voor Radio Omroep** *Dutch for* General Dutch Radio Company: the sponsors of the last major international chess tournament held before World War II. See **Avro (1938)**.

**Allgaier Gambit** an opening sequence arising out of the King's Gambit: 1. P–K4, P–K4 2. P–KB4, P×P 3. N–KB3, P–KN4 4. P–KR4, P–N5 5. *N–N5*. Black's position is usually felt to be superior. The most common continuation is: 5 . . ., P–KR3. This gambit was invented by the German chess player Johann Allgaier and was later popularized by Lionel Kieseritzky. Also called **Allgaier-Kieseritzky Gambit.**

**Allgaier, Johann** (1763–1823) German chess player and writer. He was the author of the first chess primer to be written in German, *Neue Theoretisch-Praktische Anweisung* which was published in 1795.

Allgaier was small in stature and was the secret operator of the **Turk** for several years, including 1809 when it played and defeated Napoleon.

**all-play-all** see **round-robin.**

**Alter** pseudonym of the Reverend John Owen.

**amateur** **1.** any player whose principal occupation is not chess. Unlike many other games there has never been a rigid distinction between amateur and professional players; both categories have been entitled to receive monetary prizes at tournaments. The difficulty of distinguishing between amateurs and professionals led to chess being excluded from the eighth Olympic Games (Paris, 1924) and provided the stimulus for the creation of the Chess Olympiads in which both amateurs and professionals compete.

**2.** a euphemism for a weak player.

Compare **professional.**

**Amateur World Champion** a title that was awarded in the early Chess Olympiads to the winner of an individual tournament open only to amateur players. The title was first won by Mattison of Latvia in the unofficial 1924 Chess Olympiad. The second and last holder of the title was Dr Euwe, who gained it at the 1928 Chess Olympiad. It was at this event that it was decided to end discrimination between amateur and professional chess players and the title was abolished.

**amaurosis scacchistica** chess blindness. The term was coined by Tarrasch, a doctor, in an effort to explain blunders that occur when a glaringly evident resource goes unperceived. Amaurosis scacchistica will normally decide the games between novices, but it can be found at all levels of play. For instance, Tarrasch used the term to explain, scathingly, some of his blunders in his world championship match with Lasker. A well-known example is seen in the game between Popiel and Marco at Monte Carlo (1902).

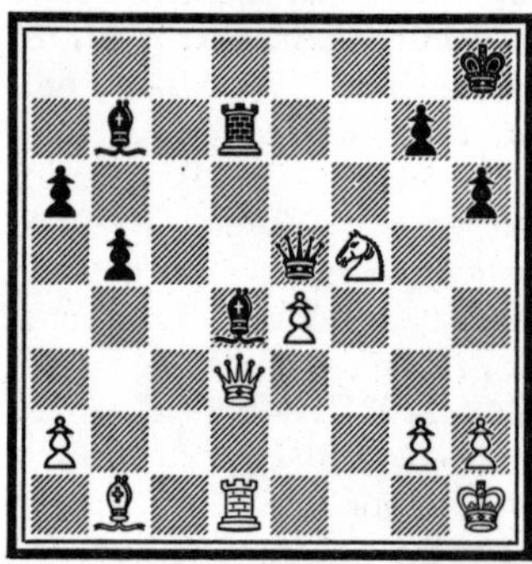

Popiel vs. Marco (Monte Carlo, 1902)

Believing that he had to lose the Bishop, Black resigned. In fact he had a forced win by: 1 . . ., B–N8! (threatening mate) 2. K × B, R × Q 3. B × R, B × P 4. B × B, Q × B.

A startling example of amaurosis scacchistica struck the future world champion Tigran Petrosian when he played Bronstein in the Candidates' tournament (1956). He simply overlooked that his Queen was attacked by a Knight and lost it! A third example, dubbed the 'mistake of the century', was seen in Skopje (1976) in the game between Rafael Vaganian and Rista Nicevski. Vaganian failed to notice a one-move checkmate and made a move that still allowed it to be delivered. (Although he resigned before it happened).

While these aberrations are galling to their perpetrators and blemishes on many otherwise beautiful games they undoubtedly cause a warm glow inside weak players everywhere. If asked how he did, a player who blundered away piece after piece can always truthfully reply, 'Why I played like a Grandmaster!'

**Amazon** a Fairy chesspiece that possesses the powers of both the Queen and the Knight. It is thus a type of Combined Chessman.

Although this piece is now seen only in Fairy Chess it was once used in orthodox chess as well. During the Middle Ages in many parts of Europe the Queen could also move like a Knight and in fact retained this power until the eighteenth century in Russia.

**American** *another name* (especially in Europe) *for* **round-robin** or **all-play-all.**

**American Championship** see **United States Championship, United States Open Championship, New York (1857).**

**American Chess Bulletin** an American chess periodical that was devoted to all aspects of chess, national and international. It was founded in 1904 by Herman Helms (1870–1963).

***Analysis of the Muzio Gambit*** a book by Ghulem Kassin and James Cochrane. It was the first work to be devoted to a single opening. It was first published in Madras, India in 1829.

**Anastasia's Mate** a mate of a castled King following the sacrifice of the Queen for a pawn. From the diagram play continues: 1. N–K7ch, K–R1 2. Q×Pch, K×Q 3. R–R1mate.

Representative position for Anastasia's Mate

This combination appeared in the German novel, *Anastasia und das Schachspiel, Briefe aus Italien* by Wilhelm Heinse (1749–1803) which was first published in 1803.

**anchor-ring** a type of Fairy chessboard which combines the characteristics of both the vertical and the horizontal cylinders, i.e., not only do the first and eighth ranks join, but also the two Rook files. This means that the Queen has eight routes by which it can return to its starting point, while the Rook and the Bishop both have four different routes. The anchor-ring is normally symbolized by a diagram which has no edges. See **Cylinder Chess.** Compare **horizontal cylinder, vertical cylinder.**

**Andersen, Börge** (b. 19 March 1934) Danish chess player; awarded the title International Master in 1964. He was Danish Champion in 1967 and 1968 and competed in the Chess Olympiads of 1954, 1958, 1964 and 1966. (1976 Elo rating: 2380)

**Anderson, Frank Ross** (b. 3 January 1928) Canadian chess player; awarded the title International Master in 1954. He was Canadian Champion in 1953 and 1955. Anderson competed in the Chess Olympiads of 1954, 1958 and 1964. In the 1954 Olympiad he obtained the best result on second board (+13 −2 =2) and repeated this feat in 1958 (+9 −1 =3). In the 1958 Olympiad he needed merely to play in the last round to obtain the minimum number of games necessary for the award of the title of International Grandmaster. The result of the game was irrelevant since Anderson would have obtained the title even if he had lost, but unfortunately he was unable to play because of illness.

**Anderssen, Adolf** (1818–1879) German chess player; born in Breslau on 6 July 1818. Although Anderssen learned to play chess at the age of nine, his chess career did not begin until he was in his thirties, for he was by profession a teacher and not a professional chess player. He graduated from Breslau University. After qualifying as a teacher in 1847, Anderssen taught mathematics at the Friedrichs-Gymnasium in Breslau until his death. He first became known as the author of a collection of chess problems, *Aufgabe für Schachspieler*, published in 1842. In 1846 he became an editor of the *Deutsche Schachzeitung*, but his active chess career began only in 1848, when he drew a match with Daniel Harrwitz (+5 −5 =0) after previously defeating him in a blindfold game. Three years later he won the **Great Exhibition tournament** by defeating Kieseritzky, Szen, Staunton and Wyvill to become generally recognized as the strongest living player. This was immediately followed by victory in another London tournament in which he played the **Immortal Game**. Anderssen may have considered becoming a chess professional, but had to support his mother and sister and returned to teaching, playing only occasionally. (The **Evergreen Game** was played during this semi-retirement from chess.)

He came out of retirement to play at Manchester (1857), but was eliminated in the second round by Löwenthal. In the following year he was decisively defeated in a match with Morphy (+2 −7 =2). Convinced of the need to play regularly in order to remain in good form, Anderssen began to compete more often. He defeated Kolisch in a match in 1861 (+4 −3 =2), came first at London (1862) and also drew matches with Louis Paulsen (+3 −3 =2) and Suhle (+3 −3 =2) in the same year. In 1865 Breslau University presented Anderssen with an honorary doctorate for his success in chess.

In 1866, Anderssen played a match in London against Wilhelm Steinitz and was defeated in a hard-fought struggle (+6 −8 =0). Steinitz's reign as World Champion is normally dated from this match. Anderssen continued to play regularly and won numerous victories, of which Baden-Baden (1870) ahead of Steinitz was the most important. Other results included a second at the Anderssen Jubilee Festival held in Leipzig in 1877 and a third at Vienna (1873). Later matches were played against Zukertort in 1868 and 1871 (+8 −3 =1 and +2 −5 =0) and against Louis Paulsen in 1876 and 1877 (+4 −5 =1 and +3 −5 =1). Anderssen died of a heart illness on 13 March 1879.

**Anderssen Attack** an opening sequence arising out of the French Defence: 1. P–K4, P–K3 2. P–Q4, P–Q4 3. N–QB3, N–KB3 4. B–KN5, B–K2 5. *B×N*, B×B 6. *P–K5*, B–K2 7. *Q–N4*. White launches a direct attack on the King side and will normally castle on the opposite wing. The variation was popularized by Adolf Anderssen and was played extensively in this century by the East German chess player Kurt Richter.

**Anderssen Opening** an opening where White plays: 1. P–QR3. White wastes a tempo to play a non-developing move, thereby handing the initiative to Black. This opening is rarely seen in contemporary chess, but was a favourite of Anderssen, who often played it successfully. In his match with Morphy he used this opening three times (+1 −1 =1).

**Andersson, Ulf** (b. 27 June 1951) Swedish chess player; awarded the titles International Master in 1970 and International Grandmaster in 1972. His results include firsts at Göteborg (1971) and the Capablanca memorial tournaments of 1974 and 1975, and seconds at Pula (1975) and Orense (1975). In 1974 he acted as second to Mecking in his Candidates' match with Korchnoi, gaining his first experience (although at second-hand) of the World Championship qualifying cycle; in the following year Andersson proved his aptitude for match-play by defeating Bent Larsen (+5 −2 =1) in eight games. In 1976 he competed in the Biel interzonal, but did not qualify for the Candidates' matches. (1976 Elo rating: 2585)

**Angel chess** a variant of chess, with an extra piece known as the Angel, on a board of 81 squares. The piece, which combines the moves of Knight and Queen, initially stands immediately to the right of the King. A player is not allowed to capture his opponent's Angel if his own Angel can be captured on the next move. This condition almost completely eliminated drawn games. Angel chess was invented in the 1930s.

**Anikayev, Yuri** Soviet chess player; awarded the title International Master in 1975. (1976 Elo rating: 2435)

**annotate** to append comments to the score of a game.

**annotations** comments appended to the score of a game; they usually indicate the psychological, strategic, and tactical reasons for the moves, evaluate their worth and point out the alternative unplayed lines including possible traps and brilliancies.

**answer** a move specifically made to meet a threat, and successfully doing so. In extreme cases, where the threat itself was incorrect, the answer may constitute a **refutation**.

**ant** (old-fashioned U.S. slang) a chess player who has memorized famous games, openings, defences and variations, but is lost when confronted by an opponent who deviates from well-known lines of play.

**antagonism of pieces** (Lasker's term) the active opposition of two rival chess pieces, especially those that are equal in absolute or theoretical value. The mutual exchange of such pieces, however, may result in a practical or positional advantage for one side.

**Anti-Meran Gambit** an opening sequence arising out of the Slav Defence to the Queen's Gambit Declined: 1. P–Q4, P–Q4 2. P–QB4, P–QB3 3. N–KB3, N–B3 4. N–B3, P–K3 5. *B–N5*. With his fifth move White offers a pawn in order to prevent the **Meran Defence.** Black usually accepts the sacrifice and then continues with a **pawn roller** on the Queen side. The most common continuation is: 5 . . ., P×P 6. P–K4, P–N4.

**Anti-Neo-Orthodox Variation** an opening sequence arising out of the Orthodox Defence to the Queen's Gambit Declined: 1. P–Q4, P–Q4 2. P–QB4, P–K3 3. N–QB3, N–KB3 4. B–N5, B–K2 5. P–K3, O–O 6. R–B1, *P–KR3* 7. *B–R4*. Compare **Neo-Orthodox Variation.**

**antipositional** term describing a move that contradicts the general principles of positional play or the strategic ideas expressed in the preceding moves. In the Sicilian Defence a Queen-side attack by White or a King-side attack by Black could be antipositional as it might reduce the effectiveness of the previous placing of the pieces and pawns. Antipositional moves can, of course, be strong if the opponent has made an error that can be taken advantage of tactically, but unless such compensation exists they are highly weakening. One of the many differences between a strong and weak player is the fact that the former knows more easily what moves are antipositional.

**Antoshin, Vladimir** (b. 14 May 1929) Soviet chess player. He was awarded the title International Master in 1964 and gained the title International Grandmaster in the same year. (1976 Elo rating: 2460)

**Antunac, Goran** (b. 16 April 1945) Yugoslavian chess player; awarded the title International Master in 1975. He was first at Zagreb (1975). (1976 Elo rating: 2450)

**Arabian Mate** one of the earliest types of mate recorded, delivered against a cornered King by a Rook with the assistance of a Knight.

**arbiter** the referee of a competition. According to *The Laws of Chess* the arbiter's duties are to: (1) ensure that the rules of play are strictly observed; (2) supervise the competition, establish that the time limit has not been exceeded, fix the order of resumption of adjourned games, supervise adjournments; (3) enforce decisions which he may make on disputes arising during the competition; (4) impose penalties on players for any fault or infraction of the rules. It is usual for any large tournament to have a chief arbiter, with one or two deputies who take responsibility for the day-to-day organisation. See also **International Judge, tournament director.**

**arch-priest of the hypermoderns** (Golombek's term) a descriptive phrase for Aron Nimzovitch (1886–1935), a member of the so-called hypermodern school of chess that flourished in the decade after the First World War. See **hypermodern.**

**Argentine Variation** an old-fashioned variation occurring in the Queen's Gambit Declined, arising out of the basic position established in the Cambridge Springs Defence. The move characterizing this variation is in italics: 1. P–Q4, P–Q4 2. P–QB4, P–K3 3. N–QB3, N–KB3 4. B–N5, QN–Q2 5. P–K3, P–B3 6. N–B3,

Q–R4 7. N–Q2, B–N5 8. Q–B2, O–O 9. *B–R4*. In this position, Alekhine recommended the following as Black's best reply: 9 . . ., P–B4.

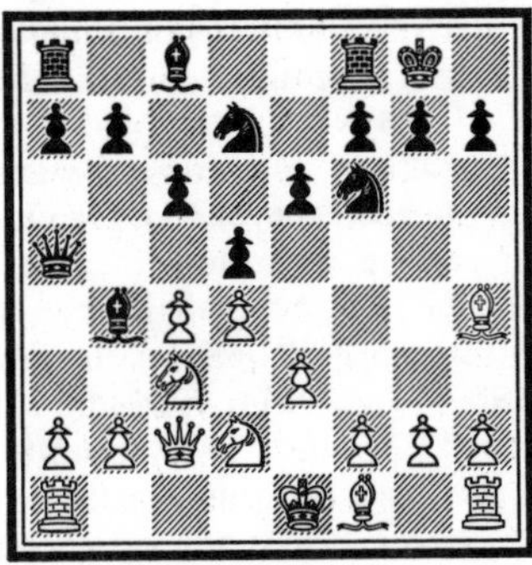

Position after 9. B–R4

**Aronin, Lev** (b. 20 July 1920) Soviet chess player; awarded the title International Master in 1950.

**Arrow Bishop** a Fairy chesspiece that moves like a normal Bishop except when giving check. It then also covers the two squares that are orthogonally adjacent to the King. For example, an Arrow Bishop on KR1 checking a King on Q5 would cover the normal squares plus Q4 and K5. It was invented by W. Hagemann of Braunschweig.

***Art of Chess, The*** a book on the endings and openings by the American master James Mason. It explains the strengths and weaknesses of each man in the ending and examines 39 openings. It was first published in 1898, quickly becoming a standard work. Later editions were modernized and revised by L. Hoffer and F. Reinfeld. It uses descriptive notation. See ***Principles of Chess***.

***Art of Chess Combination, The*** a book by Eugène Znosko-Borovsky. Its purpose is to teach the techniques of combination play through illustrations of master play. It was translated by Philip W. Sergeant and was first published in 1936. It uses descriptive notation.

***Art of the Middle Game, The*** a book by the Soviet Grandmasters Paul Keres and Alexander Kotov, dealing with attack and defence in the middle game. It also analyzes the strengths and weaknesses of various pawn positions in the centre and contains what is probably the best chapter ever written on the art of analysis. The English translation was first published in 1964 and uses descriptive notation.

**Assizes** the different sets of laws of chess that existed in the world before the introduction of a uniform code in 1929.

There were many disagreements between the various assizes over such matters as the initial pawn-move, castling, promotion, and the types of draw and win available (see **baring the King**). To prevent disputes when players of different nationalities competed against each other it was decided to abide by the rules of the nation where play took place.

**Asztalos, Dr Lajos** (1889–1956) Hungarian chess player; awarded the titles International Master in 1950 and International Judge in 1951. He was born on 29 July 1889 and became a National Master in 1912. After the First World War he emigrated to Yugoslavia and competed for that country in the Chess Olympiads of 1927 and 1931. In 1942 he returned to Hungary and was appointed vice-president of the Hungarian Chess Union and secretary of FIDE's Qualification Committee. He died in Budapest on 1 November 1956.

**Atkins, Henry Ernest** (1872–1955) British chess player; awarded the title International Master in 1950. He was British Champion in 1905, 1906, 1907, 1908, 1909, 1910, 1911, 1924 and 1925 and competed in the Chess Olympiads of 1927 and 1935. Atkins was born in Leicester on 20 August 1872 and learned to play at the age of 12. Graduating from Peterhouse, Cambridge he entered the teaching profession, eventually becoming a headmaster. For him chess was a recreation rather than a career and he competed in only three international events apart from the Chess Olympiads: Amsterdam (1899), Hanover (1902) and London (1922). His seven consecutive British Championship victories remain a record number. He died on 31 January 1955.

**Atomic Chess** a variant form of chess using a board of 144 squares (12 × 12) and the addition of two new pieces, Tanks and Aircraft. Instead of queening, a pawn on reaching the eighth rank becomes an Atomic Bomb, which can be used once only during the game to destroy all pieces in a limited area surrounding it. Destruction, instead of checkmate, is the object of the game; if a player's own King is destroyed, it is replaced by the next most valuable piece left. The game received a French patent in 1949, but fortunately this strange variant never became popular. See **variant forms of chess.**

**attack** *v.* to move a pawn or piece in a directly aggressive manner. ***n.*** any move or sequence of moves that is aggressive in intention.

**attacking move** one that is basically aggressive and thus encourages the opponent to respond defensively. Unless checkmate is imminent, however, the opponent need not respond defensively but may counter-attack or improve his position. For a classic example of ignoring attacking moves, see **Immortal Game.**

***Aufgabe für Schachspieler*** a collection of chess problems composed and compiled by Adolf Anderssen. The work is mainly interesting today as an indication of Anderssen's creative imagination during a period in which he was obviously starved for over-the-board play against worthy opponents. It was first published in 1842.

**Aufin** *Old French for* Bishop. The most common name for that piece in Europe during the Middle Ages.

**Augustin, Josef** (b. 18 May 1942) Czechoslovakian chess player; awarded the title International Master in 1976. (1976 Elo rating: 2405)

**Austrian Morphy, The** nickname of Wilhelm Steinitz, given to him in his early career before he had left Vienna.

**automaton chessplayer** a mechanism claimed to be capable of playing chess without human aid. Famous hoaxes concerning automaton chessplayers have been **Ajeeb, Mephisto,** and **the Turk.**

**Averbakh, Yuri Lvovich** (b. 8 February 1922) Soviet chess player; awarded the title International Master in 1951 and the title International Grandmaster in 1952. He became an International Judge of Chess Compositions in 1956 and has been President of the Soviet Chess Federation since 1973. (1976 Elo rating: 2530)

**Averkin, Orest** (b. 26 February 1944) Soviet chess player; awarded the title International Master in 1976. (1976 Elo rating: 2450)

**Avro (1938)** the last major international tournament to be held before World War II. It took place in several venues in Holland and was held under the auspices of the Algemeene Vereeniging voor Radio Omroep (General Dutch Radio Company). It had been intended to use the tournament to find an official challenger for a match against Alekhine. For this reason the field was extremely strong, consisting of Alekhine, Botvinnik, Capablanca, Euwe, Fine, Flohr, Keres and Reshevsky. However, in a speech made after the tournament had begun, Alekhine rejected the assumption that he would be obliged to face the tournament winner in a match in preference to other candidates. He retained the right to play others first. The tournament itself was a double-round all-play-all and was jointly won by Fine and Keres (Keres was awarded first place as he had a plus score in his two games with Fine). Botvinnik was third, Alekhine, Euwe and Reshevsky all shared fourth place, Capablanca was seventh and Flohr was last. The two surprises were the excellent form of Keres and the poor form of Capablanca; the main purpose of the tournament (to find an official challenger) was prevented by the outbreak of war.

# B

**B** *abbrev. for* Bishop: used in chess notation. This is only used in English-speaking countries as the name for this piece varies widely (e.g. it is *Fou* in France and *Laufer* in Germany). To minimize confusion many international publications, such as *Informator*, have abolished these symbols and now use figurine algebraic notation.

**back rank** a player's own first rank. One of the tactical themes of some endgames or middle-games is to place a Rook or Queen on the opponent's back rank, where it will deliver checkmate when the enemy King is hemmed in by its own pawns and by the edge of the board. This is known as a **back-rank mate** and is one of the most common traps fallen into by beginners.

**backward pawn** one that has allied pawns on adjacent files in front of it, but cannot advance to a square where these pawns will support it without the risk of being captured by enemy pawns. A backward pawn has all the weaknesses of an isolated pawn, but can be converted into a strong pawn by a successful advance. (See illustration on p.26.) See **hanging pawns, isolated pawn.**

**backward pawn**

White's Rook pawn and Black's Bishop pawn are both backward

**bad Bishop** a Bishop that is unable to function aggressively because it is impeded by its own pawns. Two of the characteristics of the Bishop are its great range and its limitation to squares of one colour. If these squares are occupied by its own pawns it loses mobility and is forced into the passive role of defending them. An extreme case of a bad Bishop is one that has been forced to defend a pawn or pawns by joining a pawn chain, thus becoming little better than a pawn itself. Compare **good Bishop**.

**Baden-Baden (1870)** an all-play-all tournament with ten competitors, held in Baden-Baden, Germany from 16 July to 4 August 1870. It was at this tournament that chess clocks were introduced, although the competitors had the option of using the old-fashioned hour-glasses. Each competitor met every other competitor twice, with draws counting for half a point. The event was won by Adolf Anderssen (with 13 points) with Wilhelm Steinitz second (with 12½ points) and Joseph Blackburne and Dr W. R. L. Neumann equal third (with 12 points). The other competitors were: Cecil de Vere, Johannes Minckwitz, Louis Paulsen, Samuel Rosenthal, Adolf Stern and Simon Winawer.

This was the first chess tournament to be disrupted by the outbreak of war – in this case, the Franco-Prussian War of 1870. The war dispersed most of the spectators, but play continued although the sound of artillery could often be distinctly heard. Manheim (1914) and the 1939 Chess Olympiad were also affected by war.

**Baden-Baden (1925)** the first major international tournament to be held in Germany after the outbreak of World War I. Originated by Tarrasch, it was undoubtedly the strongest German event since **Nuremberg (1896)** and was contested by all the leading players of the day with the exceptions of Capablanca, Lasker and Vidmar. It was won by Alekhine (+12 −0 =8), with Rubinstein in second place (+10 −1 =9) and Sämisch in third.

**Bagirov, Vladimir Konstantinovich** (b. 16 August 1936) Soviet chess player: awarded the title International Master in 1963.

Bagirov competed in the 1961 European Team Championship and in the World Student Team Championships of 1961 and 1962. (1976 Elo rating: 2490)

**Balanel, Ion** (b. 7 June 1926) Romanian chess player; awarded the title International Master in 1954. Balanel was Romanian Champion in 1950, 1953, 1955, and 1958. He played on top board at the 1956 Chess Olympiad.

**Balashov, Yuri** (b. 12 May 1949) Soviet chess player; awarded the titles International Master in 1972 and International Grandmaster in 1973. He competed in the 1974 Student Olympiad and came equal first in the Vilnius zonal to qualify for the 1976 Manila interzonal. (1976 Elo rating: 2545)

**Balinas, Rosendo** Philippine chess player; awarded the titles International Master in 1975 and International Grandmaster in 1976. (1976 Elo rating: 2365)

**Barcza, Gedeon** (b. 21 August 1911) Hungarian chess player; awarded the title International Master in 1950 and the title International Grandmaster in 1954. (1976 Elo rating: 2435)

**Barcza System** an opening sequence arising out of the Réti Opening: 1. N–KB3, P–Q4 2. *P–KN3*. White does not commit his centre pawns until he has developed his King-side pieces and castled. Black has several satisfactory replies. This variation is named after Gedeon Barcza.

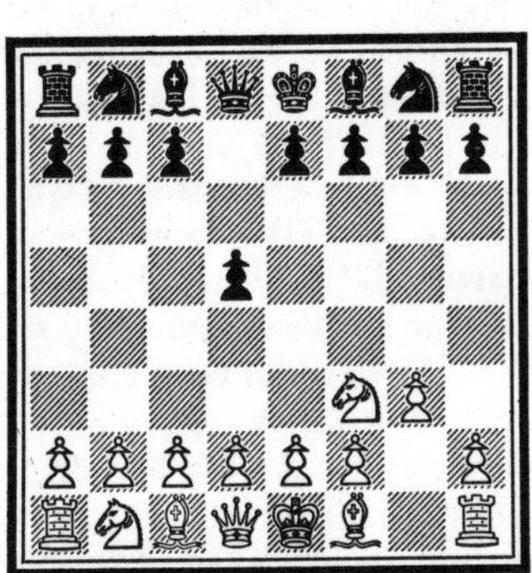

Position after 2. P–KN3

**Barczay, Laszlo** (b. 21 May 1936) Hungarian chess player; awarded the title International Master in 1966 and the title International Grandmaster in 1967. (1976 Elo rating: 2485)

**Barda, Olaf** (1909–1970) Norwegian chess player; awarded the titles International Master in 1952 and International Correspondence Chess Grandmaster in 1953. Barda was Norwegian Champion six times and competed in the 1956 Chess Olympiad.

**Bardeleben, Kurt von** (1861–1924) German chess player. He first became well-known through winning the reserve tournament at London (1883). Later results included fourths at Frankfürt (1887) and Breslau (1889), and first at Berlin (1897). Von Bardeleben competed regularly in tournaments until the First World War, but rarely finished among the prize-winners. He experienced poverty throughout his life and finally committed suicide by jumping from a window in 1924.

**Barden, Leonard William** (b. 20 August 1929) British chess player; awarded the title British Master in 1962. He was joint British Champion in 1954 and competed in the Chess Olympiads of 1952, 1954, 1960 and 1962. Barden retired from active play in 1962 to concentrate on writing about chess. He is the author of numerous works, including *The Guardian Chess Book, How Good is Your Chess?, The King's Indian Defence* (of which he was once one of the world's leading analysts) and *The Penguin Book of Chess Positions*. He is the chess columnist of *The Guardian, The Field*, the London *Evening Standard*, and *The Financial Times*.

**Bare King** the condition in which all of an opponent's chessmen have been captured, resulting in only his King being left on the board. See **Great Bare King, Little Bare King.**

**Barendregt, Professor Johan Teunis** (b. 16 February, 1924) Dutch chess player and professor of psychology; awarded the title International Master in 1962.

**baring the King** a type of win found in ancient Indian and Arabic chess. Victory was gained when all the opponent's men except his King had been captured. This type of victory (always considered inferior to checkmate) was abandoned in the Middle Ages in most parts of Europe, although it still existed in Iceland during the nineteenth century.

**Barle, Janez** (b. 21 March 1952) Yugoslavian chess player; awarded the title International Master in 1976. (1976 Elo rating: 2480)

**Barnes, Thomas Wilson** (1825–1874) British amateur chess player; member of the St George's Chess Club. He was the most successful British player to meet Morphy, winning 8 games and losing 19.

**barrier** any connected line of squares which the opposing King cannot pass. A common example is where a Rook on the seventh rank prevents the enemy King moving to the aid of its pawns. See **cordon.**

**Baseline Chess** a variant of chess in which each player arranges his men in any order on the back rank without knowing the formation adopted by his opponent. Normal chess rules then apply. This game is growing in popularity and in February 1976 a tournament was held in Brighton, England where Baseline Chess alone was played.

***Basic Chess Endings*** a treatise on the endgame by the U.S. Grandmaster Dr Reuben Fine. It systematically deals with the basic mates, the King and pawn endings, minor piece and pawn endings, minor piece endings, Rook and pawn endings, Rook and minor piece endings, and Queen endings. Each category is broken down into several characteristic types and is discussed with a profusion of analysis. It was first published in 1941 and uses descriptive notation.

***Basis of Combinations in Chess, The*** a book by Julius du Mont. It attempts to familiarize the reader with the standard combinations while making their causes easier to understand. At the same time it provides entertaining examples of combinations from top-class play. It was first published in 1938 and uses descriptive notation.

***Batsford Chess Yearbook, The*** an annual survey of world chess edited by Kevin J. O'Connell. Among the items it contains are the international rating list, the results of the major tournaments and FIDE events, a collection of the best games played during the year and a selection of the year's outstanding blunders. It was first published in 1975 and uses figurine algebraic notation.

**battery** (chess-problem term) an alignment of two men on the same rank, file or diagonal as the enemy King (with no other men intervening), when a move of the middle man would create a discovered check. It is thus similar to a **pin**, except that the middle man belongs to the attacking and not the defending forces. A simple example would be if a White Bishop and Rook stood on their K4 and KB5 squares respectively and the Black King stood on its KR2. See **half-battery**.

**Baturinsky, Victor D.** Soviet chess player; president of the Moscow Central Chess Club and author of a biography of former World Champion Mikhail Botvinnik.

**B.C.A.** or **BCA** *abbrev. for* British Chess Association.

**B.C.C.S.** or **BCCS** *abbrev. for* British Correspondence Chess Society.

**B.C.F.** or **BCF** *abbrev. for* British Chess Federation.

**B.C.F. Grading System** a method of evaluating the relative strength of a British chess player based upon his results in tournament, club and league play. The player is initially assigned a grading that is based ideally on a minimum of 30 games played with graded players over the previous year and this is adjusted annually. The grading is arrived at by aggregating the grades of all the players played against, adding 50 points for each victory and deducting 50 points for each defeat and averaging the result. This process is carried out by each regional chess union rather than by a central body.

The B.C.F. grading may be converted into an approximate Elo rating through use of the formula: Elo = 8 B.C.F. + 600 so that: B.C.F. = ⅛Elo −75. It has been estimated that an International Grandmaster with an Elo rating of 2500 would have a B.C.F. rating of 238. Compare **Elo Scale, Ingo System**.

**B.C.M.** *abbrev. for British Chess Magazine.*

**Becker, Albert** (b. 5 September 1896) Argentinian chess player; awarded the title International Master in 1953. He was Austrian Champion in 1937. Becker played for Austria in the 1931 Chess Olympiad and had the best result on fourth board (+10 −3 =1). He also competed in the 1939 Chess Olympiad as a member of the German team. This event was held in Argentina and, on the outbreak of the Second World War, Becker decided to seek asylum in Argentina and retired from tournament chess.

**Becker's Defence** an opening sequence arising out of the King's Gambit: 1. P–K4, P–K4 2. P–KB4, P×P 3. N–KB3, *P–KR3*. Black begins the attempt to form a King-side pawn chain. A common continuation is: 4. P–Q4. This defence was devised by the Argentinian International Master Albert Becker.

**Bednarski, Boguslaw Jacek** (b. 12 March 1939) Polish chess player; awarded the title International Master in 1964.

He was Polish Champion in 1963 and has competed on top board in several Chess Olympiads since 1964. (1976 Elo rating: 2425)

**beginner** any person who has only recently been introduced to chess and has yet to learn the basic principles involved in tactics and strategy. The best way for a beginner to progress in chess ability is to play against stronger opponents, especially those who are patient and willing to take time to explain the underlying principles of the game and why a particular move is weak. Most larger cities have chess clubs, which welcome novices to their ranks; in such clubs, paired against opponents of varying strengths, great progress can usually be made in one's playing ability. An alternative – especially for beginners who live in rural areas – is to participate in **correspondence chess**. See **woodpusher, duffer.**

**Belkadi, Ridha** (b. 25 April 1925) Tunisian chess player; awarded the title International Master in 1974. (1976 Elo rating: 2350)

**Bellin, Robert** (b. 30 June 1952) British chess player; awarded the title British Master in 1975. He was equal first in the 1974 British Championship, but only shared sixth place in the subsequent play-off. He was second in the Master group at Wijk aan Zee (1976), gaining his first International Master norm. (1976 Elo rating: 2360)

**Bellon, Juan Manuel** (b. 8 May 1950) Spanish chess player; awarded the title International Master in 1974. (1976 Elo rating: 2475)

**Bély, Dr Miklos** (1913–1971) Hungarian chess player; born 9 August 1913, died 27 September 1971. He was awarded the title International Master in 1956 and competed in the Chess Olympiad of that year.

**Belyavsky, Alexander** (b. 19 December 1953) Soviet chess player; awarded the titles International Master in 1973 and International Grandmaster in 1975. He gained the first title through winning the 1973 World Junior Championship, held in Teesside in the United Kingdom. Other results include a first at Leningrad (1975), a second at Las Palmas (1974) and fourths at Hastings (1974) and the Soviet Young Masters Championship (1974). He was also a member of the successful Soviet team at the 1975 Student Olympiad. (1976 Elo rating: 2560)

**Benkö Gambit** an opening sequence arising out of the Benoni Defence: 1. P–Q4, N–KB3 2. P–QB4, P–B4 3. P–Q5, *P–QN4* 4. P × P, *P–QR3* 5. P × P, *B × P*. Black sacrifices a pawn in return for quick development and open lines of attack on the Queen side. It is named after Pal Benkö, who has popularized and developed it. In the U.S.S.R. it is more commonly known by its older name of the **Volga Gambit.** Also called **Benoni Counter Gambit.**

**Benkö Opening** an opening where White plays 1. P–KN3. It is in effect the Modern Defence with a move in hand. There are many good continuations for Black. Although played by Nimzovitch, it is named after Pal Benkö who began playing it in the 1960s. Also called **King's Fianchetto Opening.**

Benkö Gambit

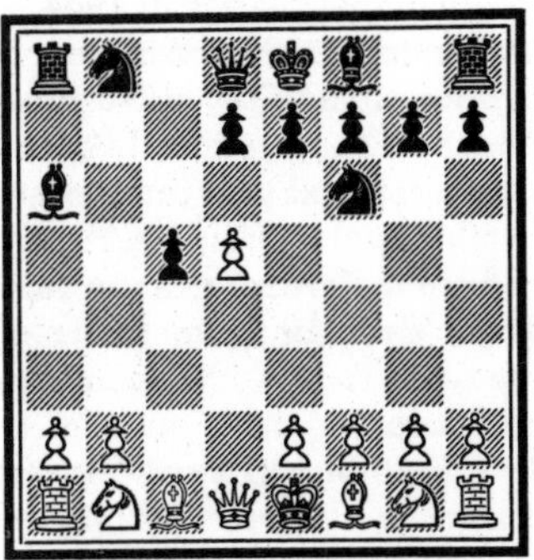

Position after 5 . . ., B×P

**Benkö, Pal** (b. 15 July 1928) United States chess player; awarded the title International Master in 1950 and the title International Grandmaster in 1958. Benkö was originally Hungarian, but emigrated in 1957. He thus possesses the unusual distinction of having been both Hungarian and United States national champion. He competed in the 1959 and 1962 Candidates tournaments. (1976 Elo rating: 2480)

**Benoni Counter Gambit** another name for the Benkö Gambit. It is sometimes also used to signify the moves: 1. P–Q4, *P–QB4*.

**Benoni Defence** a defence to the Queen pawn opening: 1. P–Q4, *P–QB4* or 1. P–Q4, N–KB3 2. P–QB4, *P–B4*. Black allows White to gain more space in the centre in return for play on the black squares and Queen side. Many variations are characterized by short tactical play.

This defence was first analyzed in a pamphlet by Aaron Reinganum (Frankfurt 1825) and was played by von der Lasa against Hanstein in 1841 and twice by Saint-Amant against Staunton in 1843. It fell into disuse in the latter half of the century, but was played by Spielmann at Bad Pistyan (1912) and rehabilitated by Alekhine in the 1930s. Since then its most influential advocate has been Tal. See also **Modern Benoni, Czech Benoni.**

**Berger, Bela** (b. 12 August 1931) Australian chess player. Originally Hungarian, Berger emigrated to Australia where he was awarded the title International Master in 1964. He competed in the 1964 interzonal tournament where he finished twenty-third.

**Berlin (1928)** a double-round tournament with seven competitors, won by Capablanca (who scored 8½) ahead of Nimzovitch (7), Spielmann (6½), Tartakover (5½), Réti (5), Rubinstein (5) and Marshall (4½).

**Berlin Defence 1.** a defence to the Bishop's Opening: 1. P–K4, P–K4 2. B–B4, *N–KB3*. Black both develops a piece and counterattacks against White's King pawn. Common continuations are: 3. P–Q3, and 3. P–Q4. This opening can easily transpose into other openings including the **Giuoco Piano**, the **King's Gambit**, and the **Vienna Game**.

**2.** a defence to the Ruy Lopez: 1. P–K4, P–K4 2. N–KB3, N–QB3 3. B–N5, *N–B3*.

**Berlin pawn** another name for **Berolina pawn**.

**Berlin Pleiades** the nickname of seven German chessplayers: L. E. Bledow (1795–1846); K. Schorn (1802–50); B. Horwitz (1807–85); Baron Tassilo von Heydebrand und der Lasa (1808–99); C. Mayet (1810–68); W. Hanstein (1811–50); and P. R. von Bilguer (1813–40).

The whole group lived in Berlin only from 1837 until early in 1839, but this was sufficient time for them firmly to establish chess in Germany through projects such as the compilation of the *Handbuch des Schachspiels* (Handbook on the Game of Chess), which was published in 1843 under the editorship first of von Bilguer and then of der Lasa, and through Bledow's annual journeys on which he visited different parts of the country. The group also created the magazine *Schachzeitung* in 1846. This still exists and is probably the oldest chess magazine regularly published.

These projects, plus Bledow's annual journeys, helped to establish chess in Germany. Although the nickname was meant as a compliment, der Lasa objected to it because this constellation shines very faintly.

**Bernstein, Ossip Samilovitch** (1882–1962) Russian émigré chess player and international lawyer; awarded the title International Grandmaster in 1950. Bernstein was born in Jitomir, the Ukraine, on 20 September 1882. In 1906 he graduated from Heidelberg University with a doctorate in law and practised in Moscow until the Russian Revolution caused him to emigrate to France. His tournament results included a first at Ostend (1907), fourths at Coburg (1904) and Barmen (1905) and a sixth at St Petersburg (1914). Bernstein withdrew from active chess for long periods, although with little apparent harm; in 1933 he drew a short training match with Alekhine after eighteen years away from chess. After another long absence he came second at London (1946) and Montevideo (1954) and won a tournament at Montevideo (1961). This was his last success; he died on 30 November 1962.

**Berolina pawn** a Fairy pawn that moves diagonally and captures orthogonally. Like an orthodox pawn it cannot retreat, can capture *en passant*, and promotes in the normal manner. The Berolina (or Berlin) pawn was invented by E. Nebermann in 1926.

**Bertok, Mario** (b. 2 September 1929) Yugoslavian chess player; awarded the title International Master in 1957.

Bertok competed in the 1960 Chess Olympiad and played in the 1962 interzonal tournament where he finished seventeenth. (1976 Elo rating: 2425)

**best game of chess** choosing the best game of chess ever played is impossible on an objective basis, although the experts have offered an abundance of candidates. Players themselves can usually pick two or three of their own games that they consider their best. When Marshall asked Capablanca to name his best game, the Cuban replied 'There are three possible types of best game – a fine attack, a brilliant defence, or a purely artistic treatment.' (Capablanca chose as his most 'artistic' game one played against Bernstein on 4 February 1914.)

**best move** a chess move considered to be the strongest choice of perhaps several alternatives for reasons of defence, position, or attack. In chess problems the best move is often in fact the only move that will satisfy the criteria established by the problem. Many moves in standard positions (especially during opening play) that were once considered best have subsequently been discarded in favour of stronger moves. See **refutation.**

**Bhend, Edwin** (b. 9 September 1931) Swiss chess player; awarded the title International Master in 1960. He won the Coupe Suisse, a national knockout competition, in 1957 and has played in numerous Chess Olympiads since 1952. He is the author of a monograph on the King's Gambit. (1975 Elo rating: 2315)

**Bielicki, Carlos** (b. 15 May 1940) Argentinian chess player; awarded the title International Master in 1959 on becoming World Junior Champion.

**Bikova** a variant spelling of **Bykova.**

**Bilek, Istvan** (b. 11 August 1932) Hungarian chess player; awarded the titles International Master in 1960 and International Grandmaster in 1962. He was Hungarian Champion in 1963, 1965 and 1971 and competed in the Chess Olympiads of 1958, 1960, 1962, 1964, 1966, 1968, 1970, 1972 and 1974. He also competed in the interzonals of 1962, 1964 and 1967. (1976 Elo rating: 2435)

**Bilguer, Paul Rudolf von** (1813–1840) German chess player and member of the Berlin Pleiades; met the other members of the group when stationed in Berlin as a lieutenant in the Prussian Army.

He was mainly responsible for the *Handbuch des Schachspiels*, but died before it was completed. Another member of the group, von der Lasa, felt him to be the most brilliant of them all. Bilguer was also a noted blindfold player.

**bind** a spatial advantage held by one side that seriously impedes the movement of the opponent's men. It is normally caused by an advanced pawn chain. See **Maróczy bind.**

**Bird, Henry Edward** (1830–1908) British chess player; born in Portsea, Hampshire on 14 July 1830. He learned to play at the age of 10 and was strong enough by 1851 to enter the **Great Exhibition Tournament,** although he was knocked out in the first round by Horwitz, who also defeated him in a match played soon afterwards (+3 −7 =4). Bird played little chess in the next 15 years, concentrating instead upon his profession of accountancy and his book *An Analysis of Railways in the United Kingdom*, which was published in 1866. He did, however, play several times against Morphy when the American visited the United Kingdom, but with little success.

Bird played several matches in his career, but the most important ones all seem to have ended in defeats. He lost to Steinitz in 1867 (+6

−7 =6), to Blackburne in 1884 (+1 −4 =0) and to Lasker in 1890 and 1892 (+2 −7 =3 and +0 −5 =0). Defeats never discouraged him; he was always ready to play anyone at any time. After his death (11 April 1908), Teichmann described his play as being 'the same as his health in always alternating between being dangerously ill and being dangerously well. England will not see his like again.'

**Bird's Defence** a defence arising out of the Ruy Lopez: 1. P–K4, P–K4 2. N–KB3, N–QB3 3. B–N5, *N–Q5*. Black attempts to prevent the advance of White's Queen pawn while preparing to support the advance of his own Queen pawn by the adjacent Bishop pawn. However, the movement of his only developed piece leaves Black behind in development. A common continuation is: 4. N×N, P×N 5. O–O, P–QB3.

This defence was pioneered by the British master, Henry Bird. Lately it has been revived by the Leningrad masters.

**Bird's Opening** an opening where White plays 1. *P–KB4*, controlling a central square, K5, and intending to launch a King-side attack. Among Black's best replies are 1 . . ., P–Q4 (when this opening is also known as the Dutch Attack, as this is a Dutch Defence with colours reversed), or From's Gambit 1 . . ., P–K4. The opening is named after the English player, Henry Edward Bird, who played it throughout his career.

**Bisguier, Arthur B.** (b. 8 October 1929) U.S. chess player; awarded the title International Master in 1950 and the title International Grandmaster in 1957. In addition he was U.S. Champion in 1954. (1976 Elo rating: 2440)

**Bishop** a chessman that moves diagonally over any number of unoccupied squares. It is confined to the same-coloured squares throughout the game as it cannot move horizontally or vertically. Each side begins with two Bishops which initially occupy the squares between the King or Queen and Knight.

Although the Bishop is in effect restricted to half the board this is compensated for by its great range. Its approximate value is equal to that of three pawns or one Knight.

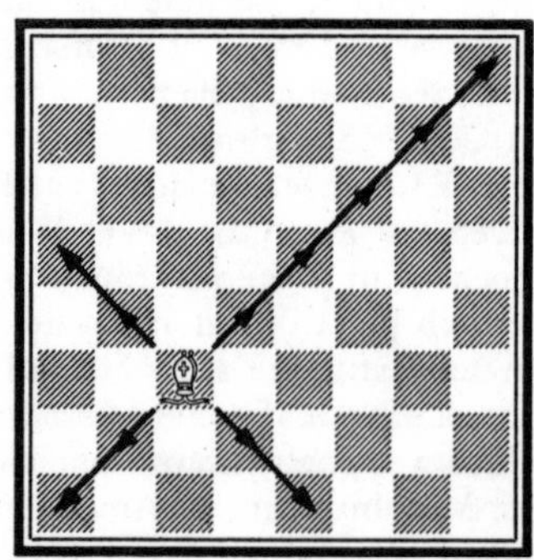

Potential moves of the Bishop over unobstructed diagonal squares

The Bishop's move and name have changed radically since the beginning of known chess. In Arabic it was called the *al-fil* (elephant) and moved by jumping to any of the squares diagonally two squares away, capturing any adjacent man over which it passed. When it was introduced into Europe the meaning of its name was forgotten and numerous titles for it were adopted including aufin, bishop, count, fool, old man, sage, spy, and thief. Indeed, this piece still has no uniform name. For instance, it is known as *fou* (fool) in France, *Laufer* (runner) in Germany, and *slon* (elephant) in the U.S.S.R. The modern move of the Bishop was created in the late 14th century. Abbrev. **B.**

**Bishops of opposite colours** enemy Bishops of the same type, i.e. two King Bishops or two Queen Bishops. When there are Bishops of opposite colours in an endgame the result is often a draw if there is only a difference of one pawn in material. Indeed, draws when one side has an advantage of two pawns are common, since neither Bishop can protect squares that are attacked by the other.

**Bishop of the wrong colour** a Bishop that travels on squares of a different colour from the queening square of the Rook pawn in the ending of King, Bishop and Rook pawn versus King. Such an ending is a draw if the lone King can reach the queening square, because it cannot be driven out.

**Bishop pair** the two Bishops when opposed by two Knights or by a Knight and Bishop. The Bishop pair has a slight but definite advantage over any other combination of minor pieces in the ending through their superior mobility, which enables them to control both wings more effectively.

**Bishop's Opening** an opening sequence: 1. P–K4, P–K4 2. *B–B4*. White attempts to create a quick attack on Black's King side. This opening has declined in popularity since the nineteenth century, but has often been played by Bent Larsen. See **Berlin Defence.**

**bi-valve** a theme in problem chess in which the movement of a defending piece to block an attacker automatically clears the way for a second attacker. For instance, a move by a Knight might block a file but at the same time unblock a diagonal.

**Black** the second player, i.e. the one who has the dark chessmen. The chessmen are not necessarily black in colour and, indeed, neither are the White pieces likely to be white, since the contrast in colours would be too harsh to be viewed comfortably for long periods of time. Until the twentieth century, the right to move first and the choice of colour of men were decided independently by lot, so in fact in many early games it was Black who moved first. Compare **White.**

**Blackburne, Joseph Henry** (1841–1924) British chess player; born in Manchester on 10 December 1841. Blackburne learned to play chess at the relatively late age of 19 and became a chess professional seven years later. His career was phenomenally long, beginning at London (1862) and ending at St Petersburg (1914).

During that period he played every player of note from Anderssen (1862) to Alekhine (1914). In his prime his aggressive play and large black beard earned him the nickname of 'The Black Death'. His greatest success was first place at Berlin (1881) in front of Tchigorin and Zukertort. He played many matches, but was less successful than in tournament play and lost to Steinitz in 1862, 1870 and 1876 (+1 −7 =2, +0 −1 =1, +0 −7 =0); lost to Zukertort in 1881 (+2 −7 =5); won a match against Gunsberg in 1881 but lost another in 1886 (+7 −4 =3, +2 −5 =6); defeated Bird in 1888 (+4 −1 =0); and lost to Lasker in 1892 (+0 −6 =0). Blackburne was also a strong blindfold player. He was the chess columnist of *The Field* from the turn of the century until his death in London on 1 September 1924.

**Blackburne Trap** another name for **Legal's Mate.**

**Black Death, The** *nickname of* Joseph Henry Blackburne.

**Blackmar-Diemer Gambit** an opening sequence arising out of the Queen pawn opening: 1. P–Q4, P–Q4 2. *P–K4*, P×P 3. N–QB3, N–KB3 4. P–B3. This attack is widely felt to be unsound, since a pawn is sacrificed for insufficient compensation. This gambit has been known for a long time, but is named after the U.S. player Blackmar and the German player Diemer, who analysed it independently.

**black-square weakness** inability to control the dark squares of the chessboard. This normally arises when the black-square Bishop (White's Queen Bishop or Black's King Bishop) has been captured or exchanged, or when too many pawns have been moved to white squares. Black square weakness allows the opponent to station his men on the dark squares where they are relatively immune from attack and often provides undefended open lines for the opponent's pieces to penetrate the defences. For instance, when the fianchettoed Bishop of a castled King is captured the enemy Queen can often move along the unguarded long diagonal to deliver checkmate.

The discovery of black and white square weaknesses was one of Steinitz's most important contributions to chess theory. Compare **white-square weakness.** See **hole.**

**Bladel Variation** an opening sequence arising out of the Dutch Defence: 1. P–Q4, P–KB4 2. P–QB4, P–KN3 3. N–QB3, *N–R3*. This was first played by Euwe against Flohr in the Réti Memorial tournament held in Bladel, Holland in 1969. Play continued: 4. P–K4, P–Q3 5. P–QN3, B–N2 6. B–N2, O–O and the game was drawn after twelve moves.

**Blau, Max** (b. 19 December 1918) Swiss chess player; awarded the title International Master in 1953.

Blau was Swiss Champion in 1953, 1955, 1956, and 1967 and has competed in several Chess Olympiads since 1954.

**Bled (1931)** an international all-play-all tournament that was held in Bled, Yugoslavia in August 1931. There were 13 competitors who played each other twice. The event was won by the World Champion Alekhine (+15 −0 =11) fully 5½ points ahead of Bogoljubov in second place. The other participants included Flohr, Kashdan, Maróczy, Nimzovitch, Pirc, Stolz and Vidmar.

**Bled (1961)** an international tournament held on the 30th anniversary of Bled (1931), from 2 September to 4 October 1961. It was won by Tal (14½), ahead of Fischer (13½), Gligorić (12½), Keres (12½) and Petrosian (12½).

**blindfold chess** chess played without seeing the board and men, although the players are not necessarily blindfolded. Normally only the stronger player will not be allowed to see the board. He plays by visualizing the initial position and modifying this image after every move.

This is testing enough, but even more exacting is a **simultaneous blindfold chess** display, where the player giving the display competes against several others who are allowed to look at their boards. If a simultaneous display consists of twenty games, the 'blindfolded' player must accurately remember the course of twenty different games, retaining the image of each distinct position in his memory until called upon to play a move in the corresponding game. In these displays the 'blindfolded' player sits out of sight of the boards. Each opponent in turn plays a move which is relayed by the referee. The player then replies with his move and this is made on the board by the referee. This routine is repeated at each board until every game has been completed.

An early example of a simultaneous blindfold display took place in January 1266 when Buzzeca (or Buzecca), a Saracen expert, visited Florence and successfully played two games blindfold and one over-the-board against Italy's best players (+2 −0 =1). Blindfold play was still known in the sixteenth century, as shown by the publication of a work by Damiano entitled *The Elements of the Art of Playing Without Seeing the Board* (1512), but by the eighteenth century had been almost completely forgotten. Thus Philidor's achievement in playing two blindfold games in 1783 caused general astonishment. Indeed, affidavits were signed to confirm this feat and Diderot wrote to Philidor begging him not to risk his sanity in such dangerous pursuits!

In 1858 Morphy played eight blindfold games simultaneously, in the same year Paulsen played ten, and in 1876 Zukertort sixteen. This record was shattered by Pillsbury, who eventually played twenty-two in Moscow in 1902 (+17 −1 =4). In 1919 Réti created a new record by playing twenty-four blindfold games in Haarlem, the Netherlands (+12 −3 =9). In quick succession the record was held by Breyer, Alekhine, and Koltanowski until 1943 when Najdorf surpassed them all and consolidated his hold on the title at Sao Paulo in 1947, by playing 45 games (+39 −2 =4) in 23½ hours. This record lasted until 13 December 1960 when Koltanowski regained the title by playing 56 games (+50 −0 =6) in 9¾ hours in San Francisco. Doubts exist regarding the validity of some blindfold records. Against weak players, of course, the task of the 'blindfolded' player is considerably easier.

Other notable blindfold events include: a tournament held in Prague in 1874 in which each competitor played blindfold, and which was won by the problemist Jan Dobrusky with 13⅛ points out of 14; a blindfold match between Mieses and Schlechter at Stuttgart in 1909 which the former won (+2 −0 =1); and Fine's display in playing and winning four simultaneous rapid transit games against experts (including Robert Byrne) in New York on 4 September 1945.

**blindness, chess** see **chess blindness** and **amaurosis scacchista.**

**Blitz** *German for* lightning. **1.** a game in which each move must be made within five or ten seconds.

**2.** *another name for* **Progressive Chess.**

**Blitz formation** (Kmoch's term) a large and menacing pawn centre which the other side has opportunities to attack. It is given this name because of the explosive character it provides in a game. See ***Pawn Power in Chess***.

**blockade** the obstruction of a pawn by a piece. Devised and popularized by Nimzovitch in such axioms as, 'First restrain, next blockade, lastly destroy', and in games such as that against Johner (Dresden 1926), it has now become a standard manoeuvre. The best blockading pieces are the Knight and the Bishop which are not impeded by a pawn in front of them, but the King can also become a good blockader in the endgame.

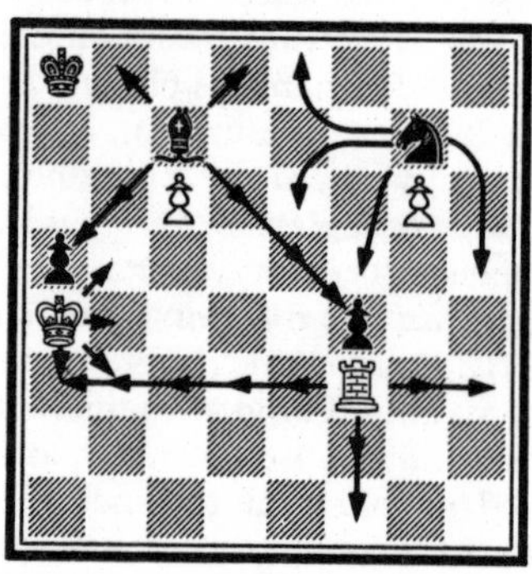

Minor pieces make the best blockaders

**block problem** a type of chess problem in which White's first move maintains or creates zugzwang for Black. If Black cannot move first without allowing mate the problem is known as a *complete block*. White must then find a waiting move that preserves all the mating threats. If he cannot achieve this he must substitute new mates for those that are dropped and the problem is known as a *mutate*. In an *incomplete block* White's first move puts Black into a zugzwang that did not previously exist.

**Blumenfeld, Benjamin Markovitch** (1884–1947) Russian chess player and theorist; regularly played in tournaments, but is mainly remembered for his contributions to the openings. Apart from the counter gambit named after him, he also made important contributions to the **Scotch Opening** and the **Meran Defence** and added to the theory of the endgame.

**Blumenfeld Counter Gambit** an opening sequence in the Benoni Deferred in which Black offers a pawn: 1. P–Q4, N–KB3 2. P–QB4,

P–K3 3. N–KB3, P–B4 4. P–Q5, *P–QN4*. White's best reply is generally considered to be 4. B–N5. It was named after Benjamin Markovitch Blumenfeld, the Russian chess player who invented it.

**Blumenfeld Variation** an opening sequence arising out of the Meran Defence: 1. P–Q4, P–Q4 2. P–QB4, P–QB3 3. N–KB3, N–B3 4. N–B3, P–K3 5. P–K3, QN–Q2 6. B–Q3, P×P 7. B×BP, P–QN4 8. B–Q3, P–QR3 9. P–K4, P–B4 10. P–K5, P×P 11. *N×NP*. The most common continuations are: 11 . . ., P×N 12. P×N, Q–N3 and 11 . . ., N×P 12. N×N, P×N. It is named after the Russian player, Benjamin Markovitch Blumenfeld.

**blunder** a move so inferior to one's normal standard of play as to be inexplicable on purely technical grounds. This is purely a relative definition; a blunder for a Grandmaster need not be a blunder for a novice.

Alexander has categorized three causes of blunders, each of which reinforces the others. They are (a) **time trouble,** when a player overlooks something in his haste to reach the **time control**; (b) technical errors, when elementary resources, such as a backward capture by a Knight, are missed; (c) psychological reasons, such as the effect of extreme nervousness or over-confidence. Most blunders will be due to more than one of these reasons and Alexander considered those caused by (b) and (c) to be the most common.

**board** **1.** another name for **chessboard.**

**2.** the position at which a player competes in a team competition. If, for instance, a league match between two chess clubs consisted of six games, play would take place on six boards and the strongest players would compete on **top board** (or **first board**), the next strongest would meet on the second board and so on down to the weakest players who would contest sixth board. In some team competitions, such as the Chess Olympiads, it is forbidden to play on a lower board than that to which the player is originally assigned. This means that a reserve player can only play on the lowest board (since no player can move downwards) and the strongest player can only contest top board.

***Bobby Fischer Teaches Chess*** a book by Bobby Fischer, Stuart Margulies and Donn Mosenfelder. It attempts to teach chess through programmed learning methods; each page has one or more diagrams either with simple passages on combinations, mating attacks, etc., or with questions for the reader which are answered on the page overleaf. By working through the book the player develops his chess abilities. It was first published in 1966 and contains no chess notation of any sort.

**Bobotsov, Milko Georguiev** (b. 30 September 1931) Bulgarian chess player; awarded the title International Master in 1960, and became the first Bulgarian to gain the title International Grandmaster in 1961. He played on first board for Bulgaria in the 1970 Chess Olympiad, but shortly after suffered a severe illness which forced him to cut down on strenuous tournament play. (1976 Elo rating: 2400)

**Boden, Samuel Standidge** (1826–1882) British amateur chess player; born in Hull. In 1858 he played two matches against the Reverend

John Owen and won both (+5 −3 =1 and +5 −1 =0). Other results included second place at Manchester (1857) and Bristol (1861), but he played in few major tournaments preferring friendly games. Morphy considered him to be the strongest of his British opponents, while Steinitz thought him to be the strongest player that Morphy competed against apart from in matches. Boden was the chess columnist of *The Field* 1857–1872 and was succeeded by Steinitz.

**Boden's Mate** a mate with two Bishops following the sacrifice of the Queen. Boden used it to win with Black against Schulder at London (1860), but it had previously been played by Horwitz against Popert at Hamburg (1844). From the diagrammed position Horwitz continued: 1. R–KR5!, Q×R 2. Q×Pch!, P×Q 3. B×Pmate.

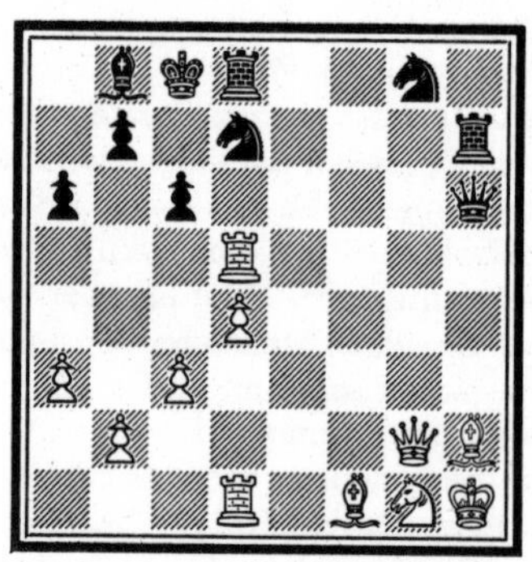

Horwitz vs. Popert (Hamburg, 1844)

**Bogdanović, Rajo** (b. 15 November 1931) Yugoslavian chess player; awarded the title International Master in 1963. (1976 Elo rating: 2430)

**Bognor Regis International Chess Congress** an annual group of tournaments held soon after Easter in Bognor Regis, in the United Kingdom. The main event of the congress, which began in 1953, was the Churchill Memorial Tournament. The last Bognor Regis Congress was held in 1969, after which its chief organizer, J. N. Fishlock-Lomax, was forced to give up his work owing to illness.

**Bogo** *nickname of* **Yefim Dmitrievich Bogoljubov**.

**Bogoljubov, Yefim Dmitrievich** (1889–1952) World Championship contender; awarded the title International Grandmaster in 1951. He was born in Russia on 14 April 1889 and was originally educated for the priesthood (appropriately his surname means 'beloved of God'), but discovered he had no vocation and decided to become a chess professional. In 1914 he was competing in the tournament at Mannheim, Germany, when the war broke out and was interned at Triberg with most of the other foreign competitors. This enforced stay with other high-calibre players immeasurably increased his strength and by the end of the war he was one of the world's strongest players. After the Russian Revolution Bogoljubov (frequently called 'Bogo') emigrated to Germany and became a naturalized citizen, although he returned to the U.S.S.R. to win the Soviet Championships of 1924 and 1925. His results also included firsts at Pistyan (1922), Carlsbad (1923), Moscow (1925), Berlin (1926) and Bad Kissingen (1928). These victories made him a worthy contender for the World Championship, but Alekhine defeated him convincingly in matches played in 1929 (+5 −11 =9) and 1934 (+3 −8 =15).

Bogoljubov's play varied erratically between the inspired and the abysmal. His innate optimism and self-confidence (as revealed in his comment, 'When I am White I win because I am White; when I am Black I win because I am Bogoljubov') could lead to a lack of objectivity or to a calmness when playing the best. Euwe has described his style as being 'primarily positional [with a] tactical talent which came into its own especially when the opponent had been outplayed strategically.' He died on 18 June 1952.

**Bogoljubov-Indian Defence** a defence to the Queen pawn opening: 1. P–Q4, N–KB3 2. P–QB4, P–K3 3. N–KB3, *B–N5ch*. This normally leads to an exchange of minor pieces.

The opening is named after its inventor Yefim Bogoljubov, but the name is slightly misleading as the distinguishing characteristic of the Indian Defences, a fianchetto of a Bishop, is lacking. Also called **Bogo-Indian Defence.** Compare **Nimzo-Indian Defence.**

**Bohatirchuk, Fedor Parthenij** (b. 14 December 1892) Canadian chess player; awarded the title International Master in 1954.

Bohatirchuk was born in Kiev. In 1927 he finished equal first in the All-Russian Championship. He was equal second in this event in 1938 and was equal third in 1912, 1923, 1924, and 1931. In 1948 he emigrated to Canada, which he represented in the 1954 Chess Olympiad.

**Böhm, Hans** (b. 15 January 1950) Dutch chess player; awarded the title International Master in 1975. (1976 Elo rating: 2425)

**Boi, Paolo** (1528–1598) Italian chess player, one of the best of his era. By 1566 Boi had defeated all the players in his home town of Syracuse and had begun his travels through Italy. He found favour with many and Pope Pius V would have granted him a rich benefice if he had entered the clergy. Soon after Leonardo's visit to Spain Boi also travelled there and in 1575 he too defeated Ruy Lopez, for which Philip II rewarded him with appointments in Sicily that yielded 500 crowns annually. On his return from Spain, Boi was captured by Algerian pirates and sold as a slave; he obtained his freedom by winning large sums for his master through his skill at chess. Boi continued to travel throughout his life; in 1598 he played Salvio at Naples. In the game he won Salvio's Queen with a five-move combination, but Salvio had seen further and won back the Queen and the game. 'Youth can more than age; you are in the prime of life and I am seventy years old,' commented Boi. Three days later he died by poisoning. A contemporary estimated his total winnings at chess to have been 30,000 crowns.

**Bolbochan, Julio** (b. 20 March 1920) Argentinian chess player;

awarded the title International Master in 1950. He was Argentinian Champion in 1938, 1946 and 1948. He competed in the Chess Olympiads of 1935, 1937, 1939, 1950, 1952, 1954, 1956, 1962 and 1966. In the 1950 Olympiad he had the best score on second board (+9 −0 =5). He took part in the 1962 interzonal tournament where he finished thirteenth.

**Boleslavsky, Isaac** (1921–1977) Soviet chess player; awarded the title International Grandmaster in 1950. He became a National Master in 1939 and in the following year tied with Botvinnik for fifth place in the 1940 Soviet Championship. Later results in this event included third place in 1944 and second place in 1945 and 1947. Boleslavsky took part in the 1948 interzonal and qualified for the 1950 Candidates' tournament. In this event he shared first place with Bronstein, but was defeated by him in a special match arranged to determine the challenger for the subsequent World Championship match (+2 −3 =9). He competed in only one Chess Olympiad, that of 1952. Boleslavsky made important contributions to the theory of the openings, of which the rehabilitation of the variation of the Sicilian Defence that is named after him is the most important. In the 1960s Boleslavsky was the chief trainer of the Soviet Chess Federation, and was the second of Petrosian during the latter's rise to the World Championship.

**Boleslavsky System** an opening sequence arising out of the Grünfeld Defence: 1. P–Q4, N–KB3 2. P–QB4, P–KN3 3. N–QB3, P–Q4 4. N–B3, B–N2 5. Q–N3, P×P 6. Q×BP, O–O 7. P–K4, *P–B3*. Black plans to force the advance of his King pawn at the same time as he drives the White Knight from its central square. He will continue with: 8 . . ., P–QN4 9 . . ., Q–R4 and 10 . . ., P–N5. The most common continuation is: 8 B–K2. This variation was devised by the Soviet theorist Isaac Boleslavsky.

**Boleslavsky Variation** an opening sequence arising out of the Sicilian Defence: 1. P–K4, P–QB4 2. N–KB3, N–QB3 3. P–Q4, P×P 4. N×P, N–B3 5. N–QB3, P–Q3 6. B–K2, *P–K4*. It was at first thought that this move merely weakened the Queen pawn by making it backward, but in the 1940s it was discovered that this was offset by Black's piece activity. The most common continuations are: 7. N–N3 and 7. N–B3. The acceptance of a backward pawn in such positions was one of the many innovations of Louis Paulsen, but it fell into disrepute until its rehabilitation by Isaac Boleslavsky.

**Bondarevsky, Igor Zakharovich** (b. 12 May 1913) Soviet chess player; awarded the titles International Grandmaster in 1950, International Judge in 1954 and International Grandmaster of Correspondence Chess in 1961. He was joint Soviet Champion in 1940.

Bondarevsky became a National Master through his performance at the 1937 Soviet Championship and jointly won this event with Lilienthal three years later. His best subsequent result was an equal third in the 1947 Soviet Championship. He has played in few international tournaments – his best performance in such an event was equal sixth place in the 1948 interzonal which qualified him for the subsequent Candidates' tournament although illness prevented him from participating.

Bondarevsky is an outstanding correspondence player and played on first board for the Soviet team in the third and fourth Correspondence Chess Olympiads. He has been a trainer to several strong players, including Boris Spassky, and is also a well-known opening theorist.

**Bonius Socius** *Latin for* Good Companion. Pseudonym of Nicholas de St Nicholai, a Frenchman who lived at the end of the thirteenth century. He is primarily remembered as the author of a vellum manuscript of 182 leaves containing 290 illustrated chess problems.

**book** all published analyses of the openings including the most widely accepted evaluations of them.

**book draw** a standard drawn position that can be found in any textbook on the endings. Examples include King and Rook versus King and Bishop and King and Queen versus a King adjacent to a Bishop pawn on the seventh rank.

A book draw

**Böök, Eero** (b. 9 February 1910) Finnish chess player; awarded the title International Master in 1950.

Böök has been Finnish Champion several times. He played in the Chess Olympiads of 1935, 1937, 1950, 1952, 1958 and 1960. In 1947 he won the Helsinki zonal and therefore qualified for the 1948 interzonal where he finished twelfth.

**book move** an orthodox move. This is a commonly played continuation in the position reached and is one that is recommended in published analyses.

***Book of Chess, A*** a wide-ranging survey of chess from its inception to the present day written by C. H. O'D. Alexander. Among the topics covered are computer chess, a profile of a Grandmaster (Bent Larsen), and the numerous variants of chess that exist. It was first published in 1973 and uses descriptive notation.

**book player** a player who will follow memorized opening sequences to excess rather than depend upon his own judgment. The term is usually derogatory, implying that the player doubts his own capability and would be in trouble once play deviates from published analysis.

**Boston 64s** a founding member of the **National Chess League**. In the league's first season the team came eighth. The team's leading members were Kenneth Rogoff, Norman Weinstein and John Peters.

**Botterill, George S.** (b. 8 January 1949) British chess player; British Champion in 1974. He played for Wales in the 1976 Olympiad.

**Botvinnik, Mikhail Moisevich** (b. 17 August 1911) Soviet chess player; World Champion from 1948 to 1957, 1958 to 1960, 1961 to 1963; awarded the titles International Grandmaster in 1950 and International Judge of Chess Compositions in 1956. He was Soviet Champion in 1931, 1933, 1939, 1941, 1945, and 1952. He competed in the Chess Olympiads of 1954, 1956, 1958, 1960, 1962 and 1964.

Botvinnik was born in St Petersburg and learned to play chess when aged 12. Two years later he defeated the World Champion, Capablanca, in a simultaneous exhibition and in the following year came equal first in the Leningrad Championship. He became a Soviet Master at the age of 16 and four years later won the Soviet Championship for the first time, while in the same period he studied electrical engineering at the Leningrad Polytechnic Institute.

Botvinnik came equal first with Flohr in front of Lasker and Capablanca at Moscow (1935) and came equal first with Capablanca at Nottingham (1936) – the first major Soviet success in international chess. He was second at Moscow (1936) and equal third at Avro (1938), after which he challenged Alekhine to a World Championship match. However, other contenders had priority and the outbreak of war suspended all negotiations. During the war Botvinnik worked in engineering, but did compete in the 1940 Soviet Championship and in the Absolute Championship and won the latter event.

After the end of the war another challenge to the World Champion was issued, but Alekhine died before a match could take place. As a result, a World Championship match-tournament was held to determine his successor and Botvinnik won with ease by defeating each of the other four contenders in their individual matches. Over the next three years Botvinnik played almost no chess, but concentrated instead on obtaining his doctorate in engineering. His first title defence was against Bronstein in 1951; the match ended in a draw, allowing Botvinnik to retain his title (+5 −5 =14). His next challenger was Smyslov in 1954; this match also ended in a draw (+7 −7 =10). Smyslov fought his way through the qualifying cycle and again met Botvinnik in a title match in 1957. This time Botvinnik was defeated (+3 −6 =13), but exercised his right to a return match in the following year and regained the title (+7 −5 =11). The next opponent was Tal in 1960 and Botvinnik was well beaten by the younger man (+2 −6 =13). Yet again Botvinnik prepared for the return match with his customary thoroughness and won back the title (+10 −5 =6). His final World Championship match resulted in a loss to Petrosian (+2 −5 =15). By this time FIDE had passed a ruling abolishing a defeated World

Champion's automatic right to a return match (sometimes known as the 'anti-Botvinnik law') and Botvinnik withdrew from the World Championship qualifying cycle, as he felt it to be too tiring.

In recent years Botvinnik has attempted to devise a computer chess program of master strength. In 1957 he was awarded the Order of Lenin. Among Botvinnik's books translated into English are *Championship Chess* and *Computers, Chess and Long-range Planning*.

**Botvinnik Variation** an opening system arising out of the Nimzo-Indian Defence: 1. P–Q4, N–KB3 2. P–QB4, P–K3 3. N–QB3, B–N5 4. Q–B2, P–Q4 5. P–QR3, B×Nch 6. Q×B, *N–B3*. Black attempts to take advantage of White's loss of a tempo. A common continuation is: 7. N–B3, N–K5 8. Q–B2, P–K4.

**Bouaziz, Slim** (b. 16 April 1950) Tunisian chess player; awarded the title International Master in 1975. (1976 Elo rating: 2355)

**Boudy-Bueno Julio** Cuban chess player; awarded the title International Master in 1975. (1976 Elo rating: 2395)

**Bouwmeester, Hans** (b. 16 September 1929) Dutch chess player; awarded the title International Master in 1954. Bouwmeester represented his country in the Chess Olympiads of 1956, 1960, 1962, 1964, 1966, 1968 and 1970. (1976 Elo rating: 2420)

**BP** *abbrev. for* Bishop pawn.

**B.P.C.F.** or **BPCF** *abbrev. for* British Postal Chess Federation.

**Braille Chess Association** an organization for blind players founded in 1933. It arranges postal chess games for its members and enters teams in the British Chess League. A Blind Players Championship is also regularly held, the winner qualifying for the World Championship for the Blind, a tournament organized by the International Braille Chess Association.

**break** a pawn-move or sequence of pawn-moves intended to gain space for the pieces or to provide one or more flight squares for the King. It is normally a defensive manoeuvre.

**breakthrough** a pawn-move or sequence of pawn-moves that creates open lines, disrupts the opposing defence, or seizes squares for use as jumping-off points by the pieces when attacking.

**Bremen System** an opening sequence arising out of the English Opening: 1. P–QB4, P–K4 2. N–QB3, N–KB3 3. *P–KN3*. White intends to strengthen his control of his own Q5 square before developing his other minor pieces such as the King Knight. This variation was devised by the West German International Master Carl Carls.

**Breslau Variation** an opening sequence arising out of the Ruy Lopez: 1. P–K4, P–K4 2. N–KB3, N–QB3 3. B–N5, P–QR3 4. B–R4, N–B3 5. O–O, N×P 6. P–Q4, P–QN4 7. B–N3, P–Q4 8. P×P, B–K3 9. P–B3, B–K2 10. R–K1, O–O 11. N–Q4, *N×KP*. Black sacrifices a piece in return for a powerful attack. The critical continuation is: 12. P–B3, B–Q3 13. P×N.

The variation was first analysed by a group of German masters, principally Tarrasch, at the turn of the century. Compare **Tarrasch trap.**

**Breyer Gambit** an opening sequence arising out of the King's Gambit: 1. P–K4, P–K4 2. P–KB4, P×P 3. *Q–B3*. White begins to align his major pieces on the half-open file for a King-side attack. However, with best play Black should equalize; this is normally achieved by a counter-attack in the centre. Although this opening is now named after Gyula Breyer, it was known for many years before his birth.

**Breyer, Gyula** (1894–1921) leading theorist and player. He was born in Budapest on 3 April 1894 and studied engineering at the university there. He entered his first international tournament in Cologne (1911) where he finished sixth. In the following year he achieved his first major successes when he won the Hungarian Championship and also tied for seventh place at Bad Pistyan.

The war interrupted his development but he still showed his strength in the post-war era, coming joint second at Vienna (1920), first at Berlin (1920), and third at Vienna (1921). His only match was against Réti and he lost by a large margin (+0 −4 =1).

Breyer was also a strong blindfold player and broke the world record in 1921, but he is primarily remembered as being a leading theoretician of the hypermodern school. His is the dictum that after 1. P–K4, 'White's game is in its last throes'. His theoretical contributions lay mainly in the openings and included the Breyer Defence to the Ruy Lopez, the Breyer Gambit, and the Budapest Defence (with Abonyi and Barasz).

Breyer died of heart disease on 10 November 1921. Réti's epitaph was that, 'A new Steinitz was all too soon snatched from us'.

**brilliancy** a game containing a series of highly original and usually surprising chess moves, valued as much for their aesthetic appeal and innovative qualities as for positional or material gain.

**brilliancy prize** an award presented for a game in which has been demonstrated the highest level of creative or innovative play. The first tournament to award a brilliancy prize was New York (1876) where it was won by Bird for his game against Mason.

***Brilliant Touch, The*** a collection of 240 brilliancies compiled by Walter Korn. Most of the combinations are from obscure games and had not been published in book form before. It was first published in 1950 and uses descriptive notation.

**Brinckmann, Alfred** (1891–1967) West German chess player, arbiter, and author; awarded the title International Master in 1953 and the title International Judge in 1951.

**Bristol theme** a motif in problem chess in which a man is moved to an apparently useless square to clear a line for another man to reach a particular square and eventually deliver checkmate. The first problem to contain this theme was devised by the English problemist F. Healey, who entered it in the Bristol problem tournament (1861) where it won first prize. See **Indian theme**.

**British Championship** the national championship of the United Kingdom. It is held in conjunction with the annual B.C.F. Congress and takes place every August. The championship began in 1866 under the auspices of the British Chess Association and was won for the first time by Cecil de Vere. It was then held every two years until 1872, when John Wisker won the championship cup outright by winning the event for the second successive time. No championship was held from 1872 until 1904, when it was revived by the newly-created British Chess Federation and won by W. E. Napier. It has since been held annually, apart from the war years, and until 1949 was an all-play-all tournament with 12 selected competitors; since then it has been run under the Swiss System. For instance, the 1976 Championship was an 11-round Swiss event with 36 contestants and was won by Jonathan Mestel – who scored 9½ points, equalling the record of Yanofsky in 1953 and Alexander in 1956.

**Bristol theme**

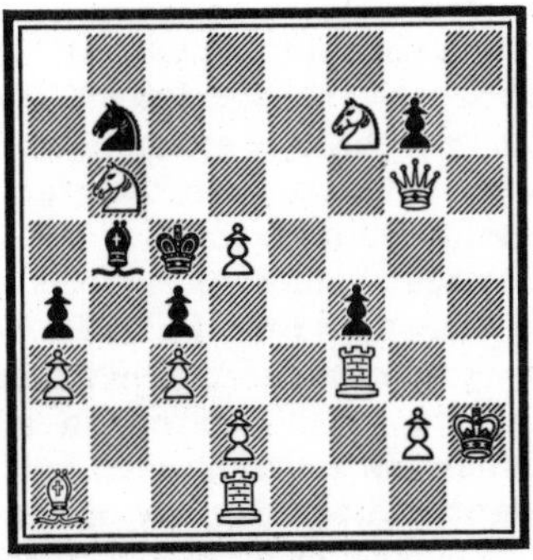

In this (the original) problem, White wins by: 1. R–R1, B–Q2 2. Q–N1, B–N4 3. Q–N1mate

**British Chess Association** an organization that was formed in 1855, originally under the name of the Chess Association, to coordinate chess within Britain. From the outset it faced the hostility of Staunton and its difficulties increased from 1865 with the creation of a hostile rival organization, the Counties' Chess Association. This internecine strife led to the collapse of both bodies in the 1890s.

The British Chess Association's officials included the Poet Laureate Lord Tennyson (who was elected President in 1885) and Sir Robert Peel, Lord Randolph Churchill and John Ruskin, who were all elected Vice-Presidents in 1885. Abbrev. **B.C.A.** or **BCA**.

**British Chess Federation** the governing organization of chess within the United Kingdom. It was created in 1904 to take the place of the defunct British Chess Association and is now responsible for the organization of the annual national championship, the promotion of tournaments and matches within the United Kingdom, and participation in FIDE events including the Chess Olympiads. It popularizes chess within the United Kingdom in numerous other ways.

The federation itself is formed from constituent units, such as the West of England Chess Union, Midland Counties Chess Union, Northern Counties Chess Union, etc., as well as smaller organizations such as the British Postal Chess Federation and the British Chess Problem Society. Abbrev. **B.C.F.** or **BCF.**

***British Chess Magazine*** one of the two leading chess periodicals in the United Kingdom. Founded in 1881, it is published monthly.

**British Chess Problem Society** a society that is concerned with all aspects of problem chess. It was founded as the Sussex Chess Problem Fraternity and became the British Chess Problem Fraternity on 2 November 1918 and adopted its present name on 8 November 1919. Its journal is *The Problemist.*

**British Correspondence Chess Championship** an annual event held under the auspices of the British Postal Chess Federation. It has one Championship section of eleven players, six Candidates' sections with nine players and up to six reserve sections containing nine players. Each section is a round-robin.

The games begin in the middle of October and can continue until 30 June, when unfinished games are adjudicated. The only games which are allowed to contravene this rule are those which would affect the first place of the Championship section; these are allowed to continue for another month before adjudication.

Entrants to this competition must be members of and recommended by an organization affiliated to the B.P.C.F. Any newcomers will normally be assigned to a reserve section. Winners of the Reserve and Candidates' sections may then compete in the Candidates' and Championship sections, respectively, in the following year.

**British Correspondence Chess Society** an organization that was formed in 1962 to encourage the playing of correspondence chess. It provides facilities for participation in national and international events and runs numerous competitions among which are a continuous tournament, a knockout competition and a tournament for Pocket Knight Chess. The association is a founder member of the B.P.C.F., to which it is affiliated. Its official publication, *Chess Post*, appears six times a year. Abbrev. **B.C.C.S.** or **BCCS.**

**British Lady Master** a title awarded by the British Chess Federation to any British woman who has shown a sufficiently high standard of play. The title is awarded to any woman who has either gained the Ladies I.M. title or who has qualified through one of the following six ways: (1) by one appearance in the B.C.F. grading list at 180 or more; (2) by two appearances in B.C.F. grading lists at 175 or more; (3) by three appearances in B.C.F. grading lists at 170 or more; (4) by four appearances in B.C.F. grading lists at 165 or more; (5) by winning a British Ladies Championship outright; or (6) by sharing the Championship with a player who has a grading of 170 or more after allowing for this result. The title was created in 1975.

**British Master** a title that is awarded by the British Chess Federation to Britons who have displayed a consistently high level of results. Abbrev. **B.M.** See **National Master.**

**British Postal Chess Federation** an organization founded in 1963 to encourage the playing of correspondence chess, organize national championships, award British titles, take part in international tournaments and matches and harmonize the efforts of the various independent British correspondence chess organizations.

The federation is affiliated to the British Chess Federation and the International Correspondence Chess Federation and itself has organizations such as the British Correspondence Chess Association, British Railways Staff Association and Postal Chess Club affiliated to it. Abbrev. **B.P.C.F.** or **BPCF.**

**Broadbent, Reginald J.** (b. 1906) British chess player; British Champion in 1948 and 1950.

**Bronstein, David** (b. 19 February 1924) Soviet chess player; awarded the titles International Grandmaster in 1950 and International Judge of Chess Compositions in 1961. He was joint Soviet Champion in 1948 and 1949, the World Championship challenger in 1951 and a competitor in the Chess Olympiads of 1952, 1954, 1956 and 1958. In addition he has taken part in five interzonals (winning two) and three Candidates' tournaments (winning one).

He was born in Belaya Tserkov and began to study chess under the direction of Soviet Master Alexander Konstantinopolsky while in the Young Pioneers. In 1938 he won the schoolboy championship of Kiev and two years later became the youngest Soviet Master since Botvinnik. Although he obtained only 6½ points out of 16 in his debut in the Soviet Championship of 1944, he came third in this event a year later and shared first place in it in 1948 and 1949, having won at Moscow (1946) in the meantime.

His victories in the 1948 interzonal and the subsequent Candidates' tournament led to a match with Botvinnik, which was drawn (+5 −5 =14) allowing Botvinnik to retain the title. Despite everyone's expectations Bronstein never again played in a World Championship match for this was the period when Smyslov dominated the chess scene. Bronstein has had numerous tournament successes including firsts at Hastings (1953), Belgrade (1954), Moscow (1959), Szombathely (1966) and Berlin (1968). An anthology of specimens of his play, *200 Open Games*, was published in 1975. (1976 Elo rating: 2540)

**Bronstein Variation** an opening sequence arising out of the Rubinstein Variation of the Nimzo-Indian Defence: 1. P–Q4, N–KB3 2. P–QB4, P–K3 3. N–QB3, B–N5 4. P–K3, P–QN3 5. N–K2, *B–R3*. Black puts pressure on the enemy Queen Bishop pawn. Common continuations are: 6. N–N3, and 6. P–QR3.

This variation was first played by Bronstein in the 1951 World Championship match, where he won with it. It was later frequently used by Smyslov in his three World Championship matches against Botvinnik.

**Browne, Walter Shawn** (b. 12 October 1946) American chess player; awarded the titles International Master in 1969 and International Grandmaster in 1970. Australian by birth, he became American Champion in 1974 and 1975 and has played in Chess Olympiads for both countries; he represented the United States in the 1976 Manila interzonal. Browne's tournament successes include firsts at Wijk aan Zee (1974), Lone Pine (1974), the Pan American Championship (1974) and Mannheim (1975). He is sometimes called the 'Swiss King' because of his success in tournaments run under the Swiss System. (1976 Elo rating: 2585)

**Buckle, Henry Thomas** (1821–1862) British historian; author of the *History of Civilization in England* (vol. 1, 1857; vol. 2, 1861), forming only the general introduction to a much larger work, which he was forced to abandon because of ill health. Buckle, as one of England's strongest chess players, was invited to participate in the **Great Exhibition tournament**, but declined because of work pressures. However, he agreed to play a match against Löwenthal, which he won (+4 −3 =0). In a match three years earlier (1848) he had defeated Kieseritzky (+3 −2 =3). Buckle had a rather dry sense of humour; when once asked if he had ever played a match against Staunton he replied, 'No, I was always careful to maintain friendly relations with him.' Following publication of the second volume of his history, he travelled to Egypt and Syria to improve his health. He died in Damascus on 29 May 1862 of typhoid fever.

**Budapest (1929)** a tournament with fourteen competitors, won by Capablanca (who scored 10½) ahead of Rubinstein (9½).

**Budapest Defence** a defence to the Queen pawn opening: 1. P–Q4, N–KB3 2. P–QB4, *P–K4* 3. P × P. Black normally continues with: 3 . . ., N–N5.

This gambit was pioneered by the Budapest masters, Abonyi, Breyer and Barasz during World War I and was first played competitively in a game between Breyer and Esser on 14 November 1916.

**buffer duo** (Kmoch's term) a joint formation of opposing duos that directly confront each other with only one rank separating them. A buffer duo would exist if White had pawns on his KR4 and KN4 and Black had pawns on his KR3 and KN3. The buffer duo is an amalgam of opposing **loose duos**. See ***Pawn Power in Chess***.

**Bukić, Enver** (b. 2 December 1937) Yugoslavian chess player; awarded the titles International Master in 1964 and International Grandmaster in 1976. He was first at Vrsac (1975). (1976 Elo rating: 2500)

**Burn, Amos** (1848–1925) British chess player; born in Hull on 31 December 1848. He learned to play chess at the age of 16, but did not play it seriously until his middle age, concentrating instead upon his career in marine insurance. His first major successes were a first at Nottingham (1886) and a second at London (1886) and these led to an invitation to compete at Frankfurt (1887) – his debut in a foreign tournament. Over the next 25 years he competed in 22 international tournaments and came first at Amsterdam (1889) and Cologne (1898) and second at Breslau (1889).

From 1913 until his death on 25 November 1925 he was the chess columnist of *The Field*.

**Burn Variation** an opening sequence arising out of the French Defence: 1. P–K4, P–K3 2. P–Q4, P–Q4 3. N–QB3, N–KB3

4. B–KN5, *P*×*P*. Black concedes superiority in the centre to White by this exchange of pawns, but has a sound position free from immediate risk. A common continuation is: 5. N×P. This variation is named after the English player Amos Burn.

**Buzzeca** (or **Buzecca**) a Saracen who, it is claimed, played and won two simultaneous blindfold games in Florence in 1266. See **blindfold chess.**

**Bykova, Elizaveta** (b. 1913) Soviet female chess player; Women's World Champion from 1953 to 1956 and from 1958 to 1962. She first won the Moscow Women's Championship in 1938 and won the Soviet Women's Championship in 1947, 1948 and 1950. She became Women's World Champion by defeating Ludmila Rudenko (+7 −5 =2), but lost the title to Olga Rubtsova in a triangular match (also with Rudenko). Bykova regained the title in 1958 by defeating Rubtsova (+7 −4 =3) and successfully defended it against Kira Zvorykina in 1960 (+6 −2 =5) before losing to Nona Gaprindashvili in 1962 (+0 −7 =4).

**Byrne, Donald** (1930–1976) American chess player; born 12 June 1930, died 8 April 1976. He was awarded the title International Master in 1962. Byrne won the U.S. Open Championship in 1953 and was also joint first in 1957. He played against the U.S.S.R. in the matches of 1954 and 1955, competed in the Chess Olympiads of 1962, 1964 and 1968, and was non-playing team captain in 1966. His brother is the International Grandmaster Robert Byrne.

**Byrne, Robert** (b. 20 April 1928) American chess player; awarded the titles International Master and International Grandmaster in 1964. One of the leading U.S. players, he reached the quarter-final of the Candidates' matches in 1974 when he was defeated by Spassky. (1976 Elo rating: 2540)

# C

**cable match** a match played by telegraph. From 1896 to 1911, 13 cable matches were played between the United States and the United Kingdom with each country winning six games and drawing one. The most famous participants were Blackburne, who played in 11 matches (+2 −4 =5), and Pillsbury, who played in eight matches (+1 −2 =5).

Between 1899 and 1924 eleven matches were played between teams representing American and British universities. This series also ended in a tie with four wins and three draws each. The most notable contestant was Capablanca, who played on first board in 1907 and drew against H. J. Rose. Compare **radio match, telex match.**

**Cadet** a Fairy pawn that cannot be promoted upon reaching the eighth rank until one of the pieces of its own colour is captured. It must then immediately promote to that piece if the promotion is legal. (It cannot promote and give check at the same time.) It was devised by P. Pratt and appears in his work, *Studies of Chess* (1825 edition).

**Café de la Régence** the centre of French chess in the eighteenth and nineteenth centuries. It was founded during the regency (1715–1723) of Philip, Duke of Orleans, after whom it was named, and quickly became a fashionable haunt. Among its frequent visitors were Voltaire, Diderot, Rousseau, Franklin and Robespierre. At this time France was the home of the world's strongest chess players, all of whom could be found at the Café de la Régence. They included Légal, Deschapelles, La Bourdonnais, Saint-Amant and Kieseritzky. It was the venue for several famous matches, notably that between Morphy and Harrwitz.

**Caïssa** the muse of chess. Caïssa was the creation of the eighteenth-century orientalist Sir William Jones, who wrote a poem with this title in 1763. It tells of the wooing of a wood-nymph named Caïssa by Mars, the god of war. His advances are rejected until Mars is advised to ask Euphron, god of sport, for assistance. Euphron invents chess which so charms Caïssa that she falls in love with Mars. The poem is believed to have been written under the inspiration of the medieval poem *Schacchia Ludus* (The game of chess) by Vida.

**Calabrese, The** *nickname of* Gioachino Greco.

**Calvo, Ricardo** (b. 22 October 1943) Spanish chess player; awarded the title International Master in 1974.

**Cambridge Springs (1904)** a major international tournament that was held from 25 April to 19 May in Cambridge Springs, Pennsylvania. It was decisively won by Marshall (who was undefeated), followed by Lasker and Janowski in equal second place, Marco in fourth place, Showalter in fifth place and Schlechter and Teichmann in sixth place. The other competitors were Barry, Delmar, Fox, Hodges, Lawrence, Mieses, Napier, Pillsbury and Tchigorin.

The main surprise was the abysmal form of Pillsbury, who was suffering from the illness that was to kill him less than two years later. It was from this date that Marshall became the leading player in the United States. Janowski's excellent performance was also slightly unexpected and probably encouraged his patron, Pierre Nardus, in his opinion that Janowski was the equal of the World Champion, Lasker. Cambridge Springs is also notable for the variation of the Queen's Gambit Declined that was played extensively there. See **Cambridge Springs Defence.**

**Cambridge Springs Defence** an opening sequence in the Queen's Gambit Declined, in which Black takes temporary advantage of the absence of White's Queen Bishop from its home square: 1. P–Q4, P–Q4 2. P–QB4, P–K3 3. N–QB3, N–KB3 4. B–N5, QN–Q2 5. P–K3, P–B3 6. N–B3, *Q–R4*. By this move, Black not only releases the pin on his Queen and pins White's Knight, but threatens on the next move to play N–K5. It was originally introduced by Harry Nelson Pillsbury before the end of the nineteenth century, although it is named after the Cambridge Springs Tournament of 1904. Also called **Cambridge Springs Variation, Pillsbury Defence.**

**Camel** a Fairy chesspiece that moves like a Knight but has a longer range. It is a type of Leaper. While a Knight moves 1 × 2 squares, a Camel moves 1 × 3 squares. A Camel on QB1 could thus move to KB2, Q4, or QN4. Compare **Giraffe, Zebra**.

**Cambridge Springs Defence**

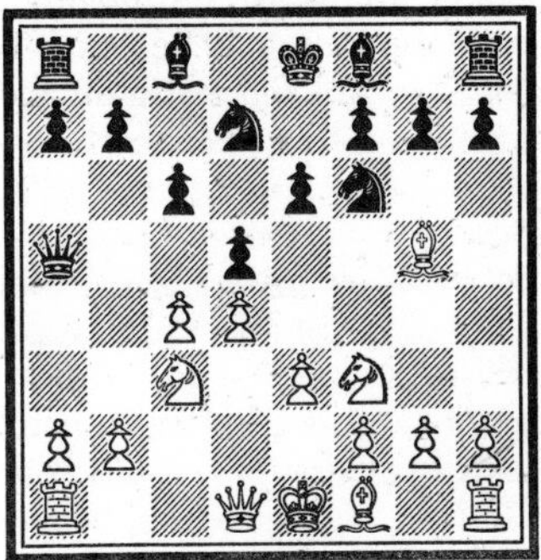

Position after 6 . . ., Q–R4

**Campos-Lopez, Mario** (b. 15 May 1943) Mexican chess player; awarded the title International Master in 1975. (1976 Elo rating: 2345)

**Canal's Variation** an opening sequence arising out of the Orthodox Defence to the Queen's Gambit Declined. In the following typical progression the characteristic move is in italics: 1. P–Q4, P–Q4 2. P–QB4, P–K3 3. N–QB3, N–KB3 4. B–N5, P–B4 5. P × QP, *Q–N3*.

**candidate** (Kmoch's term) one of two united passed pawns that is not blocked by an opposing pawn. For example, if a King pawn and a Queen pawn were faced by a King pawn, the Queen pawn would be the candidate as it would be the more likely of the two to queen, following a pawn exchange.

**Candidate Master** **1.** a title that is awarded by the British Chess Federation to Britons who have displayed a consistently high standard of play. It is a lower award than that of British Master. Abbrev. **C.M.** See **National Master.**

**2.** a title that is awarded in the U.S.S.R. and most East European countries. It is older than the British title of the same name.

**candidate move** any of a group of plausible moves that can be played in response to the opponent's move. A candidate move is similar to a **key** in problem chess. The term was coined by Alexander Kotov.

**Candidates' matches** the third stage in the three-year qualifying cycle to select a challenger in the subsequent match against the World Champion. They consist of three rounds of knock-out matches.

The competitors are the six players who finished highest in the preceding **interzonal tournament** as well as the loser of the previous World Championship match and the losing finalist of the previous series of Candidates' matches.

The Candidates' matches began in 1965, replacing the Candidates' tournaments which had existed since 1950. They were easier to organize and could be held in several countries at once; the matches closely simulated the conditions of a World Championship match; finally no player's chances could be affected by the results of any player other than his opponent which is not true of a tournament.

The first series was won by Spassky, who defeated Keres, Geller, and Tal. The 1968 series was also won by Spassky, who defeated Geller, Larsen, and Korchnoi. The 1971 series of matches was won by Fischer who scored six straight wins against Taimanov and Larsen and then defeated Petrosian. The matches in 1974 were won by Karpov, who defeated Polugayevsky, Spassky and Korchnoi. It is interesting to note that the winner of the Candidates' matches has then become the World Champion three out of four times.

**Candidates' tournament** formerly the third stage in the three-year qualifying cycle to select a challenger in the subsequent match against the World Champion. The competitors were those who had finished highest in the preceding interzonal tournament as well as the loser of the previous World Championship match and the player who was second in the previous Candidates' tournament. The winner of the Candidates' tournament became the official challenger.

The first Candidates' tournament was held in 1950 in Budapest. This was a round-robin event with ten players and was narrowly won by Bronstein after a play-off match against Boleslavsky.

The second was held in 1953 at Neuhausen and Zürich and was won by Smyslov, as was the 1956 tournament, which was held at Amsterdam and Leuwarden.

The 1959 tournament was held in Bled, Yugoslavia with one round each being played in Zagreb and Belgrade. Eight players took part and each played four games against every other competitor. It was won by Tal, who scored four wins against Fischer.

The 1962 tournament was held at Curaçao in the Dutch Antilles and was won by Petrosian. After this tournament, Fischer, who had finished only fourth, alleged that the Soviet players cheated by agreeing easy draws between themselves and fighting hard against him.

The 1965 event was not a tournament but was organized as a series of **Candidates' matches**. This met Fischer's objections, more exactly simulated the conditions of a World Championship match, and was easier to arrange since they could be split up and held in several countries.

**Capa** *nickname of* **José Raúl Capablanca**.

**Capablanca Memorial Tournament** a tournament in memory of José Raúl Capablanca which has been held annually in Havana or Cienfuegos, Cuba from 1962.

**Capablanca's freeing manoeuvre** a continuation of the Orthodox Defence of the Queen's Gambit Declined: 1. P–Q4, P–Q4 2. P–QB4, P–K3 3. N–QB3, N–KB3 4. B–N5, B–K2 5. P–K3, O–O 6. N–B3, QN–Q2 7. R–B1, P–B3 8. B–Q3, P×P 9. B×P, *N–Q4*.

Black seeks to simplify the position through exchanges, following up with: P–K4. This will 'free' his Queen Bishop, which is usually very cramped in the Queen pawn openings. The most common continuation is: 10. B×B, Q×B. This manoeuvre (now standard in the Orthodox Defence) was devised by Capablanca, who used it against Alekhine in their World Championship match.

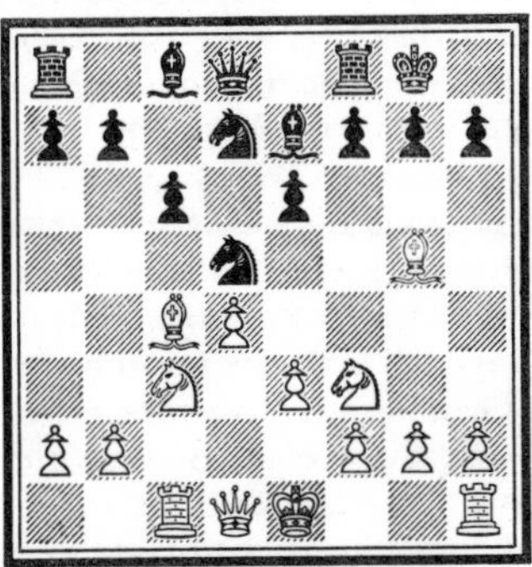

Position after 9 . . ., N–Q4

***Capablanca's Last Chess Lectures*** the transcripts of the last lectures Capablanca gave before his death in March 1942. In these 12 talks Capablanca concentrates upon the importance of studying the endings, but other topics include pawn play and an analysis of the Ruy Lopez. Although the talks were broadcast on South American radio in 1942, the English translation was not published until 1967. In this edition descriptive notation is used.

**Capablanca y Graupera, José Raúl** (1888–1942) Cuban chess player; World Champion from 1921 to 1927. He was born in Havana on 19 November 1888 and learned to play at the age of four by watching some of his father's games. Although one of the greatest of child prodigies, he played little chess in his youth; in 1901 he defeated Juan Corzo, Champion of Cuba, in a match (+4 −2 =6). After he left Columbia University in 1907 he immersed himself in chess and in 1909 won a crushing victory in a match against the U.S. Champion Frank Marshall (+8 −1 =14). This success led to his inclusion at San Sebastian (1911), one of the strongest tournaments of all time. Capablanca won this event, his first international tournament, with ease and also obtained the brilliancy prize for his first-round game against Bernstein. Shortly afterwards he entered the Cuban diplomatic service, although his main task was to publicize Cuba by playing chess.

Capablanca was now one of the chief challengers for the World Championship, but Lasker persistently avoided a match against him. They first played each other at St Petersburg (1914), where Lasker played one of the finest games of his career to defeat Capablanca and win first prize (with Capablanca second). The outbreak of the war prevented any match between them for several years, during which

Capablanca reached the height of his powers. In the decade from 1914 he lost only one game and gained a reputation for invincibility; he was referred to as 'The Chess Machine' for his unerring accuracy of play. In 1921 a World Championship match between Capablanca and Lasker was finally held; Lasker had attempted to retire without playing, but was tempted by a purse of $20,000 (the highest until 1972). The challenger was never in serious trouble and Lasker conceded defeat after fourteen games (+4 −0 =10).

During his time as World Champion Capablanca's results included firsts at London (1922) and New York (1927), a second at New York (1924) and a third at Moscow (1925). In 1927 he defended his title against Alekhine. He made no special preparations for the match – unlike his opponent who had painstakingly analysed Capablanca's play – and soon found himself in trouble. This was the longest World Championship match of all time and was unexpectedly lost by Capablanca (+3 −6 =25). Over the next fifteen years he attempted to secure a return match, but Alekhine avoided playing him.

After losing the title Capablanca's results declined slightly, perhaps because his aura of invincibility had been destroyed. However, he came first or equal first at eight tournaments, including Berlin (1928), Budapest (1928), Budapest (1929), Moscow (1936) and Nottingham (1936) and in 1931 defeated Euwe in a match (+2 −0 =8). He died in New York on 8 March 1942 after suffering a stroke at the Manhattan Chess Club.

Many consider Capablanca to be the greatest player of all time. He played chess that was positional rather than tactical and in which technique was carried almost to perfection. He was supreme in the endings and often resorted to early exchanges to simplify the position.

**capped Knight** a Knight with which the stronger player in an **odds** game undertakes to deliver checkmate. It is usually identified by being tied with string or ribbon or capped with a ring. The weaker player wins the game either by checkmating the opposing King or by capturing the capped Knight. This method of giving odds is now seldom seen.

**capped pawn** a pawn with which the stronger player in an **odds** game undertakes to deliver checkmate. The selected pawn (often the King Knight pawn) is usually identified by being tied with string or ribbon or capped by a ring. The weaker player wins either by checkmating the opposing King or by capturing the capped pawn. This method of giving odds is now seldom seen. Also called **pion coiffé**.

**capture** to remove an opposing man from the game by taking it from the square on which it stands and substituting a man of the opposite colour. Captures can be made only by men that can legally move from the squares upon which they stand to the squares on which the captures are made. Even if a move is geometrically possible, it may still be illegal because of other constraints, such as if the 'capturer' is pinned to a King and consequently unable to move legally.

While all the pieces capture in the same directions that they move the pawn can capture only on the diagonally adjacent squares in front of it. If there are no enemy men on these squares the pawn is unable to move to either of them. See **piece** (def. 1).

**Cardoso, Rodolfo Tan** (b. 25 December 1937) Philippino chess player; awarded the title International Master in 1957. He was Philippine Champion in 1958 and 1963. He won the Asian Zonal in 1958 and defeated Bronstein in the 1958 interzonal, so preventing him from qualifying. (1976 Elo rating: 2320)

**Carlsbad (1907)** a tournament with 21 competitors, narrowly won by Rubinstein (who scored 15) ahead of Maróczy (14½).

**Carlsbad (1929)** one of the major tournaments of the 1920s. It was an all-play-all event with 22 players and was won by Nimzovitch (+10 −1 =10) in his greatest tournament success. Equal second were Capablanca and Spielmann while Rubinstein was fourth. The other competitors were (in the order they finished): Becker, Euwe, Vidmar, Bogoljubov, Grünfeld, Canal, Mattison, Colle, Maróczy, Tartakover, Treybal, Sämisch, Yates, Johner, Marshall, Gilg, Thomas, and Menchik. Other tournaments at the same venue were also strong, especially Carlsbad (1923), which was won by Capablanca.

**Carls, Carl** (1880–1958) West German chess player, born on 16 September 1880 and died on 11 September 1958. He was awarded the title International Master in 1951. He was German Champion in 1934 and played in the Chess Olympiads of 1927 and 1930.

**Carls' System** another name for the **Bremen System**.

**Caro-Kann Defence** a defence to the King's pawn opening: 1. P–K4, *P–QB3*. Black attempts to establish a pawn on his Q4 without imprisoning his Queen Bishop. White's usual immediate reply: 2. P–Q4. Although mentioned by the sixteenth-century Italian player, Giulio Polerio, the opening was named after H. Caro of Berlin and M. Kann of Vienna, both of whom played it in the 1890s.

**Carroll, Lewis** *pseudonym of* Charles Lutwidge Dodgson (1832–1898), the author of *Alice's Adventures in Wonderland* (1865) and *Through the Looking Glass* (1872), both of which were written for Alice Liddell, the daughter of the Dean of Christ Church, Oxford (where Dodgson was a don). Dodgson charmed and intrigued the young Alice Liddell with some of the mysteries of chess and invented fanciful stories to illustrate the rules of the game and how the pieces move. He was later to incorporate many of these stories in *Through the Looking Glass*.

**Castaldi, Vicenzo** (1916–1970) Italian chess player, born on 15 May 1916 and died on 6 January 1970. He was awarded the title International Master in 1950. Castaldi was Italian Champion several times from 1936 and competed in the Chess Olympiads of 1937 and 1950.

**castle** 1. to move the King to KN1 or QB1 while at the same time bringing the relevant Rook over to KB1 or Q1 respectively. A player is allowed to castle only if (a) his King is not in check, (b) neither the King nor the relevant Rook has moved during the game, (c) no pieces separate the King and the relevant Rook, and (d) none of the squares over which the King travels is covered by an enemy man. To castle

King's side, i.e. moving the King to KN1, is symbolized in both algebraic and descriptive notation by O–O, while to castle Queen's side, i.e. moving the King to QB1, is symbolized by O–O–O.

The King moves only two squares in castling either King side or Queen side

**2.** a colloquial name for the Rook, based on the piece's (accidental) resemblance to a turreted tower of a castle.

**Castro, Oscar** (b. 8 April 1953) Colombian chess player; awarded the title International Master in 1975. (1976 Elo rating: 2380)

**Catalan Opening** an opening where White prepares to fianchetto his King Bishop at a very early stage: 1. P–Q4, P–Q4 2. P–QB4, P–K3 3. *P–KN3*. Black has several other opening moves that he could have made instead of those shown above; White develops his men according to a preconceived strategy. This opening is thought to have been first played in Catalonia, Spain and was given this name by Tartakover.

***Catalogue of Chessplayers and Problemists, A*** a privately printed collection of less familiar chess games and chess problems, together with the dates of birth and death of the players or composers (where available). It features lists of pseudonyms, Russian names and new-style dates (Gregorian and Julian calendars). It is compiled by the chess historian Jeremy Gaige and the first edition was published in 1969 (second edition, 1971). The third edition (1973) contained approximately 2,000 new names, bringing the total to around 6,000. (Gaige welcomes corrections and additions by chess enthusiasts; they may be sent in his care to 2313 Green Street, Philadelphia, Pennsylvania 19130, U.S.A.)

**Caxton, William** (1422?–1491) England's first printer. In 1475 he translated and printed *The Game and Playe of the Chesse*, the second book to be printed in English and the first to be written about chess. It was a translation of a work by Jacobus Cessolis and was a moral allegory using chess for illustrations. It was printed in Bruges.

**C.C.** *abbrev. for* correspondence chess.

**centralize** to develop pieces and pawns towards the centre where they can control the maximum number of squares.

**centre** the squares K4, K5, Q4, and Q5. The 12 immediately adjacent squares are also often considered to be a part of the centre (see **enlarged centre**). Control of the centre has been known to be important since the days of Steinitz. This is for several reasons including the facts that pieces stationed on these squares have a greater range than those stationed on the wings, can swiftly transfer to either wing, and can hamper the movement of enemy pieces from one wing to the other.

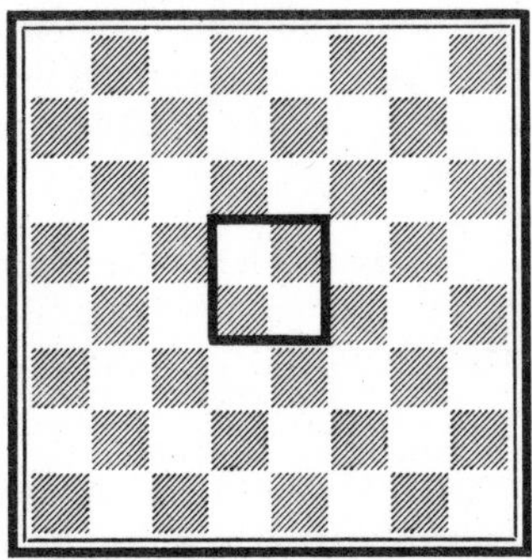

The centre squares: they can be controlled directly or (as with a Bishop on N2) from a distance

**Centre Counter Defence** a defence to the King's pawn opening: 1. P–K4, *P–Q4* 2. P×P. Black's continuation in former times was usually 2 . . ., Q×P, but nowadays 2 . . ., N–KB3 is preferred, delaying recapture of the pawn to avoid harassment of the Queen.

**Centre Game** an opening sequence: 1. P–K4, P–K4 2. *P–Q4*, P×P 3. Q×P. Black will gain time by attacking White's Queen, thus securing the advantage. Black's usual continuation is 3 . . ., N–QB3. See **Danish Gambit.**

**Centre-holding Variation** an opening sequence arising out of the Giuoco Piano. In the following typical progression the characteristic moves are in italics: 1. P–K4, P–K4 2. N–KB3, N–QB3 3. B–B4, B–B4 4. P–B3, *Q–K2* 5. P–Q4, *B–N3* 6. O–O, P–Q3. Black attempts to maintain his central pawns at the cost of conceding superiority in space to White.

**centre lever** (Kmoch's term) a **lever** on the King and Queen files. Unlike levers elsewhere, its slope does not convey an advantage to either side. Compare **inner lever, outer lever**. See ***Pawn Power in Chess.***

**centre pawns** the King and Queen pawns. They are generally more valuable than the pawns on the wings since they may be able to control the central squares, which form the most important section of the board.

**centreswap** (Kmoch's term) a type of doubling in which one centre pawn captures another. Compare **innerswap, outerswap**. See ***Pawn Power in Chess.***

**Centro Americano y del Caribe** an individual tournament open only to players from Central American or Caribbean countries. The first event was held in October 1975 in Guatemala and was won by M. Sisniega of Mexico (+9 −0 =3).

***Ceske Melodie*** a book written by Josef Pospisil (1861–1916), a well-known composer of chess problems. It was published in 1908 and discusses the philosophy behind the three-move problems of the so-called Bohemian School of problem composers.

**Cessolis, Jacobus de** a Dominican friar who lived in Lombardy in the thirteenth century. He is principally remembered for his homily, *De ludo scachorum* (On the game of chess) which used chess as a source from which to draw observations on morals in real life.

**ch** *abbrev. for* check.

**chain** see **pawn chain.**

**chainfork** (Kmoch's term) an attack by a Knight upon two pawns in a pawn chain. Kmoch writes that the tension generated in this way will often explode in sacrificial combinations. See **double attack, fork, *Pawn Power in Chess*.**

**chain lever** (Kmoch's term) a situation that exists when two levers are diagonally adjacent. A chain lever would exist if White had pawns on his QR4 and QN3 while Black had pawns on his QN4 and QB5. This formation favours the player whose leading pawn is the furthest advanced. Compare **double lever, mute chain lever.** See ***Pawn Power in Chess*.**

**Challengers' tournament** another name for **Candidates' tournament.**

**Chameleon** a Fairy chesspiece that changes its powers on each move. Unless otherwise specified, a Chameleon will take the powers of a Queen, Knight, Bishop, Rook, and Queen again on successive moves. It was invented by W. E. Lester in 1925.

**chameleon-echo** a type of chess problem where the King is checkmated on differently coloured squares in successive variations. See **Echo model.**

***Championship Chess*** the tournament book of the 1941 Soviet Championship match-tournament compiled and annotated by M. Botvinnik. This is one of the outstanding tournament books not only because of the calibre of the competitors (Botvinnik, Keres, Smyslov, Boleslavsky, Lilienthal and Bodarevsky) but also because of the quality and depth of the annotations on which Botvinnik worked for three years. It was translated by Stephen Garry and first published in English in 1950. The English edition uses descriptive notation.

**Chariot** the equivalent of the Rook both in chaturanga and in modern chess and the piece from which the Rook is descended. It was one of the four components of each player's forces (the three others being the elephants, cavalry and infantry) which accurately copied the composition of the armies of ancient India. The move of the Chariot has always been identical to that of the modern Rook, unlike most other pieces whose moves radically differ from those of their forerunners.

**Charousek, Rudolf** (1873–1900) Austro-Hungarian chess player; born in Prague on 10 September 1873. Charousek was an avid player –

apparently too poor to buy a copy of the *Handbuch des Schachspiels*, he is said to have copied it by hand from one in the public library. His first international tournament was Nuremberg (1896); he came only 12th but did beat Lasker who prophesied that he would eventually be defending his title against Charousek. Other results included a first at Berlin (1897) and second places at Budapest (1896) and Cologne (1898). Charousek died of tuberculosis at the age of 27.

***Charusim al sechok Shahmath*** a twelfth-century Hebrew poem (Verses on the Game of Chess) by Aben-Ezra.

**chaturanga** *Sanskrit for* chess; the earliest known version of chess which existed in India at least as early as the sixth century A.D. The word is a composite of *chatur* (four) and *anga* (limbs) and was the name of the standard army of ancient India. The 'four limbs' were the chariots, elephants, cavalry and infantry which were represented in chaturanga by the forerunners of the Rooks, Bishops, Knights and pawns respectively. The remaining two pieces symbolized the king and his vizier. Chaturanga was won either through checkmate or by baring the King.

**cheapo** (originally, Canadian chess slang) a swindle.

**check** 1. a compulsory warning to the opponent that his King is *en prise*. The term is derived from the Persian word *shah* (King), since it was once customary to call out the names of the pieces that were attacked by the newly moved piece.

2. an attack on the King. Abbrev. **ch**; Symbol **+**

**Checkless Chess** a type of Fairy Chess in which neither side may check a King unless it is checkmate. This condition enormously increases the power of the Kings which become dangerous attacking pieces.

**checkmate** an attack on a King that cannot be repulsed. It exists when the checking man cannot be captured, when interposition between the attacker and the King is impossible and when the King has no flight square.

Checkmate is derived from the Persian words *shah* (King), and *mat* (defeated). Also called **mate**.

**Chekhov, Valery** Soviet chess player; awarded the title International Master in 1975 upon winning the 1975 World Junior Championship. (1976 Elo rating: 2530)

**Chernev, Irving** (b. 1900) American chess player and author of several entertaining books on chess.

**chess** the origins of the game of chess are somewhat clouded in recorded and archaeological history. According to H. J. R. Murray (*A History of Chess*, 1913), 'The earliest works which make mention of chess date from the beginning of the 7th century A.D., and are associated with NW India, Persia, and Islam.' Chess is most certainly a type of war game, as philological evidence of the early names of the pieces suggests. (For example, *pawn* comes from the Latin *pedo*, meaning foot-soldier.)

Attempts to place the origins of chess further back than about the 6th century have not been totally successful and the discovery of chesslike pieces in ancient Egyptian tombs is not considered supportive evidence. Likewise, in 1973 Russian archaeologists discovered a china jar in the Uzbek Republic, near the border of Afghanistan, believed to have been made in the 2nd century; among other objects, it contained two ivory figurines that closely resemble chess pieces.

Enthusiasm for chess spread from India throughout the civilized world, reaching Europe (by means of several routes) by about the middle of the 10th century A.D. Chess was widely played during the Middle Ages and soon became extremely popular among the leisured classes of Europe. The moves, names and individual powers of the pieces changed only gradually and it was not until about the 17th or 18th century that the game began to settle down to its recognizable modern features, although many important changes were made in the 15th century. See **King, Queen, Rook, Bishop, Knight, pawn, checkmate.**

***Chess*** one of the two leading chess periodicals in the United Kingdom. It was founded in 1935 by B. H. Wood, who is still its editor, and is published monthly. Its address is Sutton Coldfield, B73 6AZ. Compare ***British Chess Magazine.***

**Chess and Checker Club of New York** one of the largest chess meeting houses in New York. At various times up to 200 people of widely-varying strengths can be found there. It is situated near Times Square at 212 West 42nd Street.

**Chess Archives** a loose-leaf classified encyclopedia of the theory and practice of chess, originally published twice-monthly and edited by Dr Max Euwe. An English translation (like the original, consisting of sixteen pages per issue) was first published in 1952.

**chess blindness** the failure to spot a normally obvious danger, such as the fact that a piece has been left *en prise*. Such blunders are frequently seen at the amateur or novice level but may also occur in games at the master level. See **amaurosis scacchistica, blunder.**

**chessboard** the board on which the game of chess is played. It consists of 64 squares, alternately light and dark, arranged into eight rows and eight columns. The light-coloured corner squares must always be on the right of the players. The number of squares on the board has not altered since the creation of chess, but the chequering of the board was a thirteenth-century European invention.

**chess clock** a device to record the exact time taken by each player during the game. It is made up of two clocks. At any time only the clock of the player whose move it is will be ticking; the player moves and presses a button or lever on the top of his clock, which stops it and sets his opponent's clock in operation. On the dial of each clock is a tiny pendulum, known as a 'flag', which is steadily pushed upwards by the minute-hand as it approaches the figure 12. Once this number is passed the flag drops indicating that the player has run out of time. The initial setting of the clocks' minute-hands will determine the time limit each player has.

The first chess clock was invented by Thomas Bright Wilson of

Manchester and was used at London (1883). Previously hour-glasses or ordinary clocks stopped and started by friends were used.

**chess column** a section of a newspaper or periodical that is concerned with chess. A typical chess column appears at weekly intervals and consists of an annotated game, one or more chess problems, and news of general interest to chess players.

The first chess column to appear in a newspaper was that of the *Liverpool Mercury* which appeared on 9 July 1813. The world's oldest chess column still extant is that of the *Illustrated London News*. It first appeared on 25 June 1842.

***Chess Companion, The*** an anthology of stories, articles, games and puzzles compiled by Irving Chernev, first published in 1949.

**Chess Endgame Study Circle** a society that is interested in all aspects of the endgame study and problem. It was revived in November 1975 after a period of eclipse. Well-known members are Edmund Peckover and Walter Korn (editor of M.C.O.). Its founder is the English study composer A. J. Roycroft.

***Chess Fever*** a two-act Soviet film comedy (1925) that satirizes the mania for chess. It was produced and directed by Vsevolod Pudovkin during an international chess tournament that was being held in Moscow and in which the future World Champion, Capablanca, was participating (he was actually seen in one of the episodes).

Pudovkin used a roving camera, focusing on tournament fans in the Moscow streets (who were seen clutching pocket chess sets and discussing chess positions) and even invading the Hotel Metropol, in which the tournament was being held. These authentic shots were mixed in rapid sequence with studio shots in which chess dominated the lives of the actors (one of whom was seen on his knees apparently about to propose to a beautiful lady, but in fact studying a chessboard on the floor).

***Chess for Fun and Chess for Blood*** articles and reminiscences by the International Master Edward Lasker. The first section (*Chess for Fun*) discusses combinations, endgame play and strategy with illustrations from the author's games. The second section (*Chess for Blood*) deals with Edward Lasker's experiences in tournaments and matches and gives in full his draw against his namesake Emanuel Lasker at New York (1924). The book was first published in 1942 and uses descriptive notation.

***Chess: Games to Remember*** an anthology of nearly 300 games compiled by I. A. Horowitz. In the author's opinion these represent the best chess played in the 1960s. It was first published in 1972 and uses descriptive notation.

**chessic** *relating to* chess.

***Chess in a Nutshell*** a concise introduction to chess by Fred Reinfeld. It sets out the rules of chess and explains the moves of the men and chess notation. From there it provides a guide to play in the opening, middle-game and ending. It was first published in 1958 and uses descriptive notation.

***Chess Informant*** *another name for* **Informator**.
**chessist** a chess player or anyone interested in chess.
***Chess Life & Review*** the chess periodical of the United States Chess Federation. It is published monthly under the editorial direction of Burt Hochberg. Its address is 479 Broadway, Newburgh, N.Y. 12550, U.S.A.
**Chess Machine, The** term by which José Raúl Capablanca is popularly described.
**chessman** a pawn or major or minor piece. See **piece**.
**chessmaster** any player who holds the title of **Master** or higher or who is of equivalent playing strength. See **International Master, International Grandmaster**.
***Chessmen*** an illustrated book on the history and development of chessmen written by A. E. J. Mackett-Beeson. It was first published in 1973.
***Chess Mind, The*** a book by Gerald Abrahams. Its purpose is to describe the intellectual processes involved when playing chess. This is supplemented by 47 annotated games. It was first published in 1951 and uses descriptive notation.
**chess notation** see **notation**.
**Chess Olympiad** a biennial tournament in which teams from all over the world meet to compete against each other. It is held under the auspices of FIDE, which selects the host nation.

An attempt to include chess in the 1924 Olympic Games failed, because of the difficulty of distinguishing between amateurs and professionals. It was left to FIDE to organize a Chess Olympics, and in 1927 London became the venue for the first successful Chess Olympiad. Olympiads were then held at irregular intervals until World War II and have been held regularly since 1950.

Any association that is affiliated to FIDE may enter the Olympiads. (In the case of the United Kingdom this means that teams from the four countries plus Guernsey can enter separately.) Each team consists of up to six players and is made up of four regular players plus reserves.

The increase in the number of competitors eventually made it impossible for each team to play every other. An early solution to the problem was to seed the teams before the competition and assign them to preliminary sections, from which the most successful progressed to the *A* finals, the next to the *B* finals, and the weakest to the *C* and *D* finals. The winner of the *A* finals received the Hamilton-Russell Cup.

This system had certain drawbacks: it was difficult to seed teams accurately and an incorrect seeding could harm or improve a team's chances markedly; secondly, a large number of games had to be played, often against extremely weak teams.

The **Swiss System** was adopted for the 1976 Olympiad at Haifa as the increasing numbers had made the previous system unwieldy, necessitating too long a tournament. Thus the Swiss was used to keep the event to thirteen rounds so that it could all be finished in less than three weeks. Also called **International Team Tournament, Tournament of**

**Nations, World Team Championship.**

**chessomania** a pathological craving for chess to the virtual exclusion of all other activities and concerns.

***Chess Openings, Theory and Practice*** an encyclopedia of the opening. It contains concise explanations of the aims behind each opening and details 2660 variations together with 439 games as illustrations. It was published in 1964 under the editorial direction of I. A. Horowitz and must now be considered slightly outdated, although still immensely valuable for all but the strongest. It uses descriptive notation.

**chessophrenetic** (nonce term) a chess fanatic.

**Chess-o-rama** a variant of chess played on four interlocking boards by eight people. The four boards together form a four-foot square with patterns representing four oceans and five continents. There are two teams with the players of the same colour acting as allies. Initially the four games are played in comparative isolation, but as they proceed there are many opportunities for cooperation. There are also special rules for air attack. The game was invented by Lawrence H. Nolte of Lebanon, Pennsylvania and won a gold medal at the International Licensing Exhibition of 1973.

**Chess Oscar** a statuette of a woman sheltering under an umbrella, awarded each year to the outstanding player. The Oscar was inaugurated in 1967 and the award is decided by the votes of the International Association of Chess Journalists (A.I.P.E.). It was won by Bent Larsen in 1967, Boris Spassky in 1968 and 1969, Robert Fischer in 1970, 1971, and 1972, and Anatoly Karpov in 1973, 1974, 1975 and 1976.

***Chess Player's Annual*** the first yearbook on chess to be published in English. It was compiled by a Charles Tomlinson and covered the year 1856.

***Chess Player, The*** a half-yearly publication containing well over 1000 top-class games as well as FIDE ratings, game endings, occasional articles, etc. It uses figurine algebraic notation.

***Chess Players, The*** a novel by Frances Parkinson Keyes based upon the life of Paul Morphy. It was first published in 1960.

**chess problem** a composed position in which a task is set for the reader. Chess problems are either orthodox and abide by the laws of chess or heterodox and contain innovations that affect the problem (see **Fairy Chess**).

Orthodox chess problems can themselves be sub-divided into problems where mate can be delivered through a forced sequence of moves and problems where the task is to reach an obviously drawn or winning position, but where there is no quick end in sight. See **endgame study**.

***Chess Questions Answered*** a collection of essays by the U.S. Grandmaster Larry Evans based upon questions sent to his column in the *Chess Life & Review*. It was first published in the United States in 1969 and in the United Kingdom in 1971. It uses descriptive notation.

***Chess Secrets*** the autobiography of Edward Lasker. It is dominated by his experiences in chess; in it he provides brief biographies and reminiscences about many of the masters he has played. Accounts of famous tournaments and matches in which he has competed are also included. Among these are the tournament at New York (1924) and the United States Championship match against Marshall, which took place in 1923. The book was first published in 1929 and uses descriptive notation.

***Chess the Easy Way*** a book by Dr Reuben Fine. Its purpose is to help a complete beginner reach the standard of an average club player. As well as detailing the moves of chess it contains chapters on each phase of the game, together with relevant problems for the reader to solve. It was first published in 1942 and uses descriptive notation.

***Chess Tournament Crosstables*** a privately printed collection of the results of international chess tournaments, compiled by the chess historian Jeremy Gaige. Volume IV (published in 1974) contains tournament results in over 810 crosstables for the decade 1921–1930. Also included are tables of national championships and recurring tournaments.

**Chicago Prairie Dogs** a founding member of the **National Chess League**. In the league's first season the team came seventh. The leading members of the team were Richard Werber and William Martz.

**Chigorin** a variant spelling of **Tchigorin**.

**Chocholous, Jiri** (1856–1930) Bohemian composer of chess problems, born in what is now part of Czechoslovakia.

**Christoffel, Martin** (b. 2 September 1922) Swiss chess player; awarded the title International Master in 1952. He was Swiss Champion in 1942, 1943, 1945, 1948 and 1952. He also won the Coupe Suisse in 1944.

**Ciocîltea, Victor** (b. 16 January 1932) Romanian chess player; awarded the title International Master in 1957. He was Romanian Champion in 1952, 1959, 1961, 1962, 1970 and 1971 and competed in the Chess Olympiads of 1956, 1962, 1964, 1966, 1968, 1970, 1972 and 1974. (1976 Elo rating: 2480)

**Circe chess** a type of Fairy Chess in which each captured piece is immediately replaced on its original square if this is unoccupied. If it is not, the piece remains off the board as in normal chess. Minor pieces are returned to the square of the identical colour to that on which the capture occurred. Pawns are returned to the second rank of the file on which they were captured. Circe chess was devised by Pierre Monréal, a Canadian, on New Year's Eve in 1967.

**Cirić, Dragoljub** (b. 12 November 1935) Yugoslavian chess player; awarded the title International Master in 1961 and the title International Grandmaster in 1965. (1976 Elo rating: 2435)

**Clare Benedict Challenge Cup** an annual West European team tournament that began in 1953. It consists of a round-robin held on four boards and is contested by six nations (the number was increased to eight in 1974), although the list of nations taking part differs each year. The tournament was regularly held in Switzerland, but since 1970 has been held in a different country each year. England was for a long time unsuccessful in this event, but eventually won it for the first time in 1974, having been taking part since 1954. The tournament is named after the late Miss Clare Benedict, who died in 1962. No country could be found to host the event in 1975 or 1976 and it was feared that the series had ended, but Denmark brought it back to life by organizing and winning the 1977 tournament.

**Clarke, Peter H.** (b. 18 March 1933) British chess player and writer. He represented England in all the Chess Olympiads from 1956 (Moscow) to 1968 (Lugano). Clarke is chess columnist for *The Sunday Times* and is the author of several books, including *100 Soviet Chess Miniatures*, *Mikhail Tal's Best Games of Chess* and *Petrosian's Best Games of Chess*. (1976 Elo rating: 2350)

**classical** a description of a style of play that evolved in the late nineteenth century. It stressed the importance of swift development and of occupying and controlling the centre by pawns. Leading members of the classical school were Steinitz and Tarrasch. By the early twentieth century these principles were becoming too dogmatically laid down and were increasingly challenged by the members of the hypermodern school. Compare **hypermodern.**

**Classical Benoni Defence** an opening sequence arising out of the Benoni Defence: 1. P–Q4, P–QB4 2. P–Q5, *P–K4* 3. P–K4, *P–Q3*. Black closes the centre and attempts to free his game by later advancing his King Bishop pawn. There are numerous continuations. Although this variation was regularly played by Alekhine, he considered it one of his 'chess sins' and inferior for Black.

**Classical Variation (Orthodox Defence)** an opening sequence arising out of the Orthodox Defence to the Queen's Gambit Declined. The following is the typical progression: 1. P–Q4, P–Q4 2. P–QB4, P–K3 3. N–QB3, N–KB3 4. B–N5, B–K2 5. P–K3, O–O 6. N–B3, QN–Q2 7. R–B1, P–B3 8. B–Q3, P×P 9. B×P, N–Q4 10. B×B, Q×B 11. O–O, N×N 12. R×N, P–K4. See **Orthodox Defence.**

**C.L.&R.** *abbrev. for Chess Life & Review.*

**Cleveland Kinghunters** a founding member of the **National Chess League.** In the league's first season the team, which included Milan Vukcevich and Dumitru Ghizdavu, came third.

**clock** see **chess clock.**

**Closed Defence** a defence to the Ruy Lopez in which Black attempts to avoid exchanges and to maintain a pawn on his K4, characterized by the moves 3 . . ., P–QR3 4. B–R4, N–B3 5. O–O, B–K2. Possible plans of action are numerous, depending on whether White chooses the King or Queen side as his principal base of activity.

**closed file** a file that has pawns from both sides upon it. Initially all files are closed, but at least some will be converted to half-open or open files as the game proceeds unless there is a very quick decision. See **file.**

**closed formation** (Kmoch's term) a pawn formation in which all the pawns are on the board, at least one of which has crossed the frontier line. Compare **open formation.** See ***Pawn Power in Chess.***

**closed game** a position with extensive interlocked pawn chains and little room for manoeuvre by the pieces. Most men will still be on the board and most of the pieces will be behind the pawns creating a cramped position with few opportunites for exchanges. Closed games are more likely to result from the Queen pawn opening and the flank openings than from the King pawn opening. Compare **open game**.

**closed Knight's tour** a **Knight's tour** in which the last move of the knight lands it upon its starting square. The formulation of closed Knight's tours was first studied by the great eighteenth-century Swiss mathematician Leonard Euler. Also called **Euler**.

**Closed Variation (Tarrasch Defence)** an opening sequence arising out of the Orthodox Defence to the Queen's Gambit Declined: 1. P–Q4, P–Q4 2. P–QB4, P–K3 3. N–QB3, P–QB4 4. *P–K3*. See **Tarrasch Defence.**

**Cobo, Eldis** (b. 5 September 1929) Cuban chess player; awarded the title International Master in 1967. (1976 Elo rating: 2370)

**Colle, Edgar** (1897–1932) Belgian chess player; born 18 May 1897 and died after an operation for a gastric ulcer. He was Belgian champion in 1924. Other successes included firsts at Merano (1926), Scarborough (1927), Hastings (1928), and Scarborough (1930). Colle is especially remembered for his contributions to opening theory and for his successes with the system named after him.

**Colle System** an opening sequence: 1. P–Q4, P–Q4 2. N–KB3, N–KB3 3. *P–K3*. White concentrates on creating a secure centre and developing his pieces although his Queen Bishop is restricted by the pawns. This opening is named after Edgar Colle, the Belgian chess player who popularized it.

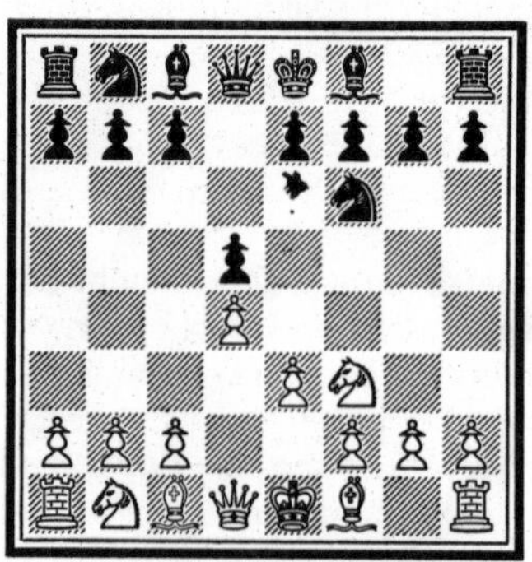

Position after 3. P–K3

**Combe, Robert F.** (b. 16 August 1912) British chess player; British Champion in 1946.

**combination** a coordinated series of moves involving two or more chess pieces, designed to capture enemy pieces, force checkmate, or just gain a positional advantage. A common characteristic of a combination is the initial sacrifice of a piece, thereby opening direct lines of assault on the exposed King. See also **brilliancy**.

***Combinations: the Heart of Chess*** a book by Irving Chernev. Its purpose is to teach the art of combination by citing examples from tournament play. After progressing from easy to difficult combinations, the book shows combinations hidden in the annotations of games as well as disastrous combinations suggested by kibitzers and boomerang combinations where the combiner did not see far enough. The book then examines examples from the play of 14 major players from Anderssen to Botvinnik. It was first published in 1960 and uses descriptive notation.

**combine** to move pieces and pawns into alignment for a combination.

**Combined Chessman** any Fairy chesspiece that possesses the powers of two distinct pieces. Combined Chessmen can be divided into three groups. First there are pieces that can move and capture with the powers of two pieces – examples being the Amazon, Dragon, Empress, Gryphon or Griffen, Gnu, and Princess. Secondly there are pieces that can move like one man and capture like another – examples being the pieces that move like a Bishop and capture like a Rook and vice versa, and the pieces that move like a Knight and capture like a Rook and vice versa. These pieces do not have particular names in English, but hybrid designations such as Bishop-Mover/Knight-Capturer. Thirdly there are the Hunters, which are pieces that possess the powers of one piece when advancing and of another when retreating.

**Commission for Chess Compositions** a body that functions independently within the framework of FIDE. It confers the titles of International Arbiter for Chess Compositions, International Master for Chess Compositions, and International Grandmaster for Chess Compositions, which are ratified by FIDE at its congresses.

**Commons, Kim** (b. 23 July 1951) American chess player; awarded the title International Master in 1976. He was equal first in the 1975 American Open tournament and was a member of the gold-medal winning U.S. team at the 1976 Haifa Olympics. (1976 Elo rating: 2420)

**compensation** an advantage that counterbalances a disadvantage elsewhere. The compensation might be of a different nature to the disadvantage as, for example, in gambits where a gain of a tempo is considered adequate compensation for a loss of a material. However, compensation can be in the same element. For example, the loss of a Rook might be compensated for by the capture of a Bishop and two pawns.

**compensation, law of** the possession of a good square tends to be offset by the opponent's possession of a good square. This axiom has been stated in this form by G. Abrahams.

***Complete Book of Chess, The*** a collection of essays and chess problems compiled by I. A. Horowitz and P. L. Rothenberg. It covers a wide range of topics from the origins of chess to the age factor in master chess. It also includes numerous problems and endgame studies as well as 41 examples of *amaurosis schacchistica* committed by master players. The book was first published in 1969 and uses descriptive notation.

***Complete Games of World Champion Anatoly Karpov, The*** the definitive collection of Karpov's recorded games (541) up to 1975 when it was published. It was compiled by K. J. O'Connell, D. N. Levy and J. B. Adams and uses figurine algebraic notation.

**composed ending** see **endgame study.**

**compound** (Kmoch's term) a formation that contains elements of more than one pawn formation. For instance, a **cross lever** could also be regarded as a type of **duo** or **ram.** See ***Pawn Power in Chess.***

**Computer Chess Championship** the first world computer chess championship was held in August 1974 in Stockholm under the control of the International Federation for Information Processing. Thirteen programs from eight nations competed in the tournament, which was a four-round Swiss event. The championship was won by Kaissa (a Soviet program from the Institute of Control Science, Moscow). Second was the U.S. champion, Chess 4.0, from Northwestern University, Illinois; and the Canadian champion, Ribitt, was third. The tournament revealed a rise in the standard of computer chess in recent years (Chess 4.0 was estimated to be approximately 1600 on the Elo scale) and was the scene of the first recorded instance of a positional piece sacrifice by a computer (by the U.S. computer, Chaos, in its game with Chess 4.0).

**condensed algebraic** see **algebraic notation.**

**congress** any large event which contains more than one tournament and in which competitors from more than one location or club are eligible to participate. The usual chess congress in the United Kingdom is a week-end or holiday event organized under the Swiss system. A typical example is the annual Southend chess congress, which contains open, major, minor and junior tournaments, as well as the southern counties championship.

**connect** (of Rooks) to bring Rooks of the same colour onto a common rank, with no pawns or pieces separating them. In the opening, Rooks will normally be connected on the first rank; this is accomplished by castling and then developing the Queen and minor pieces onto squares in front of the first rank. Connected Rooks can be much stronger than the sum of their parts when separate. See **unite.**

**connected passed pawns** another name for **united passed pawns.**

**consolidate** to make and retain secure positional or material advantages gained during the course of the game.

**consolidation** the process of retaining and making secure positional and tactical advantages gained during the course of the game.

**consultation chess** a game in which there are two or more players on one or both sides who act jointly, deciding their move out of earshot of their opponent or opponents.

Consultation games have a venerable history. Both the Scotch Opening and the French Defence originated in consultation games. Morphy won a sparkling game against the combined efforts of the

Duke of Brunswick and Count Isouard; he also met Staunton in some offhand consultation games (his team won).

However, playing in a team in a consultation game does not appear to give the advantage that one would suppose. More brilliancies are known where the partners were the losers against a single expert than vice versa. Perhaps playing by committee creates special problems, such as indecisiveness or perhaps it is merely a reflection of the fact that players who are given such odds are likely to be appreciably weaker than their opponent anyway. The game between Alekhine and four unknown players is an outstanding example of a Grandmaster seizing a heaven-sent opportunity: 1. P–K4, P–QB3 2. P–Q4, P–Q4 3. N–QB3, P×P 4. N×P, N–Q2 5. Q–K2, KN–B3?? 6. N–Q6 mate.

**continental notation** another name for **algebraic notation.** This form of notation is used throughout the Continent with the exception of Spain, where a form of descriptive notation is employed.

**control** domination of a square or group of squares, enabling a piece to be maintained there or an enemy piece to be kept away. If one player's connected Rooks control an open file they cannot be driven away and may eventually be able to penetrate the enemy position. Control of the centre (directly by pawns or at a longer range by pieces) is one of the main objectives of each player in the opening.

**cook** a flaw in a chess problem. Perhaps the problem could be solved by more than one key or mating sequence, or alternatively a possible defence may have been overlooked by the problemist. Although the term is often thought to be named after the nineteenth-century problemist E. B. Cook, it is probably derived from the word's English slang meaning (to tamper with or falsify). See **dual.**

**Cook, Nathaniel** nineteenth-century British designer and close friend of Howard Staunton. In 1835, Cook designed the chessmen known then and today as 'Staunton chessmen', a name originally sanctioned by Staunton himself. See **Staunton chessmen.**

**cooperating Bishops** the Bishop pair, especially when working along adjacent diagonals. See **Horwitz Bishops.**

**cordon** any barrier that cuts a King off from a section of the board. In the endgame the winning procedure against a lone King is to form a cordon around him with the pieces and King and force him to move to the edge of the board, where he can be mated easily. See **barrier.**

**correspondence chess** chess played by post. This is common not only for international encounters but also flourishes within the United Kingdom and the United States. There is little difference between the laws and conventions governing correspondence chess and orthodox chess. Minor differences deal with analysis and the time limit.

In correspondence chess it is permissible to consult texts when analysing a position. This is illegal in chess played over the board.

Time is measured from the moment a player receives notice of his opponent's move up to the time he posts his reply. Time spent while the move is in transit is ignored.

Correspondence chess is less demanding of nervous energy than chess played over the board, and is often played by those who are prone to fatigue or tension.

The first match to be played by post took place between the London and Edinburgh Chess Clubs in 1824 and was the scene of the debut of the Scotch Game. Abbrev. C.C. Also called **postal chess.**

**Correspondence Grandmaster of the Blind** a title awarded to any blind player who wins the **IBCA Correspondence World Championship** more than three times. It has so far been awarded only to R. W. Bonham.

**correspondence notation** a method of recording the moves of a game that has been authorized by FIDE for use in correspondence chess. Each square is given a unique two-figure combination to identify it, with the first figure showing its file and the second figure showing its rank from White's viewpoint. A move is recorded by showing the starting square and the final square, so that 1. P–K4, N–KB3 (Alekhine's Defence) is shown by 1. 5254, 7866. O–O and O–O–O by White are shown by 5171 and 5131, i.e. only the move by the King is recorded.

Correspondence notation is invaluable for international games where there might be no agreement as to the abbreviations and symbols of the men and no common system of notation. Compare **Udemann Code.**

**Black**

| 18 | 28 | 38 | 48 | 58 | 68 | 78 | 88 |
|---|---|---|---|---|---|---|---|
| 17 | 27 | 37 | 47 | 57 | 67 | 77 | 87 |
| 16 | 26 | 36 | 46 | 56 | 66 | 76 | 86 |
| 15 | 25 | 35 | 45 | 55 | 65 | 75 | 85 |
| 14 | 24 | 34 | 44 | 54 | 64 | 74 | 84 |
| 13 | 23 | 33 | 43 | 53 | 63 | 73 | 83 |
| 12 | 22 | 32 | 42 | 52 | 62 | 72 | 82 |
| 11 | 21 | 31 | 41 | 51 | 61 | 71 | 81 |

**White**

**Correspondence World Championship** a competition to determine the world's strongest player of correspondence chess. It is organized by the ICCF. The finalists, who will have qualified from preliminary tournaments, participate in a round-robin tournament of approximately sixteen players. All the games are played concurrently and the final lasts for nearly three years. The winner becomes the **Correspondence World Champion** and is awarded the title of International Grandmaster of Correspondence Chess if he does not possess it already.

The first championship final lasted from 1 May 1950 to 31 March 1953 and was won by the Australian player Cecil John S. Purdy. It is interesting to note that the domination which the Soviet players exert over the other championships has not been transmitted to the Correspondence World Championship. Soviet players have won the title only in a minority of cases. Also called **World Correspondence Chess Championship**.

**Cortlever, Nicolaas** (b. 14 June 1915) Dutch chess player; awarded the title International Master in 1950. He competed in the Chess Olympiads of 1939, 1950, 1952 and 1954. Cortlever's best results in the Dutch Championship were second places in 1938, 1947, 1954 and 1958.

**Counsellor** a translation of the original Indian name of the piece known in English as the Queen. The meaning of its Arabic name (*firzān* or *firz*) was soon forgotten by the Europeans and the new name was suggested from the adjacency of the piece to the King.

**counter gambit** **1.** a defence to a gambit in which the White pawn is ignored and a pawn is offered in return. Playing a counter gambit is often psychologically justified since it forces White into a role that is likely to be less congenial for him; White must decide how to defend instead of sacrificing a pawn and attacking as he originally intended. Well-known counter gambits are the Falkbeer Counter Gambit and the Albin Counter Gambit.

**2.** any gambit carried out by Black, whether White has opened with a gambit or not. An example is the Queen's Pawn Counter Gambit.

**counterpawn** (Kmoch's term) an enemy pawn that opposes a pawn on the same file. Compare **sentry**. See ***Pawn Power in Chess***.

**counterplay** attacking counterchances existing in an inferior or defensive position. Counterplay is almost always present to some degree.

**Counter-thrust Variation** a rare name for an opening sequence arising out of the King's Indian Defence: 1. P–Q4, N–KB3 2. P–QB4, P–KN3 3. P–KN3, B–N2 4. B–N2, *P–Q4*. Black creates a similar pawn formation to that occurring in the Grünfeld Defence, of which this was an early form. This variation was first played at Carlsbad (1923).

**Courier Game** a medieval variant of chess devised in Germany in the fifteenth century. Play took place on a board of 96 squares (8 × 12). Each player had the conventional pieces as well as four extra pawns which shielded two Couriers, a Jester, and a Sage. The Courier moved in the same manner as a modern Bishop (a medieval Bishop was more limited). The Jester moved one square vertically or horizontally. The Sage moved one square in any direction. The game was popular for several centuries, as shown by *The Chess Players*, painted by Lucas van Leyden about 1510, which depicts a Courier Game in progress.

**Cozio Defence** a defence to the Ruy Lopez: 1. P–K4, P–K4 2. N–KB3, N–QB3 3. B–N5, *KN–K2*. Black attempts to set up a solid, albeit cramped, defensive formation. The most common continuation is: 4. P–Q4. This defence is named after Count Carlo Cozio, an Italian chess player of the eighteenth century. Unfashionable for many years, this variation finally gained some popularity only recently, following Larsen's successful adoption of it in a number of games.

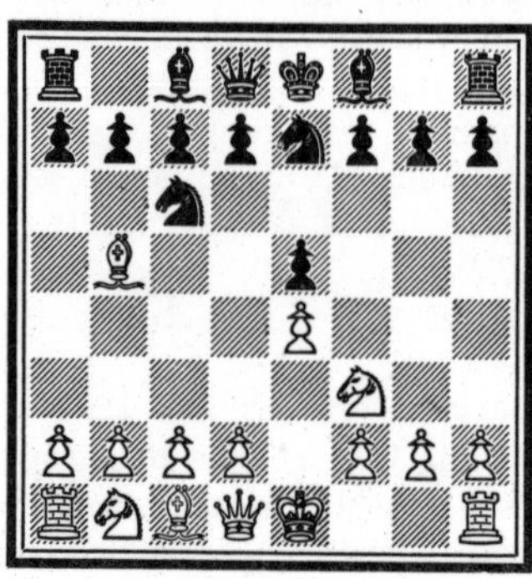

Position after 3 . . ., KN–K2

**cramped game** a game in which the men have little room to manoeuvre. In this position writers recommend exchanging pieces to clear space and blunt any attack that could arise because of this weakness.

**creeping move** a surprising move that apparently threatens nothing, but definitely transforms an even position into a winning position for its exponent. The term was coined by Alexander Kotov in *Think Like a Grandmaster*. See **quiet move.**

**crippled majority** a formation of pawns with at least one weakness that prevents the creation of any passed pawn by normal means, despite outnumbering the opposing pawns. Characteristic weaknesses of a crippled majority are doubled pawns and backward pawns.

**critical position** **1.** a position reached in an opening upon the evaluation of which is based the judgment of that opening variation. If the critical position is obviously favourable for one side the onus is on the other to introduce an innovation to prevent this position being reached.

**2.** any point of the game from which a decisive sequence of moves begins.

**cross-board** another name for **over the board.** See **O.T.B.**

**cross check** any move which nullifies a check and simultaneously gives check to the enemy King.

**cross lever** (Kmoch's term) a formation that occurs when two friendly adjacent pawns are immediately opposed by two hostile adjacent pawns. An example would be if White had pawns on his K4 and Q4 and Black had pawns on his K4 and Q4. The most important feature of this formation is the constant likelihood of exchanges. Compare **duo, ram, lever.** See ***Pawn Power in Chess***.

**crosstable** a special tabular representation of the results of a tournament. Each player's name is entered on the left-hand side and at the top of the table and the resulting ranks and columns form a grid on which the results are shown. A player's results against his opponents are entered in the rank beside his name at the intersection with the appropriate column bearing each opponent's name. Each result is recorded twice, since it appears in the rank of each of the two competitors, and is shown by 1 for a win, ½ for a draw and 0 for a loss. Since a player obviously cannot play against himself, the intersection of each player's own name is filled by a cross. A final column shows the end results of the tournament.

**Crosstable**

*Wijk aan Zee (1977) – Grandmaster Section*

| | Geller | Sosonko | Timman | Kurajica | Olafsson | Bohm | Kavalek | Miles | Nikolac | Sigurjonsson | Ligterink | Barczay | Totals |
|---|---|---|---|---|---|---|---|---|---|---|---|---|---|
| Y. Geller *(U.S.S.R.)* | x | ½ | ½ | 1 | ½ | ½ | 1 | 0 | 1 | 1 | 1 | 1 | 8 |
| G. Sosonko *(Holland)* | ½ | x | ½ | ½ | 1 | ½ | 1 | ½ | 1 | ½ | 1 | 1 | 8 |
| J. Timman *(Holland)* | ½ | ½ | x | ½ | 0 | 1 | ½ | 1 | 1 | ½ | 1 | 1 | 7½ |
| B. Kurajica *(Yugoslavia)* | 0 | ½ | ½ | x | ½ | ½ | 1 | 1 | 1 | ½ | 1 | ½ | 7 |
| F. Olafsson *(Iceland)* | ½ | 0 | 1 | ½ | x | ½ | ½ | ½ | ½ | ½ | ½ | 1 | 6 |
| H. Bohm *(Holland)* | ½ | ½ | 0 | ½ | ½ | x | 0 | ½ | 0 | ½ | 1 | 1 | 5 |
| L. Kavalek *(U.S.A.)* | 0 | 0 | ½ | 0 | ½ | 1 | x | ½ | 1 | ½ | ½ | ½ | 5 |
| A. Miles *(England)* | 1 | ½ | 0 | 0 | ½ | ½ | ½ | x | 0 | 1 | ½ | ½ | 5 |
| J. Nikolac *(Yugoslavia)* | 0 | 0 | 0 | 0 | ½ | 1 | 0 | 1 | x | 1 | ½ | 1 | 5 |
| G. Sigurjonsson *(Iceland)* | 0 | ½ | ½ | ½ | ½ | ½ | ½ | 0 | 0 | x | ½ | ½ | 4 |
| G. Ligterink *(Holland)* | 0 | 0 | 0 | 0 | ½ | 0 | ½ | ½ | ½ | ½ | x | ½ | 3 |
| L. Barczay *(Hungary)* | 0 | 0 | 0 | ½ | 0 | 0 | ½ | ½ | 0 | ½ | ½ | x | 2½ |

**Crutch Odds** a rarely used term that describes the offer by White of astounding odds. Before the start of the game, White removes from the board all but four of his pawns (QRP, QNP, KNP and KRP remain) and all four of his minor pieces (leaving only the two Rooks, Queen and King on the back rank). White castles on the King side, bringing his Rook to bear down on the half-open KB file. Depending on Black's opening move, White then moves his Queen to KB3. Against extremely weak, unwary or slightly demented opponents, White has checkmate on the next move (Q × KBPmate).

This highly bizarre and bracing offer by White of all but his major pieces is surprisingly effective (once only!) against woodpushers or duffers of all shapes and sizes. See **odds**.

**Csom, Istvan** (b. 2 June 1940) Hungarian chess player; awarded the title International Master in 1967 and the title International Grandmaster in 1973. He first competed in the Chess Olympiads in 1970 when he scored the third highest percentage (75%) as first reserve. Csom has also competed in the European Team Championships; in 1973 at Bath he scored the best result for fifth board. (1976 Elo rating: 2490)

**Cuellar Gacharna, Miguel** (b. 18 November 1916) Colombian chess player; awarded the title International Master in 1957. He played in the Chess Olympiads of 1954, 1956, 1958, 1964 and 1972 on top board and competed in the interzonal tournaments of 1962, 1967, and 1973. (1976 Elo rating: 2345)

**cumulative tie-breaking method** a tie-breaking system occasionally adopted in tournaments run under the **Swiss System**. It discriminates in favour of those players who win early in the tournament and thus face harder opposition in the later rounds than do those players who win later in the tournament. The method consists of summing the cumulative score of the players with an equal number of points. For example, a player who successively obtains win, loss, loss and draw has a cumulative score of 4½ (1+1+1+1½), while a player who successively obtains a draw, a loss, loss and win has a cumulative score of only 3 (½+½+½+1½). Compare **Sonneborn-Berger system**.

**Cunningham Gambit** an opening sequence arising out of the King's Gambit: 1. P–K4, P–K4 2. P–KB4, P×P 3. N–KB3, *B–K2*. Black has developed a piece and, after White's most common immediate reply: 4. B–B4, used to play 4 . . ., B–R5ch?! but now 4 . . ., N–KB3 is preferred. The opening is named after the eighteenth-century diplomat and historian Alexander Cunningham, who popularized it. It was first given this name in *The Noble Game of Chess* by Captain Joseph Bertin, published in London in 1735.

**Cutty Sark Grand Prix** an annual prize of £1,000 awarded to the player who collects the most points in domestic tournaments in the United Kingdom within the year. The results of the more important events are given weights. Thus, points scored in the 1975 London Open were multiplied sevenfold in counting for the Cutty Sark Grand Prix. The Grand Prix is sponsored by the makers of Cutty Sark whisky and began in 1974. The first winner was Tony Miles.

**Cylinder Chess** a type of Fairy Chess in which the edges of the board are imagined to be joined, so forming a cylinder. Pieces can thus move from one side to the other without crossing the centre of the board. Cylinder Chess can take place on a vertical cylinder on which the Rook files are imagined to be joined, on a horizontal cylinder on which the first and eighth ranks are joined, or on an anchor-ring which combines both characteristics. Although physically possible, the endless circulation of a cylindrical board is prohibited by the Piran Codex unless specifically stipulated. See **anchor-ring, horizontal cylinder, vertical cylinder.**

**Czech Benoni** an opening sequence arising out of the Benoni Defence: 1. P–Q4, N–KB3 2. P–QB4, P–QB4 3. P–Q5, P–K4 4. N–QB3, P–Q3 5. P–K4, *B–K2*. Black prepares to force the advance of either the King Bishop pawn or Queen Knight pawn and eventually hopes to exchange his bad Bishop. However, he has a cramped position and often must defend against a King-side attack. This variation was often used by the Czech players Vlastimil Hort and Vlastimil Jansa in the 1960s.

**Czech Defence** formerly another name for **Slav Defence**.

**Czerniak, Moshe** (b. 3 February 1910) Israeli chess player; originally Polish, he emigrated to Palestine in 1934. He was Palestinian Champion in 1936 and Israeli Champion in 1955. He has competed in numerous Chess Olympiads since 1935. (1976 Elo rating: 2385)

# D

**Dake, Arthur W.** (b. 8 April 1910) U.S. chess player; awarded the title International Master in 1954. He competed in the Chess Olympiads of 1931, 1933, and 1935 and played for the United States in the radio match against the U.S.S.R. in 1945. (1976 Elo rating: 2360)

**Damiano** sixteenth-century Portuguese apothecary, known only for his book, *Questo Libro e da imparare giocare a scachi*. The first work in Italian on chess, it was printed in Rome in 1512 and analysed several openings.

**Damiano's Defence** a defence to the King's pawn opening: 1. P–K4, P–K4 2. N–KB3, *P–KB3*. This is clearly dubious, robbing the King Knight of its best square and opening a diagonal on to the Black King. White can play either 3. N × P, or 3. B–B4 with the better game. The opening is named after Damiano who first analysed it.

**Damjanović, Mato** (b. 23 March 1927) Yugoslavian chess player; awarded the title International Master in 1962 and the title International Grandmaster in 1964. (1967 Elo rating: 2425)

**Danish Gambit** an opening sequence arising in the Centre Game: 1. P–K4, P–K4 2. P–Q4, P × P 3. *P–QB3*, P × P 4. B–QB4, P × P 5. B × NP. White gets a rapid development in return for the pawns that he sacrifices, but Black can often equalize with an eventual P–Q4. The opening is named in recognition of the Danish players, especially Severin From, who developed it in the nineteenth century.

**Darga, Klaus** (b. 24 February 1934) West German chess player; awarded the title International Master in 1957 and the title International Grandmaster in 1964. (1976 Elo rating: 2500)

**dbl ch** *abbrev. for* double check.

**'Dean of American Chess'** *descriptive phrase for* Herman Helms.

**decoy** a name sometimes given to an outside passed pawn that can be caught only by the enemy King. While the King is chasing the pawn the opposing King usually gains a decisive advantage on the other side of the board.

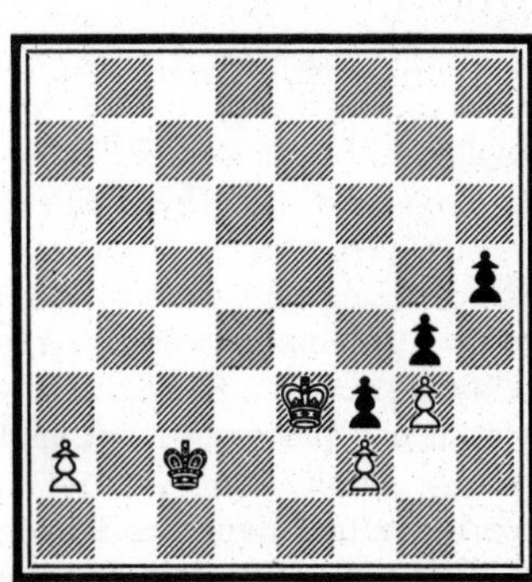

Black chases the decoy while White captures his pawns

**defence** a move or sequence of moves intended to nullify the opponent's threats. 'Defence' is sometimes included in the name of an opening sequence when it is Black's moves that create the characteristic position of that opening. *U.S. spelling* defense.

***Defence, The*** a novel by Vladimir Nabokov published in 1964. It describes the hero's life from his introduction to chess when a child in czarist Russia up to his suicide, itself caused by his obsession with the game. The book is regarded by many as being the finest work of fiction ever written about chess. Compare ***Dragon Variation, The; Master Prim; Royal Game, The.***

**defensive player** a passive player who prefers to repulse his opponent's attacks rather than fight for the initiative. When successful such a policy will avoid early dangers but may result in a high proportion of draws. Notable defensive players are Reshevsky and Petrosian.

**deflation of titles** See **title inflation.**

**De Greiff, Boris** (b. 13 February 1930) Colombian chess player; awarded the title International Master in 1957. He played in the Chess Olympiads of 1954, 1956, 1958, 1966 and 1976. (1976 Elo rating: 2320)

**Delayed Exchange Ruy Lopez Deferred** another name for the **Exchange Variation Double Deferred.**

**Delmar, Eugene** (1841–1909) American amateur chess player. He defeated several masters in single games, including Bird and Tchigorin, and won a match against the great problem-composer Sam Loyd (+6 −2 =0).

***De Ludis Orientalibus*** *Latin for* On Oriental games. A two-volume work by Thomas Hyde, it was the first systematic study of the history of chess, although it confined itself to a study of the game in the East. It was first published by the Oxford University Press in 1694.

***De ludo scachorum*** *Latin for* On the game of chess. One of the earliest sermons on moral conduct that used chess as an allegory for human conduct. It was written in the thirteenth century by Jacobus de Cessolis, a Dominican friar in Lombardy.

**Dely, Peter** (b. 5 July 1934) Hungarian chess player; awarded the title International Master in 1962. He was Hungarian Champion in 1970. (1976 Elo rating: 2430)

**demonstration chessboard** a large vertically mounted chessboard on which games, positions, etc., can be shown to an audience. Chess symbols are usually attached magnetically. The first demonstration chessboard was used in New York for the World Championship match between Steinitz and Zukertort.

**Denker, Arnold S.** (b. 20 February 1914) U.S. chess player; U.S. Champion from 1944 to 1946, and was awarded the title International Master in 1950. (1976 Elo rating: 2360)

**DERLD** *acronym for* **Delayed Exchange Ruy Lopez Deferred.**

**Deschapelles, Alexander Louis Honoré Lebreton** (1780–1847) the strongest French chess player in the early nineteenth-century. Born on 7 March 1780, he was the son of a marshal of France. He lost a hand while fighting the Prussians in the Napoleonic Wars. After the restoration of the Bourbon monarchy he became a farmer. He boasted of having learned chess in three days, in which he reached his full strength, but was generally disbelieved. From 1798 he was the strongest player at the Café de la Régence for two decades and in 1807 was successfully able to give odds of a Rook to the strongest members of the Berlin Chess Club. He later only played odds games and when in 1821 a former pupil, La Bourdonnais, was able to beat him, Deschapelles withdrew from the game. In 1836 he issued a challenge after the match between La Bourdonnais and McDonnell offering a pawn and two moves to any English player, but no match took place.

Deschapelles also composed music, of which none has survived, and was also a good whist player – being the inventor of the 'Deschapelles coup'. He was a staunch anti-Bourbonist and was arrested in 1832, but was freed after writing to the King. He died on 27 October 1847.

**descriptive notation** a system of notation based upon the names of the men and the places they occupy in the opening position.

The pieces are represented by their initial letters so that R stands for Rook, B stands for Bishop, K stands for King and so on. The Knight is identified by Kt, N, or S (the last because of its German name Springer) to minimize confusion with the King. Where these designations are ambiguous, the pieces may be distinguished according to their original place (for example, KB is King Bishop and QB is Queen Bishop).

The pawns are named in the same way, but each pawn has three different groups of letters instead of two. Thus the same pawn can be noted as P, BP, or QBP depending upon the circumstances of the game.

The eight files are identified by the pieces which originally stood upon them and the ranks are numbered from one to eight counting from each player's first rank. This means that each square has two names, one for each player. For instance, White's QR5 is also Black's QR4.

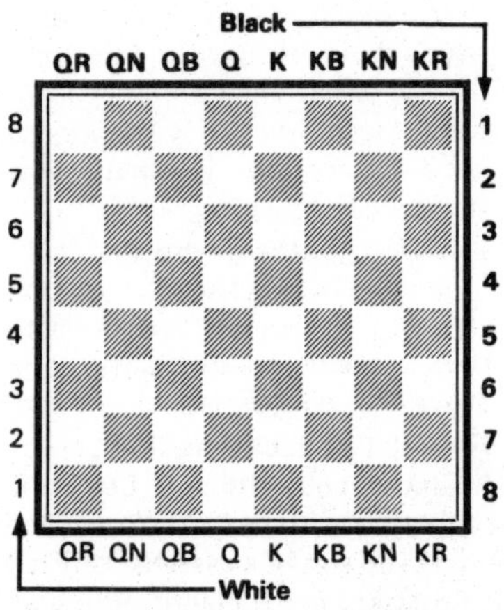


(White's QR5 is also Black's QR4)

A move is recorded by giving the name of the man and the square to which it moves; e.g., R–KB4 means that a Rook has moved to the fourth square of that player's King Bishop file. When two similar pieces can move to the same square, the square of departure is also shown, e.g. R(Q4)–KB4. Each move is written down from the viewpoint of the player making it.

Symbols used are O–O and O–O–O, which mean castling on the King side and Queen side, respectively; x, which indicates a capture; ch or +, which shows a check; and mate or ++, which signifies checkmate. These symbols are also used in algebraic notation.

Algebraic notation is undoubtedly more concise (in its usual shortened form), more understandable, less open to confusion, and much more widespread internationally. However, descriptive notation is the most widely used system in the English-speaking countries and so is used in this book. Also called **English notation.** See **symbols.**

**desperado** a piece that is certain to be captured. It can be used to inflict as much damage as possible, since there is nothing to lose that is not already lost and anything captured represents a gain of some kind. For instance, after the opening moves 1. P–K4, P–K4 2. N–KB3, N–QB3 3. N–B3, B–B4 4. N×P, since 4 . . . N×N is met by 5. P–Q4 regaining the piece, Black can choose the desperado 4 . . ., B×Pch 5. K×B, N×N in the hope of exposing the White King.

***De Tafel van der Kersteure*** a text drawing moralistic parallels between chess and real life, first published in the Netherlands about 1410. It drew heavily on the work of Jacobus de Cessolis, and is also notable for the twenty-four miniature paintings that it contains.

***Deutsche Schachzeitung*** the leading chess periodical in West Germany. It was founded in 1846 and is consequently the oldest surviving chess magazine. Among its editors have been Anderssen, Mieses, Schlechter and Teschner. It appears every month.

**develop** to move the chessmen from their initial positions to squares where their offensive and defensive potential is greater.

**development** the movement of the chessmen from their initial positions to squares where their offensive and defensive potential is greater. Judgements as to what constitutes good development have changed greatly, but according to Chernev and Harkness good development means placing pieces on squares where they will be safe from attack and will cause a threat.

***Development of Chess Style, The*** a book by Dr M. Euwe. It traces the growth and development of chess from the early seventeenth century to the 1960s and traces in particular the contributions of Steinitz as well as the characteristics of the leading players of the last half century. It was translated from Dutch by W. H. Cozens and was first published in 1966. It uses descriptive notation.

**de Vere, Cecil** (1845–1875) British chess player; born in Montrose, Scotland on 14 February 1845. De Vere was taught to play chess at the age of 12 by Francis Burden, a strong London player, and soon became a regular visitor to the Divan. When he was 19 the City of London

Chess Club sponsored a match between him and Steinitz, with Steinitz giving odds of pawn and move. De Vere was the victor.

In 1866 the newly-formed British Chess Association organized the first British Championship; the event was won by de Vere, who remained the youngest holder of the title British Champion for over a century. Other results included a fifth at Paris (1867) and a third at Dundee (1867) in front of Steinitz. He died of tuberculosis on 9 February 1875.

**deviant forms of chess** see **variant forms of chess**.

**Deže, Anton** (b. 22 March 1940) Yugoslavian chess player; awarded the title International Master in 1976. (1976 Elo rating: 2415)

**diagonal** any contiguous line of squares along which a Bishop can move. Each Bishop must always be at the intersection of two diagonals when in play, and since these diagonals must always be of unequal length they are differentiated by being referred to as the long and the short diagonals. The term the long diagonals also refers to the squares QR1–KR8 and KR1–QR8, which are the two diagonals on the board that contain the most squares. Control of them is the main purpose of the **fianchetto**.

**diagonal power** the ability to move diagonally in all directions. This especially applies to the Bishops, which can move in no other way, but also belongs to the King and Queen. Compare **rectangular power**.

**Diaz, Joaquim** (b. 1950) Cuban chess player; awarded the title International Master in 1975. (1976 Elo rating: 2385)

**dice chess** an obsolete variant of chess in which dice were thrown to determine the type of man to be moved. In his 98-page manuscript *Libro del Acedrex*, (or 'Juegos de Axedrez, dados y tablas'), written in 1283, Alfonso X of Castile wrote that the numbers one to six meant that the pawn, Bishop, Knight, Rook, Queen and King should be moved respectively. If the indicated move was impossible the dice were thrown again, while if only one man could legally be moved it was moved without throwing the dice. Dice chess had reached Europe from the East by the eleventh century and swiftly became as popular as orthodox chess. The use of dice may partially explain the mediaeval Church's disapproval of chess as a gambling game.

***Die Neuen Ideen im Schachspiel*** *German for* New Ideas in Chess, a book written by Richard Réti and published in 1922. It examines the styles of the best players in the history of chess up to that date and analyzes the contributions of each one. Indirectly it reflects the author's own beliefs and judgements, which were those of the hypermodern school.

**Diez del Corral, Jesus** (b. 6 April 1933) Spanish chess player; awarded the titles International Master in 1967 and International Grandmaster in 1974. (1976 Elo rating: 2490)

**direct mate** a task in problem chess in which White plays first and must mate Black within the specified number of moves despite Black's defence.

**direct opposition** see **opposition**.

**dis ch** *abbrev. for* discovered check.

**discovered attack** an attack that occurs when a piece or pawn moves and uncovers another piece that poses a threat. If the move itself contains a threat, the danger to the defender is that much greater. A discovered check is a discovered attack in which the attacked piece is the enemy King. A particularly dangerous form of discovered attack is the double check.

**discovered check** a type of check that occurs when a man moves thus uncovering a piece that checks the King. While the King protects itself the first man has a freer time than would otherwise be the case. Abbrev. **dis ch.**

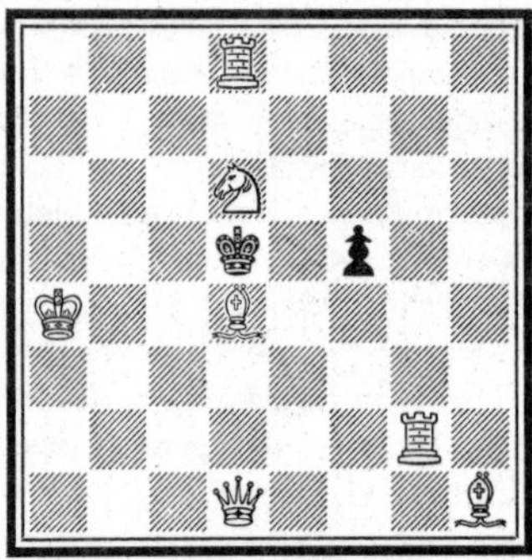

In this position (by T. Row) White has 35 possible discovered checks

**dispersion** (Kmoch's term) disruption of the pawn structure through captures of the pawns and captures by the pawns. This will lead to doubled pawns and the isolation of one or more pawns. Compare **distortion**. See ***Pawn Power in Chess***.

**distant opposition** see **opposition**.

**distortion** (Kmoch's term) disruption of the pawn structure through the uneven advance of the pawns. Although this may be remediable by the advance of the rearmost pawns, it may be impossible to carry out. Distortion enables the enemy pieces to manoeuvre behind the strung-out pawns and attack them from behind with protection only from the pieces. Compare **dispersion**. See ***Pawn Power in Chess***.

**Divan, the** London's major chess meeting-place in the nineteenth century. It was founded in the 1820s by Samuel Ries, a Portugese, and occupied rooms at 101 the Strand. Although it began as a place of general interest, it soon became the British equivalent of the Café de la Régence and was visited by all the leading players. In 1847 the chess rooms were transferred from the ground floor to the floor above and soon became known as Simpson's Divan after the rooms' head-waiter, who was later to buy the premises. When he opened Simpson's restaurant in 1886 the chess room was moved one floor higher up and the Divan slowly began to decline. In the early years of the twentieth century the rooms were closed for rebuilding; when they were re-opened, chess was no longer encouraged.

**Djurasević, Božidar** (b. 26 April 1933) Yugoslavian chess player; awarded the title International Master in 1957. He was Yugoslavian Junior Champion in 1950 and competed in the Chess Olympiads of 1956 and 1958.

**Dobrusky, Jan** (1853–1907) Bohemian composer of chess problems, born in what is now part of Czechoslovakia.

**Doda, Zbigniew** (b. 22 February 1931) Polish Champion in 1964 and 1967; awarded the title International Master in 1964. He has competed in several Chess Olympiads since 1962. (1976 Elo rating: 2405)

**Donner, Jan Hein** (b. 6 July 1927) Dutch chess player; awarded the title International Master in 1952 and the title International Grandmaster in 1959. (1976 Elo rating: 2475)

**Döry Defence** a defence to the Queen pawn opening: 1. P–Q4, N–KB3 2. P–QB4, P–K3 3. N–KB3, *N–K5*. Since it commits the sin of moving a piece twice in the early opening, this defence has never found great favour, although Keres was once an exponent of it. It can often transpose into the Queen's Indian Defence. The most common continuation is: 4. P–K3.

**double attack** an attack by a man on two of the opposing force. The fork is a type of double attack. The double attack can be made by any man with the exception of the Rook pawn.

**double check** a simultaneous check from two men. This occurs only when one man moves and checks at the same time uncovering a piece which also gives check. The only escape is to move the King. Abbrev. **dbl ch.** Compare **discovered check**.

**double corridor** an addition to the chessboard suggested by F. V. Morley in his book *My One Contribution to Chess*. He proposed adding a 'corridor' of six squares to each side of the board from the second to seventh ranks. This would allow the Rook pawns to capture in two directions as can all other pawns and would also prevent many stalemate positions by providing the Kings with more room to manoeuvre.

**doubled pawns** two pawns of the same colour that are on the same file. They are weak since they cannot defend each other, can only advance as quickly as the leading pawn, and can be blockaded by a single pawn or piece. These drawbacks may be compensated for if the half-open or open file which is inevitably created by the doubling can be seized by the Rooks or the Queen. (See illustration on p. 84)

**Double Fianchetto** any opening variation in which one side fianchettoes both of his bishops.

**double lever** (Kmoch's term) a formation that exists when the pawn of one side may be captured by two pawns from different levers. A double lever would exist if White had pawns on his Q4, K3 and KB4 while Black had pawns on his Q3, K4 and KB3 since Black's King pawn could be captured in either of two ways. Compare **lever, chain lever**. See ***Pawn Power in Chess***.

**Double-move Chess** any type of Fairy Chess where each player makes two moves consecutively. In one version each player plays both White and Black in his turn. For instance, A plays one White move in his first turn; B then plays one Black move and one White move; A then plays one Black move and one White move, etc. The winner is the first to checkmate either King.

Another type of Double-move Chess is **Marseillaise Chess.**

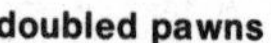
**doubled pawns**

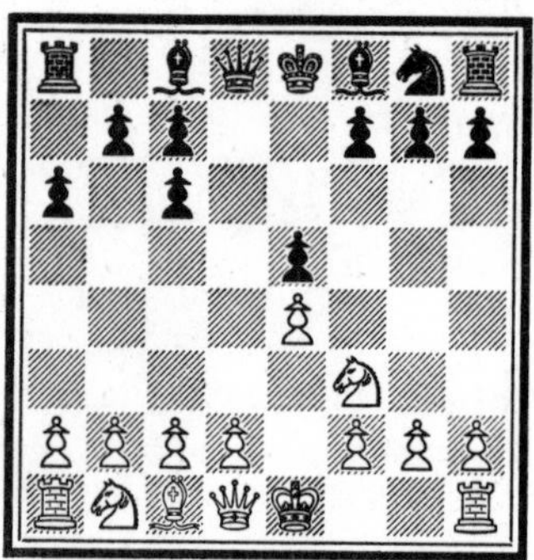

In the Exchange Variation of the Ruy Lopez, Black is left with doubled pawns on his QB2 and QB3

**Double-move Queen** a Fairy chesspiece that moves alternately like a Bishop and Rook or vice versa. Its abbreviation is **DQ**. This piece was invented by A. W. Baillie and T. H. Willcocks.

**double-round** a tournament in which each competitor plays every other competitor twice.

**doubling** **1.** moving a pawn onto a file shared by a pawn of the same colour. See **doubled pawns.**

**2.** placing both Rooks on the same file or rank, particularly on open or half-open files, or the seventh rank.

**down-float** the pairing of a player with someone who has a lower score in a tournament organized under the Swiss System. Players should always be matched against those with an equal score, but this is sometimes impossible. For instance, there might be an unequal number of competitors with the same score, an otherwise suitable player might have been matched against an opponent with a higher score (who has had a down-float himself), or the players might have been matched earlier in the tournament and consequently be ineligible to play each other. When a down-float is arranged the player in question normally meets the highest eligible competitor in the group immediately behind him, but pairing is made at the discretion of the arbiter and pairing committee.

**Dragon** a Fairy chesspiece that possesses the powers of both the pawn and the Knight. It is thus a type of Combined Chessman.

**Dragon Bishop** the Black King Bishop when posted at KN2 in the Dragon Variation of the Sicilian Defence.

**Dragon Variation** a variation of the Sicilian Defence, reputedly so called because of Black's serpentine pawn structure after the opening moves. The two moves in italics are specifically characteristic of this variation: 1. P–K4, P–QB4 2. N–KB3, P–Q3 3. P–Q4, P×P 4. N×P, N–KB3 5. N–QB3, *P–KN3* 6. B–K3, *B–N2*.

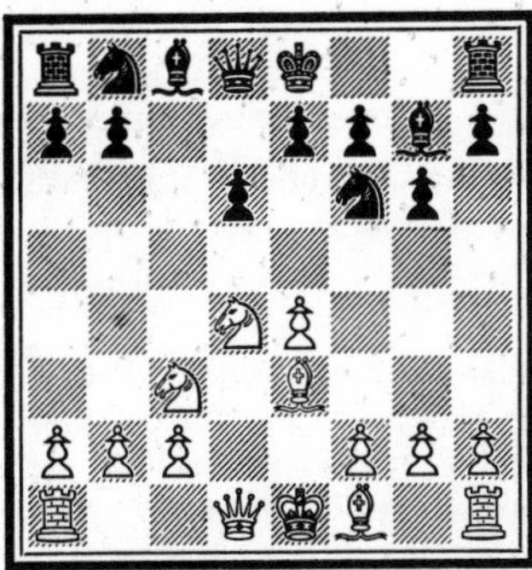

Position after 6 . . ., B–N2

***Dragon Variation, The*** a novel by Sir Anthony Glyn which was published in 1969. It is centred on the experiences of a 19-year-old natural player who is discovered and sponsored by a wealthy American. Real people, such as Leonard Barden, Pal Benkö, Mikhail Tal and B. H. Wood also appear in the book. Compare ***Defence, The; Master Prim; Royal Game, The***.

**draw** *n*. a completed game which neither player has won. *vb*. to complete a game without having won or lost it. It is possible to draw a game in four ways: (1) when there is stalemate; (2) by mutual agreement; (3) at the request of one of the players when the same position appears three times and each time the same player has the move (see **repetition of position**); (4) when the player whose turn it is to move proves that at least fifty moves have been played without any capture and without a pawn having been moved, although there are certain exceptions (see **fifty-move rule**).

**'draw death'** an expression coined by Capablanca, who believed chess to be played out. He thought that a player would always be able to obtain at least a draw because of the perfection of technique. To prevent this he suggested rendering all opening theory obsolete by adding two extra pawns and new pieces to each side: one combining the moves of Rook and Knight and one combining the moves of Bishop and Knight. This proposal aroused little enthusiasm and the necessity for it was challenged by the hypermodern players, who instead developed new openings based upon new concepts under the slogan, 'No draw death!'

**Drawing Master, The** term by which Carl Schlechter is popularly described. It has since been used for masters of later generations, including Trifunović and Petrosian.

**Dresden (1926)** a round-robin tournament with ten competitors, won by Nimzovitch (8½ points) well ahead of the others, who were led by

Alekhine. Immediately after the tournament Nimzovitch challenged Capablanca to a World Championship match, and was given nine months to raise the stake money.

**Drimer, Dolfi** (b. 18 October 1934) Romanian chess player; awarded the title International Master in 1961. He has played in several Chess Olympiads since 1960.

**dual** the presence of two or more forced mates in a chess problem. Consequently the problem has at least a dual solution. A dual will exist if, for instance, a piece has two or more mating moves or if several men are able to deliver checkmate. Aesthetically this is felt to be a defect in a chess problem.

**Dubinin, Pyotr Vassilievich** (b. 30 June 1909) Soviet chess player; awarded the title International Master in 1950 and the title International Correspondence Grandmaster in 1962, when he finished second in the third Correspondence World Championship.

**Dubois, Serafino** (1817–1899) strongest Italian player of the late nineteenth century. In 1862 he entered the London tournament and came joint fourth with MacDonnell. In the same year he played a match with Steinitz, which he lost (+3 −5 =1).

**Duckstein, Dr Andreas** (b. 2 August 1927) Austrian chess player; awarded the title International Master in 1956 and was Austrian Champion in 1954 and 1956. Duckstein has competed in several Chess Olympiads, notably that of 1956 when he scored the highest percentage on second board. (1976 Elo rating: 2425)

**duffer** a hopeless or inept chess player. See **woodpusher**.

**Dunkelblum, Arthur** (b. 23 April 1906) Belgian chess player; awarded the title International Master in 1957 and was Belgian Champion in 1949. He has competed in numerous Chess Olympiads. (1976 Elo rating: 2250)

**Dunst Opening** an opening where White plays: 1.*N–QB3*. It is named after the New York master T. A. Dunst who analysed it extensively. Also called **Queen Knight Opening**.

**duo** (Kmoch's term) two adjacent friendly pawns. This is the strongest possible arrangement of two pawns; two such duos on the same rank can sometimes cover all the squares of the rank in front of them. See ***Pawn Power in Chess***.

**Duplex** a type of chess problem in which either King may be mated. If White moves first he can effect a forced mate of Black and vice versa. Duplexes will often consist of two **helpmates** which have been merged into one problem.

**Durao, Joaquim** (b. 12 October 1938) Portuguese chess player; awarded the title International Master in 1975. (1976 Elo rating: 2325)

**Duras, Oldrich** (1882–1957) Czechoslovakian chess player; awarded the title International Grandmaster in 1950. He was born in Humny, Bohemia on 30 October 1882. Duras gained the Master title at the Barmen **Hauptturnier** (1905) and quickly became one of the strongest of pre-war players with results that included firsts at Vienna (1908),

Prague (1908) and Breslau (1912) and second places at Nuremberg (1906) and Hamburg (1910). Unfortunately his tournament career ended in 1914. Although Lasker had predicted that Duras would eventually play him in a World Championship match, Duras was not a chess professional and after the war could not afford the time to play in tournaments. He was invited to compete at Moscow (1925), but was refused a leave of absence from his work in the civil service. However, he remained active as a composer of endgame studies and problems. Duras died in Prague on 5 January 1957.

**Durkin Attack** an opening where White plays: 1. N–QR3. It is named after the New Jersey player R. T. Durkin who played it widely in tournaments and in postal chess competitions.

**Dutch Attack** another name for **Bird's Opening.**

**Dutch Defence** a defence to the Queen's pawn opening: 1. P–Q4, *P–KB4*. Black plans an attack on the King side. This move controls a central square and provides a base for any pawn storm. Its main disadvantage is that it weakens Black's King side. White has a choice of many continuations and will usually attack in the centre. The defence was analysed by Elias Stein of Holland in his work, *Nouvel essai sur les échecs* ('A New Essay on Chess').

**Dutch Indian** another name for the **Leningrad Variation** of the **Dutch Defence.**

**Dutch Stonewall** an opening sequence arising out of the Dutch Defence: 1. P–Q4, P–KB4 2. N–KB3, P–K3 3. P–KN3, N–KB3 4. B–N2, B–K2 5. O–O, O–O 6. P–B4, *P–Q4*. The **Stonewall formation** of pawns on Black's Q4, K3, and KB4 gains control of the K5 square and at least partially fixes the centre, enabling him to launch a King-side attack. In his turn, White will normally attack on the Queen side and can also direct operations against Black's weak K4 square and against his weak black squares. The most common continuations are: 7. P–N3, 7. QN–Q2 and 7. N–B3. Compare **Leningrad Variation.**

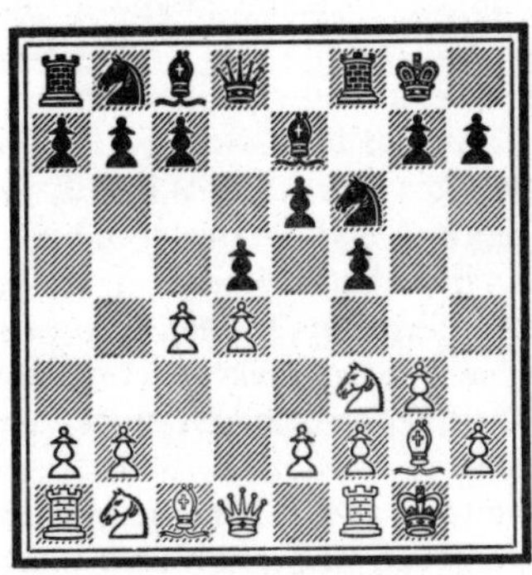

Position after 6 . . ., P–Q4

**Dvoretsky, Mark** (b. 9 December 1947) Soviet chess player; awarded the title International Master in 1975. He came first at the Wijk aan Zee Masters tournament (1975). (1976 Elo rating: 2540)

***Dynamic Chess*** a book by R. N. Coles. It describes the historical development of the hypermodern school of play and its development into dynamism, which is the characteristic of Soviet play. First published in 1956 and revised in 1966, it uses descriptive notation.

**dynamism** a style of play in which positional weaknesses are accepted in return for aggressive counterplay. A concrete example of this style is the Boleslavsky Variation of the Sicilian Defence in which Black deliberately weakens his Q4 square to obtain greater activity for his pieces. This was considered unsound until Boleslavsky demonstrated that the weakness could not be exploited successfully. Dynamism developed from the **hypermodern** revolt against the **classical** dogmas of Steinitz and Tarrasch and is felt to be especially characteristic of the Soviet players.

# E

**Echo model** a type of chess problem where two or more variations illustrate the same theme. Examples would be symmetrical mates by the Knights, the compelling of defending pieces to switch positions in different variations, and the creation of a pin by a succession of pieces. See **chameleon-echo.**

**E.C.O.** *abbrev. for Encyclopaedia of Chess Openings.*

**edge** **1.** the perimeter of the chessboard, comprising the first and eighth ranks and both Rook files.

**2.** (colloquial) a small advantage.

**Edge, Frederick Milne** nineteenth-century British journalist and correspondent on the *New York Herald*; acted as assistant secretary for the First American Chess Congress (1857) in New York. It was there that he first met Paul Morphy; during Morphy's legendary matches in London and Paris (1858–59), Edge was his constant companion and friend. His contemporary account of the brilliant successes of the young chess genius, *Paul Morphy, the Chess Champion*, was published by William Lay in 1859. It is now available under the title *The Exploits and Triumphs in Europe of Paul Morphy, The Chess Champion.*

**Edgehog** a Fairy chesspiece that moves in a similar way to the Queen, but must always begin or end a move at the edge of the board. This means that an Edgehog that is already at an edge can move like a normal Queen, but an Edgehog in the centre will have to move to an edge. The Edgehog is always represented on diagrams by a Queen that has been rotated one quarter-turn anti-clockwise. It was invented by John Driver in 1966.

***8×8*** German surrealist film (1957) made by Hans Richter, in which eight episodes of a strange story are linked by ideas and associations relating to chess and an actual game of chess.

**Eight-Queens Problem** eight Queens can be placed on a chessboard so that they fail to attack one another. Several solutions exist to this problem, one of which is shown in the diagram:

***Elements of Chess, The*** a book whose author was probably William Blagrove, a nephew of the original publisher. This was the first American chess book that was written by a United States citizen. One of its most interesting suggestions was the proposal that the men should be renamed so as not to offend 'our feelings as citizens of a free republic'. For instance, King would be replaced by Governor and Queen by General. It was first published in Boston in 1805.

**Elephant** a translation of the original Indian name of the piece known in English as the **Bishop**. In Arabic sets the piece was represented by a figure with two horns to represent the tusks of an elephant. In European sets this design was progressively altered until, in the Staunton chessmen, the split head resembles a bishop's mitre rather than an elephant's tusks.

**Eley, Brian R.** British chess player; British Champion in 1972.

**Eliskases, Erich** (b. 13 January 1913) Argentinian chess player; awarded the titles International Master in 1950 and International Grandmaster in 1952. He was born in Innsbruck and competed for Austria in the Chess Olympiads of 1930, 1933 and 1935 (when he had the best score on third board). After the union of Austria and Germany, Eliskases became German Champion in 1938 and 1939 and competed for Germany in the Chess Olympiad in 1939. This event was in progress when the Second World War began and Eliskases was one of the many competitors who decided to remain in the host country of Argentina rather than return to Europe. He eventually became a naturalized citizen and played for Argentina in the Chess Olympiads of 1952, 1958, 1960 and 1964.

**Elo, Arpad E.** (b. 1903) lecturer in physics and astronomy at the University of Wisconsin; Chairman of the U.S.C.F. Ratings Committee since 1959; Secretary of the FIDE Qualification Committee. El was the chairman of the Ratings Committee when it revised the U.S.C.F. ratings system and was the originator of the **Elo Scale** (or **system**). He was in the physics department at Marquette University for 37 years before retiring from there as Associate Professor in 1969. He was State Champion of Wisconsin eight times between 1935 and 1961.

**Elo list** another name for **International Rating List.**

**Elo Scale** or **System** a method of evaluating the relative strength of a chess player based primarily on his past results in tournament play. He is assigned a rating (Elo rating) derived from a mathematical analysis of his total number of wins, draws and losses, and the strengths of his opponents. The system is named after Prof. Arpad E. Elo, chairman of the committee appointed by the United States Chess Federation to revise its former method of grading players, and is soundly based in statistical theory. The magnitude of Elo ratings is completely arbitrary, being carried over from the U.S.C.F. system that preceded the Elo System. It is not their absolute level that is important, but the difference between the ratings of two competitors. The following table sets out the results that can be predicted when players with known Elo ratings play a series of games.

| *Rating difference between players* | *% score expected* | | *Rating difference between players* | *% score expected* | |
|---|---|---|---|---|---|
| | *Higher player* | *Lower player* | | *Higher player* | *Lower player* |
| 0–3 | 50 | 50 | 198–206 | 76 | 24 |
| 4–10 | 51 | 49 | 207–215 | 77 | 23 |
| 11–17 | 52 | 48 | 216–225 | 78 | 22 |
| 18–25 | 53 | 47 | 226–235 | 79 | 21 |
| 26–32 | 54 | 46 | 236–245 | 80 | 20 |
| 33–39 | 55 | 45 | 246–256 | 81 | 19 |
| 40–46 | 56 | 44 | 257–267 | 82 | 18 |
| 47–53 | 57 | 43 | 268–278 | 83 | 17 |
| 54–61 | 58 | 42 | 279–290 | 84 | 16 |
| 62–68 | 59 | 41 | 291–302 | 85 | 15 |
| 69–76 | 60 | 40 | 303–315 | 86 | 14 |
| 77–83 | 61 | 39 | 316–328 | 87 | 13 |
| 84–91 | 62 | 38 | 329–344 | 88 | 12 |
| 92–98 | 63 | 37 | 345–357 | 89 | 11 |
| 99–106 | 64 | 36 | 358–374 | 90 | 10 |
| 107–113 | 65 | 35 | 375–391 | 91 | 9 |
| 114–121 | 66 | 34 | 392–411 | 92 | 8 |
| 122–129 | 67 | 33 | 412–432 | 93 | 7 |
| 130–137 | 68 | 32 | 433–456 | 94 | 6 |
| 138–145 | 69 | 31 | 457–484 | 95 | 5 |
| 146–153 | 70 | 30 | 485–517 | 96 | 4 |
| 154–162 | 71 | 29 | 518–559 | 97 | 3 |
| 163–170 | 72 | 28 | 560–619 | 98 | 2 |
| 171–179 | 73 | 27 | 620–735 | 99 | 1 |
| 180–188 | 74 | 26 | over 735 | 100 | — |
| 189–197 | 75 | 25 | | | |

As can be seen, if there is a gap of 100 points between the players the stronger player can be expected to win 64% of the points, which is the approximate equivalent of winning two and losing one out of every three games. (This would apply whether the two players were Grandmasters or novices; it is the disparity in the grades rather than the absolute level that matters.) If there is a difference of 192 points, the stronger player can be expected to collect 75% of the points. If there is a difference of 735 points or more, the stronger player can be confidently expected to defeat his opponent every time. It must be remembered that while this system can forecast the outcome of a series of games surprisingly accurately it can never definitely predict the result of one game – no statistical technique can do that.

This system allows a player's Elo grading to be continuously adjusted on the basis of his most recent results. When he enters a tournament he will find that it will be assigned a grading, which is based upon the average of the ratings of the people that he will be matched against. Assume that this is 10 points less than the player's. We should expect him to gain 51% of the points, i.e. 2½ points in a tournament of five rounds. If he were to have a disastrous event, losing all his games, his Elo rating would fall by k(2½–0) where 2½ was his expected score, 0 was his actual score, and k was a weighting of between 45 and 10. A competitor will be assigned a relatively large weighting at the beginning of his career, so each tournament can substantially affect his grading, but once he has reached a consistent level his weighting will be reduced.

The major divergence between the Elo (and the Ingo) system and the B.C.F. grading method is that the former allows for a continual reassessment of players' strengths, while the latter only alters gradings annually. The reason is that much more club chess is played in the United Kingdom than the United States, and since these results are not processed as swiftly as tournament results are, anomalies can easily arise. There are therefore no plans in the United Kingdom to transfer to the Elo system, but for purposes of comparison the gradings can be converted into each other by the formula: Elo = 8B.C.F. + 600.

The Elo system was first adopted in the United States in 1960, replacing the former U.S.C.F. method, which had begun to show defects. It has been so successful that it was adopted by FIDE in September 1970 to form the basis for the award of the titles of International Grandmaster and International Master. It has also enabled an international Rating List to be published for the first time, giving accurate estimates of the strengths of the world's leading players.

**Empress** a Fairy chesspiece that possesses the powers of both the Rook and the Knight. It is thus a type of Combined Chessman.

***Encyclopaedia of Chess, The*** single-volume encyclopedia, compiled by Anne Sunnucks, featuring biographies of leading chess players, selected openings, and a wide variety of general subjects of interest to chess players. It was first published in 1970 (second edition, 1976) and uses both descriptive and algebraic notation.

**Encyclopaedia of Chess Openings** a five-volume reference work on opening theory compiled under the general editorship of Alexander Matanovic, with contributions from a team of International Grandmasters. Each volume uses figurine algebraic notation supplemented by 45 symbols which are used to evaluate the final position – essential, since this international work contains no prose in any language (except for a multilingual introduction). The use of algebraic notation rather than descriptive notation also allows a greater efficiency in the use of space.

**Volume A** covers all openings that begin with moves other than 1. P–K4 or 1. P–Q4 and unusual replies to 1. P–Q4; **Volume B** covers all half-open defences except the French Defence; **Volume C** covers all openings that arise after 1. P–K4, P–K4 and 1. P–K4, P–K3; **Volume D** covers all openings that arise after 1. P–Q4, P–Q4 as well as the Grünfeld Defence; **Volume E** covers the Bogoljubov-Indian, King's Indian and Nimzo-Indian Defences.

Volume C (the first issued) was first published in 1974. Abbrev. ***E.C.O.*** Compare ***Modern Chess Openings***.

**endgame** another name for **ending.**

**endgame study** a composed position in which White must find a win or draw according to the particular stipulation. Unlike the chess problem, White does not have to checkmate in a stated number of moves, but instead must bring about a winning (or drawn) position. Endgame studies are normally more realistic than problems and thus may be more beneficial to the player.

Endgame study by Rinck
White draws by: 1. R–K1, Q–Q7 2. K–B1, K–N6 3. R–K3ch, Q × R
4. R–R3ch, K × Rstalemate

**ending** the final phase of the game. It is characterized by a paucity of material, especially pieces, making it almost impossible to carry out checkmate. Consequently, the most common motif is **pawn promotion**; to help attain this, the King is able to function more aggressively than in the opening or middle-game. It is to this phase of the game that certain manoeuvres and features belong, of which manoeuvring to gain the **opposition, triangulation** of the King and **zugzwang** are the most common. Like the opening, it is possible to categorize endings extensively and so discover the winning techniques in many cases. Also called **endgame**. Compare **opening, middle-game**. See ***Basic Chess Endings, Pocket Guide to Chess Endgames***.

**Enevoldsen, Jens** (b. 23 September 1907) Danish chess player and arbiter; awarded the title International Master in 1950 and the title International Judge in 1960. He was Danish Champion in 1940, 1943, 1947, 1948 and 1960 and competed in the Chess Olympiads of 1933, 1935, 1937, 1939, 1952, 1956 and 1966.

**English notation** another name for **descriptive notation**.

**English Opening** an opening where White plays: 1. *P–QB4*, controlling the central square, Q5. Black usually responds with either 1 . . ., P–K4, 1 . . ., P–QB4, or 1 . . ., N–KB3. It received this name because it was first seriously played by Howard Staunton in his match with St Amant (1843), in the England-France match (1843), and in the London Tournament (1851). In some parts of Europe it was known as the Sicilian Attack, since this move mirrors Black's first move in the Sicilian Defence.

**enlarged centre** the four central squares plus the twelve squares forming their periphery. They are: KB3, KB4, KB5, KB6, K6, Q6, QB6, QB5, QB4, QB3, Q3, and K3. The fight for control of the enlarged centre is one of the main themes of opening play. See **centre**.

**en passant** *French for* in passing. This is a privilege accorded to a player who has a pawn on the fifth rank. Such a pawn attacks two squares on the sixth rank and is allowed to capture any enemy pawn that passes across one of these squares without remaining there (because of its ability to move two squares on its first move).

In this case the pawn may act as if the enemy pawn had moved only one square and so may capture it *en passant* by moving to that square. This privilege can be used only on the move immediately following the advance of the enemy pawn. In one game at the Haifa 1976 Chess Olympiad an *en passant* capture was made two moves after the advance of the enemy pawn. The illegality went unnoticed both by players and arbiters and was discovered only after the conclusion of the game. This is the only recorded instance of an '*en passant* deferred'. *Abbrev.* **e.p.**

**en prise** *French for* in a position to be taken. A man is *en prise* if it can be captured without loss. This type of chess blindness can occur at all levels.

**e.p.** *abbrev. for* ***en passant***.

**epaulet mate** any mate where the checkmated King stands at the edge of the board and is immediately flanked by two defending pieces that bar its escape. For example, a typical epaulet mate would occur when the checkmated King is on K1 with Rooks on KB1 and Q1 and an enemy Queen on its K6. Such a position is reminiscent of a soldier wearing shoulderstraps or epaulets, hence the name. Also **epaulette, epaulette mate**. (See illustration on p. 94)

epaulet mate

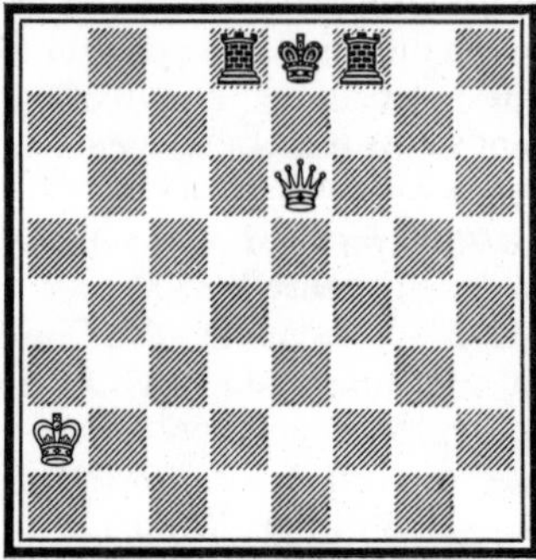

**equality** a situation existing when neither side has a decisive advantage. Black's first objective in the opening is to obtain equality by negating the initiative which White possesses through having the first move.

**Equihopper** a Fairy chesspiece that can move like any orthodox man, but needs to leap-frog a man in its move. This man will exactly bisect the length of the move. The Equihopper is represented on diagrams by a symbol of a Queen rotated 90° to the right.

**Ermenkov, Evgenni** (b. 29 September 1949) Bulgarian chess player; was awarded the title International Master in 1974. (1976 Elo rating: 2435)

**Eschécs de la Dame Enragée** *French for* chess of the angry Queen. This epithet was applied to the modernized version of chess, which was invented in the late fifteenth century. Its main differences were the increased ranges of the Queen (hence the nickname) and the Bishop. These alterations radically changed the game by quickening it and by making detailed analysis of the opening necessary for the first time – in the older game the opposing forces often did not come into contact for 15 moves, but in the new game checkmate could be delivered in only two moves. Within a very short period of time the new game had replaced the old.

**Escher, Maurits C.** (b. 17 June 1898) Dutch design artist, born in Leeuwarden; famous for his technical mastery of graphic processes and analytic compositions in which natural forms meld into one another – for example, his birds gradually become fish – and his use of cleverly concealed perspective, in which water appears to flow uphill or steps appear to go upwards and downwards at the same time. One of Escher's most famous woodcuts (see **Metamorphosis**) incorporates a chess motif, used by Hugh Alexander for the endpapers of his *A Book of Chess* (1973).

**Estrin, Yakov** (b. 1923) Soviet chess player; awarded the title International Master in 1975. (1976 Elo rating: 2450)

**etiquette** good manners in chess should not differ from the everyday observance of fairness, courtesy and general adherence to established social conventions. Even though Ruy Lopez, the famous 16th-century Spanish priest, advocated placing the chessboard so that the sun shines in the opponent's eyes (and Lasker was known to annoy opponents with the smoke from his ever-present cigar), it is best to exhibit a generous degree of social decorum and not selfishly distract your opponent. This includes the control of any urge to hum, whistle, tap your fingers on the table, laugh at his stupid (or excellent) moves, spill coffee in his lap, or punch him on the nose after you have been checkmated. Good losers can also become good winners.

**Euler** another name for the **closed Knight's tour.**

**Euratom Committee** a committee under the chairmanship of Dr Max Euwe. One of its tasks was to 'investigate the possibilities of programming chess for a computer' (a task that has also been of great interest to another former World Chess champion, Mikhail Botvinnik).

**Europa Cup** a trophy awarded by FIDE to the victorious team in the European Team Championship. It has consistently been held by the U.S.S.R. since its first presentation in 1957.

**European Club Cup** an annual international knock-out tournament held to discover Europe's best club. The event was created in 1974 and is open to national club champions or to clubs nominated by the national chess federations. Play takes place on six boards and each match consists of two rounds. In 1975, sixteen teams competed in the event which was won by Burevestnik of the U.S.S.R. The 1976 event was jointly won by Burevestnik and Solingen SG 1868 of West Germany.

**European Junior Championship** an annual international tournament held in Groningen, Holland to discover Europe's best player aged 21 or less. The Championship was first officially held from 20 December 1971 to 7 January 1972 (previously it had been run outside the auspices of FIDE) and was won by Gyula Sax (Hungary). Since then it has been won by Oleg Romanishin (U.S.S.R.), Tony Miles (United Kingdom), John Nunn (United Kingdom) and Kochiev (U.S.S.R.). The event itself is divided into two sections: the preliminaries, which consist of seven rounds conducted under the Swiss system; and the A, B and C finals which are organized on an all-play-all basis. Compare **World Cadet Championship, World Junior Championship.**

**European Team Championship** a triennial event held to discover the strongest teams in Europe. It first took place in 1957 when four teams competed in the final in Vienna and Baden, Austria. Now the Championship is comprised of preliminary tournaments from which eight teams qualify to compete in the final. This is a round-robin tournament held on eight boards.

Many believe that this event provides a more accurate gauge of the current strength of the European nations than does the Chess Olympiad, since more players compete in each team. Compare **Pan-American Team Championship.**

**Euwe, Maghielis (Max)** (b. 20 May 1901) Dutch chess player; World Champion from 1935 to 1937; awarded the titles International Grandmaster in 1950, International Judge in 1951, President of FIDE in 1970. Dr Euwe learned to play chess when aged four and won his first tournament six years later. He became Dutch Champion in 1921 and won the title on each of the 12 subsequent occasions he competed. He took part in many Chess Olympiads including the very first, which was held in 1927.

Euwe's first major successes were a second at Gothenburg (1920) and a drawn match with Maróczy in 1921 (+2 −2 =8). Euwe was always an amateur rather than a professional chess player; in 1923 he became a teacher of mathematics, gaining his doctorate in 1926. Consequently, he could play only during school vacations (usually with inadequate preparation) and in this light his match record is remarkably good. He defeated Colle in 1924 and 1928 (+5 −3 =0 and +5 −0 =1); narrowly lost to Alekhine in 1926 (+2 −3 =5); lost to Bogoljubov in 1927 and 1928 (+2 −3 =5 and +1 −2 =7); lost to Capablanca in 1932 (+0 −2 =8); defeated Spielmann in 1932 and 1935 (+2 −0 =2 and +4 −2 =2); and drew with Flohr in 1932 (+3 −3 =10).

In 1935 Euwe met Alekhine in a World Championship match and, despite his good past record against Alekhine, caused general surprise by winning a narrow victory (+9 −8 =13) to become the only amateur World Champion in chess history. In marked contrast to most of his predecessors, Euwe immediately offered a return match, which was played in 1937. In a hard-fought contest, Alekhine regained the title after an exhausted Euwe had lost four and drawn one of the last five games (+4 −10 =11). Euwe remained in Holland during the war and refused to play in tournaments sponsored by the Germans. After the end of the war he returned to tournament chess and had an excellent result at Groningen (1946), finishing only half a point behind Botvinnik and well in front of the other competitors. However, he was in abysmal form in the World Championship match-tournament two years later and came last of the five competitors (+1 −13 =6).

After this, Euwe competed less frequently although he did play in the Chess Olympiads and in the 1953 Candidates' tournament. From 1961 to 1963 he was President of the Eurotom Committee on computer chess and in 1970 he was elected President of FIDE.

Euwe's style was precise and logical, but was marred by a frequent tendency to blunder in winning positions. He was especially strong in the opening and was the founder of *Chess Archives*, which he edited until 1967. Euwe is a prolific author; included among his works are *The Development of Chess Style* and *The Middle Game*.

**Evans Gambit** an opening sequence arising in the Giuoco Piano: 1. P–K4, P–K4 2. N–KB3, N–QB3 3. B–B4, B–B4 4. *P–QN4*. White offers a pawn in return for rapid development, a stronger centre, and control of the long diagonal by a fianchetto of the Queen Bishop. This opening was devised by Captain William D. Evans in about 1827 and was described by a contemporary as 'A gift of the gods to a languishing chess world', but is now rarely seen in competitive chess.

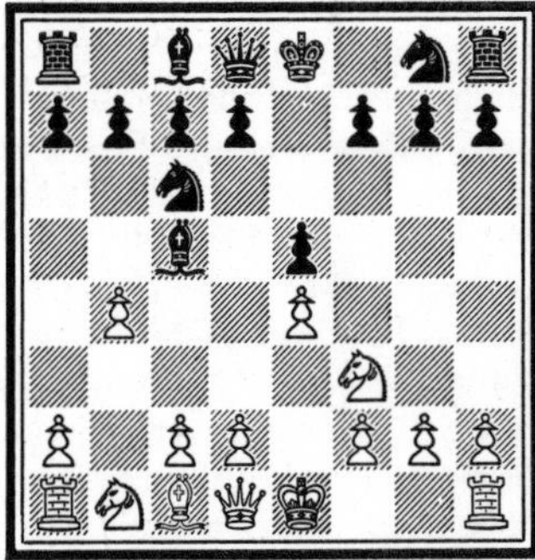

Position after 4. P–QN4

**Evans, Larry** (b. 22 March 1932) U.S. chess player; awarded the titles International Master in 1952 and International Grandmaster in 1957. He has been U.S. Champion several times. (1976 Elo rating: 2540)

**Evans, William Davies** (1790–1872) British amateur chess player; born in Milford. Evans was an officer in the British navy and served as a Commander in H.M. Royal Mail Packet Service at Milford. He later joined the P & O company. Although Evans was apparently a weak player, he was the inventor of the gambit named after him – one of the most popular openings of the nineteenth century. See **Evans Gambit.**

**Evergreen Partie** or **Game** the name given to a game played between A. Anderssen and J. Dufresne, an authority on the openings, in Berlin in 1852. Anderssen was White: 1. P–K4, P–K4 2. N–KB3, N–QB3 3. B–B4, B–B4 4. P–QN4, B × P 5. P–B3, B–R4 6. P–Q4, P × P 7. O–O, P–Q6 8. Q–N3, Q–B3 9. P–K5, Q–N3 10. R–K1, KN–K2 11. B–R3, P–QN4 12. Q × P, R–QN1 13. Q–R4, B–N3 14. QN–Q2, B–N2 15. N–K4, Q–B4 16. B × P, Q–R4 17. N–B6ch, P × N 18. P × P, R–N1 19. QR–Q1!, Q × N 20. R × Nch, N × R? 21. Q × Pch!, K × Q 22. B–B5ch, K–K1 23. B–Q7ch, K–B1 24. B × Nmate.

The game was given this name by Steinitz in tribute to its eternal freshness and charm. It has been described as the most brilliant Evans Gambit ever played. Compare **Immortal Game.**

**Excelsior theme** a motif in problem chess consisting of the promotion of a pawn standing on its original square at the beginning of the problem. The word itself is derived from Latin and means higher. This theme was used by Sam Loyd in a famous problem devised in 1858.

**exchange** the swapping of one man for another, usually of equal value. Winning (or losing) the exchange takes place when a man is swapped for another of greater (or lesser) value. The term is especially used to describe the exchange of Knight or Bishop for Rook. See **minor exchange.**

**Exchange Variation** **1.** an opening sequence arising out of Alekhine's Defence: 1. P–K4, N–KB3 2. P–K5, N–Q4 3. P–QB4, N–N3 4. P–Q4, P–Q3 5. *P×P*. This variation is widely believed to be too passive for White, since the exchanges that ensue will allow Black to equalize by playing normal developing moves. The most common continuation is: 5 . . ., BP×P, though 5 . . ., KP×P has also had periods of popularity.

**2.** an opening sequence arising out of the Caro-Kann Defence: 1. P–K4, P–QB3 2. P–Q4, P–Q4 3. *P×P, P×P*. The most common continuations are: 4. P–QB4, and 4. B–Q3. In the former case this variation has transposed into the Panov-Botvinnik Attack, which at one time was thought to pose a severe threat to the Caro-Kann Defence. The alternative move is less ambitious and aims merely to hamper Black's Queen Bishop. There are opportunities for minority attacks on opposite flanks, but little immediate tension in the position.

**3.** an opening sequence arising out of the English Opening: 1. P–QB4, N–KB 2. N–QB3, P–Q4 3. *P×P, N×P*. The most common continuation is: 4. P–KN3, after which Black must decide what to do with this Knight. This variation was adopted in the third World Championship match between Botvinnik and Smyslov and usually led to good positions for Black following the immediate exchange of Knights.

**4.** an opening sequence arising out of the French Defence: 1. P–K4, P–K3 2. P–Q4, P–Q4 3. *P×P*. This line is satisfactory for Black, since his French Bishop is freed from its cramped position. Very often the result of the game will be a draw as the major pieces are exchanged on the open file. The most common continuation is 3 . . ., P×P.

**5.** an opening sequence arising out of the Grünfeld Defence: 1. P–Q4, N–KB3 2. P–QB4, P–KN3 3. N–QB3, P–Q4 4. *P×P, N×P* 5. P–K4. White's fifth move leads to further exchanges which both relax the tension and allow Black to train his pieces on the centre. The most common continuation is: 5 . . ., N×N 6. P×N.

**Exchange Variation Double Deferred** an opening sequence arising out of the Ruy Lopez: 1. P–K4, P–K4 2. N–KB3, N–QB3 3. B–N5, P–QR3 4. B–R4, N–B3 5. O–O, B–K2 6. *B×N*. White exchanges his Bishop for the Knight only after developing his pieces. Black's best immediate reply: 6 . . ., QP×B. Also called **Delayed Exchange Ruy Lopez Deferred.**

**Exchange Variation (Orthodox Defence)** an opening sequence arising out of the Orthodox Defence to the Queen's Gambit Declined. The following is a typical progression, although the exchange of pawns (from which the name is derived) may be deferred: 1. P–Q4, P–Q4 2. P–QB4, P–K3 3. N–QB3, N–KB3 4. P×P, P×P 5. B–N5, P–B3 6. Q–B2, B–K2 7. P–K3, QN–Q2 8. B–Q3. See **Orthodox Defence.**

***Exploits and Triumphs in Europe of Paul Morphy, The Chess Champion*** reprint title (1973) of a book originally written in 1859 by Morphy's friend and companion Frederick Milne Edge, under the title

*Paul Morphy, the Chess Champion.* The primary value and interest of this work is its contemporary account of the dazzling successes of Morphy against the leading players of London and Paris. It also recounts the story behind Morphy's futile attempts to engage Howard Staunton in match play.

# F

**Fabel, Karl** (1905–1975) West German mathematician and civil judge; awarded the titles International Master for Chess Compositions in 1967 and International Judge of Chess Compositions in 1964. He was a prolific composer of chess problems and wrote several books on the subject. Fabel's contributions to Fairy Chess problems (particularly retrograde analysis) made him one of the best-known names among problemists.

**Fairhurst, William A.** (b. 21 August 1903) British chess player; British Champion in 1937 and many times Scottish champion.

**Fairy Chess** any variant of chess that fundamentally differs from orthodox chess. There are four main variations of Fairy Chess: (1) where new pieces have been added to the game (see **Amazon, Grasshopper, Nightrider**) or orthodox pieces have been given extra powers (see **Progressive Chess, Total Chess**); (2) where the chessboard has been altered, either by changing its size and/or shape (see **anchor-ring, Cylinder Chess**); (3) where artificial conditions have been imposed, either on the moves of the pieces or on the objective of the game which is no longer to checkmate the opposing King (see **Checkless Chess, Maximummer, Helpmate**); (4) retrograde analysis, where no moves are made, but instead the objective is to deduce Black's last move.

Fairy Chess has existed for as long as orthodox chess, but it only became popular in the twentieth century. This was mainly due to the efforts of T. R. Dawson (1889–1951), who popularized it through his numerous contributions to chess periodicals and his creation of *The Fairy Chess Review*. In 1958 FIDE decided that Fairy Chess was a legitimate area of problem chess and included a set of rules covering Fairy Chess problem composition in the Piran Codex. Also called **heterodox chess.**

**Fajarowicz Variation** an opening sequence arising out of the Budapest Defence: 1. P–Q4, N–KB3 2. P–QB4, P–K4 3. P×P, *N–K5*. This line was first played in 1928. The most common continuation is: 4. N–KB3, N–QB3.

**faker** (Kmoch's term) a **half-free** pawn that cannot be helped to promote by other pawns.

**Falkbeer Counter Gambit** an opening sequence arising out of the King's Gambit in which Black also offers a pawn: 1. P–K4, P–K4 2. P–KB4, *P–Q4*. A common continuation is: 3. KP×P, P–K5 4. P–Q3, N–KB3.

This opening gives Black scope for his pieces and contests White's aggressive plans. It is one of the most popular choices against the King's Gambit. It was invented by the nineteenth-century player

Ernest Falkbeer, but analysed by Jänisch by whose name it is also known.

**Falkbeer, Ernest** (1819–1885) Austro-Hungarian chess player; born in Brunn, Austria and emigrated to England where he became the editor of *The Chess Players' Magazine* and wrote the chess column of *The Sunday Times*.

At Birmingham (1858), he came second behind Löwenthal, but ahead of Staunton. In 1856 and 1857 he played Bird in two matches losing the first (+1 −2 =0), but winning the second (+5 −4 =4) in his style of romantic aggression. In 1864 he returned to Vienna, becoming a sub-editor on an Austrian periodical, and gave up chess. He died in Vienna on 14 December 1885.

**family check** an attack by a Knight where the enemy King is checked while one or more major pieces are simultaneously attacked. The term was devised by Bogoljubov.

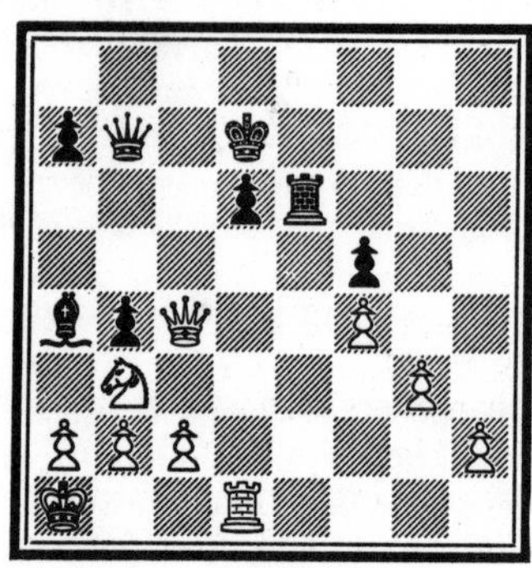

Tal vs. Klaman (Moscow, 1957)
After 35. N–B5ch, Black resigned as the Knight attacked the Queen, Rook and Bishop as well

**Faragó, Ivan** (b. 1 April 1946) Hungarian chess player; awarded the titles International Master in 1974 and International Grandmaster in 1976. He was equal first at the Amsterdam Masters' tournament (1975). (1976 Elo rating: 2420)

**Farré, Mallofre Miguel** (b. 23 February 1936) Spanish chess player; awarded the title International Master in 1959. He competed in the World Junior Championships of 1953 and 1955 and played in the Chess Olympiads of 1958 and 1960.

**Father of Modern Chess, The** a descriptive phrase often applied to Aron Nimzovitch because of his highly original teachings on chess.

**Fazekas, Dr Stefan** (1898–1967) British amateur chess player; born in Hungary on 23 March 1898. He was awarded the title International Master in 1953 and became an International Correspondence Chess Master and also British Champion in 1957. Fazekas died on 3 May 1967.

**Fédération Internationale des Échecs** the international organization, founded in Paris in 1924, responsible for governing all aspects of international chess competition and for drafting the rules for such play. The Federation organized the first Chess Olympiads within three years of its founding, and since 1948 has had total control over the conduct of the World Championship matches. It awards various titles, the most important of which are International Grandmaster and International Master. There are 97 member countries and the organization has its headquarters at Amsterdam. Abbrev. **F.I.D.E.** or **FIDE**.

**Fegatello (Attack)** an opening sequence arising out of the Two Knights' Defence: 1. P–K4, P–K4 2. N–KB3, N–QB3 3. B–B4, N–B3 4. N–N5, P–Q4 5. P×P, *N×P* 6. *N×BP*, K×N. By capturing the pawn, Black allows an extremely dangerous Knight sacrifice, which presages an attack that often drives Black's King into the centre of the board. Fegatello is derived from the Italian word *fegato* (literally meaning liver and figuratively meaning guts or courage). While White shows courage in sacrificing the Knight it is usually Black's liver that gets 'fried' in the onslaught. Also called **Fried Liver Attack, Polerio's Gambit.**

**feint** a manoeuvre in which the player achieves one objective by seeming to attempt another. For instance, a King gets within capturing distance of a passed pawn by appearing to be moving to protect his pawn.

By this manoeuvre Lasker drew an important game against Tarrasch (St Petersburg 1914).

**Fernandez, Ciro** Cuban chess player; awarded the title International Master in 1975. (1976 Elo rating: 2360)

**Fernandez, Juan** Cuban chess player; awarded the title International Master in 1975. (1976 Elo rating: 2370)

**fianchetto** *vb.* to develop a Bishop to KN2 or QN2. *n.* a developing move characterized by moving the King's or Queen's Bishop to one of these squares. The Bishop is sometimes fianchettoed on the second move, after the preparatory move of the Knight's pawn to KN3 or QN3. See **Robatsch Defence.**

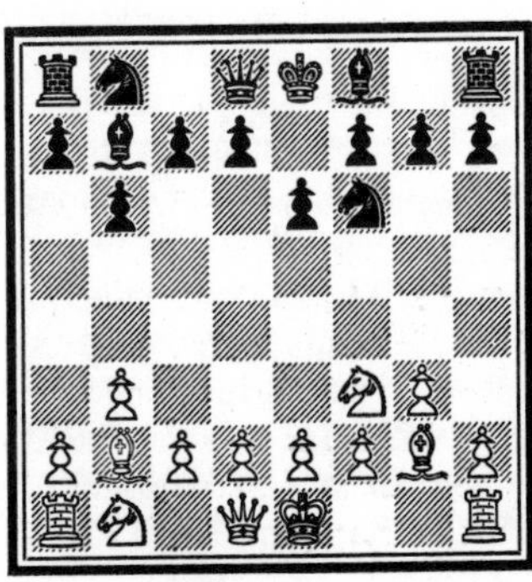

Fianchetto (by Black) and double fianchetto (by White)

**Fianchetto del Rey** a former name for the **Robatsch Defence.**

**Fichtl, Jiri** (b. 16 February 1921) Czechoslovakian chess player; awarded the title International Master in 1959. He was Czechoslovakian Champion in 1950 and 1960 and competed in the Chess Olympiads of 1954, 1958, 1960, and 1962. (1976 Elo rating: 2345)

**F.I.D.E.** or **FIDE** Fédération Internationale des Échecs.

**fifty-move rule** a law of chess which deems that when a player demonstrates that 50 moves have been recorded without a capture or a move of a pawn the game may be deemed a draw. If a capture or move of a pawn is made the counting must start afresh. There are certain infrequent cases where a mate is possible in greater than 50 moves and for these an exception is sometimes made, but only when specified in advance in the tournament conditions. The rule has to be applied only infrequently, usually where one player is continuing in a theoretically drawn ending such as rook and bishop against rook, which nevertheless demands accurate defence.

**figurine algebraic notation** a variant of algebraic notation in which each man is symbolized by the figure that represents it on a diagram. This means that a Knight will be shown by a miniature horse's head and so on. This type of notation minimizes confusion as, while the name and hence the initial of each man varies from country to country, the symbols are based on the Staunton chess men which is the only set allowed by FIDE to be used in international tournaments. The ranks and files are lettered and numbered in the same way as in normal algebraic notation since there is less variation in the alphabets and none at all in the system of numerals. This type of notation is used by *Informator*.

**file** one of the eight columns of squares that run vertically up the chessboard. Each is a path that initially connects the same opposing pieces, such as the two King Rooks. Indeed, each file is named after the piece that originally stands on it, for example the King Rook file. See **closed file, half-open file, open file.** Compare **rank.**

**Filip, Dr Miroslav** (b. 27 October 1928) Czechoslovakian chess player; awarded the titles International Master in 1953 and International Grandmaster in 1955. He was Czechoslovakian Junior Champion in 1947 and Czechoslovakian Champion in 1950, 1952 and 1954. Filip competed in every Chess Olympiad from 1952 to 1974 and also took part in the European Team Championships of 1957 and 1961. He made his debut in the interzonals with Göteborg (1955) and has since appeared in the interzonals of 1958, 1962 (when he was equal fourth) and 1970. He took part in the 1962 Candidates' tournament finishing in equal seventh place. (1976 Elo rating: 2495)

**Filipowicz, Andrzej** (b. 13 May 1938) Polish chess player; awarded the title International Master in 1975. (1976 Elo rating: 2385)

**Fine, Reuben** (b. 11 October 1914) American chess player; awarded the title International Grandmaster in 1950. He was U.S. Open Champion in 1932, 1933, 1934 (with Reshevsky), 1935, 1939 and 1940 and competed in the Chess Olympiads of 1933, 1935 and 1937. His other results include firsts at Hastings (1935) and Zandvoort (1936) and seconds at Hastings (1936) and at Avro (1938) after a tie-break with Keres. In 1937 he acted as Euwe's second in the return match with Alekhine. Fine was undoubtedly one of the world's strongest players in the late 1930s and in 1948 was invited to compete in the tournament to decide the next World Champion, but declined in order to concentrate upon his work as a psychologist. Since then he has played no serious chess. His books include *Basic Chess Endings*, *Bobby Fischer's Conquest of the World Chess Championship*, *Chess the Easy Way*, *The Ideas Behind the Chess Openings* and *Psychology of the Chessplayer*.

**fingerfehler** *German for* finger-slip. It is used to describe any obvious but bad move that is made unthinkingly.

***Fireside Book of Chess, The*** an anthology of articles, stories, and games of chess compiled by Irving Chernev and Fred Reinfeld. The games range from fiercely contested battles in World Championship matches to a six-move brevity played in the 19th century; the articles and stories include everything from an encapsulated history of the game to a ghost story. It was first published in 1949 and uses descriptive notation.

**First American Chess Congress** the first chess tournament to be held in America. It began on 4 October 1857 and was held in Descombe's Rooms, 704 Broadway, New York under the sponsorship of the New York Chess Club. The tournament, which was restricted to American players, was a four-round knockout competition with 16 players competing and was easily won by Paul Morphy who defeated Louis Paulsen in the final (+5 −1 =1). Second was Paulsen, third was Theodor Lichtenheim of New York, and fourth was Dr B. I. Raphael of Louisville.

**first board** another name for **top board**.

**first move** the first move in a game of chess is nowadays always made by the person using White (or the light-coloured pieces). In tournament play, the colours are generally pre-determined; but in match play lots may be drawn to allocate the white pieces. In friendly or offhand games, it is traditional for the two opponents to decide who plays White by one of them first mixing one Black and one White pawn in his cupped hands and then offering one of each in his closed fists to the other player. In subsequent games the players usually alternate who has the White pieces (and thus the first move). Other methods of determining who has the first move are sometimes used as well.

**Fischer, Robert (Bobby) James** (b. 9 March 1943) American chess player; World Champion from 1972 to 1975; awarded the title International Grandmaster in 1958. He was American Champion in 1958, 1959, 1960, 1961, 1963, 1964, 1966 and 1967 and competed in the Chess Olympiads of 1960, 1962, 1966 and 1970. He has taken part in four interzonals (winning two), two Candidates' tournaments and one series of Candidates' matches.

Born in Chicago and brought up by his divorced mother, Fischer learned to play at six by puzzling out the rules with his 11-year-old sister after she had bought a chess set. In 1950 he joined the Brooklyn Chess Club, and began playing in tournaments in 1955. His early results were unremarkable, but in 1956 he won the United States Junior Championship and some months later became famous by playing the **game of the century** against International Master Donald Byrne. In 1957 he won in quick succession: the United States Junior Championship, the United States Open Championship and the United States Championship itself, to qualify for the 1958 interzonal where he became the youngest International Grandmaster ever in coming equal fifth and qualifying for the subsequent Candidates' tournament where he also came fifth.

Fischer left school at 16 to become a chess professional and scored numerous tournament successes. In 1961 Mrs Piatigorsky sponsored a 16-game match between him and Reshevsky, but Fischer forfeited the match after the score was tied 5½–5½ in protest at a game being rescheduled to suit the sponsors. Throughout his career Fischer has been prepared to sacrifice his personal interests if he believes himself to be in the right.

Fischer won the 1962 interzonal by a large margin and was confident of winning the following Candidates' tournament. However, he came only fourth and in an angry article in *Sports Illustrated* magazine accused the Soviet players of cheating by taking short draws among themselves in order to conserve their strength to fight against him. The ensuing controversy was one cause of a short-lived FIDE law banning draws under 30 moves and was a reason for the replacement of Candidates' tournaments by Candidates' matches. Fischer almost completely withdrew from chess over the next two years and refused to participate in the 1964 interzonal. In 1967 he entered the Sousse interzonal, but withdrew while in the lead after a dispute with the organizers over their refusal to re-schedule his games. (Fischer refuses to play chess on his Sabbath.) Again he partially withdrew from international chess for two years, although he did work on a collection of his games.

In March 1970 he came out of retirement to play on second board in the **match of the century** and defeated Petrosian (+2 −0 =2). It was apparent that he was stronger than ever and had eliminated former weaknesses, such as a tendency to go astray in tactical complications, or drift when no strategic plan was available. After a heated debate, FIDE allowed him to enter the interzonal without qualifying and Fischer came an easy first, 3½ points ahead of the next players. This was followed by sensational results in the Candidates' matches where he defeated Taimanov (+6 −0 =0) and Larsen (+6 −0 =0); in the finals of the Candidates' matches he met Petrosian. After winning the first game, Fischer had gone 18 games without a loss or draw – an unprecedented run of victories, but Petrosian won the second game and had better chances in the draws that followed. Fischer then won the final three games to become Spassky's challenger for the World Championship match in Iceland in 1972 (+5 −1 =3).

The 1972 World Championship match was one of the most acrimonious on record. Fischer did not turn up for the opening ceremony and arrived only after British financier James Slater had doubled the stakes. During the match itself there was a continuing series of arguments – mainly between Fischer and the promoters, although the exasperated Soviet contingent did counter-accuse the Americans of influencing Spassky to play badly. In play, though, Fischer was at the peak of his form. After losing the first two games (the second by a forfeit) he overpowered Spassky in the first half of the match to build up a lead that Spassky was unable to destroy in the latter half of the match (+7 −3 =11).

Fischer had announced his intention to defend his title as often as possible, but in fact played no chess before the time was due for his first title defence, against the Soviet player Anatoly Karpov. Fischer then resigned his title after he and FIDE were unable to reach agreement on the conditions under which he should defend it.

Fischer has been described as combining the best of Capablanca and Alekhine. Equipped with a burning will to win, he plays at maximum intensity at all times. Like Capablanca he is an extremely fast player and this too increases the pressure on his opponents. He is particularly good in the exploitation of minute advantages (the sixth game of the World Championship match is a fine example of this), but the match with Spassky also showed his capacity for the sustained calculation of variations and his tactical ability.

Fischer has written two books: *Bobby Fischer Teaches Chess* (with S. Margulies and D. Mosenfelder) and *My 60 Memorable Games* (with L. Evans). (1975 Elo rating: 2780)

***Fischer-Spassky Move by Move*** an account of the 1972 World Championship match by Larry Evans and Ken Smith. Each move in the match is accompanied by a diagram with a comment, and can thus be followed without the need for a chess set. There are a total of 1,800 diagrams. The book was first published in 1973 and uses descriptive notation.

***Fischer v. Spassky, Reykjavik 1972*** an account of the 1972 World Championship match by C. H. O'D. Alexander. In addition to an analysis of each game it contains reports on the upsets and arguments around the match as well as illustrated biographies of the players. It was first published in 1972 and uses descriptive notation.

**five-minute chess** chess in which a player must complete all his moves within five minutes. Unlike **five-second chess** there is a time limit for the whole game rather than for each move.

**Five-Queen Check** five Queens can be placed on a chessboard so that they attack every square. The diagram printed on p.106 gives the solution to this common problem.

**five-second chess** chess played at the rate of five seconds per move. See **Blitz, lightning chess.**

**flag** a component of a chess clock that is found on each of its faces. It is a miniature pendulum that hangs down from a point near 12 o'clock. As the minute hand of the clock approaches the figure 12 it pushes this tiny pendulum upwards. Once the minute hand reaches and passes the figure 12 the flag can no longer be supported by the minute hand and consequently falls. This provides an easy way of discovering exactly when the time limit has been passed and if the stipulated number of moves to be made has in fact been made. If not, the game is lost on time. See also **time** (def. 1), **time control.**

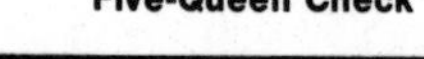

**Five-Queen Check**

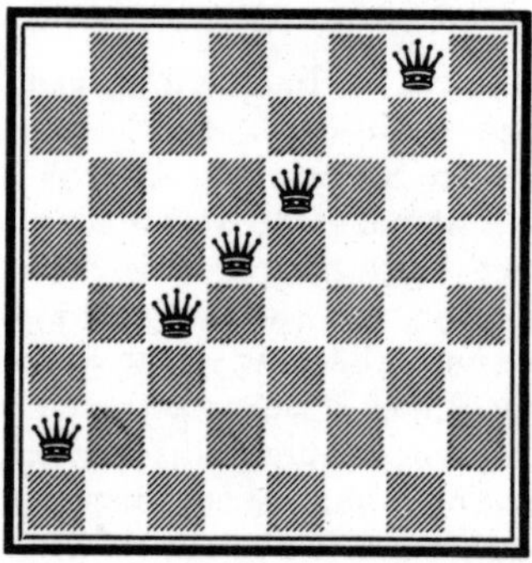

All free squares are under attack

**flank** the three outer files on one of the sides of the chessboard. Also called **wing.** See **centre, enlarged centre.**

**flank development** development on one or both wings. This term is principally used to describe the fianchetto of the Bishops.

**flank openings** those openings where White refrains from an early advance of the two central pawns, preferring instead to develop on the wings by means of a fianchetto on one or both flanks. These openings often have strategies behind them similar to those of the King's Indian Defence and the Modern Defence.

Two flank openings are the **English Opening** and the **King's Indian Attack.**

**Flea House, The** *nickname of* the Chess and Checker Club of New York.

**Flesch, Janos Laszlo** (b. 30 September 1933) Hungarian chess player; competed in the 1964 Chess Olympiad. Flesch is an outstanding blindfold chess player; in 1960 he gave a simultaneous display against 52 opponents (+31 −3 =18). (1976 Elo rating: 2390)

**flight square** any square that a King can use to escape from a check. A King is checkmated if it has no flight square, cannot capture the attacker, and cannot interpose a man. See also **plus-flight theme, star-flight theme.**

**Flohr, Salo** (b. 21 November 1908) Soviet chess player; awarded the titles International Grandmaster in 1950 and International Judge in 1963. He competed in the Chess Olympiads of 1930, 1931, 1933, 1935 and 1937 (obtaining the best score on first board in the last two events) and took part in the 1948 interzonal.

He was born in Horodenka in Russian Poland and was evacuated to Czechoslovakia after being orphaned in the First World War. By 20 he was both a professional chess player and reporter and often covered the events in which he played. His first big success was second place behind Rubinstein at Rogaska Slatina (1929); a long series of victories followed, among which were firsts at Hastings (1931 and 1934) and equal first with Botvinnik at Moscow (1934). By this time he was a national hero; Flohr cigarettes, Flohr pastries, Flohr slippers and many other products could be seen on sale in Czechoslovakia. In 1937 FIDE selected him as Alekhine's next challenger. Although the decision was not binding upon the World Champion, negotiations were begun, only to be interrupted by the German invasion of Czechoslovakia and then by the outbreak of war. After the invasion in 1938, Flohr fled to the U.S.S.R.; he became a Soviet citizen in 1942.

Flohr was never again a serious challenger for the World Championship and this has been ascribed to his change in style; in the 1930s he was a combinative player, but as he grew older he increasingly attempted to avoid complications and relied upon technique. While this reduced the likelihood of defeat, it also reduced the chances of victory. In later years Flohr concentrated upon his work as a writer on chess.

**Flórián, Tibor** (b. 2 March 1919) Hungarian chess player; awarded the title International Master in 1950. He was Hungarian Champion in 1945. Flórián competed in the 1952 Chess Olympiad and in the 1961 European Team Championship.

**fluid pawn centre** a position where the centre pawns are able to advance or be exchanged for other pawns. A fluid pawn centre is a feature of open games. See **pawn storm**.

**Foltys, Jan** (1908–1952) Czechoslovakian chess player; competed in the Chess Olympiads of 1937 and 1939 and was Czechoslovakian Champion in 1943. He was awarded the title International Master in 1950 and in 1951 qualified for the 1952 Interzonal, but died before he could compete.

**Fool's Mate** the shortest possible game ending in checkmate: 1. P–KN4, P–K3 2. P–KB3, Q–R5 mate! It has been known for centuries and was mentioned in Arthur Saul's *Famous Game of Chesse Play,* published in 1614. See also **Scholar's Mate**.

**Footsoldier** a translation of the original Indian name of the man known in English as the pawn. In Arabic it was known as the *baidaq* (footsoldier) and this meaning was retained in some European countries, including Britain, on the introduction of chess since many variants of the name, including *pawn*, derive from the Latin *pedes* (footsoldier).

**force** the total strength of one player's material. For instance, if White has one piece more than Black he has a greater force. This is one of the three basic elements in which players attempt to gain an advantage, the other two being space and tempo (or time).

**forced move** or **sequence** a move or series of moves for which there are no alternatives or whose alternatives are demonstrably inferior. If the forced move or sequence leads to an inferior position then the player is initially in zugzwang.

**forcing move** a move that compels the opponent to play a move or consecutive series of moves. A forcing move may create a threat that can only be parried in one way as, for example, when a lone King can only retreat to the edge of the board when attacked by two united Rooks.

**Forintos, Gyözö** (b. 30 July 1935) Hungarian chess player; awarded the titles International Master in 1963 and International Grandmaster in 1974. (1976 Elo rating: 2490)

**fork** a double attack in two directions. Every man is capable of carrying out a fork with the exception of the Rook pawns, but some men are able to carry out more valuable forks than others. For instance, the King and Queen are only useful in forking unprotected men because of their great value. For this reason they are the worst pieces to carry out forks.

The best are the pawn and the Knight. The pawn is dangerous, because its lack of value enables it profitably to capture any piece it forks whether that piece is guarded or not. The comparative unimportance of the Knight is also a factor in its favour in this case; another advantage is the fact that no attacked piece can attack the Knight (unless it is itself another Knight).

**fork trick** a combination that may win a pawn. A minor piece is able to capture an apparently protected central pawn since its own capture would allow a fork by a pawn.

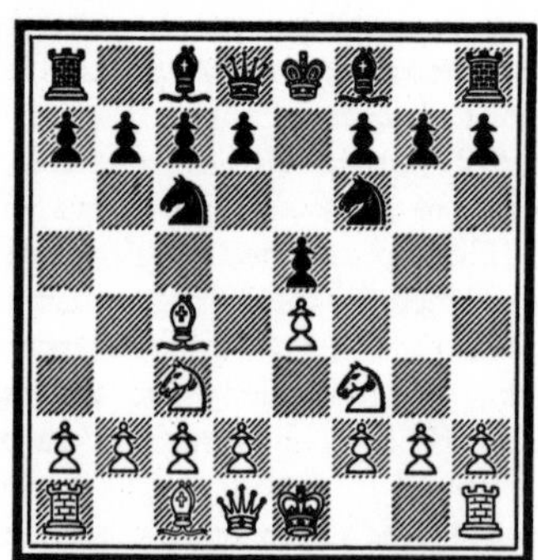

In the diagram the fork trick would be: 1 . . ., N×P 2.N×N, P–Q4. This combination is usually found in the centre in the opening, due to the congestion that often occurs.

**Forsyth notation** a concise method of recording the position reached in a game (unlike algebraic notation and descriptive notation which record the moves of a game). Beginning with the top left-hand corner, i.e., Black's QR1, the position of the men as well as the vacant spaces are written down rank by rank. Black's men are written in small letters and White's in capitals to avoid confusion. Thus a checkmate of Black's King on its K1 by a King on White's K6 and a Queen on KR8 would be recorded in Forsyth notation as: 4k2Q/8/4K3/40. The numbers refer to the number of vacant squares that exist, so that '40' means that there are five consecutive ranks that are bare of men. This system of notation was invented by the Scottish player, David Forsyth, in the nineteenth century.

**Fou** *French for* jester. English equivalent, Bishop. This piece received this name because it was reminiscent of a jester's cap. In French diagrams it is often represented by a cap and bells.

**Founder of the Soviet school of chess, The** a descriptive phrase often applied to Mikhail Tchigorin, whose aggressive style of play showed a willingness to evaluate each position separately rather than rely upon dogmatic judgments that might be disproved by exceptions. His ideas were later adopted by the Soviet players, who consider him to be the founder of their dynamic school of play.

**four-handed chess** a variant of chess for four players. It is played on a chessboard with three rows added to each edge so that it consists of 160 squares. A set of men is arranged on each edge with one player in control of each.

The players form two teams and work together to checkmate both opposing Kings, but the partners may neither consult each other nor move each other's men. Players cannot capture their partner's men and so their Kings may occupy adjacent squares.

The objective is to mate both opposing Kings. Once one King has been mated, both it and its men must remain motionless and in this state they can neither check, capture, nor be captured. This will continue until the mate is relieved by the partner. If the partner's King is mated before this can happen the game is over.

Pawns are promoted only on the back ranks of the opponents. As these are on either side of the partners this must involve captures. If instead a pawn reaches the back rank of the partner, the pawn must move backwards until it reaches the second rank, when it can advance again. A pawn blocked by a partner's pawn may leapfrog over it.

Four-handed chess was devised in the United Kingdom in the nineteenth century and has two basic variants: the Hughes Game and the Verney Game.

Although this game is a fairly recent introduction, its four handedness represents a reversion to the much older game of **chaturanga**. See **variant forms of chess.**

**Four-Handed Chess Club** a nineteenth-century chess club in London devoted to playing four-handed chess. It met at the Holborn Restaurant and numbered among its members M. E. Hughes-Hughes, who introduced one of the basic variants of the game in 1888.

**Four Knights' Game** an opening sequence: 1. P–K4, P–K4 2. N–KB3, N–QB3 3. *N–B3, N–B3*. White relies on his extra tempo and develops swiftly, but with proper play Black faces few problems.

Although drawish, this opening was a favourite of both Akiba Rubinstein and Mikhail Botvinnik.

**Four Pawns Attack (Alekhine's Defence)** an opening sequence arising in Alekhine's Defence: 1. P–K4, N–KB3 2. P–K5, N–Q4 3. P–Q4, P–Q3 4. P–QB4, N–N3 5. *P–B4*. Despite the harrying of the Knight, White's primary intention is to gain an advantage in space leading to a decisive attack on the King side. Black is prepared to suffer a cramped opening for the sake of an extended target in the strungout pawns. Black's possible immediate replies include 5 . . ., B–B4, P–N3; and P × P.

**fractional notation** a system of notation in which White's moves are recorded as the numerator of a fraction and Black's moves are recorded as the denominator. The moves: 1. P–K4, P–K4 2. N–KB3, N–QB3 would be shown as: 1. $\frac{\text{P–K4}}{\text{P–K4}}$ 2. $\frac{\text{N–KB3}}{\text{N–KB3}}$ This system is now used only infrequently

**Franco-Benoni Defence** a defence to the Queen pawn opening: 1. P–Q4, P–K3 2. P–K4, *P–QB4*. This is a hybrid of the French Defence and Benoni Defence, hence the name. It can transpose into several other openings apart from these two, although it is probably most likely to develop into a Benoni Defence after 3. P–Q5, or a Sicilian Defence after 3. N–KB3.

**Franco-Indian Defence** a defence to the Queen pawn opening: 1. P–Q4, *P–K3*. This is regarded as combining the French Defence and Nimzo-Indian Defence, hence its name. There are numerous possibilities of transposition to many other openings as well as the two mentioned above.

**Frankenstein-Dracula Variation** a humorous name for an opening sequence arising out of the Vienna Game: 1. P–K4, P–K4 2. N–QB3, N–KB3 3. B–B4, N × P 4. Q–R5, N–Q3 5. B–N3, N–B3 6. N–N5, P–KN3 7. Q–B3, P–B4 8. Q–Q5, Q–K2 9. N × Pch, K–Q1 10. N × R, P–N3. Black sacrifices the exchange to obtain a lead in development. The most common continuation is: 11. P–Q3. This old-established variation received its new name 'because it is terrifying for both sides, and like these two famous gentlemen, has an incredible facility for rising from the grave' (*Batsford Chess Yearbook*, 1975, p.53). Compare **Adams Gambit**.

**Franklin, Benjamin** (1706–1790) the famous scientist, statesman, and philosopher who was described by Daniel Willard Fiske as being, 'the first known chess player and chess writer of the New World'. Franklin was an enthusiastic and inveterate player. In his biography, Carl Van Doren records that he frequently played from six in the evening until sunrise and in his autobiography Franklin recalls how he used chess to learn Italian. He played with a fellow student on the condition that the loser would have to learn a piece of Italian grammar before the next game and, writes Franklin, 'As we played pretty equally we thus beat each other into that language'. Franklin is also known to have played while in Europe. He often visited the Café de la Régence and is mentioned in Boswell's journal for 15 September 1769 as playing chess with Sir John Pringle, his travelling companion. Franklin's opinions on chess are encapsulated in an essay entitled the *Morals of Chess* which he wrote in 1779. He firmly believed that chess was very beneficial in developing the character of those who played it as it taught foresight, circumspection and caution. In addition, it showed the players that they should never become discouraged since the 'game is so full of events, there is such a variety of turns in it, the fortune of it is so full of vicissitudes, and one so frequently, after contemplation, discovers the means of extricating one's self from a supposed unsurmountable difficulty, that one is encouraged to continue the contest to the last, in hopes of victory from our skill; or, at least, from the negligence of our adversary . . .' Franklin also laid down certain rules that should be followed when playing, such as never to demand indulgences from the other player that you are unwilling to give, never to take advantage of an opponent's oversight but instead point out the mistake, never to hurry an opponent by such strategems as whistling, singing, looking at your watch, or picking up a book to read, and if a game has been lost never to make excuses such as lack of practice, being confused by the opening, or the men being of unusual size since 'A man of proper pride would scorn to account for his being beaten by one of these excuses, even were it true; because they have all so much the appearance, at the moment, of being untrue.'

**Frankenstein-Dracula Variation**

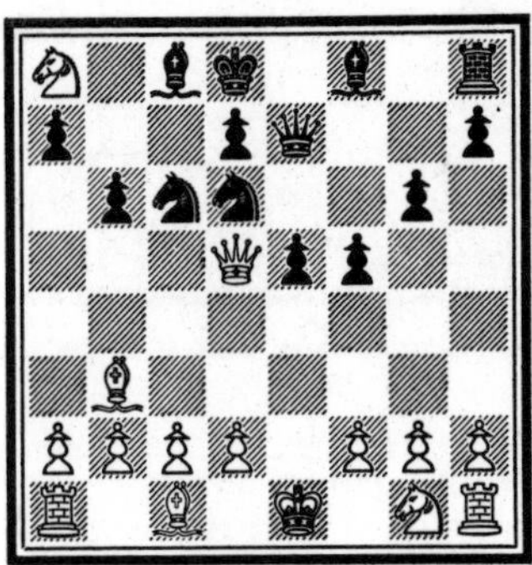

Position after 10 . . ., P–N3

**free** (Kmoch's term) relating to a **passed pawn**. Compare **half-free, unfree.** See ***Pawn Power in Chess***.

**free a game** obtain greater room for the pieces to manoeuvre when the player has a cramped game.

**free castling** an early method of castling adopted in Rome in the seventeenth century. The Rook could be moved to any square up to and including K1 while simultaneously the King could be moved to any square on the other side of the Rook up to and including KR1. Free castling persisted in many parts of Italy until the late nineteenth century. Compare **castle, King's leap.**

**free formation** (Kmoch's term) a pawn formation where all the pawns are on the board, none of which has crossed the **frontier line**. Compare **closed formation**. See ***Pawn Power in Chess***.

**freeing manoeuvre** see **Capablanca's freeing manoeuvre.**

**French Bishop** Black's Queen Bishop in the French Defence. Invariably this is Black's weakest piece, being hemmed in by a Black pawn on K3. How to free or exchange it is one of Black's major problems in this defence. Compare **Dragon Bishop, Lopez Bishop.**

**French Defence** a defence to the King's pawn opening: 1. P–K4, *P–K3* 2. P–Q4, *P–Q4*. White is invited to gain space by advancing his King pawn, after which Black hopes to react with pressure against the pawn chain. Common variations are 3. P–K5 (Nimzovitch), 3. N–Q2 (Tarrasch), 3. N–QB3, B–N5 (Winawer) and 3. N–QB3, N–KB3 (Classical). The French Defence appeared in the work of Lucena, the fifteenth-century Spanish writer on chess, but takes its name from the London-Paris correspondence game of 1834, when it was adopted by the French players, who won.

Position after 2 . . ., P–Q4

**Frey, Kenneth** Mexican chess player; awarded the title International Master in 1975. (1976 Elo rating: 2295)

**Fried Chicken Tournament** a tournament sponsored by Bill Church (chairman of Church's Fried Chicken Inc.) and organized by George Koltanowski. It was held at San Antonio, Texas, from 18 November to 11 December 1972, and was one of the strongest tournaments ever to take place in the United States, with ten Grandmasters competing. It was won by Anatoly Karpov and Tigran Petrosian (U.S.S.R.) and Lajos Portisch (Hungary), each with 10½ points out of 15.

**Fried Liver Attack** another name for the **Fegatello Attack.**

**Friends of Chess** a fund-raising organization devoted to increasing the strength of British chess, especially at the international level. Among their activities, Friends of Chess have helped to sponsor international tournaments and matches, such as the Hastings and Teesside grandmaster tournaments, the Clare Benedict tournament, and matches against West Germany. They have also aided players competing abroad. The organization was founded in 1969 and is independent of the British Chess Federation.

**From's Gambit** one of the most energetic responses to Bird's Opening. It arises in the following manner: 1. P–KB4, *P–K4* 2. P×P, *P–Q3* 3. P×P, *B×P*, leaving Black with a clear advantage in development as compensation for the pawn. White must play extremely carefully to survive; for example, if White continues with 4. N–QB3, Black has a mating attack by 4 . . ., Q–R5ch 5. P–N3, Q×Pch 6. P×Q, B×P mate. In this continuation White's best fourth move is generally thought to be: 4. N–KB3, although the Knight is a ready target for Black's King Knight pawn. The opening is named after the nineteenth-century Danish player, Severin From, who invented it.

**frontier line** an imaginary line separating the fourth and fifth ranks. It is sometimes used to estimate which side has the advantage. This is carried out by counting how many squares each player controls or occupies across the frontier line, i.e. in the opponent's half of the board. The player who controls or occupies the most squares has an advantage in space and this gives him the superior game if his opponent has no compensation elsewhere. This term was first used by Nimzovitch.

**frontspan** (Kmoch's term) the squares of a file that are in front of a pawn. Compare **interspan, rearspan**. See ***Pawn Power in Chess***.

**front-twin** (Kmoch's term) the foremost member of a pair of doubled pawns. Compare **loose twin, rear-twin, sham twin, tight twin, twin**. See ***Pawn Power in Chess***.

**Frydman, Paulino** (b. 26 May 1905) Argentinian chess player; awarded the title International Master in 1955. Frydman was originally Polish and played for that country in the Chess Olympiads of 1928, 1930, 1931, 1933, 1935, 1937 and 1939. The 1939 Olympiad was interrupted by the outbreak of World War II and the whole Polish team decided to remain in the host country of Argentina.

**Fu** *Japanese for* soldier. The Fu is the equivalent of the pawn in chess. It can only move forward one square at a time, but when promoted it becomes a To-Kin and moves like a Kin. See **Shogi**.

**Fuchs, Reinhardt** (b. 28 September 1934) East German chess player; awarded the title International Master in 1962. He competed in the Chess Olympiads of 1956, 1958, 1960, 1962, 1964 and 1966 and in the Student Olympiads of 1958 and 1959.

**Fuderer, Andrija** (b. 13 May 1931) Yugoslavian chess player; awarded the title International Master in 1952. He was joint Yugoslavian Junior Champion in 1947 and competed in the Chess Olympiads of 1952, 1954 and 1958.

**full algebraic** see **algebraic notation**.

**functional weakness** any weakness causing a restriction in the mobility of pawns and the area they control. It may be either temporary or permanent according to whether the pawns are able to advance. This term is applied to dynamic features, such as isolated and backward pawns, rather than static features, such as permanent defects in pawn structure. It was coined by Euwe. Compare **organic weakness.**

**Furman, Semyon** (1920–1978) Soviet chess player; awarded the titles International Master in 1954 and International Grandmaster in 1966. His results in the Soviet Championship include third place in 1949 and equal fourth place in 1964. Recently he has been best known as the principal trainer and second of Karpov. (1976 Elo rating: 2555)

# G

**Gaige, Jeremy** (b. 9 October 1927) American chess historian and compiler of *A Catalogue of Chessplayers and Problemists* (third edition, 1973) and *Chess Tournament Crosstables* (Vol. IV, 1974).

**gambit** a sequence of opening moves in which the first player risks or sacrifices a chessman, usually a pawn, with the hope of securing a more advantageous position later in the game. True gambits, where the sacrificed pawn cannot be compensated for by recapture of an opponent's pawn, are rare at the master level.

**Gambit of Aleppo** an older name for the **Queen's Gambit.**

***Game and Playe of the Chesse, The*** the second book to be printed in English. It was a translation of a work by Jacobus de Cessolis and was a moral allegory, using chess for illustration. It was translated by William Caxton and was printed in 1475.

***Game of Chess, The*** a primer on chess by H. Golombek. As well as an introductory chapter on the game it contains chapters on the opening and ending and an extensive section on the middle-game. It also has chapters on tournament chess and the great players from Anderssen to Botvinnik. Methods of notation, the chess organizations in the United Kingdom and a digest of the laws of chess are included in the appendices. It was first published in 1954 and uses descriptive notation.

**game of the century** the name given by Hans Kmoch to a game played between Bobby Fischer and Donald Byrne in the 1956 Rosenwald tournament. In it the 13-year-old boy sacrificed his Queen and Rook to carry out a mating attack against the International Master. Although Fischer came only eighth in this tournament, this game made him famous. Byrne was White: 1. N–KB3, N–KB3 2. P–B4, P–KN3 3. N–B3, B–N2 4. P–Q4, O–O 5. B–B4, P–Q4 6. Q–N3, P×P 7. Q×BP, P–B3 8. P–K4, QN–Q2 9. R–Q1, N–N3 10. Q–B5, B–N5 11. B–KN5, N–R5 12. Q–R3, N×N 13. P×N, N×P 14. B×P, Q–N3 15. B–B4, N×QBP 16. B–B5, KR–K1ch 17. K–B1, B–K3! 18. B×Q, B×Bch 19. K–N1, N–K7ch 20. K–B1, N×Pch 21. K–N1, N–K7ch 22. K–B1, N–B6ch 23. K–N1, P×B 24. Q–N4, R–R5 25. Q×P, N×R 26. P–KR3, R×P 27. K–R2, N×P 28. R–K1, R×R 29. Q–Q8ch, B–B1 30. N×R, B–Q4 31. N–B3, N–K5 32. Q–N8, P–QN4 33. P–R4, P–R4 34. N–K5, K–N2 35. K–N1, B–B4ch 36. K–B1, N–N6ch 37. K–K1, B–N5ch 38. K–Q1, B–N6ch 39. K–B1, N–K7ch 40. K–N1, N–B6ch 41. K–B1, R–B7mate.

***Games of Robert J. Fischer, The*** a collection of all the importan

"SOLITUDE IN CHECK" – GOUACHE AND PASTEL ON CANVAS
BY CANADIAN ARTIST ÉRIC GODIN, 1994

BORN IN MONTREAL in 1964, Eric Godin is equally at home as a painter, illustrator and graphic designer – and as an editorial cartoonist. Lively and light-filled, his works often display a whimsical take on everyday life. A prime example of Godin's style is "Solitude in Check."

games of Bobby Fischer, co-edited by Robert Wade and Kevin O'Connell. It was first published in 1972 and uses descriptive notation.

**Gaprindashvili, Nona** (b. 3 May 1941) Soviet chess player; awarded the title International Master in 1962 on becoming Women's World Champion by defeating Elizaveta Bykova 9–2. She has since defended this title successfully four times (in 1965, 1969, 1972 and 1975). She defeated Alla Kushnir on the first three occasions, winning 8½–4½, 8½–4½, 8½–7½, and Nana Alexandria on the most recent occasion. Gaprindashvili has also had several tournament successes, notably Hastings (1964) where she came fifth in the Premier, i.e. the main tournament, defeating all four U.K. entrants and drawing with the winner Keres. She had qualified for this event by winning the Challengers' tournament the previous year, when she had also won the lightning tournament, defeating Tal in the final round. Gaprindashvili is undoubtedly one of the strongest female chess players in the history of chess, rivalled only by Vera Menchik. Her style has been described as aggressive and tactical rather than positional. (1976 Elo rating: 2425)

**Garcia, Guillermo** (b. 9 December 1953) Cuban chess player; awarded the titles International Master in 1974 and International Grandmaster in 1976. He was Cuban Champion in 1974 and was first at Zürich (1975) and Plovdiv (1975). (1976 Elo rating: 2475)

**Garcia, Silvino** (b. 4 July 1944) Cuban chess player; awarded the titles International Master in 1969 and International Grandmaster in 1975. He has competed in several Chess Olympiads; other results include an equal first at Costa Brava (1975), a fourth at the twelfth Rubinstein memorial tournament, Polanica Zdroj (1974) and a fifth at Arrecife de Lanzarote (1974). (1976 Elo rating: 2430)

**Geller, Yefim** (b. 8 March 1925) Soviet chess player; awarded the titles International Master in 1951 and International Grandmaster in 1952. He was Soviet Champion in 1955 and competed in the Chess Olympiads of 1952, 1954, 1956, 1962 and 1968. In addition he took part in the interzonals of 1952, 1955, 1962, 1967, 1970, 1973 (in Petropolis) and 1976 (in Biel); in the Candidates' tournaments of 1953, 1956 and 1962; and in the Candidates' matches of 1965, 1968 and 1971. Among his long list of tournament victories were three of the strongest events of recent years: Moscow (1975), Teesside (1975) and Las Palmas (1976). (1976 Elo rating: 2620)

***gens una sumus*** *Latin for* we are one family: the official motto of FIDE.

**Georgadze, Tamaz** (b. 9 November 1947) Soviet chess player; awarded the title International Master in 1975. His tournament results include an equal first at Tbilisi (1974). (1976 Elo rating: 2475)

**Gereben, Ernö** (b. 18 June 1907) Swiss chess player; awarded the title International Master in 1950. Gereben was originally Hungarian. (1976 Elo rating: 2325)

**Gheorghiu, Florin** (b. 6 April 1944) Romanian chess player; awarded the titles International Master in 1963 and International Grandmaster in 1965. He was World Junior Champion in 1963 and has won the

Romanian Championship on eight occasions. (1976 Elo rating: 2540)

**Ghitescu, Teodor** (b. 24 January 1934) Romanian chess player; awarded the title International Master in 1961 and was Romanian Champion in 1963. He has competed in numerous Chess Olympiads since 1956. (1976 Elo rating: 2430)

**Giam, Choo Kwee** (b. 7 May 1942) Singapore chess player; awarded the title International Master in 1976. He came equal first in the Asian Masters Championship (1975). (1976 Elo rating: 2265)

**Gilg, Karl** (b. 20 January 1901) West German chess player; awarded the title International Master in 1953. He was born in Czechoslovakia and represented that country in the Chess Olympiads of 1927, 1928 and 1931. He emigrated to Germany in the late 1930s and competed for that country in the 1957 European Team Championship.

**Gin** *Japanese for* silver general. Each side has two Gin in the game of Shogi. The Gin can move one square in any diagonal direction, and can also move one square forward in the same way as a Fu. When promoted it becomes a Nari-Gin and moves like a Kin. See **Shogi**.

**Gipslis, Aivar Pyetrovich** (b. 8 February 1937) Soviet chess player; awarded the title International Master in 1963 and the title International Grandmaster in 1967. (1976 Elo rating: 2535)

**Giraffe** a Fairy chesspiece that moves like a Knight but has a longer range. It is a type of Leaper. While a Knight moves 1 × 2 squares, a Giraffe moves 1 × 4 squares. A Giraffe on QB1 could thus move to QN5, Q5 or KN2. Compare **Camel, Zebra**.

**Giuoco Pianissimo** *Italian for* quietest game. This is an opening sequence arising in the Giuoco Piano: 1. P–K4, P–K4 2. N–KB3, N–QB3 3. B–B4, B–B4 4. *P–Q3*. Both players can develop their pieces easily without fear of immediate threats.

**Giuoco Piano** *Italian for* quiet game. This is one of the oldest and most overtly aggressive of the King's pawn openings: 1. P–K4, P–K4 2. N–KB3, N–QB3 3. *B–B4*, B–B4. White controls Q5 and attacks KB7. The Giuoco Piano appears in the Göttingen manuscript (1490) and was analysed by Damiano (1512), Ruy Lopez (1561), and Greco (1600). Its longevity means that it now contains few surprises for the prepared player and, because of this rather than from any inherent defect, it is now rarely played at the highest level. Nevertheless, the Giuoco Piano can disprove its name and explode into fireworks if White or Black plays weakly.

**Giustolisi, Alberto Mario** (b. 17 March 1928) Italian chess player; awarded the title International Master in 1962. He was Italian Champion in 1961, 1964 and 1966. Giustolisi competed in the Chess Olympiads of 1950 and 1968.

**giving up the exchange** the deliberate sacrifice of a Rook for a minor piece in order to gain a positional advantage. Compare **losing the exchange**.

**Gligorić, Svetozar** (b. 2 February 1923) Yugoslavian chess player; awarded the titles International Master in 1950 and International Grandmaster in 1951. He has been Yugoslavian Champion on eleven occasions and competed in every Chess Olympiad between 1950 and 1974. Gligorić has played in nine interzonals and qualified for the Candidates' tournaments of 1953 and 1959 and the Candidates' matches of 1968.

Gligorić was born in Belgrade and learned to play chess at the age of 11, using a home-made set carved from bottle corks. By the age of 15 he was the champion of Belgrade and the following year became a National Master. During the war he fought with the partisans and was twice decorated for bravery. His first major international tournament was Prague (1946) where he was equal fourth. This was followed by a first at Warsaw (1947) in front of Boleslavsky, Pachman and Smyslov. Since then Gligorić has had many tournament successes, including five firsts at Hastings (1951, 1956, 1959, 1960 and 1962). As a match player he has been slightly less successful. In 1949 he defeated Stahlberg (+2 −1 =9); in 1952 he lost to Reshevsky (+2 −1 =7); in 1968 he defeated Donner (+3 −0 =7); and in 1968 he lost to Tal in the quarter-finals of the 1968 Candidates' matches (+1 −3 =5).

Gligorić was for many years the foreign news commentator of a leading Yugoslavian weekly and has written several books on chess, including *The Sicilian Defence* (with V. Sokolov), *Selected Chess Masterpieces* (with R. G. Wade), *The World Chess Championship* and *Fischer v. Spassky*. (1976 Elo rating: 2575)

**Giuoco Piano**

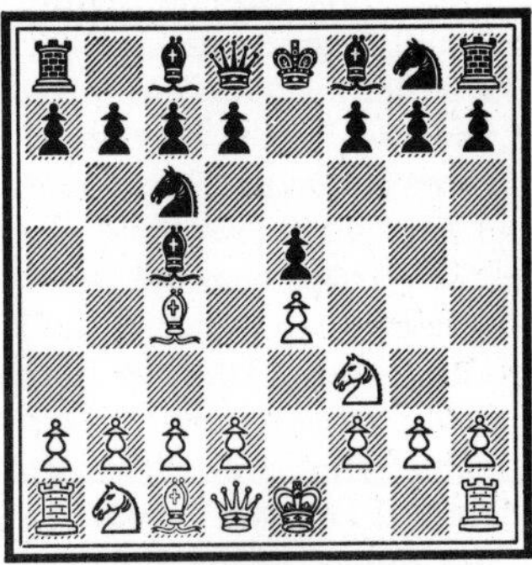

Position after 3 . . ., B–B4

**G.M.** or **GM** *abbrev. for* (International) Grandmaster.

**Gnu** a Fairy chesspiece that possesses the powers of both the Camel and the Knight. It is thus a type of Combined Chessman.

**Go** a Japanese board game for two people. It is played on a board with 361 intersections, using counters (originally black and white stones). The object is to control the larger part of the board by surrounding territory and capturing the opponent's counters.

***Golden Dozen, The*** a book by Irving Chernev. In it he ranks the players he believes to be the twelve best of all time, beginning with Nimzovitch and culminating with Capablanca. Each player is represented by a brief biography and a selection of his games. In total there are 115 annotated games. The book was first published in 1976 and uses descriptive notation.

**Golden Knighter** a correspondence chess player who has participated in the Golden Knights Postal Chess Championship, i.e. the United States Open Postal Chess Championship sponsored by the U.S.C.F., and reached the final round after completing his playing schedule. He will then receive a lapel button with an emblem of a Golden Knight and may also receive a cash prize.

***Golden Treasury of Chess, The*** an anthology of 575 games compiled by I. A. Horowitz. The collection includes games from the fifteenth century up to (in the latest edition) the early 1960s. It was first published in 1943 and uses descriptive notation.

**Golombek, Harry** (b. 1 March 1911) British chess player; awarded the titles International Master in 1950 and International Judge in 1954. He was British Champion in 1947, 1949 and 1955 and competed in the interzonal of 1952 and in the Chess Olympiads of 1952, 1954, 1958, 1960 and 1962.

Golombek learned to play chess at the age of 12 and won the London Boys' Championship in 1929; he became the youngest player to win the championship of Surrey two years later. As well as being a strong player, he is a noted arbiter and acted as a judge in the World Championship matches of 1954, 1957, 1958, 1960, 1961 and 1963.

Golombek is a member of the Central Committee of FIDE and is a member of the Permanent Commission for the Rules of Play.

He is also a prolific writer on chess. From 1938 to 1939 he was the editor of the B.C.M.; he later served as its games editor and editor of overseas news and is now one of its directors. He is the chess columnist of *The Times* and *The Observer* and has written numerous works on chess, among which are *The Game of Chess* and *World Championship Chess 1957* and has translated several Soviet works. In 1966 he was awarded the O.B.E. (Order of the British Empire) for his services to chess.

**good Bishop** a Bishop that is not impeded by its own pawns and thus is potentially highly mobile. The pawns should be stationed on squares opposite in colour to those on which the Bishop travels, since although they cannot be protected by the Bishop this is more than compensated for by the Bishop's increased range. When each player has a Bishop of the same colour as well as extensive pawn chains a good Bishop on one side is likely to be balanced by a bad Bishop on the other. The difference in their values is likely to be directly related to the number of pawns blockaded and to increase as the other minor pieces are exchanged. Compare **bad Bishop**.

***Good Companion*** an American periodical that flourished during the first quarter of the twentieth century. It was mainly devoted to chess problems.

**Good Companions Chess Problem Club** an international society of chess problem composers that existed from 1913 to 1924. It was founded by James Magee of Philadelphia and organized frequent composing tournaments, as well as regularly classifying and publishing problems.

**good Bishop**

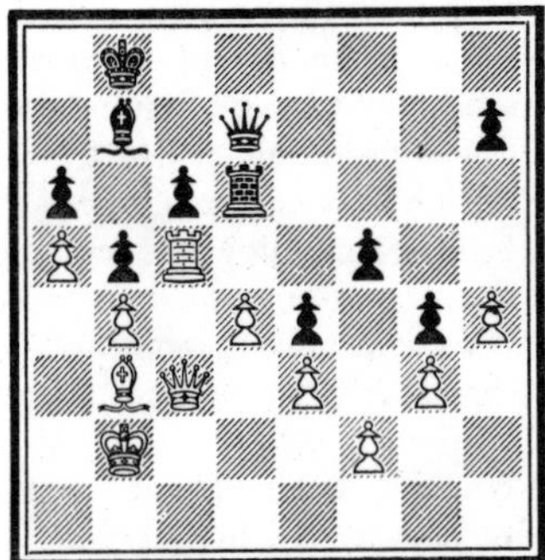

White has a good Bishop; Black has a bad Bishop

**Goodman, David** (b. 25 February 1958) British chess player; World Cadet Champion in 1975. He was British Lightning Champion in 1975 and came first in the Berlin junior international tournament (1975). He is the brother-in-law of Raymond Keene. (1976 Elo rating: 2260)

**Göring Gambit** an opening sequence arising out of the Scotch Game in the following manner: 1. P–K4, P–K4 2. N–KB3, N–QB3 3. P–Q4, P×P 4. *P–B3*. White is prepared to sacrifice a pawn to eliminate Black's King pawn and control the centre. The opening was pioneered by Dr C. Göring, who was a dean of philosophy at the University of Leipzig in the nineteenth century. Like most genuine gambits, it has never attained much popularity at the highest levels.

**Göteborg Variation** an opening sequence arising out of the Sicilian Defence, Najdorf Variation: 1. P–K4, P–QB4 2. N–KB3, P–Q3 3. P–Q4, P×P 4. N×P, N–KB3 5. N–QB3, P–QR3 6. B–KN5, P–K3 7. P–B4, B–K2 8. Q–B3, *P–R3* 9. B–R4, *P–KN4*. The most common continuation is 10. P×P.

This variation was devised by the Argentinian players Najdorf, Panno, Pilnik, Bolbochan, and Guimard. It was first seen in competitive play at the Göteborg (Gothenburg) interzonal (1955). In this tournament Najdorf, Panno, and Pilnik were scheduled to play Black against three Soviet players (Spassky, Geller, and Keres respectively) and in the same round. They thought that this variation would come as a complete surprise, but unfortunately each was brilliantly defeated by his Soviet opponent. Also called Gothenburg Variation.

**Gothenburg Variation** *English spelling of* **Göteborg Variation.**

**Gothic Defence** an unusual opening sequence arising out of the Three

Knights' Game: 1. P–K4, P–K4 2. N–KB3, N–QB3 3. N–B3, *P–B4*. Black attempts to wrest the initiative by transposing into a delayed Latvian Gambit. The most common continuations are: 4. P × P, and 4. P–Q4.

**Göttingen manuscript** a manuscript thought to date from the late fifteenth century or the early sixteenth century. Its author is believed to be Lucena.

The manuscript, which consists of 33 pages written in Latin, analyses 12 openings and provides the first mention of the Ruy Lopez. It also contains 30 chess problems culled from other sources. The manuscript deals with the newer type of chess, characterized by the increased power of the Queen, which was replacing the older version at this time.

The manuscript was eventually donated to the library of the university of Göttingen in 1752 by Dr Frederick Borner, a native of that city.

**graded player** one who has been awarded a rating by his national federation. There are several hundred graded players in both the United Kingdom and the United States. The strongest graded players will usually appear on the International Chess Federation's Grading List. In 1976 this contained nearly 1400 names. See also **B.C.F. Grading System, Elo Scale, Ingo System.**

**grading** a numerical evaluation of the strength of a player based upon his results against other graded players. The initial grading is revised by adding or deducting a number, weighted by the opponent's grade, after the win or loss. Few grading systems existed before the Second World War; the first B.C.F. grading list did not appear until March 1954. At about the same time the U.S.C.F. introduced a grading system of its own but by the 1960s it had begun to show serious inaccuracies and was replaced by the Elo System named after Professor Arpad E. Elo, who was mainly responsible for devising it. This is the only international grading system existing today. See **B.C.F. Grading System, Elo Scale, Ingo System.**

**Grandmaster** shortened form of **International Grandmaster.**

**Grandmaster draw** a quick draw agreed to by the players although both still have attacking chances. The term was initially applied only to draws at the highest level, but is now used for any such draw. In a tournament a Grandmaster draw allows each player to conserve energy while gaining a half point and it has been argued that this allows the other games to be played with more vigour – indirectly raising standards. In general they have been condemned, but are difficult to eradicate. Attempts have included rules that forbid draws of less than 30 moves or of draws made without the permission of the arbiter, but these efforts have been unsuccessful. After all, draws could be arrived at legitimately before the 30-move limit, or the players could contrive a repetition of position or could just manoeuvre aimlessly until the limit is passed.

**Grandmaster of Chess** a title awarded in 1914 by Czar Nicholas II to the five finalists of the **St Petersburg (1914)** tournament. These were: Alekhine, Capablanca, Lasker, Marshall and Tarrasch. See **International Grandmaster.**

**Grandmaster of the U.S.S.R. among women** a title created in November 1975 by the U.S.S.R. State Committee for Physical Education and Sport. The main criterion for gaining it is to become Women's World Champion. The first person to be awarded this title was Nona Gaprindashvili.

***Grandmasters of Chess*** a history of modern chess by Harold C. Schonberg. It traces the development of modern chess from Philidor up to the inauguration of Karpov as World Champion in 1975, in an account that is replete with anecdotes about the great chess players. It was first published in 1974 and uses descriptive notation.

**Grasshopper** a Fairy chesspiece that moves like a Queen except that it always leaps over one piece (of either colour) to the square beyond when moving or capturing. It was invented by T. R. Dawson in 1912 and is now the most common Fairy chesspiece. It is represented on diagrams by an inverted Queen.

**Great Bare King** a type of win in **baring the King** in which checkmate and a bare King occur on the same move. See **Little Bare King.**

***Great Chess Masters and Their Games, The*** a collection of biographies by Fred Reinfeld. It describes the life and style of play of seven players: Anderssen, Morphy, Steinitz, Lasker, Capablanca, Alekhine and Euwe, and also contains a collection of their games plus their tournament and match records. It was first published in 1952 and uses descriptive notation.

**greatest chess player** much disagreement exists about who is or was the greatest chess player of all time. Most experts could name their favourite ten choices or so with little hesitation, but find it difficult to assign a ranking order towards the very top. However, it would be surprising if four names failed to be on every list: Morphy, Capablanca, Alekhine and Fischer. Among other players often mentioned as being among the greatest are Lasker, Rubinstein, Botvinnik and Keres. Some potential candidates for such a list are brilliant but inconsistent (for example Tal, whose health problems have prevented him from engaging in exhausting tournaments).

**Great Exhibition tournament** the official title of the tournament held in London in 1851 in conjunction with the Great Exhibition at the Crystal Palace. This was the first ever international tournament and was entered by players from all over Europe, including Anderssen from Germany, Kieseritzky from France, Löwenthal from the United States and Szén from Hungary. Jänisch travelled from Russia to compete but arrived too late.

The event was organized by Staunton and the St George's Club and was a knockout tournament with the best of three games deciding the winner of each match. It was decisively won by Anderssen, who defeated in succession Kieseritzky, Szén, Staunton and Wyvill. Also called **London (1851).**

**Great Moments in Modern Chess** a survey of the international chess scene in the late 1940s, written by Reuben Fine. Particular attention is paid to chess in the United States, U.S.S.R. and Europe and to the radio matches between the United States and the U.S.S.R. The book was first published in 1948 and uses descriptive notation.

**Greco Counter Gambit** another name for the Latvian Gambit. It is called after the seventeenth century player Gioachino Greco who, it was once thought, had invented it. However, since this opening was named Polerio's manuscript has been found. This manuscript mentioned the gambit and attributed it to Giovanni Leonardo, who was born approximately sixty years before Greco.

**Greco, Gioachino** (1600–c.1634) a leading Italian chess player of the seventeenth century. He was born in Celico, Calabria and became known as 'the Calabrese' in later life.

Greco, who came from a poor family, may have been one of the world's first chess professionals. In 1621 he travelled to France and reputedly won 5,000 francs at the court of the Duke of Lorraine. In later years he visited England, Spain and again France.

Greco wrote numerous manuscripts on chess, but none was published until after his death. Written in atrocious Italian they were not pieces of original research, but openings and games drawn from earlier sources such as the works of Ruy Lopez. Nevertheless they became very popular and spread through Europe. Because of this many opening variations are named after Greco although he invented none of them.

**Greco-Philidor Gambit** another name for **Philidor Gambit**.

**Greco Variation** an opening sequence arising out of the Giuoco Piano: 1. P–K4, P–K4 2. N–KB3, N–QB3 3. B–B4, B–B4 4. P–B3, N–B3 5. P–Q4, P×P 6. B×P, B–N5ch 7. *N–B3*, N×KP 8. *O–O*. This pawn sacrifice was for a long time believed to be unsound after: 8 . . ., B × N, but this allows the strong **Möller Attack** which was discovered in the nineteenth century. The most common continuation is: 8 . . ., N×N. This variation was originally from an analysis of Greco dating from about 1625.

**Greek Gift Sacrifice** a combination that offers a Bishop in return for driving the enemy King into the centre of the board or for checkmate. A typical scheme is illustrated in the diagram on p. 123 with play continuing: 1. B×Pch, K×B 2. N–N5ch, K–N1 3. Q–R5 and mate follows shortly. The Black King could have moved to N3 on the second move, but this too normally leads to a quick defeat because of the King's extreme vulnerability.

**Grefe, John** (b. 6 September 1947) American chess player; awarded the title International Master in 1975. In 1973 he became joint U.S. champion with Kavalek. In 1974 he came equal second at the Lone Pine Tournament. (1976 Elo rating: 2420)

**Gregoriou, Miltiadis** (b. 23 March 1935) Greek chess player; awarded the title International Master in 1975. (1976 Elo rating: 2355)

**grid chess** a type of Fairy Chess in which the board is imagined to be divided into segments of four squares. A move is possible only if a line of the grid is crossed. Thus a King is not in check from an enemy Queen in the same segment, but she can check by moving away! It is also possible for the Kings to be adjacent to each other if they are in the same segment.

**Greek Gift Sacrifice**

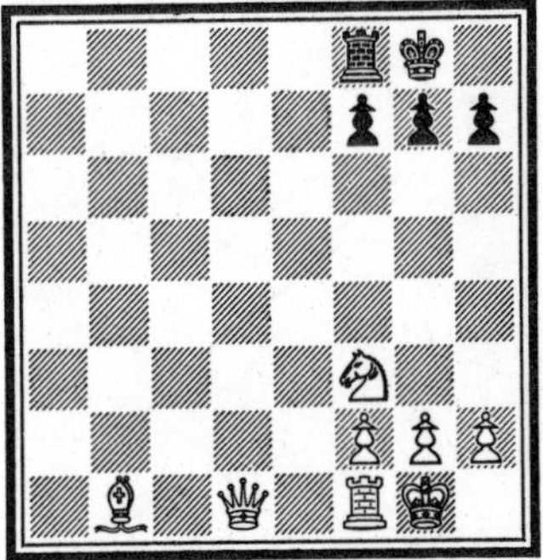

A typical scheme

**Griffith, Richard C.** (1872–1955) British chess player; British Champion in 1912. He was co-author (with J. H. White) of the early editions of *Modern Chess Openings*.

**Grimshaw theme** a theme in chess problems in which two defenders fatally hinder each other. For instance, in one variation a defending Rook might be forced to move and block a defending Bishop which would otherwise prevent checkmate, and vice versa in a second variation. It is named after Walter Grimshaw, a nineteenth-century British problem composer who first employed it. See **interference**.

**Grob, Henri** (1904–1974) Swiss chess player; awarded the title International Master in 1950. Grob was Swiss Champion in 1939 and 1951 and represented Switzerland in the Chess Olympiads of 1927, 1935, and 1952. He played postal games extensively, in which he pioneered eccentric opening ideas. One such was **Grob's Angriff**, 1. P–KN4, on which he subsequently wrote a book. He died in July 1974.

**Grob's Attack** another name for the **Spike.** It is named after Henri Grob, who studied it.

**Groningen** a town in Holland; the annual venue of the European Junior Championship.

**Groningen (1946)** the first major international tournament to be played after World War II, although the radio match between the United States and the U.S.S.R. preceded it. It was an all-play-all tournament of twenty players and was won by Botvinnik with 12½ points followed by Euwe in second place with 12 points and Smyslov far behind in third place. This was both Botvinnik's first unshared victory in a major Western tournament and Euwe's last major success.

**Grünfeld Defence (Grünfeld-Indian Defence)** a defence to the Queen's pawn opening: 1. P–Q4, N–KB3 2. P–QB4, P–KN3 3. N–QB3, *P–Q4*. As with other hypermodern defences, White is allowed to establish a strong centre which Black then attempts to immobilize and destroy. It was created in the early 1920s by the Viennese grandmaster and theoretician Ernst Grünfeld.

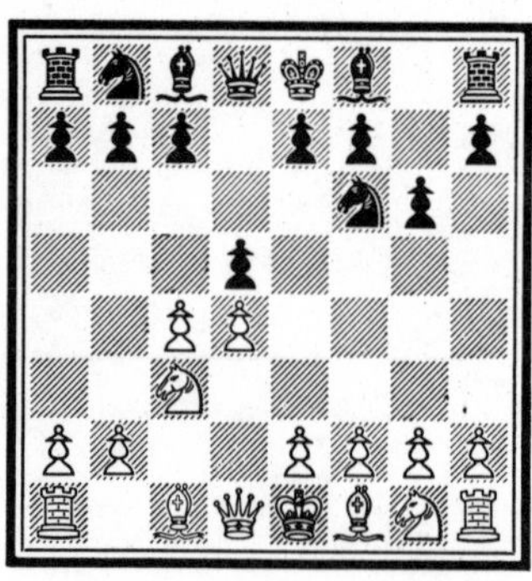

Position after 3 . . ., P–Q4

**Grünfeld, Ernst** (1893–1962) Austrian chess player; awarded the title International Grandmaster in 1950. He was born on 21 September 1893. His major tournament successes began in the early 1920s and included firsts at Margate (1923), Meran (1924 and 1934), Vienna (1927) and Mahrisch-Ostrau (1933). Grünfeld also played on first board for Austria in the Chess Olympiads of 1927, 1931, 1933 and 1935. Despite these successes, his most important contributions were in opening theory, of which he had a profound knowledge. (It was thought that he knew from memory every opening that had ever been played). He died in Vienna on 3 April 1962.

**Gryphon or Griffin** a Fairy chesspiece that possess the powers of both the pawn and the Bishop. It is thus a type of Combined Chessman.

***Guardian Chess Book, The*** a chess primer by the *Guardian* chess columnist, Leonard Barden. As well as explaining the moves and descriptive notation for the novice, it gives general advice and suggests suitable openings for the average club player. The concluding section contains 20 of Barden's favourite puzzles. It was first published in 1967 and uses descriptive notation.

**Guéridon** *French for* pedestal table. A mating position where the King is diagonally flanked by two defenders and is confronted by an adjacent and protected enemy Queen. The formation is thought to resemble a table. Compare **epaulet mate.**

**Gufeld, Eduard Yefimovich** (b. 19 March 1936) Soviet chess player; awarded the title International Master in 1964 and the title International Grandmaster in 1967. (1976 Elo rating: 2545)

***Guide to Fairy Chess, A*** an introduction to Fairy Chess by Anthony Dickens. The author lists the different types of Fairy chessmen, boards, etc., that have been invented and provides information about every aspect of Fairy Chess. In addition there are over 200 problems and puzzles for the reader to attempt to solve. The book was first published in 1969 and uses descriptive notation.

**Guimard, Carlos E.** (b. 6 April 1913) Argentinian chess player; awarded the titles International Master in 1950 and International Grandmaster in 1960. He was Argentinian Champion in 1947, 1949 and 1953 and competed in the Chess Olympiads of 1937, 1939, 1950 and 1954. He also played in the 1955 interzonal, when he came 12th.

**Gulko, Boris** (b. 9 February 1947) Soviet chess player; awarded the titles International Master in 1975 and International Grandmaster in 1976. He was Moscow Champion in 1974, came equal first at Sombor (1974), and won at Kishinev (1975). Gulko participated in the 1976 Biel interzonal, where he was equal 13th. (1976 Elo rating: 2530)

**Gumpel, Charles Godfrey** the creator of **Mephisto**, a chess-playing 'automaton'. Gumpel was by profession a manufacturer of artificial limbs.

**Gunsberg, Isidor** (1854–1930) one of the leading players of the late nineteenth century. Gunsberg was born in Budapest on 2 November 1854, but his family emigrated to Britain when he was nine.

He was sufficiently strong while young to be taken to Paris by his father at the age of 12 and introduced to the Café de la Régence as a child prodigy. In 1878 Gunsberg became a chess professional and was hired by Charles Godfrey Gumpel to operate the newly created **Mephisto**. With Gunsberg inside it Mephisto did not lose a game and, indeed, it entered and won the English Counties' Association Handicap tournament (1878).

Gunsberg's first tournament on his own was a minor section of the London tournament (1883). In this and at Nuremberg (1883) he failed to do well, but at Hamburg (1885) he took first place. This was followed by first place at the British Chess Association tournament (1888) and third place at New York (1889).

His match record was also strong. In 1881 he had lost to Blackburne (+4 −7 =3), but avenged himself in 1886 (+5 −2 =6). He also played two matches with Bird in 1886 and 1889 and won fairly easily both times (+5 −1 =3 and +3 −0 =2). In 1890 he drew a match with Tchigorin thus further establishing himself as a World Championship contender. Gunsberg's match-career culminated with a match against Steinitz in 1890–1891. Gunsberg who was an orthodox player, unlike Steinitz, lost although not by a large margin (+4 −6 =9).

Gunsberg continued to play competitive chess for almost another quarter of a century, but ill-health prevented him from recapturing the power of his youth. Notable tournaments in which he competed included Hastings (1895) and St Petersburg (1914), which was his last tournament. He died on 2 May 1930.

**Gurgenidze, Bukhuti** (b. 13 November 1933) Soviet chess player; awarded the titles International Master in 1966 and International Grandmaster in 1970. (1976 Elo rating: 2500)

**Gyoku** *Japanese for* jewelled general. In Shogi it is the equivalent of the King. See **Shogi**.

# H

**Haag, Ervin** (b. 11 January 1933) Hungarian chess player; awarded both the title International Master and the title International Correspondence Chess Master in 1961. (1976 Elo rating: 2430)

**half-battery** (chess-problem term) an alignment of men identical to the formation of a **battery** except that two attacking men are interposed between the other piece and enemy King. If one of these men moved away the grouping would become a battery.

**Half-Classical Variation (Orthodox Defence)** antiquated name for an opening sequence arising out of the Orthodox Defence to the Queen's Gambit Declined. The following is a typical progression: 1. P–Q4, P–Q4 2. P–QB4, P–K3 3. N–QB3, N–KB3 4. N–B3, P–B4.

**half-closed formation** (Kmoch's term) a pawn formation that has open files and one or more pawns that have crossed the **frontier line**. See ***Pawn Power in Chess***.

**half-free** (Kmoch's term) relating to a pawn that is not opposed by an enemy pawn on the same file, but is faced by at least one enemy pawn on an adjacent file. This pawn must be removed before the pawn can become a passed pawn. See **sentry, *Pawn Power in Chess***.

**Half Giuoco Game** an opening sequence arising out of the Giuoco Piano: 1. P–K4, P–K4 2. N–KB3, N–QB3 3. B–B4, *P–Q3*. The most common continuation is: 4. P–Q4. This variation was introduced by Alekhine.

**half-open file** a file that has pawns of only one colour upon it. These pawns may form a target on which the Rooks can be aligned. See **file**.

**half-open formation** (Kmoch's term) a pawn formation where each side has one half-open file. Kmoch divides all half-open formations into two classes: the **ram formation** and the **jump formation**. See ***Pawn Power in Chess***.

**half-passed pawn** a pawn that is not confronted by an enemy pawn, but is confronted by at least one on an adjacent file.

**half-pin** a pin in which the pinned man is free to move along the rank, file, or diagonal that it shares with the attacker. This term was devised by Comins Mansfield, who is an International Grandmaster for Chess Compositions.

**Hamilton-Russell Cup** a gold-plated trophy held by the victorious team in the Chess Olympiad. It was donated by an English fan the Hon. F. G. Hamilton-Russell at the first Chess Olympiad, which was held in London in July 1927.

***Handbuch des Schachspiels*** a German handbook on chess openings conceived by Baron Tassilo von Heydebrand und der Lasa (1808–1899) and completed by him after initial contributions by P. R. von Bilguer (1813–1840). It was published in 1843. See **Berlin Pleiades**.

**hanging** (colloquial) relating to any man that is unprotected and able to be captured with little or no loss of time. See ***en prise***.

**hanging pawns** two adjacent allied pawns on the fourth rank that are unable to be supported by other pawns and can be attacked directly on one or two half-open files. Hanging pawns have strong advantages and disadvantages. In the middle-game they can often disrupt the opponent's defence by advancing and driving away the enemy pieces, while at the same time opening lines for the attacking pieces. In the ending they become weak since they cannot mutually protect each other and must be defended by pieces.

The possessor of hanging pawns should try to avoid exchanges of pieces (as these might be needed for the defence of the hanging pawns) and should constantly be prepared for an advantageous advance of the pawns to the fifth rank. In contrast, the opponent should avoid exchanges, should fianchetto his Bishops (where they can attack centre hanging pawns in relative safety), and should attack the pawns with his major pieces along the half-open file. Equally important, he should attempt to compel one of the pawns to advance so that he can place a piece in the comparative safety of the newly created hole.

Hanging pawns tend to occur mainly in closed games, especially the Queen's Gambit.

**Hanham, James Moore** (1840–1923) a leading American amateur chess player and Major in the United States army. Born in Woodville, Mississippi, he competed in many New York tournaments at the turn of the century. The Hanham Variation of Philidor's Defence is named after him.

**Hanham Variation** an opening sequence arising out of Philidor's Defence: 1. P–K4, P–K4 2. N–KB3, P–Q3 3. P–Q4, *N–Q2*. Black builds up a cramped but solid position. The most common continuation is: 4. B–QB4. This variation is named after Major James Moore Hanham.

**Hanstein Gambit** an opening sequence arising out of the King's Gambit: 1. P–K4, P–K4 2. P–KB4, P×P 3. N–KB3, P–KN4 4. B–B4, B–N2 5. *O–O*. White intends to open the King Bishop file through the advance of his King Knight pawn and possibly sacrifice the Knight if Black attacks it with his King Knight pawn. The most common continuation is: 5 . . ., P–Q3. This gambit is named after W. Hanstein, a member of the **Berlin Pleiades.**

**Harandi, Khossrow** (b. 11 September 1950) Iranian chess player; awarded the title International Master in 1975. (1976 Elo rating: 2380)

**Harrwitz, Daniel** (1823–1884) German chess player; born in Breslau. He first became well-known as a blindfold player, but by 1846 was thought strong enough to play matches against Horwitz and Williams (winning both) and Staunton (+0 −7 =0). Two years later he drew a match with Anderssen (+5 −5 =0). In 1849 Harrwitz moved to London and there founded the *British Chess Review*. Through this he conducted a heated dispute with Staunton and this culminated in a match against Löwenthal, Staunton's friend, which Harrwitz won

(+11 −10 =12) after being seven points behind. In 1856 Harrwitz was hired by the Café de la Régence and there, two years later, he played against Morphy. After winning the first two games he was outclassed and broke off the match (+2 −5 =1). Soon afterwards he lost a match with Kolisch (+1 −2 =1) and retired from chess. He died in Bozen, Austria, on 9 January 1884.

**Hartston, Dr Jana** (née Malypetrová) (b. 9 December 1947) one of the strongest female players outside the U.S.S.R.; born in Prague. She twice won the Czech Ladies Championship (1966 and 1968) before her marriage to William R. Hartston and emigration to England in 1970. After that she won the British Ladies Championship for a record consecutive five years (1970–1974) and also in 1976. She finished sixth in the 1973 Ladies interzonal tournament and in Haifa (1976) came second to Alla Kushnir on top board. (1976 Elo rating: 2230)

**Hartston, William Roland** (b. 12 August 1947) British chess player; awarded the title International Master in 1972. He was British Champion in 1973 and 1975 and competed in the Chess Olympiads of 1966, 1970 (where he had the highest score on third board), 1972, 1974 and 1976. He also played in the Student Olympiads of 1966, 1967, 1968 and 1969 and played on first board in the 1973 European Team Championship. Hartston is the Games Editor of the B.C.M. and has written several books on chess, including *The Benoni, The Grünfeld Defence, How to Cheat at Chess* and *Karpov-Korchnoi 1974* (with R. D. Keene). (1976 Elo rating: 2445)

**Hasin, Abram** (b. 15 February 1923) Soviet chess player; awarded the title International Master in 1964.

**Hastings** a town in Sussex, England; famous as William the Conqueror's landing place in England, from which he fought the Battle of Hastings (1066). It has been the venue for many chess tournaments: the Hastings Christmas Chess Congress was held annually (either here or at nearby St Leonards-on-Sea) from 1920 to 1966, with the exception of the war years. From 1967, *The Times* co-sponsored tournaments with the Hastings and St Leonards Corporation (Times-Hastings International Chess Congress).

In the Premier tournament at Hastings (1925–1926), Alekhine and Vidmar both scored 8½ out of 9 (they drew against each other); this was the closest any participants at Hastings have come to a clear (100%) score.

**Hastings (1895)** one of the strongest chess tournaments ever held in England. It was an all-play-all tournament with 22 competitors and was won by Pillsbury, with Tchigorin in second place and Lasker third. The other competitors included Albin, Bardeleben, Bird, Blackburne, Burn, Gunsberg, Janowski, Mason, Mieses, Schiffers, Schlechter, Steinitz, Tarrasch, Teichmann, Samuel Tinsley and Benjamin Vergani. The victory of Pillsbury, an unknown, was completely unexpected and caused a sensation. The result launched him on his short international career by prompting his invitation to compete at St Petersburg (1895). The tournament also proved that Lasker's feat in winning the World Championship was not a fortuitous accident.

**Hauptturnier** *German for* major tournament; formerly an annual tournament held to determine the next German player to be awarded the title of Master. It first began in 1908 and the entrants to the Hauptturnier were the winners of strong regional tournaments. Its winner was then eligible to compete in the next Masters' tournament and if he gained a third of the points there he was awarded the title of Master.

**Haygarth, Michael J.** (b. 11 October 1934) British chess player; British Champion in 1964.

**head-duo** (Kmoch's term) two pawns on the same rank and adjacent files at the front of one side's pawn formation. When the pawn formation is headed by diagonally adjacent pawns, the supporting pawn strives to advance in order to form a head-duo. Compare **buffer duo, loose duo, tight duo.** See ***Pawn Power in Chess***.

**head-pawn** (Kmoch's term) the leading pawn in a pawn formation. See ***Pawn Power in Chess***.

**heavy piece** another name for **major piece**. The heavy pieces are the Queens and the Rooks.

**Hecht, Hans Joachim** (b. 29 January 1939) West German chess player; awarded the title International Grandmaster in 1973. (1976 Elo rating: 2495)

**Heinicke, Herbert** (b. 14 March 1905) West German chess player; awarded the title International Master in 1953. He competed in the 1952 Chess Olympiad and 1957 European Team Championship.

**Helms, Herman** (1870–1963) American amateur chess player, journalist and weekly columnist (*New York World-Telegram & Sun*); editor and publisher of the *American Chess Bulletin*. He was active in chess, particularly rapid-transit games, right up until his death. He was often referred to as the 'Dean of American Chess'.

**helpmate** a type of Fairy Chess problem in which both sides cooperate to find the quickest method of delivering checkmate by White. By convention Black moves first and therefore Black's moves are written down before White's. This type of problem was invented by the nineteenth-century player, Max Lange. Compare **selfmate**.

Helpmate in two by F. Abdurahmanović: 1. B×N, B–N2 2. O–O, Q–N6mate

**Henneberke, Franciscus Wilhelmus Johannes** (b. 23 May 1917) Dutch chess player; awarded the title International Master in 1962.

**Hennig-Schara Gambit** an opening sequence arising in the Tarrasch Defence to the Queen's Gambit: 1. P–Q4, P–Q4 2. P–QB4, P–K3 3. N–QB3, P–QB4 4. BP × P, *BP × P*. Practice has shown that White can take the offered pawn and survive the ensuing complications, but it is very easy to go astray.

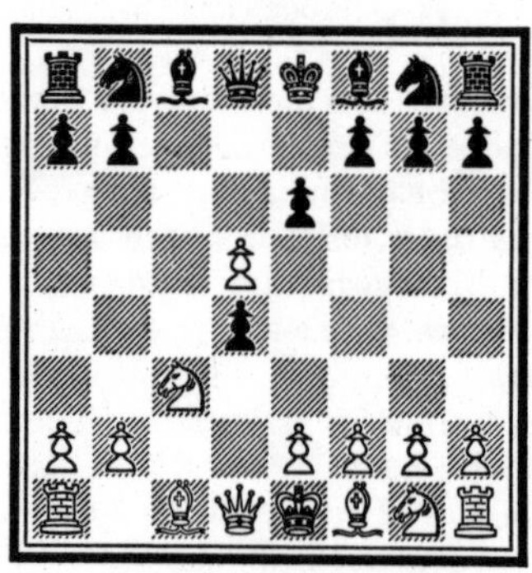

Position after 4 . . ., BP × P

**Hernandez, Roman** (b. 23 November 1949) Cuban chess player; awarded the title International Master in 1975. (1976 Elo rating: 2300)

**heterodox chess** another name for **Fairy Chess**.

**Hexagon Chess** a variant form of chess, one version of which was perfected by Wladyslaw Glinski, a Polish émigré living in England. It comprises a hexagonal board consisting of 91 smaller hexagons on which the chessmen move. The pieces have moves similar to regular chess, although there are nine pawns and three Bishops on each side in addition to the normal number of other pieces.

**Heydebrand, von** see **Lasa, Baron Tassilo von Heydebrand und der.**

**Hippogriff** a Fairy chesspiece that possesses the powers of both the Knight and the Grasshopper. It is thus a type of combined chessman. The Hippogriff was invented by a Canadian, P. Monréal, in 1964.

**Hippopotamus** an eccentric defence devised and practised in the 1950s by the English amateur J. J. Thompson. A typical progression is: 1 . . ., P–KN3 2 . . ., B–N2 3 . . ., P–Q3 4 . . ., N–Q2 5 . . ., P–KB3 6 . . ., N–R3 7 . . ., N–B2. Similar openings have been played at the highest level despite their outlandishness. Such a defence was adopted by Spassky in the twelfth game of his first world championship match with Petrosian (Spassky drew). The opening is presumably so called because the outline of Black's position is said to resemble the outline of a hippopotamus emerging from the water.

**Hisha** *Japanese for* flying chariot. Each side has one Hisha in the game of Shogi. It moves in the same way as does a Rook in Chess and becomes a Ryu when promoted, then moving in the same way as a King and Rook. See **Shogi**.

***History of Chess, A*** **1.** a monumental history of the game of chess by H. J. R. Murray. It has three purposes: to present a comprehensive record of all the varieties of chess that have ever existed; to investigate the origin of chess; and to trace its evolution from the Indian game of chaturanga. *A History of Chess* took Murray 13 years to complete, during which period he learned Arabic to further his research. The work has been described as the greatest book ever written on the game. It was first published in 1913 and uses algebraic notation.

**2.** a collection of 20 essays written by Jerzy Gizycki. Among the topics dealt with are chess and mathematics, chess in poetry and prose and **living chess**. Its English editor, Baruch H. Wood, has also added a chapter on chess in the United Kingdom. Written in Polish, the English edition was first published in 1972 and uses descriptive notation.

***History of Chess, The*** a survey of the game of chess from its origins to the present day, written by H. Golombek. Its topics include the development of the men, the evolution of styles of play, a description of various chess sets (both historical and contemporary) and seminal works of chess. It was first published in 1976.

**hold** to defend a square or group of squares successfully, allowing a piece or pieces to be placed there. Thus, a player might hold the centre or hold an open file.

**hole** a square in an important position (especially on the third rank) which can no longer be guarded by a pawn and on which an enemy piece can be stationed. Also called **weak square**.

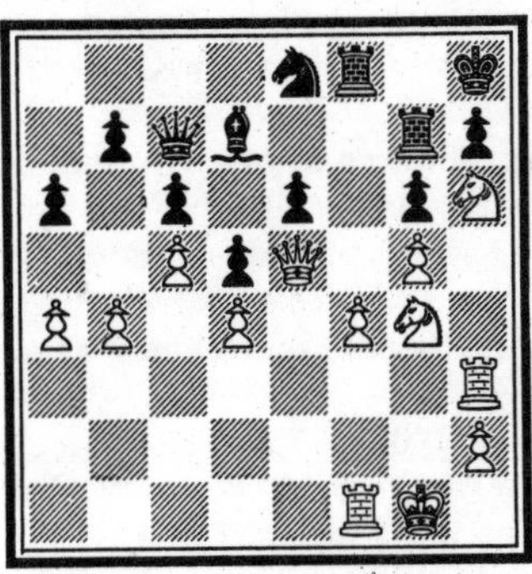

Schlecter vs. John (Barmen, 1905)
Black has four holes on the third rank

**Holmov** a variant spelling of **Kholmov**.

**home pawns** (Kmoch's term) the pawns protecting a castled King. Compare **centre pawns, rangers**. See ***Pawn Power in Chess***.

**home side** (Kmoch's term) the flank on which the King has castled. Kmoch believes that this term and its opposite – **ranger side** – convey more information than King side and Queen side since it is the position of the Kings that determines the players' plans. See ***Pawn Power in Chess***.

**Honfi, Károly** (b. 25 October 1930) Hungarian chess player; awarded the title International Master in 1962. Honfi came second in the Hungarian Championship in 1958 and competed in the Chess Olympiad in 1962. (1976 Elo rating: 2460)

**Hoogoven chess tournament** an annual tournament first held in 1938; named after the Hoogoven steel firm, which sponsors it. It consists of a Grandmaster tournament, a Master tournament and several open tournaments. From 1946 to 1970 it was held at Beverwijk; from 1971 the venue has been Wijk aan Zee (the Netherlands).

**Hopper** one of the three main types of Fairy chesspiece. It moves like a Rider except that it must hop over at least one piece in its move. There are no examples of Hoppers in orthodox chess, although the Rook does move like a Hopper when it is used in castling. Examples of heterodox hoppers are the Grasshopper, Equihopper, and the Locust. Compare **Leaper, Rider.**

**horizontal cylinder** a type of Fairy chessboard where the first and eighth ranks are joined. It can be imagined as a board wrapped around the rim of a small wheel. This means that a Rook on QR3 can move to QR6 without crossing the middle ranks, while a Bishop on KR3 can move via QB8 to QN1. The board is usually symbolized by an ordinary diagram without borders at the top and bottom. See **Cylinder Chess.** Compare **anchor-ring, vertical cylinder.**

**horizontal switch** (Kmoch's term) the manoeuvre by which a major piece moves along an open file to penetrate the opponent's defences and then attacks along a rank. Once a Rook reaches the seventh rank it will employ the horizontal switch to attack the enemy pawns from the side and rear and to confine the enemy King to its first rank. See ***Pawn Power in Chess.***

**Horse** **1.** a translation of the name (used in some countries) of the chess piece known in English as the Knight. The original Arabic name of this piece was *faras* (horse), the name still used in several countries of the Middle East. In many chess sets (including those of the popular Staunton design) this piece is represented by a horse's head.
**2.** (colloquial) a Knight.

**Horowitz, Israel Albert** (1907–1973) American chess player and chess writer, born in New York on 15 November 1907; awarded the title International Master in 1950. Horowitz was winner of the United States Open Championship in 1936 and 1948; in 1941 he lost a match against Reshevsky for the United States Championship (+0 −3 =13). He competed in the Chess Olympiads of 1931, 1935, 1937 and 1950. Horowitz was a prolific writer and was also the founder and editor of the chess magazine *Chess Review*. He died on 18 January 1973.

**Hort, Vlastimil** (b. 12 January 1944) Czechoslovakian chess player; awarded the titles International Master in 1961 and International Grandmaster in 1965. His results include firsts at Kecskemet (1965), Marianske Lazne (1965), Hastings (1967 and 1974), Sombor (1968), Venice (1969), Slanchev Breag (1974) and Vincovci (1976). Hort played in the interzonals of 1967, 1970, 1973 (in Petropolis) and 1976 (in Manila) and qualified for the 1977 series of Candidates' matches. (1976 Elo rating: 2600)

**Horwitz, Bernhard** (1807–1885) chess player and problemist. He was born in Mecklenburg-Streilitz, Germany and by the 1820s had moved to Berlin to study art, where he became a member of the influential group of German chess players known as the Berlin Pleiades. After graduating, Horwitz emigrated to the United Kingdom to continue as an artist, but continued to play chess extensively. In 1846 he played and lost a match to Staunton (+7 −14 =3), who afterwards became a friend and patron. Later in the year he lost matches to Harrwitz (+5 −6 =1) and Kieseritzky (+4 −7 =0). He competed at London (1851) and was knocked out in the second round by Josef Szén after defeating Henry Bird in the first. In 1860 he played a match against Kolisch which he lost (+1 −3 =0).

Horwitz was a noted problemist and expert on endings and edited a section on endings in *The Chess Monthly*.

**Horwitz Bishops** Bishops of the same colour occupying adjacent diagonals. A typical manoeuvre of the Horwitz Bishops is seen when one attacks an enemy pawn and compels it to advance, so coming under attack from the second Bishop. Bishops of this type were frequently seen in the games of Bernhard Horwitz.

**hourglass** another name for **sandglass.**

**House of Games** a chess meeting house in New York that is open to all. It is situated on West 72nd Street between Broadway and Columbus Avenue.

**Houston Helpmates** a founding member of the **National Chess League.** In the league's first season the team lived up to its name by coming bottom in ninth place.

***How Chess Games Are Won*** a collection of 60 of Reshevsky's games selected by Reshevsky himself. All the games were played in the decade 1951–1960. It was published in 1962 and uses descriptive notation.

***How Not to Play Chess*** a book by Eugène Znosko-Borovsky, in which he defines and illustrates typical chess mistakes and presents the basis of positional analysis (material being equal). In the revised edition (1949), which uses descriptive notation, Fred Reinfeld added twenty problems from master games.

***How to Beat Bobby Fischer*** a book by the United States International Master Edmar Mednis containing all 61 of the games that Fischer lost after becoming United States Champion at the age of 14 in 1957–8. It was published in 1975 and uses descriptive notation.

***How to Cheat at Chess*** a collection of humorous articles by British. International Master W. R. Hartston. The book covers all aspects of gamesmanship and (yes) even outright cheating! It was first published in 1976 and uses descriptive notation.

***How to Open a Chess Game*** a book on play in the opening written by seven Grandmasters. Each wrote independently and consequently adopted a different approach. For instance, Tigran Petrosian writes on the inadvisability of relying upon book variations learned by rote, while Paul Keres reveals how an innovation is prepared and used against suitable opponents. The other contributors are Larry Evans (who also helped compile a glossary of common chess terms), Svetozar Gligorić, Vlastimil Hort, Bent Larsen and Lajos Portisch. The book was first published in 1974 and uses descriptive notation.

***How To Play the Chess Openings*** a work on the openings by Eugène Znosko-Borovsky. It analyses numerous openings and features some common traps. It was published in 1935 and uses descriptive notation.

***How to Play the Opening in Chess*** a book by D. N. Levy and R. D. Keene which explains the strategy behind 12 major openings and analyzes in detail four variations for each opening. It was first published in 1974 and uses descriptive notation.

***How to Think Ahead in Chess*** a book by I. A. Horowitz and Fred Reinfeld. Its purpose is to provide a specialized opening repertoire for the amateur player and so concentrates upon one opening (the Stonewall Attack) and two defences (the Dragon Variation of the Sicilian Defence and Lasker's Variation) in reply to the King pawn opening and Queen pawn opening, respectively. It was first published in 1952 and uses descriptive notation.

***How to Win in the Chess Openings*** a primer on nine major openings, written by I. A. Horowitz. The basic principles behind each opening are revealed and a main line in each opening is studied thoroughly. This is followed by complete games beginning with these openings. It was first published in 1948 and uses descriptive notation.

***How to Win in the Middle Game of Chess*** a work on the middle-game by I. A. Horowitz. It concentrates upon combinations and situations that are commonly found during this phase; examples are double attack, discovered attack and interference. It was published in 1955 and uses descriptive notation.

**Hübner, Robert** (b. 6 November 1948) West German chess player; awarded the titles International Master in 1969 and International Grandmaster in 1970. He competed in the Chess Olympiads of 1968, 1970 and 1972 and in the last event obtained the best score on first board (+12 −0 =6). He was also the West German representative in the World Junior Championships of 1965 and 1967 and played in the Student Olympiads of 1968, 1970 and 1972.

Hübner is one of the strongest players in the West and has competed in the interzonals of 1970, 1973 (in Leningrad) and 1976 (in Biel). He qualified for the Candidates' matches of 1971 and met Petrosian in the quarter-finals, but withdrew after seven games in protest at the excessive noise in the playing-hall so leaving Petrosian the winner by default (+0 −1 =6). (1976 Elo rating: 2585)

**Hughes-Hughes, M. E.** a nineteenth-century British chess player. In 1888 he introduced the members of his club to a variation of four-handed chess, known today as the **Hughes Game**. (For details of the rules of the game, see Sunnucks' *Encyclopaedia of Chess*.) See **four-handed chess.**

**Hulak, Krunoslav** (b. 25 May 1951) Yugoslavian chess player; awarded the titles International Master in 1974 and International Grandmaster in 1976. His tournament successes include an equal first at Varna (1974). (1976 Elo rating: 2470)

**Hungarian Defence** a defence to the King pawn opening: 1. P–K4, P–K4 2. N–KB3, N–QB3 3. B–B4, *B–K2*. This opening is very infrequently seen.

**Hunter** a Fairy chesspiece that possesses the powers of one piece when advancing and of another when retreating. For instance, the N/B Hunter would advance as a Knight and retreat as a Bishop. No Hunter can move laterally. The Hunter was invented by K. Schulz in 1943.

**Hutton, Rev. G. D.** (1866–1929) inventor of the Hutton Method of Pairing. He graduated from Edinburgh university and served as a minister there until he moved to Melbourne, Australia. He returned to Scotland in 1883 and served at Bathkenner, Stirlingshire until his retirement in 1919. He first suggested the Hutton Method of Pairing in 1921 when he mentioned it to L. P. Rees, the then Secretary of the B.C.F., who secured its adoption in the 1922 Counties and District Correspondence Chess Championship.

**Hutton Method of Pairing** a system of pairing players that is employed in team tournaments. Each player has one game only and is matched, wherever possible, against another player on the same board. The pairings are arranged so that each team competes against a composite of the other teams. Ideally, the number of players in each team should be one less than the number of teams competing or be a multiple of this number to ensure that each team meets an identical number of players from every other team. Thus, if eight teams are competing the ideal sizes of the teams are 7, 14, 21, etc.

This system was devised by the Rev. G. D. Hutton and was first used in the Counties and District Correspondence Chess Championship. Also called **Jamboree Pairing Method.**

**Hydra** a Fairy chesspiece that has two Knight-leaps in its move. It is created from a pawn that reaches the eighth rank before any pieces of its colour have been captured. It was invented by Peter Pratt and appears in his book, *Studies of Chess* (1803). Compare **Cadet.**

**hypermodern** a description of a style of play that flourished in the decade after the First World War. It challenged much orthodox dogma, for instance the preference for controlling the centre from a distance with pieces rather than occupying it with pawns. Indeed, hypermodern players felt that the anchoring of pawns in the centre merely provided a static target for the opponent.

Famous members of the hypermodern school were Breyer, Nimzovitch, Réti and Tartakover (who coined this term).

# I

**I.B.C.A.** or **IBCA** *abbrev. for* International Braille Chess Association.

**IBCA Correspondence World Championship** a tournament lasting for several years to discover the world's best correspondence chess player. The first such event began in 1955 and was won by R. W. Bonham. Indeed, R. W. Bonham has been so successful in this event that in 1972 at the Pula Olympiad he was made the first **Correspondence Grandmaster of the Blind** for having won the event more than three times.

**IBCA Individual Championship** an international tournament of individuals, organized under the **Swiss System**, held to find the world's strongest blind player. The first Championship was held in 1966 at Timmendorfer Strand, West Germany and was won by a Yugoslavian player, Cabarkapa. The second Championship was held in 1970 at Ermelo, the Netherlands and was also won by Cabarkapa. In the first Championship, 22 players from 17 countries competed; 22 players from 19 countries competed in the second Championship.

**IBCA Olympiad** a quadrennial tournament in which national teams of blind players meet to compete against each other.

The first Olympiad was a round-robin tournament held in 1961 at Meschede, West Germany, when seven nations competed. By the fourth Olympiad, which was held in 1972, the number of teams entering had increased to 22, although they still came only from Europe. Because of the size of the tournament it was decided to hold preliminary rounds from which the teams qualified for the *A*, *B* and *C* finals.

Of the four Olympiads that have so far been held, Yugoslavia has won the first two and the U.S.S.R. has won the last two. The best individual result attained in any IBCA Olympiad so far was the performance of Turukin on fourth board for the U.S.S.R. in the third Olympiad where he scored 11/11. Also called **Olympiad for the Blind**.

**IBM tournament** an annual and very strong Grandmaster tournament (with a subsidiary Master tournament) held in Amsterdam.

**I.C.C.F.** or **ICCF** *abbrev. for* International Correspondence Chess Federation.

**ideal mate** **1.** any chess problem where all the men on the board have a definite role to play in the final position. Even the White King and White pawns must fulfil the condition and usually guard possible flight squares or hamper defending pieces. It can be any type of chess problem. If it exists, it is usually regarded as adding to the beauty of the composition.

**2.** The term is also applied loosely to game positions where the mating condition is relaxed to exclude King and pawns.

**ideal position** a point in an opening sequence where the advantage held by one side is at its maximum. Consequently, one player will attempt to reach this position while his opponent will try to prevent it. The term was coined by Fine.

***Ideas Behind the Chess Openings*** a book by Reuben Fine. It seeks to clarify the purposes and themes of the openings and also provides comprehensive analyses of many variations. It was first published in 1948 and uses descriptive notation.

**ideal mate**

An ideal mate

**I.F.S.B.** or **IFSB** *abbrev. for* Internationaler Fernschachbund.

**I.G.M.** or **IGM** *abbrev. for* International Grandmaster.

***Il giuoco degli scacchi*** *Italian for* the game of chess. A book by the Italian player Giambattista Lolli. It was the first modern encyclopaedia of the openings and arose out of Lolli's revision of the work of del Rio. It was first published in Modena in 1750.

**Ilivitsky, Georgy** (b. 30 April 1921) Soviet chess player; awarded the title International Master in 1955.

**illegal move** any move that breaks one of the laws of chess. If it is discovered before the conclusion of the game, the position that existed before the move was made must be recreated and the game continued from there. If the correct position cannot be recreated, the game must be abandoned and a new one played.

**illegal position** one that has not arisen legally from a game of chess. Illegal positions can be created in several ways: through an **illegal move**; through incorrect replacement of displaced men; through the incorrect arrangement of men either at the beginning of the game or after an adjournment; or through an incorrect positioning of the chessboard. This position must be corrected if at all possible. If it cannot be corrected a new game must be played.

Some composed positions could not have arisen from an orthodox game of chess, and thus also represent examples of illegal positions.

**I.M.** or **IM** *abbrev. for* International Master.

**Imitator** a Fairy chesspiece that cannot be used by either side and which moves concurrently and in exact imitation of the moves that are played. The Imitator can neither capture nor check and if, for this reason or because a legal move is impossible, it cannot imitate a move then that move itself is illegal. The Imitator is usually represented on diagrams by a large black dot. It was invented by Dr T. Kok.

**Immortal Game** the name given to a game played in 'the Divan' between Anderssen and Kieseritzky. Anderssen had recently won the

London tournament of 1851 and had knocked out Kieseritzky in the first round. Consequently in this game, which was played in a less important London tournament, Kieseritzky was seeking revenge. Anderssen was White: 1. P–K4, P–K4 2. P–KB4, P×P 3. B–B4, Q–R5ch 4. K–B1, P–QN4 5. B×NP, N–KB3 6. N–KB3, Q–R3 7. P–Q3, N–R4 8. N–R4, Q–N4 9. N–B5, P–QB3 10. P–KN4!, N–B3 11. R–N1!, P×B 12. P–KR4, Q–N3 13. P–R5, Q–N4 14. Q–B3, N–N1 15. B×P, Q–B3 16. N–B3, B–B4 17. N–Q5, Q×P 18. B–Q6!, Q×Rch 19. K–K2, B×R 20. P–K5!, N–QR3 21. N×Pch, K–Q1 22. Q–B6ch, N×Q 23. B–K7mate.

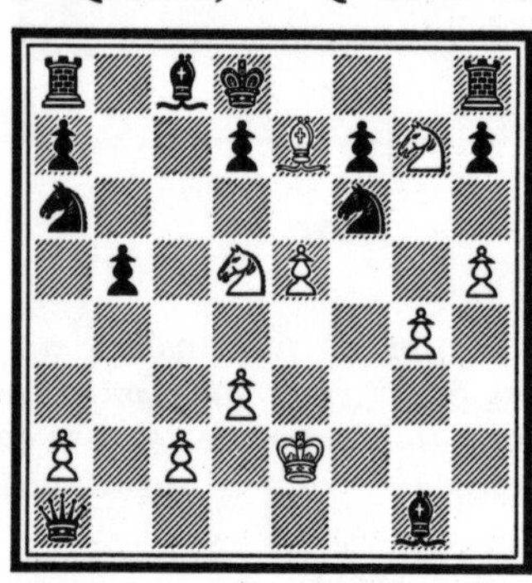

Position after 23. B–K7mate

Despite losing, Kieseritzky was so enchanted with the game that he immediately cabled the moves to his chess club in Paris. Compare **Evergreen Partie**.

**Indian Defence** originally any defence which has a Bishop in fianchetto, but later extended to embrace all defences to 1. P–Q4 other than the Queen's Gambit. It derives its name from the older openings of India where this was a normal method of development for the Bishops. They were not regularly played in modern chess until the 1920s. See **King's Indian Defence, Nimzo-Indian Defence, Queen's Indian Defence.**

**Indian in Reverse** any opening system by White, usually beginning 1. N–KB3, in which White adopts a development plan corresponding to that of Black in one of the Indian defences. The early moves in such cases tend to preserve flexibility, thus allowing frequent transposition to other openings.

**Indian theme** a theme in problem chess in which checkmate must be delivered although stalemate seems inevitable.

The first example of the Indian theme is thought to have been composed in 1845 by an Anglo-Indian chaplain named Loveday. He sent it anonymously from India to a periodical in the United Kingdom where it was greeted with great acclaim.

**inflation of titles** See **title inflation.**

***Informator*** a twice-yearly periodical containing approximately 700 games in each issue, classified by opening. Although it covers topics of

Indian theme

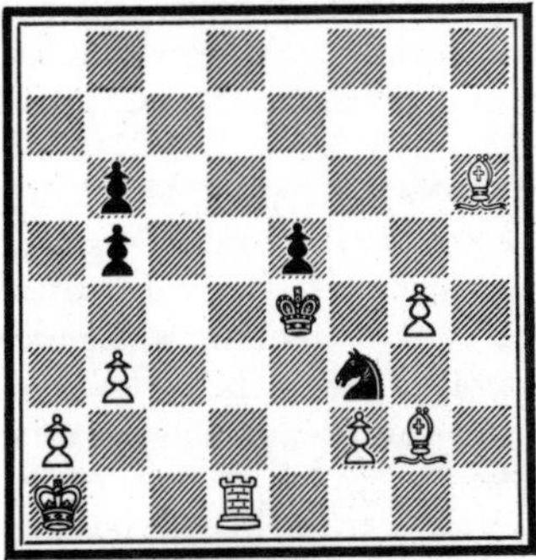

In this (the original) Indian problem, White wins by: 1. B–N5, P–N5 2. B–B1, P–N4 3. R–Q2, K–B5 4. R–Q4mate

middle-game and endgame interest it specializes in analysis of the openings. Each issue also contains FIDE news, cross-tables of the international tournaments that took place in the six months covered by the issue, and the ranking list of the world's leading players. Informator was first published in 1966 and is under the editorial direction of Alexander Matanovic. It uses figurine algebraic notation. Also called ***Chess Informant***.

**Ingo System** a method of grading players that is used in West Germany. Each player is assigned a grading which consists of a rolling average of tournament results with the result from the latest tournament being weighted by a factor of a quarter and the aggregate of all previous tournaments being weighted by a factor of three-quarters. The system was devised in the late 1940s by Herr Hoesslinger of Ingolstadt. It can be converted to the B.C.F. grading system by the formula: Ingo=280−B.C.F.

**initiative** a lead in development of an advantage in space that throws the opponent onto the defensive. At the beginning of a game White holds the initiative by having the first move. For this reason symmetrical defences are often felt to be dangerous for Black as they allow White to retain the initiative while developing and, if the symmetrical defence is continued for long enough, eventually White will be able to advantageously break the symmetry through use of his extra tempo. The initiative is a transient advantage which its possessor will attempt to increase and then exchange for a more obvious advantage, perhaps a gain of material, a mating attack, or a won ending.

**inner lever** (Kmoch's term) a **lever** that slopes towards the centre. Obviously what will be an inner lever for one player will not be for the other. The inner lever is slightly superior to one that slopes away from the centre since a pawn capture would take that pawn nearer the centre and hence increase its importance. Compare **loose lever, outer lever, tight lever**. See ***Pawn Power in Chess***.

**innerpawn** (Kmoch's term) a pawn on any file except those of the Rooks. In King and pawn endings an innerpawn has a greater chance of reaching the eighth rank than a rimpawn, since its King has greater room for manoeuvre with which to drive away the defending King. See ***Pawn Power in Chess***.

**innerswap** (Kmoch's term) a type of **doubling** in which the pawn captures towards the centre. For example, an innerswap would take place if a Rook pawn captured a Knight pawn. The innerswap is normally the strongest type of doubling since the weakness caused by the creation of doubled pawns is partially compensated for by increased control of the centre. Compare **centreswap, outerswap**. See ***Pawn Power in Chess***.

**innovation** a new move in an established opening sequence. It may be objectively better than the previous continuation, but may also be played for psychological reasons – to unsettle the opponent, perhaps by forcing the game into uncongenial channels for him, and make him consume more time. The innovation may cause a re-evaluation of that opening variation, but may instead be met by a **refutation.**

**interference** restriction on the movement of one piece by the movement of another of the same colour. For example, in the following position reached in a game between Tarrasch and three amateurs in Naples in 1914:

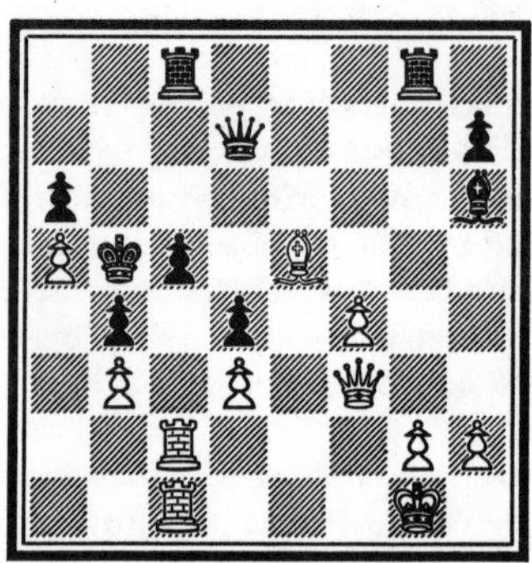

Tarrasch vs. Amateurs (Naples, 1914)

The Queen guards QN2 and the Rook guards QB4. Tarrasch played: 1. B–B7 and the amateurs resigned as the piece that captures will interfere with the other, allowing mate after either 1 . . ., R × B 2. Q–N7ch!, R × Q 3. R × P or 1 . . ., Q × B 2. R × Pch!, Q × R 3. Q–N7ch, K × P 4. R–R1.

**International Braille Chess Association** an international organization for blind players that encourages the playing of chess among the blind, organizes international competitions, and provides a governing body to deal with aspects of the game affecting blind players. Founded in 1951 by R. W. Bonham, it became affiliated to FIDE in 1964.

Among the events the International Braille Chess Association organizes are the **IBCA Olympiads**, the **IBCA Correspondence World Championships**, and the **IBCA Individual Championships**. Abbrev. **I.B.C.A.** or **IBCA**. See **Braille Chess Association**.

***International Championship Chess*** a complete record of FIDE events compiled by Bozidar M. Kazic. It contains a brief history of FIDE and provides information on all the chess olympiads, women's chess olympiads, world student team championships and the World Championship qualifying cycles and matches. It has chapters on the International Correspondence Chess Federation and the International Braille Chess Association, provides lists of International Grandmasters, International Masters, International Judges, etc., and has 273 games and positions from FIDE events. It was first published in 1974 and uses descriptive notation.

**International Chess Federation** See **Fédération Internationale des Echecs.**

**International Correspondence Chess Federation** the world organization of correspondence chess. It was created in 1946 by FIDE to replace the IFSB and is primarily responsible for the Correspondence World Championship, the Correspondence Chess Olympiad, and the award of the titles of International Master of Correspondence Chess and International Grandmaster of Correspondence Chess. Abbrev. **I.C.C.F.** or **ICCF.**

**Internationaler Fernschachbund** *German for* International Federation for Correspondence Chess; an international organization that was founded in 1927 by FIDE. It was responsible for correspondence chess within Europe. In 1946 it was superseded by the **International Correspondence Chess Federation**. Abbrev. **I.F.S.B.** or **IFSB.**

**International Grandmaster** a title that is awarded by FIDE to each of the world's strongest players. It is often shortened to Grandmaster. The title is awarded automatically to those players who qualify in the interzonal tournaments for the Candidates' matches. It is also awarded to those International Masters who achieve performances of Grandmaster standard in either two or three tournaments of recognized calibre (at least 25 games must be played) within three years of each other. (Although the Elo ratings of the players are not directly taken into consideration a player of Grandmaster standard would be expected to have a rating of at least 2500 points.)

According to Dr Ossip S. Bernstein the title was first used to describe the competitors at Ostend (1907), which was an exceptionally strong tournament. It was first awarded as a title in 1914 when Czar Nicholas II bestowed the title of Grandmaster of Chess on each of the finalists of the St Petersburg tournament. From then until World War II it was loosely used to describe any player who was of world championship class. The title was awarded by FIDE from 1950 at its own discretion, while from 1957 it has been presented by FIDE on the basis of the conditions mentioned above (although these have not always remained constant). Compare **International Master**. See **St Petersburg (1914).**

**International Judge** a title awarded by the FIDE Qualification Committee to a candidate who is deemed capable of organizing an international tournament. Each International Judge must have: 1) a perfect knowledge of the rules of play and of all FIDE regulations; 2) absolute objectivity in directing; 3) proficiency in at least two FIDE languages (English, French, German, Russian, or Spanish); 4) experience in controlling at least four important chess events, of which at least two must have been international. The title was first awarded in 1951.

**International Master** a title that is awarded by FIDE to a player of international standard who is not strong enough to be awarded the title of Grandmaster. It is awarded automatically to the Woman World Champion, the World Junior Champion, any player who qualifies for the interzonal tournament from a zonal tournament, and any player who scores 66⅔% at a zonal tournament. It is also awarded to players who achieve performances of International Master standard in either two or three tournaments of recognized calibre (at least 25 games must be played) within three years of each other. (Although the Elo ratings of the players are not directly taken into consideration a player would be expected to have a rating of at least 2400 points.) Compare **International Grandmaster.**

**International Rating List** an annual compilation by FIDE of the world's strongest players. The first list was published in July 1971 and contained the names of 600 players; since then the list has been greatly expanded and now includes over 1600 players, i.e. every player with an Elo rating of 2200 or more, or in the case of the list of women players, with a rating of 1800 or more.

The list is also used to determine the number of points needed in a tournament to obtain an I.M. or G.M. norm. Norms will vary among tournaments because of the difference in the size and strength of the competition; the International Rating List helps the latter factor to be allowed for and through the list the tournament is placed in a category between one (for the weakest) and 15 (for the strongest). As the category number increases, the size of the norm needed to gain a title falls, since the opposition is correspondingly stronger than in a lower-category tournament. Abbrev. **I.R.L.** Also known as the **Elo list.**

**International Team Tournament** another name for **Chess Olympiad.**

**International Woman Grandmaster** a title created in November 1976, during the Plenary Congress of FIDE in Haifa, and awarded to the world's strongest female players. The first players to receive this title were Nana Alexandria, Nona Gaprindashvili, Alla Kushnir, Irena Levitina and Milunka Lazarevic. One of the new title holders, Alla Kushnir, feels that there is no real need for this title and has stated that 'a female grandmaster title is a formality of purely nominal value' (*Chess Life & Review*, July 1976). *Abbrev.* **I.W.G.** or **IWG.** See **title inflation.**

**interspan** (Kmoch's term) the number of squares on a file that separate two opposing pawns. The greatest interspan is found at the start of a game when it is four squares on each rank; when the interspan is nil the pawns block each other. Compare **frontspan, rearspan.** See ***Pawn Power in Chess.***

**interzonal tournament** the second stage in the three-year qualifying cycle to select a challenger in the subsequent match against the World Champion.

Interzonal tournaments began in 1948; since then they have varied in certain features, including size and composition. The present system consists of two interzonal tournaments, rather than the one held formerly. Each interzonal consists of eighteen players, so that thirty-six are in contention. Of these, twenty players qualify through the ten **zonal tournaments.** The other sixteen are directly nominated by FIDE and consist of the six participants in the previous Candidates' matches, two youth world Champions, and eight players selected by FIDE.

The three highest competitors in each of the interzonal tournaments then enter the **Candidates' matches** together with the loser of the last World Championship match and the defeated finalist from the previous Candidates Cycle. The interzonal tournament itself is a round-robin. (Otherwise there would be little point in reducing the size of the event). Also called **interzonal.**

**Inverted Hanham** an opening sequence arising out of the King pawn opening: 1. P–K4, P–K4 2. N–KB3, N–QB3 3. B–K2, N–B3 4. P–Q3, P–Q4 5. *QN–Q2*. In this reversed form of the **Hanham Variation** it is White who creates a solid although cramped position. The most common continuation is: 5 . . ., P–KN3 6. P–B3, B–N2. This variation is named after the American player James Moore Hanham.

**inverted opening** an opening where White adopts a defence with the advantage of a move in hand. Examples are the English Opening (an inverted Sicilian Defence) and Bird's Opening (an inverted Dutch Defence). Also called **reverse openings.**

***Invitation to Chess, An*** a picture guide to chess by Irving Chernev and Kenneth Harkness. In the first part of the book the rules of chess are explained with the help of numerous diagrams and illustrations. In the same way the rest of the book discusses more difficult topics, ending with a section on combinations. It was first published in 1947 and uses descriptive notation.

**I.R.L.** abbrev. for International Rating List.

**irregular defence** a defence that deviates from the orthodox moves, either slightly or radically. If correct, an irregular defence may later become established as a standard opening. Many of the present day's most common defences, such as the King's Indian and the Modern, were not long ago considered irregular. Alternatively, an irregular defence might be inferior but be played for psychological reasons, perhaps to take weaker players out of the book as swiftly as possible or to put a stronger player under pressure and possibly into time trouble.

**isolani** another name for **isolated pawn.**

**isolated pawn** a pawn that has no allied pawns on the adjacent files. Since it cannot be defended by other pawns it must be supported by pieces. Even where it is not captured so much material may be tied down in defending it that the initiative passes to the opponent: the possessor must defend the pawn for as long as it is attacked, but the attacker can switch his offensive to other targets at any time. When he does, the defender may not be able to react in time. Another weakness is that any minor piece, especially a Knight, posted on the square in front of the isolated pawn can block it and is normally very difficult to dislodge. Also called **isolani.**

**Italian Game** another name for **Giuoco Piano.**

**Ivanović, Bozidar** (b. 24 August 1946) Yugoslavian chess player; awarded the title International Master in 1976. (1976 Elo rating: 2385)

**Ivkov, Borislav** (b. 12 November 1933) Yugoslavian chess player; awarded the titles International Master in 1954 and International Grandmaster in 1955. In 1951 he became the first player to win the World Junior Championship. Ivkov took seventh place in the 1964 interzonal tournament to qualify for the following year's series of Candidates matches, but he lost in the first round (5½–2½) to Larsen. (1976 Elo rating: 2520)

**I.W.G.** or **IWG** *abbrev. for* International Woman Grandmaster.

# J

**j'adoube** *French for* I adjust; phrase spoken during the game before touching a chessman that one does not intend to move officially, as for purposes of adjusting it on its square, flicking dust from the King's crown, etc. See also **touch-move.**

**Jaenisch** a variant spelling of **Jänisch.**

**Jamboree Pairing Method** another name for **Hutton Method of Pairing.**

**Jamieson, Robert** (b. 7 July 1952) Australian chess player; awarded the title International Master in 1975. (1976 Elo rating: 2420)

**Jänisch, Carl Andreyevich** (1813–1872) Russian chess player and theoretician who lived several years in Paris. He published a two-volume work in which several openings were analysed: *Analyse Nouvelle des Ouvertures du Jeu des Echecs* (1842–1843). Among the openings discussed were Petroff's Defence and what is known today as the Falkbeer Counter Gambit (Falkbeer was a contemporary of Jänisch). He died on 17 March 1872.

**Jänisch Defence** another name for the **Schliemann Defence.** It is named after Carl Andreyevich Jänisch, who developed it extensively. This is the more common name on the Continent.

**Janosevic, Dragoljub** (b. 8 July 1923) Yugoslavian chess player; awarded the title International Master in 1964 and the title International Grandmaster in 1965. (1976 Elo rating: 2435)

**Janowski, David Markyelovitch** (1868–1927) French chess player, born in Volkovysk, Poland on 25 May 1868. He emigrated to France when young and eventually settled in Paris. His debut in a major tournament took place at Leipzig (1894) where he came sixth; later results included firsts at Monte Carlo (1901), Paris (1902), Hanover (1902), Barmen (1905) and seconds at London (1899), Cambridge Springs (1904), Schevingen (1913) and New York (1916). Janowski was an inveterate gambler and is said to have often lost at the roulette table the prize money won at chess; this quirk was reflected in his style of play which was aggressive and sacrificial. This ferocity attracted an enthusiastic patron in Pierre Nardus, a rich painter who sponsored World Championship matches against Emanuel Lasker in 1909 and 1910. Janowski was easily beaten on both occasions by Lasker (+1 −7 =1 and +0 −8 =3), who could always tempt Janowski to overreach himself and fasten on the subsequent weaknesses. His inferiority of play was remarked upon by Janowski himself who described his own game as being, '. . . like Mary Queen of Scots – beautiful but unfortunate.' He was, however, one of only two players (the other being Tarrasch) to win games against Steinitz, Lasker, Capablanca and Alekhine.

Janowski won no tournaments after 1907, but still competed regularly. He died of tuberculosis on 15 January 1927 on the eve of a small chess event in the South of France.

**Jansa, Vlastimil** (b. 27 November 1942) Czechoslovakian chess player; awarded the titles International Master in 1965 and International Grandmaster in 1974. (1976 Elo rating: 2490)

**Japanese Chess** another name for **Shogi**.

**Jibber** a Fairy chesspiece that moves like a normal Queen except that it always halts at the square before the first man that bars its path – i.e., it jibs as a horse might at a fence. It was invented by C. D. Locock.

**Jimenez, Zeroquera Eleazar** (b. 25 June 1928) Cuban chess player; awarded the title International Master in 1963. He competed in the Chess Olympiads of 1960, 1962, 1964, 1966, 1968 and 1970. (1976 Elo rating: 2375)

**Johannessen, Svein** (b. 17 October 1937) Norwegian chess player; awarded the title International Master in 1961. He was several times Norwegian Champion (1976 Elo rating: 2420)

**Johannsson, Ingi R.** (b. 5 December 1936) Icelandic chess player; awarded the title International Master in 1963. He competed in the Chess Olympiads of 1952, 1954, 1956, 1958, 1966, 1968, 1970, 1972 and 1974. (1976 Elo rating: 2395)

**Johner, Hans** (b. 7 January 1889) Swiss chess player; awarded the title International Master in 1950. He was Swiss Champion in 1908, 1923, 1928, 1929, 1931, 1932, 1934, 1935, 1937, 1938, 1947 and 1950. He competed in the Chess Olympiads of 1927, 1931 and 1956. He was also at one time director of the Zurich Philharmonic Orchestra.

**Joke Opening** a contemptuous name given by Alekhine to what is now known as the Modern Defence. In the tournament book of New York (1924) he wrote that this 'Joke Opening . . . naturally has no independent significance.'

**Joker** a Fairy chesspiece that assumes the powers of the last piece moved by the opponent. The most common type is probably the *Joker King* which assumes the capabilities of the last piece moved and can move and attack in accordance with them, although it cannot move into check and so cannot capture any man that is guarded.

**Jones, Sir William** (1746–1794) judge, linguist and famous Orientalist;

author of **Caïssa**. He was born in London 28 September 1746 and educated at Harrow where he revealed an enormous capacity for languages. Caïssa was composed in 1763 in the year before Jones entered University College and in the next decade he published numerous translations and original works in classical, European and Asian languages. In 1774 he qualified as a barrister, but his support of the Americans in the War of Independence harmed his career. In 1783 he was knighted and appointed a judge of the Supreme Court of Judicature in Calcutta. There Jones began the study of Sanskrit and made the discovery that Sanskrit and the European languages sprang from a common root; in consequence he is regarded as the founder of comparative linguistics. He died in Calcutta on 27 April 1794.

**jump formation** (Kmoch's term) a **half-open formation** of pawns in which the two pawn structures are separated by an open rank and each side's leading pawn is separated from the other by the equivalent of a Knight's jump. See ***Pawn Power in Chess***.

**Junior Tournament of the Americas** an annual international tournament held to discover the strongest young player from the American continent. It was inaugurated in January 1974 when the first event was held in Puerto Rico. The tournament was run under the Swiss System and was won by Gildardo Garcia of Colombia. The 1975 tournament was won by Jaime Sunye Neto of Brazil.

# K

**K** *abbrev.* for King; used in descriptive notation in English-speaking countries.

***Kagans Neueste Schachnachrichten*** *German for* Kagan's Chess Newssheet. A German periodical that appeared between 1921 and 1932. It was founded, published and edited by Bernhard Kagan, an affluent Berlin businessman, and contained contributions from all the leading players of the day. It ceased publication on Kagan's death.

**Kaila, Osma Ilmari** (b. 11 May 1910) Finnish chess player; awarded the titles International Master in 1952, International Judge in 1954 and International Judge of Chess Composition in 1958. He was Finnish Champion in 1939 and 1954. Kaila was elected President of the Finnish Problem Society in 1959, became a National Master of Chess Compositions in 1966 and was elected to the FIDE Permanent Commission for Chess Compositions in 1966.

**Kaku** *Japanese for* moving at an angle. Each side has one Kaku in the game of Shogi. It moves in the same way as the Bishop in Chess and becomes an Uma when promoted, after which it moves like a combined King and Bishop. See **Shogi**.

**Kaldor, Avraham** (b. 20 May 1947) Israeli chess player; awarded the title International Master in 1975. He came first at the Netanya Masters tournament (1975). (1976 Elo rating: 2395)

**Kamikaze Chess** a type of Fairy Chess in which each piece and pawn is removed from the board once it captures an opposing man.

**Kan, Ilya Abramovich** (b. 4 May 1909) Soviet chess player; awarded the titles International Master in 1950 and International Judge in 1956.

**Karaklajić, Nicola** (b. 24 February 1926) Yugoslavian chess player; awarded the title International Master in 1955. He was Yugoslavian Champion in 1955 and was the winner of the Royal Belgian Chess Federation Championship in 1960. When not playing chess he works as a disc jockey for Belgrade radio. (1976 Elo rating: 2455)

**Karasev, Vladimir** (b. 17 June 1938) Soviet chess player; awarded the title International Master in 1976 (1976 Elo rating: 2495)

**Karpov, Anatoly Evgenyevich** (b. 23 May 1951) Soviet International Grandmaster; World Champion from 1975. Karpov developed an early interest in chess, learning the moves at the age of four. By the age of eleven he had become a Candidate Master and, after four years of schooling under the direction of Botvinnik, became the youngest master of the U.S.S.R. His international career began through a curious mistake. In 1967 he was sent as the Soviet representative to a junior tournament at Třinec, Czechoslovakia. On arrival it was discovered that the tournament was for adults. Karpov nevertheless competed and, astonishingly, came first without a single loss. It was at the end of this year that he won the European Junior Championship in the tournament in Groningen, Netherlands. Again he was undefeated. In 1969 he defeated Vaganian and Steinberg in a three-player tournament to become the U.S.S.R.'s representative in the World Junior Championship.

His main events in 1970 were the tournament at Caracas where he came joint fourth and his winning of the R.S.F.S.R. title which qualified him to enter the Soviet championship in 1971. In the championship he came fourth, a performance which he followed with two sensational results: equal first with Stein in the Alekhine Memorial Tournament (the strongest tournament for over thirty years), followed by an equal first place at Hastings – this time with Korchnoi. In 1972 he competed in both the Students' Olympiad and the 20th Olympiad, winning the prize for the best performance on fifth board in the latter.

In 1973, after coming second at the international tournament at Budapest, he entered his first qualifying events for the world championship. He came joint first in the Leningrad interzonal to qualify with Korchnoi and Byrne. The year 1974 was dominated by the assault on the championship. In his first match, Karpov met Polugayevsky in a domestic quarter-final. Under the amended rules the victor would be the first to score three wins, with draws counting for nothing. Karpov achieved the target surprisingly easily, the match lasting only eight games. He then met Spassky, who had knocked out Byrne. Spassky, with Black, easily won the opening game – Karpov's first defeat with White in two years. Undaunted, he won the third game and, by intelligent choices of openings and superb play, defeated Spassky in eleven games to meet Korchnoi and the candidate's final.

The match against Korchnoi consisted of a maximum of twenty-four games, the winner being the player who gained 12½ points or five wins. After seventeen hard-fought games, Karpov had won three and drawn fourteen. Korchnoi then began a magnificent comeback and won two of the next four games, but Karpov held on and drew the last three games to gain the right to challenge Fischer as the official candidate. The games in the match with Korchnoi were his last as the challenger. Negotiations about the match broke down and Karpov was proclaimed the World Champion on 3 April 1975.

Karpov's style of play, apparently much more defensive, is in marked contrast to that of his two immediate predecessors, Fischer and Spassky, showing reliance on strategy rather than tactics, and a preference for ultra-solid positional play to double-edged attacking positions. His most trusted defences are the Breyer Variation of the Ruy Lopez, the Caro-Kann, the Nimzo-Indian, and the Queen's Gambit Declined.

**Kashdan, Isaac** (b. 19 November 1905) U.S. chess player; awarded the title International Master in 1950 and the title International Grandmaster in 1954. In 1960 he was appointed an International Judge by FIDE and now plays infrequently.

**Kasparian, Genrik M.** (b. 27 February 1919) Soviet chess player; awarded the titles International Master in 1950, International Judge of Chess Compositions in 1956, International Master for Chess Compositions in 1960 and International Grandmaster for Chess Compositions in 1972. Kasparian has been Armenian Champion on numerous occasions and has competed in the Soviet Championship several times since 1931. His outstanding achievements are in the composition of endgame studies, of which he is perhaps the world's leading exponent.

**Katetov, Dr Miroslav** (b. 7 March 1918) Czechoslovakian chess player; awarded the title International Master in 1950. He was champion of Prague in 1943 and came second in the 1946 Czechoslovakian Championship.

**Kavalek, Lubomir** (b. 9 August 1943) Originally Czechoslovakian, but since 1969 American chess player. He was awarded the titles International Master and International Grandmaster in 1965. (1976 Elo rating: 2540)

**Kažić, Bozidar** (b. 6 February 1921) Yugoslavian chess player, journalist and author of chess books. In 1954 he won the Yugoslavian Correspondence Chess Championship. He is a prominent chess official in his country and since 1960 has been a permanent delegate to FIDE. The important matches where Kažić was chief arbiter include U.S.S.R. v Rest of the World (Belgrade, 1970) and the Fischer-Taimanov match (Vancouver, 1971). Among his books on chess are *A Chess Handbook* (with M. Yudovich) and *International Championship Chess*, a complete record of FIDE events up to 1973.

**KB** *abbrev. for* King Bishop.

**KBP** *abbrev. for* King Bishop pawn.

**Keene, Raymond D.** (b. 29 January 1948) British chess player; awarded the titles International Master in 1972 and International Grandmaster in 1976. He was British Champion in 1971 and competed in the Chess Olympiads of 1966, 1968, 1970, 1972, 1974 and 1976. He was joint British Under-18 Champion in 1964 and competed in the 1965 World Junior Championship. He took part in several Student Olympiads and also played in the 1973 European Team Championship. Keene is the author of several books, including *A. Nimzovitch: A Reappraisal*, *Learn from the Grandmasters* (ed), *Karpov-Korchnoi 1974* (with W. R. Hartston), *Chess Olympiad Skopje 1972*, *Siegen Chess Olympiad*, *Chess Olympiad Nice 1974* and *How to Play the Opening in Chess* (the last four with D. N. L. Levy). By making norms at the Olympiads of 1974 and 1976 he became the second British player to be awarded the title of International Grandmaster. (1976 Elo rating: 2465)

**Kei** *Japanese for* honourable horse. Each side has two Kei in the game of Shogi. It can move like a Knight, but only to the two squares directly in advance of the Kei. When promoted it becomes a Nari-Kei and moves like a Kin. See **Shogi**.

**Keller, Dr Dieter** (b. 19 July 1936) Swiss chess player; awarded the title International Master in 1961. He was Swiss Champion in 1958, 1960, 1961 and 1963. He competed in the Chess Olympiads of 1956, 1958 and 1968. (1976 Elo rating: 2415)

**Kemeri (1937)** a tournament with eighteen competitors; equal first place was shared by Flohr, Petrov and Reshevsky (scoring 12 points each) ahead of Alekhine (11½) and Keres (11½).

**Kentucky Lion, The** *nickname of* Jackson Whipps Showalter.

**Keres Gambit** another name for the **Mason Gambit**.

**Keres, Paul Petrovitch** (1916–1975) Soviet chess player; awarded the title International Grandmaster in 1950. He was Estonian Champion in 1934 and competed for Estonia in the Chess Olympiads of 1935, 1937 and 1939. He was Soviet Champion in 1947, 1950 and 1951 and competed for the U.S.S.R. in every Chess Olympiad from 1952 to 1964. In addition, Keres took part in the 1948 World Championship match-tournament, in five Candidates' tournaments (coming second four times) and in one series of Candidates' matches.

He was born in Narva, Estonia on 7 January 1916 and learned to play chess at the age of four. At the age of 11 he won the lightning championship of Parnu with a perfect score and soon afterwards began to play correspondence chess to extend himself (playing up to 150 games simultaneously). His victory in the 1934 Estonian Championship led to his selection to play on first board in the subsequent Chess Olympiad, where he made a sensational debut by winning more games than any other player (+11 −5 =3). In the next two years Keres had a string of successes (of which Semmering was the most important) and in 1938 was invited to play in the Avro tournament. Here he tied for first place with Fine, but was placed ahead on a tie-breaking system. FIDE nominated him for a match with Alekhine, but Alekhine avoided any commitment on the grounds of a prior agreement to play Flohr.

In 1940, Estonia was merged into the U.S.S.R. and Keres became a Soviet citizen. He came second in the 1941 Absolute Championship and came third in the 1948 World Championship match-tournament. Subsequently, he played in numerous Candidates' tournaments but was always edged out of a match against the World Champion, first by

Smyslov (twice) and then by Tal and Petrosian. Keres died in Helsinki on 5 June 1975, shortly after his victory in the Vancouver Open.

**Kestler, Hans Günter** (b. 12 December 1939) West German chess player; awarded the title International Master in 1976. (1976 Elo rating: 2450)

**Kevitz-Trajković Defence** a defence to the Queen pawn opening: 1. P–Q4, N–KB3 2. P–QB4, N–B3. Like Alekhine's Defence, it tempts White to establish an advanced pawn centre which Black will later attack. The most common continuations are: 3. N–KB3, P–Q3 and 3. N–QB3, P–K4. It was devised by A. Kevitz and Trajković and has been played by the Soviet Grandmaster Anatoly Lutikov.

**key** the only initial move in a chess problem that allows it to be solved. Opinions as to what constitutes a good key have changed over the years. In the nineteenth century, dramatic sacrifices were the most highly regarded, but now quieter keys are preferred. Indeed, many now feel that keys that check or capture are too primitive and inartistic to be satisfying.

**Khan, Mir Sultan** see **Sultan Khan, Mir.**

**Kholmov, Ratmir Dmitrievich** (b. 13 May 1925) Soviet chess player; awarded the titles International Master in 1954 and International Grandmaster in 1960. His tournament career includes many first prizes, among them Belgrade (1967), Havana (1968) and Budapest (1976). (1976 Elo rating: 2550)

**kibitz** **1.** to comment on a game of chess within the hearing of its players. Kibitzing may take place during the game or in analysis afterwards.

**2.** any remark (especially if humorous) made by an onlooker during a game or in analysis afterwards.

Kibitz is derived from the Yiddish word *kiebitz* (see **kibitzer**).

**kibitzer** a bystander whose comments on a game of chess are clearly audible to its players. The term is derived from the Yiddish word *kiebtiz* (literally meaning peewit or lapwing and figuratively meaning busybody).

**kick** (slang) to attack a piece with a pawn. It is more commonly found in the United States than in the United Kingdom.

**Kieninger, Georg** (b. 5 June 1902) West German chess player; awarded the title International Master in 1950. He was German Champion in 1937 and 1940 and West German Champion in 1947.

**Kieseritzky Gambit** an opening sequence in the King's Gambit: 1. P–K4, P–K4 2. P–KB4, P×P 3. N–KB3, P–KN4 4. P–KR4, P–N5 5. *N–K5*. White has converted Black's advanced pawns into weak hanging pawns and if he can regain his gambit his strong centre will usually give him superiority. Black's best immediate reply: 5 . . ., N–KB3. This opening appears in Polerio and was analyzed by both Salvio and Philidor, but is named after the Livonian player, Lionel Kieseritzky, who played it often.

**Kieseritzky, Lionel** (1806–1853) a leading Livonian chess player. He was born in Dorpat, Estonia, but by 1839 had moved to Paris where he became a regular visitor to the Café de la Régence. Here he was soon recognized as the strongest player. Among his contributions to opening theory was the invention of the Kieseritzky Gambit and detailed research into the Bishop's Opening.

In 1851 he was invited to compete at the international chess tournament in London and was knocked out by Anderssen in the first round. After the tournament had ended he again played Anderssen and lost what is now known as the Immortal Game. Despite his defeat, Kieseritzky was delighted with the game and immediately cabled the moves to his friends in Paris. Two years later he died, insane and a pauper, in Paris. Only one person came to his funeral – a waiter from the Café de la Régence.

His style of play was of the romantic school. He was described by the Reverend Wayte as being 'essentially a gallery player, dealing chiefly in fireworks against weak opponents'.

**Kin** *Japanese for* gold general. Each side has two Kin in the game of Shogi. The Kin can move one square vertically, horizontally, or diagonally forwards, but cannot move diagonally backwards. It cannot be promoted. See **Shogi**.

**King** the only indispensable chessman, since rendering it helpless by means of checkmate is the object of chess. It is theoretically the weakest piece, being able to move only one square at a time in any direction except when castling. In the endgame, however, the King often becomes a highly aggressive piece and its skilful manipulation can be the deciding factor in the game. Symbol: **K**.

Potential moves of the King over unobstructed squares

**King-hunt** a sustained attack on a King which drives it from its defensive position across the board in an attempt to find safety. King-hunts often involve sacrificial combinations and, almost invariably, long sequences of checks.

***King, Queen and Knight*** an anthology of references to chess in prose and poetry compiled by Norman Knight and Will Guy. The pieces that it includes span several centuries and numerous countries. It was first published in 1975.

**King's Bishop Gambit** an opening sequence arising in the King's Gambit: 1. P–K4, P–K4 2. P–KB4, P×P 3. *B–B4*. White is prepared to lose his right to castle following a check from Black's Queen in return for discouraging the advance of Black's pawn to his Q4, with the consequent reduction in space. However, by playing 3 . . ., N–KB3 followed by P–B3 and P–Q4, Black can force the swapping of White's King pawn, after which his superior mobility should give him equality.

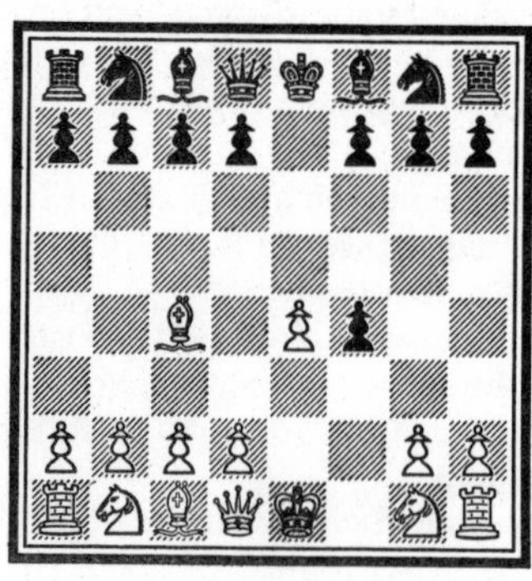

Position after 3. B–B4

**King's Fianchetto Defence** another name for the **Robatsch Defence.** This defence is characterized by a King-side fianchetto.

**King's Fianchetto Opening** another name for the **Benkö Opening.**

**King's Gambit** an opening sequence: 1. P–K4, P–K4 2. *P–KB4*. White offers a pawn for a stronger centre, a lead in development, and open lines of attack on the King side. This opening is first seen in Polerio's manuscript of the sixteenth century. It reached its zenith of popularity in the nineteenth century, but has now almost disappeared from competitive play due to the improvement in defensive technique.

**King's Gambit Declined** an opening sequence in which Black declines the immediate offer of White's pawn in the King's Gambit. Black has various ways of declining the King's Gambit of which the commonest is: 1. P–K4, P–K4 2. P–KB4, *B–B4*. Here Black attempts to retain his King pawn and hinder King-side castling by White. Other second moves used in declining the gambit are: 2 . . ., *P–Q3* and 2 . . ., N–KB3. The Falkbeer Counter Gambit illustrates another approach in declining the gambit by offering a pawn in return.

**King side** the files originally occupied by the King, King Bishop, King Knight and King Rook. Also called **King's wing.**

**King's Indian Attack** an opening sequence in which White adopts the typical formation of the King's Indian defence. For example: 1. N–KB3, P–Q4 2. P–KN3, P–QB4 3. B–N2, N–QB3 4. P–Q3, or 1. P–K4, P–K3 2. P–Q3, P–Q4 3. N–Q2, P–QB4 4. KN–B3, N–QB3 5. P–KN3. The characteristic difference between this and the Réti Opening is the intention of placing a pawn on K4 in the King's Indian Attack in place of the usual P–QB4 of the Réti.

**King's Indian Defence** a defence to the Queen's pawn opening: 1. P–Q4, N–KB3 2. P–QB4, P–KN3 with a later . . . P–Q3 by Black, distinguishing it from the Grünfeld with . . . P–Q4. Black will fianchetto his King Bishop, allow White to create a strong pawn centre and proceed to attack it. Other common features are Black's attempts to open the black-squared long diagonal and a pawn storm by Black's King-side pawns. Meanwhile White will use his advantage in space to squeeze Black's position. This is an extremely fluid defence; attacks may occur on the King side in one game and on the Queen side in another.

This defence was introduced by Louis Paulsen at Leipzig (1879) and was often played by Tchigorin, but was rarely seen until the hypermodern era, when it was played by the British players as well as by Réti and Tartakover. After New York (1927) it almost vanished from tournament play until Boleslavsky and Bronstein resurrected it in the 1940s. It is now one of the commonest openings.

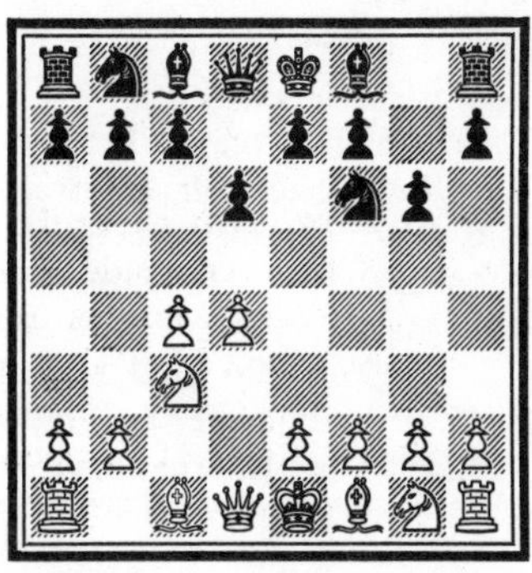

Position after 2 . . ., P–KN3 3. N–QB3, P–Q3

**King's Indian in Reverse** another name for **King's Indian Attack.**

**King's leap** a forerunner of castling in which the King was allowed to leap to another square once during the game. The rules concerning the King's leap varied over time and between regions – the Göttingen manuscript shows the King as being able to jump to any square that was two squares away; it could only do this once in a game, could not do it if the King had already moved or was in check and could not capture on the leap. This manuscript gives five examples of a King's leap to KN1 after the King Rook has moved to KB1, which is in effect King-side castling in two moves rather than one. Castling was invented in the late sixteenth century and had replaced the King's leap nearly everywhere by the beginning of the eighteenth century. Compare **castle, free castling.**

***King's Little Tragedy, The*** a unique German amateur film (1936) made by Richard Groschop. It is the only film about chess in which a game in progress is featured without players. The stone chessmen move about the board in a furious battle that eventually ends with the death of the White King.

**Kings of Chess** an account of the World Championship matches of the first half of the twentieth century written by William Winter. This is supplemented by brief biographies of the World Champions of this period: Lasker, Capablanca, Alekhine, Euwe and Botvinnik. It was first published in 1954 and uses descriptive notation.

**King's wing** another name for **King side**.

**Kirov, (Ivanov) Nino** (b. 11 September 1945) Bulgarian chess player; awarded the titles International Master in 1972 and International Grandmaster in 1975. He took part in the 1963 World Junior Championship and also in the 1974 Chess Olympiad. Other results include a second at the twelfth Rubinstein memorial tournament, Polanica Zdorj (1974). He was Bulgarian champion in 1973. (1976 Elo rating: 2485)

**KKt** *abbrev. for* King Knight used in descriptive notation in English-speaking countries. It is only used when **Kt** could also signify the Queen Knight. See also **KN**.

**KKtP** *abbrev. for* King Knight pawn used in descriptive notation in English-speaking countries. See also **KNP**.

**Klein, Ernst** (b. 1910) British chess player; British Champion in 1951.

**Klovan, Yanis** (b. 1935) Soviet chess player; awarded the title International Master in 1976. (1976 Elo rating: 2490)

**Kluger, Gyula** (b. 15 January 1914) Hungarian chess player; awarded the title International Master in 1954. He competed in the Chess Olympiads of 1954 and 1960. (1976 Elo rating: 2335)

**Kmoch, Hans** (1894–1973) American chess player; awarded the titles International Master in 1950 and International Judge in 1951. He was born in Austria on 25 July 1894 and competed for that country in the Chess Olympiads of 1927, 1930 and 1931. In the 1930s Kmoch emigrated to Holland and then to the United States. In 1950 he was the chief judge at the Dubrovnik Chess Olympiad.

Kmoch wrote several books, including *Rubinstein's Chess Masterpieces* and *Pawn Power in Chess*. In the latter work he attempted to explain the factors determining the proper deployment of the pawns and, to do this, devised a host of neologisms which have been included in this dictionary with the label 'Kmoch's term'. He died on 14 February 1973.

**KN** *symbol for* King Knight used in descriptive notation in English-speaking countries. It is only written down when **N** could also signify the Queen Knight. See also **KKt**.

**Knaak, Rainer** (b. 16 March 1953) East German chess player; awarded the titles International Master in 1973 and International Grandmaster in 1975. He was East German Champion in 1974 and competed in the 1972 Chess Olympiad. Other results include seconds at Halle (1974), Bucharest (1975) and the East German Championship (1975) and a fourth at Camaguey (1974). (1976 Elo rating: 2520)

**Kneževič, Milorad** (b. 1936) Yugoslavian chess player; awarded the title International Grandmaster in 1976. He was first at Olomouc (1975) and equal first at Čoka (1975) and Budapest (1975). (1976 Elo rating: 2460)

**Knight** a chessman that moves either one square horizontally and two squares vertically or two squares vertically and one square horizontally. Each side begins with two Knights which initially occupy the squares between the Rook and Bishop.

The Knight's move gives it certain peculiarities. Unlike the other men, it cannot be blocked although it too cannot land on a square already occupied by one of its own men. It can cover a maximum of eight squares when in the centre of the board, but this decreases to two when the Knight is on a corner square. Thus a Knight on the edge of the board is always in danger of being hemmed in and captured. Another unique property is that it lands on an opposite-coloured square with each move. The Knight's power varies during the game and with the position; it is strongest in the middle-game (when it is comparatively unhindered by pawn chains) and least effective in the endgame (when its lack of range can be a decisive weakness). Its approximate value is equal to that of three pawns or one Bishop.

The move of the Knight has remained unchanged throughout the history of chess and the meaning of its name has varied only slightly. Its Arabic name was *faras* (horse) and this was translated literally in many countries; in Europe, a word for 'horseman' was normally adopted. Interestingly, in many sets (including the Staunton chessmen) the piece is still symbolized by a horse rather than by its rider. Abbrev. **N** or (formerly) **Kt**.

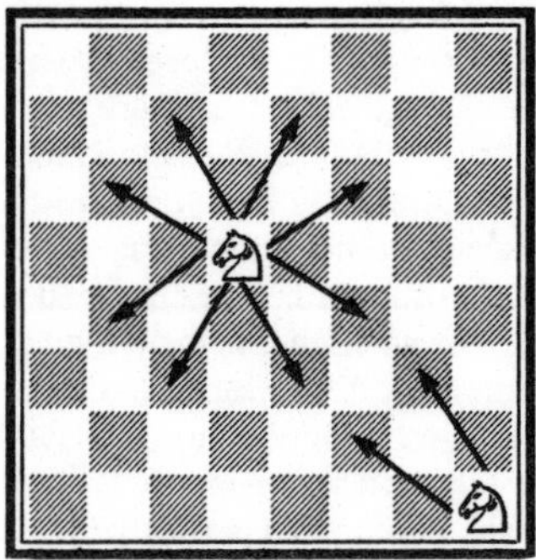

A Knight positioned at the edge of the board is severely restricted in its potential moves

**Knight fork** any double attack by the Knight. This is the most dangerous of all forks since the only attacked piece that can retaliate is another Knight. The possibility of a decisive Knight fork is the cause of the vast majority of underpromotions. See **fork**.

**Knight's tour** a chess problem in which a Knight must traverse the board, landing on each square once only. This is one of the most venerable tasks in chess, having been known since the Middle Ages. I. A. Horowitz and P. L. Rothenberg have stated that the number of possible Knight's Tours lies somewhere between 122,802,512 possibilities and 168!/(105!)(63!) where ! is the factorial symbol. Nevertheless, it is extremely difficult to discover a Knight's Tour unaided. One recommendation is to place the Knight initially on the edge of the board and then move it in the same direction wherever possible to the square from which there are the fewest exits.

| | | | | | | | |
|---|---|---|---|---|---|---|---|
| 34 | 47 | 22 | 11 | 36 | 49 | 24 | 1 |
| 21 | 10 | 35 | 48 | 23 | 12 | 37 | 50 |
| 46 | 33 | 64 | 55 | 38 | 25 | 2 | 13 |
| 9 | 20 | 61 | 58 | 63 | 54 | 51 | 26 |
| 32 | 45 | 56 | 53 | 60 | 39 | 14 | 3 |
| 19 | 8 | 59 | 62 | 57 | 52 | 27 | 40 |
| 44 | 31 | 6 | 17 | 42 | 29 | 4 | 15 |
| 7 | 18 | 43 | 30 | 5 | 16 | 41 | 28 |

An example of a Knight's tour

**Knight wheel** **1.** a common motif in problem chess in which a Knight achieves some objective by moving to a new square on each successive move, finally returning to its starting-point.

**2.** the eight squares covered by a Knight in the centre of the board.

**knock-out** a tournament in which the losers of the games played in that round or the holders of the lowest scores are progressively eliminated. In the former case this means that draws have to be replayed until decisive results are obtained. This is the oldest and simplest of tournaments, but has grave weaknesses. Strong players who are temporarily off-form will be eliminated before they can recover. If seeding is absent or inadequate the strongest players may eliminate one another before the final round. Both of these defects were met at London (1851): Löwenthal arrived from the United States in poor health after a journey of several weeks and was eliminated in the first round, Staunton was knocked out by Anderssen in the third round. Although proper seeding can eliminate the second difficulty other types of tournament are now more common. See **round-robin, Swiss System**.

**KNP** *symbol for* King Knight pawn used in descriptive notation in English-speaking countries. See also **KKtP**.

**Koch, Berthold** (b. 22 February 1899) East German chess player; awarded the titles International Master in 1950 and International Correspondence Master in 1959. He was East German Champion in 1951 and 1952 and competed in the Chess Olympiads of 1952 and

1956. Koch participated in the second Correspondence World Championship and came equal seventh.

**Koch notation** a concise method of recording the position, but not the moves, of a game. Each file and rank is assigned a number from one to eight counting from White's side of the board. Thus the Queen Rook file is given the number one, the Queen file is given the number four, the King Knight file is given the number seven, etc. In the same way, White's first rank (and thus Black's eighth rank) is given the number one, his fourth rank is given the number four, his seventh rank is given the number seven, etc. The men are identified by their normal abbreviations and each square is shown by a two-figure combination whose first number identifies the file and whose second number identifies the rank. This means that a checkmate position with White's King and Queen on his K6 and QR8 respectively and with Black's King on his K1 would be written down as – White: K56, Q18, Black: K58.

This system of notation was invented by the nineteenth-century player J. F. W. Koch. Compare **Forsyth notation.**

**Kochiev, Alexander** (b. 23 March 1956) Soviet chess player; awarded the title International Master in 1975. He was first at Lvov (1974) and equal first at Sochi (1975). (1976 Elo rating: 2460)

**Kolarov, Atanas Stefanov** (b. 2 March 1934) Bulgarian chess player; awarded the title International Master in 1957. He competed in the Chess Olympiads of 1956, 1960, 1962, 1966 and 1968. (1976 Elo rating: 2435)

**Kolibri Opening** another name for the **Spike**.

**Kolisch, Ignatz von** (1837–1889) one of the leading Austro-Hungarian chess players of the nineteenth century. Kolisch was born in Pressburg, Hungary. By 1858 he was in Paris and visiting the Café de la Regence where he learned to play chess. He quickly became good enough to become a chess professional and to draw a match against Anderssen. A prospective match with Morphy did not materialize as Kolisch refused to play without a stake and Morphy refused to play with one. In 1860 Kolisch visited England where he defeated Horwitz in a match (+3 −1), lost to Anderssen (+3 −4 =2), and drew by agreement with Paulsen after 31 games (+6 −7 =18). His match against Anderssen was notable as being the first to be played with a set time limit for a number of moves rather than for a limit for each move; the players each had to make 24 moves in two hours.

Kolisch's tournament results were erratic. At Bristol (1861) he could only finish seventh, but at Paris (1867) he came first in front of Steinitz. Many believed Kolisch to be a stronger player than Steinitz and certainly a more exciting one. According to Zukertort, 'Kolisch is a tiger who jumps at your throat, while Steinitz is a pickpocket who steals a pawn and keeps it'.

In 1868 Kolisch retired from active chess to become a banker under the patronage of Baron Albert Rothschild. His active chess career barely lasted a decade. However, he sponsored several tournaments including Baden-Baden (1870) and Vienna (1882). Kolisch became a

Baron of the Austrian Empire in 1881 and died in Vienna in 1889, reputedly a millionaire.

**Koltanowski, George** (b. 17 September 1903) American chess player; awarded the titles International Master in 1950 and International Judge. He was Belgian Champion in 1923, 1927, 1930, 1932 (with K. Dyner) and 1936 and competed in the Chess Olympiads of 1927 and 1928. Koltanowski (nicknamed 'Kolti') is a strong blindfold player and in 1937 created a new world record by playing 34 blindfold games simultaneously (+24 −0 =10). An American citizen for many years, Koltanowski is President of the U.S.C.F. He has written several books among which are *Adventures of a Chess Master* and *With the Chess Masters*.

**Kolti** *nickname of* **George Koltanowski.**

**König, Anton** (1836–1911) Bohemian composer of chess problems, born in what is now part of Czechoslovakia.

**König, Imre** (b. 9 February 1901) British chess player; awarded the title International Master in 1951. He was born in Kula, Hungary and became a Yugoslavian citizen when this region became part of Yugoslavia after the First World War. In 1938 König emigrated to the United Kingdom, becoming a naturalized citizen 11 years later; in 1953 he moved to the United States. König competed for Yugoslavia in the Chess Olympiads of 1931 and 1935 and in the former event had the best percentage result of any reserve player (+5 −1 =2). He has written several books, including *The Queen's Indian Defence* and *Chess from Morphy to Botvinnik*.

**Konstantinopolsky, Alexander Markovich** (b. 19 February 1910) Soviet chess player; awarded the title International Master in 1950. His best results were equal second in the 1937 U.S.S.R. Championship, equal fourth in the 1945 U.S.S.R. Championship and fifth in the 1950 U.S.S.R. Championship. He is also a well-known trainer, his pupils having included Bronstein and Lipnitsky.

**Korchnoi, Victor Lyovich** (b. 23 July 1931) awarded the titles International Master in 1954 and International Grandmaster in 1956. He was Soviet Champion in 1960, 1962 and 1964 and competed in the Chess Olympiads of 1960, 1966, 1968, 1970, 1972 and 1974. He has taken part in three interzonals, a Candidates' tournament and three series of Candidates' matches.

Korchnoi was born in Leningrad and learned to play chess at the comparatively late age of 13. Within three years he was Soviet Junior Champion and in 1950 came second in the Leningrad Championship. Korchnoi became a Soviet Master in 1951 and came second in the 1954 Soviet Championship.

In 1962 Korchnoi competed in his first interzonal and qualified for the subsequent Candidates' tournament, in which he came fifth. In the 1967 interzonal, Korchnoi came third and in the following Candidates' matches defeated Reshevsky (+3 −0 =5) and Tal (+2 −1 =7) before losing to Spassky (+1 −4 =5).

In the 1971 Candidates' series of matches Korchnoi defeated Geller in the quarter-finals (+4 −1 =3), but then lost to Petrosian (+0 −1 =9). Korchnoi won the 1973 Leningrad interzonal and defeated Mecking (+3 −1 =9) and Petrosian (+3 −1 =1), before meeting Karpov in the finals of the Candidates' matches. This became, in effect, a World Championship match due to Fischer's relinquishment of his title and Korchnoi narrowly lost (+2 −3 =19). In June 1976 after coming equal first at the I.B.M. tournament in Holland, Korchnoi defected to the West. (1976 Elo rating: 2670)

**Kostich, Boris** (1887–1963) Yugoslavian chess player; awarded the title International Master in 1950. He was born in Vrsac on 24 February 1887. His results included firsts at Stockholm (1913), Hastings (1921), Trentschin-Teplitz (1928) and Ljublijana (1938). Between 1913 and 1918 he travelled throughout North and South America and was very successful in chess. He won a match against Showalter in 1916 (+7 −2 =5), and this, plus his record in tournaments against Capablanca (+0 −0 =5), led to a match between the two in 1919, but after losing the first five games Kostich withdrew. He later competed in the Chess Olympiads of 1927, 1931, 1935 and 1937. Kostich was also a strong blindfold player and in 1916 broke the then current world record by playing twenty blindfold games simultaneously. He died in Belgrade on 3 November 1963.

**Kotov, Alexander** (b. 12 August 1913) Soviet chess player; awarded the titles International Grandmaster in 1950 and International Judge in 1951. He was joint Soviet Champion in 1948 and competed in the Chess Olympiads of 1952 and 1954. Kotov took part in the interzonals of 1948 and 1952 and in the latter event set a record that lasted eighteen years by going undefeated through the event, finishing three points ahead of Petrosian and Taimanov, who shared second place. He qualified for the subsequent Candidates' tournaments, which were held in 1950 and 1953, and finished in sixth place on both occasions.

Kotov has written a number of books on chess subjects, among which *The Soviet School of Chess* (written in collaboration with M. Yudovich), *Think like a Grandmaster*, and *Alexander Alekhine* have been translated. (1976 Elo rating: 2500)

**Kottnauer, Cenek** (b. 24 February 1910) British chess player, awarded the titles International Master in 1950 and International Judge in 1951. Originally Czechoslovakian, he represented that country in the 1952 Chess Olympiad where he had the best result of any player (+10 −0 =5). In 1953 he sought asylum in Switzerland and later emigrated to the United Kingdom. He competed for England in the Chess Olympiads of 1964 and 1968.

**Kouatly, Bachar** Lebanese chess player; awarded the title International Master in 1975. (1976 Elo rating: 2370)

**Kovacevic, Vladimir** (b. 26 March 1942) Yugoslavian chess player; awarded the titles International Master in 1970 and International Grandmaster in 1976. (1976 Elo rating: 2480)

**Kovács, László** (b. 5 October 1938) Hungarian chess player; awarded the title International Master in 1965. (1976 Elo rating: 2405)

**Kozma, Julius** (b. 1 June 1929) Czechoslovakian chess player; awarded the title International Master in 1957. He competed in the Chess Olympiads of 1958 and 1960 and was Czechoslovakian Champion in 1967. (1976 Elo rating: 2375)

**KP** *abbrev. for* King pawn.

**KR** *abbrev. for* King Rook.

**KRP** *abbrev. for* King Rook pawn.

**Kraidman, Yair** (b. 1 November 1932) Israeli chess player; awarded the titles International Master in 1965 and International Grandmaster in 1976. He has competed in several chess Olympiads since 1958 and his tournament results include a first at Netanya (1974). (1976 Elo rating: 2465)

**Kramer, Haije** (b. 24 November 1917) Dutch chess player; awarded the title International Master in 1954. He competed in the Chess Olympiads of 1950, 1952, 1956, 1958, 1960 and 1962. (1976 Elo rating: 2330)

**Kriegspiel** *German for* wargame. A variant of chess in which each player knows only the position and strength of his own forces and must deduce the position and strength of the opposing forces, which are out of sight. A third person is needed to act as umpire and keep track of the whole position on a third board. The umpire announces when a move has been made together with certain extra information. He informs both players when a capture has been made as well as identifying the square where the capture occurred, but discloses neither the capturing nor the captured man. Checks are also announced as well as the direction from which they come – e.g. on a rank, file, long or short diagonal, or by a Knight. The umpire will also warn a man when he is attempting to make an illegal move, such as moving to a square already occupied by an opposing man. The only information the players may seek is to ask if any captures by their pawns are possible. If the answer is yes the questioner must make at least one attempt to capture with a pawn. Kriegspiel strains each player's deductive faculty at least as much as it does his ability in playing chess. It was devised during the Boer War at the beginning of the century by Michael Henry Temple, a British journalist. The name was adopted from wargaming, which is a hobby involving the manoeuvring of model soldiers on artificial terrain with each player having only partial knowledge of his opponent's movements.

(1976 Elo rating: 2570)

**Krnić, Zdenko** (b. 2 October 1947) Yugoslavian chess player; awarded the title International Master in 1976. (1976 Elo rating: 2400)

**Krogius, Nikolai** (b. 22 July 1930) Soviet chess player; awarded the titles International Master in 1963 and International Grandmaster in 1964. Krogius is a professional psychologist and acted in this capacity when he was Spassky's second in the world championship match (1972).

**Kt** *symbol for* Knight used in chess notation. See also **N.**

**Kuijpers, Franciscus Antonius** (b. 27 February 1941) Dutch chess player; awarded the title International Master in 1964. He was Dutch

Champion in 1963 and competed in the Chess Olympiads of 1964, 1968 and 1976. (1976 Elo rating: 2430)

**Kupper, Josef** (b. 10 March 1932) Swiss chess player; awarded the title International Master in 1955. He was Swiss Champion in 1954, 1957, and 1962. He competed in the Chess Olympiads of 1954, 1958, 1964 and 1968. (1976 Elo rating: 2380)

**Kuprejanov, George** (b. 6 March 1938) Canadian chess player; awarded the title International Master in 1972. (1976 Elo rating: 2365)

**Kurajica, Bojan** (b. 15 November 1947) Yugoslavian chess player; awarded the titles International Master in 1965 (on becoming World Junior Champion) and International Grandmaster in 1973. His tournament results include firsts at Wijk aan Zee Masters tournament (1974) and Costa Brava (1974). (1976 Elo rating: 2525)

**Kushnir, Alla** (b. 11 August 1941) Israeli chess player. She was awarded the title International Master in 1962 and unsuccessfully contested the women's World Championship Final in 1965, 1969 and 1972. Kushnir was born in Georgia in the U.S.S.R., but has now emigrated to Israel where she plays under her married name of Stein. Her style of play has been described as positional in direct contrast to that of Gaprindashvili. (1976 Elo rating: 2320)

**Kuzmin, Gennady** (b. 19 January 1946) Soviet chess player; awarded the title International Grandmaster in 1973. He competed in the 1973 Leningrad interzonal, where he came seventh. (1976 Elo rating: 2565)

**Kyo** *Japanese for* pikeman. Each side has two Kyo in the game of Shogi. It can move forwards like a Rook, but cannot move sideways or retreat. When promoted it becomes a Nari-Kyo and moves like a Kin. See **Shogi**.

# L

**La Bourdonnais, Louis Charles Mahé de** (1797–1840) French chess player; world's strongest player from 1821 until his death. La Bourdonnais learned the game from visits to the Café de la Régence and was soon befriended by Deschapelles. By 1821 the latter could no longer successfully give La Bourdannais odds of pawn and two moves and retired rather than play on even terms. La Bourdannais, now a chess professional, was by then the strongest player in France and played every opportunity. Between noon and midnight on any day he could be found playing chess at his special table at the Régence when he was in Paris. From 1825 he regularly visited London and in 1834 he played six matches with Alexander McDonnell, London's strongest player, and won decisively (+45 −27 =13). La Bourdannais was also the author of *Une Traité sur le Jeu des Échecs (A Study of the Game of Chess)*, the founder and editor of *Le Palamède*, and a noted blindfold player. By 1840 prolonged ill-health had left him penniless and he accepted an invitation to work at the Divan in London for two guineas a week. However, his health broke down soon after arriving and he died in London 13 December 1840.

**Landstrasse Gambit** another name for the **Alfred Wolf Gambit**. Landstrasse is German for highway.

**Lange, Max** (1832–1899) German chess player and author of several books on chess. He won first prize in international tournaments at Aix la Chapelle (1867) and Hamburg (1868). Among the new modes of opening play he invented is the one now known as the **Max Lange Attack**.

**Langeweg, Kristian** (b. 7 March 1937) Dutch chess player; awarded the title International Master in 1962. He competed in the Chess Olympiads of 1960, 1962, 1964, 1966 (when he scored the highest percentage on fourth board with 80%), 1968, 1970, 1972 and 1974. (1976 Elo rating: 2450)

**LARA chess congress** an annual London chess congress sponsored by the Lambeth Arts and Recreations Association. It first took place in 1974 (when the open tournament was won by A. J. Miles) and normally consists of at least three separate tournaments.

**Larsen, Bent** (b. 4 March 1935) Danish chess player; awarded the titles International Master in 1955 and International Grandmaster in 1956. He has won the Danish Championship on each of the six occasions that he has played in it and has competed in the Chess Olympiads of 1954, 1956, 1958, 1966, 1968 and 1970. He has played in six interzonals (winning three) and qualified for four series of Candidates' matches.

Larsen represented Denmark in the 1951 World Junior Championship and finished in equal fourth place; two years later he again played in this competition and finished in equal fifth place. In 1954, after winning the Danish Championship for the first time, he played on first board in that year's Chess Olympiad and performed well enough to become an International Master. Two years later he obtained an even better result in this competition by obtaining the highest score on first board (+11 −1 =6) to become an International Grandmaster.

Larsen first played in an interzonal in 1958, when he came sixteenth; subsequently, he came first in the interzonals of 1964, 1967 and 1976. Apart from Fischer, Larsen is the strongest Western chess player of the last two decades. His play is consistently creative and aggressive and ends much more often in victory or defeat, rather than in a draw, than the play of most of his contemporaries. Although he is a better tournament than match player, he was the first non-Russian to defeat a Soviet Grandmaster in a match by beating Geller in 1966 (+3 −2 =4). Other match results include a victory over Ivkov in 1965 (+4 −1 =3); a loss to Tal in 1965 (+2 −3 =5), but a win over him in 1969 (+4 −1 =3); a victory over Portisch in 1968 (+3 −2 =5); a loss to Spassky in the same year (+1 −4 =3); a victory over Uhlmann in 1971 (+4 −2 =3); a loss to Fischer in 1971 (+0 −6 =0); and a loss to Andersson in 1975 (+2 −5 =1). His tournament successes are numerous and include firsts at Le Havre (1966), Havana (1967), Winnipeg (1967), Monte Carlo (1968), Büsum (1969), Teesside (1972), Hastings (1972) and Orense (1975). (1976 Elo rating: 2625)

**Larsen's Opening** an opening where White plays 1. P–QN3. White waits for Black to commit himself in the centre before developing his men. There are many good continuations for Black. This opening has become popular in the last decade, following its adoption by the Danish Grandmaster Bent Larsen (after whom it is named). Also called **Nimzovitch Attack, Queen's Fianchetto Opening.**

**Lasa, Baron Tassilo von Heydebrand und der** (1818–1899) German chess historian and theoretician. In 1836 he joined the Berlin Chess Club, where he met the six men who eventually formed the famous Berlin Pleiades with him. Von der Lasa conceived the idea of compiling and publishing a German handbook on chess openings, which he finished after initial contributions by P. R. von Bilguer (1813–1840). It was published in 1843 under the name *Handbuch des Schachspiels*. In 1853, Von der Lasa won a match (+3 –4 =3) against Howard Staunton.

After a career in the diplomatic service (1845–1865), Von der Lasa retired to concentrate on writing about chess and assembled a vast library on all aspects of the game. He died in 1899.

**Lasker, Edward** (b. 3 December 1885) American chess player; awarded the titles International Judge in 1956 and International Master in 1963. Originally German, Lasker was working in London as an engineer at the outbreak of World War I and moved to the United States, where he became a citizen in 1921. He was Berlin Champion in 1909, London Champion in 1914, New York Champion in 1915, and Western States Champion in 1916, 1917, 1919, 1920 and 1921. In 1923 he narrowly lost a match against Marshall for the U.S. Championship (+4 –5 =9), but his excellent performance led to his inclusion at New York (1924) in which he came fifth, drawing with Alekhine, Capablanca and Emanuel Lasker.

Undoubtedly the oldest international player of all time, Lasker took part in the 1976 telex match between London and New York at the age of 90. He has written several books including *The Adventure of Chess*, *Chess, Chess for Fun and Chess for Blood* and *Chess Secrets* (his autobiography).

**Lasker, Emanuel** (1868–1941) German chess player, World Champion from 1894 to 1921; born in Berlinchen on 24 December 1868. The son of a cantor, Lasker was sent to Berlin at the age of 11 to study mathematics and was there taught to play chess by his elder brother, Berthold. He was soon a frequent visitor at the Café Kaiserhof, a chess meeting-place, and in 1889 became a German Master by winning the Breslau ***Hauptturnier***. From then until his emigration to the United States in 1892 he successfully competed in several tournaments and matches, defeating Blackburne and Bird among others. In 1893 Lasker won all his games in the tournament at New York and challenged Steinitz to a match for the title. The outcome surprised almost everyone for the relatively unknown Lasker won comfortably (+10 –5 =4) and won the return match two years later even more decisively (+10 –2 =5). Many ascribed these results to Steinitz's age, but Lasker proved himself a worthy champion by coming third at Hastings (1895) and first at St Petersburg (1895) – the two strongest tournaments up to that time. Other results in the period up to 1914 included firsts at London (1899), Paris (1909) and St Petersburg (1909 and 1914).

Lasker never considered himself to be exclusively a chess player; in 1909 he gained his Ph.D. in mathematics at the university of Erlange. During this period he also wrote three works on philosophy. This partially accounted for the hiatus between his second match with Steinitz and his next title defence; but within four years from 1907 he defended his title six times! In 1907 he played Marshall after four years of negotiations and won easily (+8 −0 =7). In 1908 he at last met Tarrasch. A great antipathy existed between the two players and they refused to talk to each other during the match. By this time Tarrasch was past his peak and Lasker won with little difficulty (+8 −3 =5). Lasker played matches against Janowski in 1909 and 1910 and won both times (+7 −1 =2 and +8 −0 =3). These matches were separated by the hardest match of Lasker's career. In January 1910 he met Carl Schlechter in a short match of ten games. Schlechter took the lead in the fifth game and needed only to draw the last game to become World Champion. Tragically for Schlechter he obtained a winning position, but eventually lost the game, allowing Lasker to retain the title (+1 −1 =8). Schlechter refused an offer to extend the match for reasons of fatigue and ill-health.

Negotiations for a match against Rubinstein or Capablanca were suspended after the outbreak of World War I and after it Capablanca had become the obvious contender. Negotiations were finally concluded, but in 1920 Lasker conceded the title without a fight. His poverty as a result of the war led him to be persuaded to change his mind, but in the match he played listlessly and conceded the title after 14 of the 24 games (+0 −4 =10).

Lasker spent two years in retirement and then in 1923 (at the age of 55) returned to chess. In an unprecedented come-back he came first at Mahrisch-Ostrau (1923) and New York (1924) and came second at Moscow (1925), easily holding his own against the new generation of players. Satisfied, he retired again; but the rise of Hitler turned Lasker and his wife into impoverished refugees and Lasker was forced to support himself by chess yet again.

In this third phase of his career Lasker came fifth at Zurich (1934), third at Moscow (1935) – only half a point behind Botvinnik and Flohr – sixth at Moscow (1936) and seventh at Nottingham (1936), all impressive performances in extremely strong events. After Nottingham, Lasker finally retired and settled first in the U.S.S.R. and then in the United States. He died in New York on 11 January 1941.

Lasker had no overt disciples, unlike Steinitz or Tarrasch, and there is not even general agreement as to the characteristics of his style of play. Réti maintained that he played the psychologically best moves if not the objectively best ones and that he forced games into the most uncongenial channel for his opponent. Others maintain that Lasker played the board and not the man and saved himself from losing positions by his enormous fighting spirit rather than as the result of a deliberate plan of campaign. Undoubtedly for Lasker chess was not primarily a game, art or science, but a fight which the more determined player won.

**Lasker's Defence** an opening sequence arising out of the Queen's Gambit Declined: 1. P–Q4, P–Q4 2. P–QB4, P–K3 3. N–QB3, N–KB3 4. B–N5, B–K2 5. P–K3, O–O 6. N–B3, P–KR3 7. B–R4, *N–K5*; 8. B × B, *Q × B*. The wholesale exchanges that are likely to result in this variation increase the freedom of Black's pieces, although theory maintains that White can keep a small advantage. The most common continuation is: 9. P × P, N × N 10. P × N, P × P. This defence was devised by the former World Champion Emanuel Lasker.

***Lasker's Manual of Chess*** a textbook on chess by the former World Champion Emanuel Lasker. Although it teaches the basic rules of the game, it is mainly of value to the advanced and intermediate player. Of particular interest is its exposition of the theories of Steinitz. The English edition, which was translated by Lasker himself, was first published in 1932 and uses descriptive notation.

**Lasker's Variation** see **Lasker's Defence.**

**Lasker trap** a trap that arises in the Albin Counter Gambit in the following way: 1. P–Q4, P–Q4 2. P–QB4, P–K4 3. P × KP, P–Q5 4. P–K3?, *B–N5ch* 5. B–Q2, *P × P!* 6. B × B, *P × Pch* 7. K–K2, P × N=Nch! with a winning position.

Position after 7 . . ., P × N=Nch (if the Rook captures, 8 . . ., B–N5ch, winning White's Queen)

**Las Palmas** the major town of Grand Canary in the Canary Isles; the scene of an annual international chess tournament since 1972. This tournament is mainly sponsored by the Caja de Ahorros (Savings Bank). The winners of Las Palmas tournaments have been as follows: 1972, Portisch; 1973, Stein and Petrosian; 1974, Ljubojevic; 1975, Ljubojevic; 1976, Geller.

**Last Knight of the King's Gambit, The** *descriptive phrase for* Rudolf Spielmann.

**Latvian Gambit** an opening sequence that arises in the King's pawn opening in the following way: 1. P–K4, P–K4 2. N–KB3, *P–KB4*. White has many promising replies, including 3. N × P, 3. B–B4 and 3. P–Q4, any of which should gain the advantage. Polerio attributed the invention of this gambit to Giovanni Leonardo, but it is named after the Latvian masters, led by K. Behting, who have analysed it in this century. Also called **Greco Counter Gambit**.

**Laufer** *German for* runner. English equivalent: Bishop. See **Bishop**.

***Laws of Chess, The*** an authorized English translation of the official rules or laws of chess as established by FIDE, edited and revised by H. Golombek (a member of the FIDE Rules Commission). The fourth edition was published in 1975.

**Lazarević, Milunka** (b. 1 December 1932) Yugoslavian female chess player; awarded the title International Woman Grandmaster in 1976. She took part in every Women's Candidates' tournament and Candidates' competition between 1955 and 1971. (1976 Elo rating: 2200)

**Leaper** one of the three main types of Fairy chesspiece. It moves directly from starting square to destination and jumps over any interposing man. An orthodox leaper is the Knight. Examples of heterodox leaper are the Camel, Giraffe and Zebra. Compare **Rider, Hopper**.

***Learn Chess from the Masters*** a collection of ten games compiled by Fred Reinfeld. Each game has points assigned to every move and sound alternative. By totalling up the score of the moves he guessed correctly, the reader is able to discover his approximate playing strength. The book was first published in 1946 and uses descriptive notation.

**Lederman, Leon** (b. 25 May 1947) Soviet-born but now Israeli chess player; awarded the title International Master in 1976. (1976 Elo rating: 2420)

**lee** (Kmoch's term) that part of a rank divided by a pawn, which has the fewer squares. Compare **luff**. See ***Pawn Power in Chess***.

**Lee, Peter N.** (b. 21 November 1943) British chess player; British Champion in 1965.

**Légal's Mate** a mating sequence that was first recorded as being played by M. de Kermar, Sire de Légal (1702–1792). An example of it took place in the game between Légal and Saint Brie in 1750. From the diagrammed position printed on p.167, play continued: 1. N × P, B × Q 2. B × Pch, K–K2 3. N–Q5 mate.

**Lehmann, Dr Heinz** (b. 20 October 1921) West German chess player; awarded the title International Master in 1961. He competed in the Chess Olympiads of 1958 and 1960. (1976 Elo rating: 2375)

**Lein, Anatoly Yakovlenich** (b. 28 March 1931) Soviet-born chess player, now resident in the United States; awarded the titles International Master in 1964 and International Grandmaster in 1968. (1976 Elo rating: 2515)

**Lemberg Gambit** another name for the **Zukertort Gambit**.

**Lengyel, Levente** (b. 13 June 1933) Hungarian chess player; awarded the titles International Master in 1962 and International Grandmaster in 1964. He played in the 1964 interzonal tournament, where he finished in 12th place. (1976 Elo rating: 2400)

**Légal's Mate**

Légal vs. Saint Brie (1750)

**Leningrad Variation** **1.** an opening sequence arising out of the Dutch Defence: 1. P–Q4, P–KB4 2. N–KB3, N–KB3 3. P–KN3, *P–KN3*. Black attempts to transpose into a favourable variant of the King's Indian Defence with control of the long diagonal by the King Bishop and an advanced King Bishop pawn, which can form the start of a King-side pawn storm. However, Black's third move weakens Black's King side; White will also eventually usually be able to move his Queen pawn forward to Q5 creating a hole for Black on his K3.

This variation was devised in the 1950s by a group of Leningrad players which included Kopylov, Korchnoi and Vinogradov.

**2.** another name for the **Spassky Variation**.

**Leo** a Fairy chesspiece that moves like a normal Queen except when capturing. To capture a piece the Leo must jump over it, landing on any square that is directly on its path. The Leo can move without capturing, when it moves like an orthodox Queen. The Leo, the Pao and the Vao were introduced from Chinese chess by T. R. Dawson.

**Leonardo, Giovanni** (1542–1587) Italian chess player, one of the best of his era. Leonardo left his home in Cutri, Calabria to study law in Rome, but soon became well-known as a chess player. There he was nicknamed 'il Puttino' (the boy). By 1560 he had become sufficiently famous for Ruy Lopez to play him twice when he visited the city in that year. Leonardo lost both games and, it is said, was so upset by this that he spent the next two years studying the game. In 1574 he travelled to Spain with two other players and defeated Ruy Lopez in the presence of Philip II. By 1587 Leonardo had become agent to the prince of Bisignano and it was there that he was poisoned by a rival.

**Lesser Bishop's Gambit** an opening sequence arising in the King's Gambit: 1. P–K4, P–K4 2. P–KB4, P×P 3. *B–K2*. After 3 . . ., P–Q4 Black can equalize with little difficulty.

**Letelier, Martner René** (b. 21 February 1915) Chilean chess player; awarded the title International Master in 1960. He has frequently won the Chilean Championship and competed in the Chess Olympiads of 1939, 1950, 1956, 1960 and 1966. (1976 Elo rating: 2350)

**leucopenia** (Kmoch's term) insufficient control of the light squares. This normally arises when the light-squared Bishop has been exchanged and the pawns placed on black squares. Compare **melanpenia, monochromy**. See ***Pawn Power in Chess***.

**Levenfish, Grigori** (1889–1961) Soviet chess player; awarded the title International Grandmaster in 1950. Levenfish was born on 9 March 1889. His first international tournament was Carlsbad (1911) where his style of play was likened to Tchigorin's. Levenfish's tournament career lasted for nearly fifty years and included numerous successes. Undoubtedly his greatest achievement was drawing a match with Botvinnik in 1937, since this meant that he retained the Soviet Championship, which he had won in 1934. Levenfish was a supreme tactician, but also made many contributions to opening theory. He died on 9 February 1961.

**lever** (Kmoch's term) a situation that exists when hostile pawns are diagonally adjacent. This means that each can capture the other, but frequently the one who captures first weakens his pawn formation relative to that of his opponent. As a result, each will often try to make the other capture first and this tension is comparable to the stress on a lever; hence the term. Compare **centre lever, chain lever, double lever, inner lever, loose lever, mute chain lever, outer lever, pincer lever, tight lever**. See ***Pawn Power in Chess***.

**Levitina, Irina** (b. 8 June 1954) Soviet female chess player; awarded the title International Woman Grandmaster in 1976. She was the Soviet reserve in the 1972 Women's Olympiad and in 1975 narrowly lost to Alexandria (+3 −4 =10) in a match to decide the qualifier for the subsequent World Championship match. (1976 Elo rating: 2335)

**Lewis chessmen** a collection of chessmen discovered in 1831 on the Isle of Lewis in the Outer Hebrides. There are 67 men, forming the remnants of at least four sets, made of natural ivory and undifferentiated in colour. The men have slightly different markings to distinguish them. The origin of the Lewis chessmen is uncertain, but they were probably made in either the British Isles or Iceland in the twelfth century. They are now in the British Museum.

**Lewis, William** (1787–1870) British chess player and writer; born in Birmingham, England on 9 October 1787. In his youth Lewis was a pupil of J. H. Sarratt and upon Sarratt's death was regarded as the strongest player in the country. In 1819 he briefly operated the Turk and in 1821 visited France where he defeated Deschapelles (+1 −0 =2). Lewis opened some chess rooms in 1825, but went bankrupt two years later and turned increasingly to writing. The Second Series of his *Progressive Lessons*, an amalgam of the ideas of the Italian and Philidorean schools, was published in 1832 and greatly influenced the development of chess, becoming the basis of the *Handbuch des*

*Schachspiels*. Lewis rarely played chess in later life; he died on 22 August 1870.

**Liberzon, Vladimir** (b. 23 March 1937) Israeli chess player; awarded the titles International Master in 1963 and International Grandmaster in 1965. He was born in the Soviet Union, but emigrated to Israel in 1973 and represented that country on first board in the Olympiads of 1974 and 1976. He was Israeli champion in 1975 and qualified for the Biel (1976) interzonal tournament by winning a toss-up after a drawn play-off match with Parma.

**Lichtenhein, Theodor** (1829–1874) American amateur chess player; born in Königsberg, Prussia. He emigrated to the United States as a youth and took up residence in New York. Lichtenhein competed in the First American Chess Congress and came third, being knocked out by Morphy in the third round. In 1858 he was elected president of the New York Chess Club.

**lightning chess** a general term for any quick game of chess, with or without timing of the game. It refers particularly, however, to **five-second chess, ten-second chess,** or **five-minute chess.**

**light piece** another name for **minor piece**. The light pieces are the Knights and the Bishops.

**Lilienthal, Andrei Arnoldovich** (b. 5 May 1911) Soviet chess player; awarded the title International Grandmaster in 1950. Lilienthal was born in Moscow, but his family emigrated to Hungary two years later. Consequently he played for Hungary in the Chess Olympiads of 1933 (where he had the highest score for a reserve player), 1935 (where he had the highest score on second board) and 1937 (where he played on first board).

Lilienthal competed at Moscow (1935) and was impressed by the widespread interest in chess; in 1939 he became a Soviet citizen. He was joint Soviet Champion with Bondarevsky in 1940; his other results include a first at Barcelona (1934), a second at Budapest (1934) and a fourth at Moscow (1936). Lilienthal now rarely plays tournament chess, concentrating instead upon his work as a chess trainer and writer. He returned to Hungary in 1976.

**Lipschütz, Solomon** (1863–1905) American chess player, U.S. Champion 1891–1894. Lipschütz was the leading American player at New York (1891) where he finished sixth, and claimed the title of U.S. Champion upon George Mackenzie's death later in the year. J. W. Showalter disputed the claim, but was defeated in a match for the title (10½–4½). In 1895, however, Showalter defeated him in a second championship match. Lipschütz's other major success was victory in the Manhattan Chess Club tournament (1900) when Marshall finished in eighth and last place.

**liquidation** **1.** a policy of exchanging men to blunt the opponent's attack. Reasons for liquidation could include the need to free a cramped defensive position, to ease tension in the centre, and to catch up in development by exchanging off the opponent's more developed pieces. The term was coined by Nimzovitch.

**2.** a policy of exchanging men to increase the value of a material advantage by simplifying to an easily won ending. For example, the winning of the exchange may prove insignificant in the middle-game, but as men are exchanged the material advantage will steadily increase in importance and may eventually become the decisive winning factor.

**Lisitzin, Georgi** (1909–1972) Soviet chess player; awarded the title International Master in 1950. Lisitzin won the Leningrad Championship three times and won the Soviet Trade-Union Championship of 1936. He was at one time a leading exponent of Réti's Opening. He died on 20 March 1972.

**Little Bare King** a type of win in which the capture involved in baring the King does not deliver checkmate. See **Great Bare King**.

**'Little Olympiad'** a team tournament of nations held together with the third FIDE Congress in Budapest in July 1926. Only four teams had time to enter, because of a delay in issuing invitations. Consequently, the competition, which was held on four boards, was not recognized by FIDE as an official Chess Olympiad. Hungary came first with nine points followed by Yugoslavia with eight points, Romania with five points, and Germany with two points.

***Liverpool Mercury*** the first English newspaper to publish a chess column. The column lasted from 9 July 1813 to 20 August 1814.

**living chess** a game played with people as the pieces and pawns, moving as ordered by the players. The Sultan Mohammed is believed to have played such a game in Grenada in 1408. There are also descriptions of living chess in *Hypnerotmachia Poliphili*, a mystical work written by Francisco Colonna, a Dominican, in 1467 and in the fifth book of *Pantagruel* by Rabelais, which was first published in Lyons in 1564.

There have been many displays of living chess in the twentieth century. A game was played annually at the Wawel in Cracow for many years. In the United Kingdom the most notable display took place at Hurlingham in 1936 when games were played between the universities of Cambridge and Oxford, the House of Commons and the House of Lords, the Army and Navy, and the national boy and girl champions. In 1945 a game was played in Hollywood, California between a team of North American players (including Reuben Fine) and a team of Latin American players (including Herman Pilnik). In March 1962 a game was played at the Moscow Sports Palace between Botvinnik and Smyslov with ballet dancers as the pieces and pawns. Displays of living chess have also been seen at Chess Olympiads.

**Ljubojević, Ljubomir** (b. 2 November 1950) Yugoslavian chess player; awarded the title International Grandmaster in 1971. He competed in the Student Olympiad of 1969, the Chess Olympiads of 1972 and 1974, the 1973 Petropolis interzonal and the 1976 Manila interzonal. Ljubojević's aggressive and sacrificial style of play has won him many tournaments, including Orense (1974), Las Palmas (1974 and 1975), Montreal (1974), the Amsterdam IBM tournament (1975), Manila (1975) and Hoogoven (1976). (1976 Elo rating: 2620)

**local majority** (Kmoch's term) a **majority**. See ***Pawn Power in Chess***.

**Locock, C. D.** (1862–1946) British chess problem composer; born in Brighton on 27 September 1862. His forte was the construction of artificial games fulfilling certain given criteria. Locock's books include *120 Chess Problems and Puzzles, 70 More Chess Problems and Puzzles, One Hundred Chess Maxims,* and *Imagination in Chess*. He died on 13 May 1946.

**Locust** a Fairy chesspiece that moves like a Grasshopper except that the piece over which it leaps must be an enemy (this piece is then captured) and the square on which the Locust lands must be vacant. The Locust is a type of Hopper.

***Logical Chess Move by Move*** a collection of games compiled by Irving Chernev. It contains 33 games played between 1895 and 1945, each of which is annotated move by move. The games were selected to illustrate either the King-side attack, a Queen pawn opening or where the theme of the game is clearly carried out. The book was first published in the United Kingdom in 1958 and uses descriptive notation.

**Lokvenc, Josef** (b. 1 May 1899) Austrian chess player; awarded the title International Master in 1951. He was German Champion in 1943 and Austrian Champion in 1953. He represented Austria in the Chess Olympiads of 1927, 1928, 1930, 1931, 1952, 1954, 1956, 1958, 1960 and 1962.

**Lombard, André** (b. 19 September 1950) Swiss chess player; awarded the title International Master in 1976. He was Swiss Champion in 1975 and won the Zürich national tournament in 1976. (1976 Elo rating: 2420)

**Lombardy, William** (b. 4 December 1937) U.S. chess player; automatically gained the title International Master on becoming World Junior Champion in 1957 and was awarded the title International Grandmaster in 1960. For many years Lombardy was a priest and not a chess professional and consequently played less frequently than most players of his calibre. He is, however, a regular columnist of *Chess Life & Review*. (1976 Elo rating: 2520)

**London (1851)** another name for the **Great Exhibition tournament**.

**London (1862)** a round-robin tournament with fourteen competitors, won by Anderssen (who scored 12) ahead of Paulsen (11) and Owen (10). Steinitz came sixth, his international debut.

**London (1899)** a double-round tournament with fifteen competitors, won by Lasker (who scored 23½) ahead of Maróczy, Pillsbury and Janowski (all of whom scored 19 for equal second place).

**London (1922)** a tournament with sixteen competitors, won by Capablanca (who scored 13) ahead of Alekhine (11½).

**London Chess Club** one of the leading chess clubs of the nineteenth century. Founded on 6 April 1807, and meeting at Tom's Coffeehouse in the City of London, it swiftly gained pre-eminence, overshadowing Parsloe's. This was a clash of styles: Parsloe's naturally played in the Philidorian style, while the members of the London Chess Club introduced and adopted the more open and attacking

Italian system, with its emphasis on free play and sacrifices. It is hardly surprising that it was the London Chess Club that was triumphant. In 1824 the club broke new ground by playing a series of correspondence games with the Edinburgh Chess Club. It lost by two games to one with two games drawn, Edinburgh playing first in four of the games. This match saw the debut of the Scotch Game – an opening embodying all the principles of the Italian system of play. It was also in 1824 that a club member, Captain W. D. Evans, introduced his gambit.

The club's supremacy was challenged towards the middle of the century by the rise of the St George's Club, of which Howard Staunton was the leading member. The acrimony and petty jealousy between the two did nothing but harm to English chess. For instance, the London Chess Club boycotted the London Chess Tournament of 1851 because it had been organized by Staunton and supported by the St George's Club, so preventing Harrwitz from playing. The London Chess Club finally closed it doors in 1870.

**London System** an opening sequence arising out of the King's Indian Defence: 1. P–Q4, N–KB3 *2. N–KB3*, P–KN3 *3. B–B4*. Although not inferior, its main value is the psychological one of taking weaker opponents out of memorized book-lines. This system, adopted by Black at London (1922), is now used to describe this White opening.

**Lone Pine** a town in California; since 1971 it has been the annual venue for a strong international chess tournament. See **Louis D. Statham Masters-Plus Tournament.**

**long castling** castling on the Queen side. The Rook moves three squares – one more than when castling on the King side. Symbol **O–O–O**. Compare **short castling.**

**longest game** the game containing the most number of moves at the top level lasted for 191 moves. It was played between Hermann Pilnik and Moshe Czerniak in 1950 at Mar del Plata, Argentina, and ended in a draw. Its duration of 20 hours was 1½ hours less than the time taken by a game between Vladimir Makagonov and Vitalij Tchehover at Baku, U.S.S.R., in 1945 (171 moves, ending in a draw). The longest game ending in a win (168 moves) was won by Heinrich Wolf against Oldrich Duras in 1907 at Carlsbad, Austria, and lasted for 22½ hours. Compare **shortest game.**

**looking-glass chess** any chess game or method of play reminiscent or suggestive of the whimsical and fantastic game in Lewis Carroll's *Through the Looking Glass*.

**loose duo** (Kmoch's term) a **duo** that has no pawns in contact with the enemy pawns. In this situation the pawn structure is still fluid. Compare **tight duo.** See ***Pawn Power in Chess.***

**loose lever** (Kmoch's term) a **lever** in which both sides have the choice of capturing or bypassing the enemy pawn. Compare **inner lever, outer lever, tight lever.** See ***Pawn Power in Chess.***

**loose twin** (Kmoch's term) a doubled pawn that may be able to move to another file during the course of the game. Compare **sham twin, tight twin, twin.** See ***Pawn Power in Chess.***

**Lopez Bishop** White's King Bishop in the Ruy Lopez (Opening). It can often exert pressure on the centre and King side after being chased to White's QN3 by Black's pawns.

**Lopez, Ruy** the strongest Spanish player of the sixteenth century. Born in Segura, he became a priest in Esteradura and in 1559 visited Rome on the accession of Pope Pius IV. There he proved his superiority to the Italian players and read Damiano's book on chess for the first time. Within two years he had published *Libro de la invencion liberal y arte del Juego del Acedrez* (Alcala 1561). It consisted of four sections which respectively discussed the origin and worth of chess and provided general advice to players (such as to place the board so that the sun shines in the opponent's eyes), analysed several openings (including the one that is now known as the Ruy Lopez, which he recommended for the many traps it contains) and two sections that criticize Damiano's analyses.

Ruy Lopez was the strongest player in Spain, then the world's leading chess power, for nearly two decades and is known to have played before Philip II, who rewarded him with a benefice. He was decisively defeated in 1587 by Giovanni Leonardo (whom he had previously beaten during his stay in Rome) in the presence of Philip II. Allegedly, Leonardo intentionally lost the first two games and then won the next three to underline his superiority.

**Los Angeles Stauntons** a founding member of the **National Chess League**. In the league's first season the team came only fifth (despite its excellent name). The leading members of the team were Larry Christiansen, Kim Commons, Peter Biyiasas and Anthony Saidy.

**Losing Chess** a variant of chess in which the winner is the first player to lose all his men. The Kings can be captured without ending the game. Captures must be made if at all possible, but if there are two or more possibilities the capturer may choose which man to take.

**losing the exchange** being forced to lose a Rook while receiving a minor piece in exchange.

**Louis D. Statham Masters-Plus Tournament** a strong tournament held annually (since 1971) at Lone Pine, California. Petrosian came first in 1976 (5½ out of 7); Liberson came first in 1975 (7½ out of 10); and Browne came first in 1974 (6 out of 7). In 1975 a record number of 22 International Grandmasters competed. Also called **Lone Pine tournament.**

**Löwenthal, Johann Jakob** (1810–1876) leading nineteenth-century chess player; born in Budapest in July 1810. He was taught to play chess by a schoolfriend, Josef Szen, and with him and Vincenz Grimm represented Budapest in a correspondence game with the Paris Chess Club from 1842 to 1846. Their victory enormously increased their prestige and shortly thereafter Löwenthal toured Europe, playing Von der Lasa among others. After the collapse of Kossuth's abortive uprising, Löwenthal was forced to flee Hungary and eventually settled in the United States, where he met the young Paul Morphy, who defeated him three times. In the following year he travelled to London for the

**Great Exhibition tournament**, but arrived tired and ill and was eliminated in the first round by Williams. His poor form also showed in matches he played soon afterwards against the historian H. T. Buckle (+3 −4 =0) and against Williams (+7 −5 =4). Disheartened by his failure in the tournament, Löwenthal decided to remain in London as a chess professional rather than return to the United States. He was soon a protegé of Staunton, who influenced his appointment as Secretary of the St George's Club, but the friendship cooled after Löwenthal lost a rancorous match to Daniel Harrwitz, an enemy of Staunton, (+10 −11 =2) after leading by seven points and after Löwenthal had indiscreetly suggested in print that he had a plus score against Staunton. He later won tournaments at Manchester (1857) ahead of Anderssen and Birmingham (1858) in front of Staunton and Falkbeer. Also in 1858 he lost a match to Morphy (+3 −9 =2).

After this he played little chess, but was still active as the chess columnist of *The Era*, *Illustrated News of the World* and *Family Herald*. He was mainly responsible for organizing the 1862 tournament, edited *Chess Magazine* from 1863 to 1867, and was the Manager of the B.C.A. from 1865 to 1869. In 1872 he became the only chess professional to be elected President of the City of London Chess Club. In the same year a reconciliation took place between him and Staunton. Löwenthal died on 21 July 1876, bequeathing all he had to be used 'to promote the interests of English Chess'.

**Lucena** the Spanish author of the oldest known printed work containing chess analysis. The book, *Repeticion de Amores e Arte de Axedres con CL iuegos de partido*, was printed in Spain in 1497 and forms a bridge between mediaeval and modern chess. It consists of two sections, which contain love poetry and discuss chess respectively. The chess section details the laws of chess and outlines the difference between the old chess and the new; it analyses eleven openings played by the new laws and gives 150 chess problems, which are a mixture from old and new chess. Lucena is also believed to be the author of the **Göttingen manuscript**.

**Lucena position** a well-known type of Rook and pawn ending in which a win for White can be demonstrated. White's problem is to vacate the queening square without exposing the King to an endless series of checks. From the diagrammed position printed on p.175 play continues: 1. R–B4, R–B8 2. K–K7, R–K8ch 3. K–Q6, R–Q6ch 4. K–K6, R–K8ch 5. K–Q5, R–Q8ch 6. R–Q4 and White wins.

This position can be found in Lucena's compilation of problems, which was printed in 1497.

**luff** (Kmoch's term) the part of a rank divided by a pawn, which has the more squares. Compare **lee**. See ***Pawn Power in Chess***.

**Luft** *German for* air; figuratively, breathing space. A **flight square** created for a King that is under heavy attack, or simply to avoid a later possible back-rank mate.

**Lukacs, Peter** (b. 9 July 1950) Hungarian chess player; awarded the title International Master in 1976. (1976 Elo rating: 2430)

Lucena position

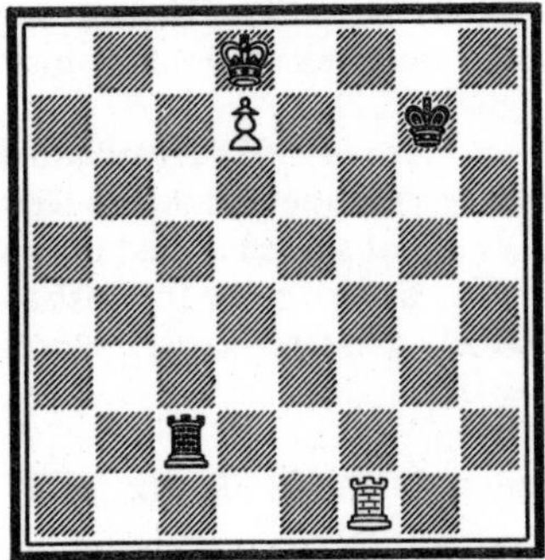

**Lundin, Erik** (b. 2 July 1904) Swedish chess player; awarded the title International Master in 1950. He was Swedish Champion in 1941, 1942, 1945, 1946, 1960, 1961 and 1964. Lundin competed in the Chess Olympiads of 1930, 1931, 1933 (when he scored the highest percentage of those on third board), 1935, 1937, 1939, 1952, 1954 and 1960. He also played in the 1948 interzonal. (1976 Elo rating: 2365)

**Lutikov, Anatoly** (b. 5 February 1933) Soviet chess player; awarded the titles International Master in 1967 and International Grandmaster in 1974. (1976 Elo rating: 2500)

**Lvov Gambit** another name for the **Zukertort Gambit**.

# M

**MacCutcheon Variation** an opening sequence arising in the French Defence: 1. P–K4, P–K3 2. P–Q4, P–Q4 3. N–QB3, N–KB3 4. B–N5, *B–N5*. Black indirectly continues his attack on White's King pawn by pinning its sole defender, the Queen Knight. The usual continuation is 5. P–K5, P–KR3 6. B–Q2. It is named after John Lindsay MacCutcheon, a nineteenth-century American player.

**MacDonnell, Rev. George Alcock** (1830–1899) Irish chess player and chess columnist; born in Dublin on 16 August 1830. He was appointed a curate in London in 1856 and soon became well-known in the chess clubs of the city. He came third at Dundee (1867) and fourth at London (1862 and 1872). He played two matches against Wisker in 1873 and 1874, winning the first (+3 –0 =1) but losing the second (+4 –7 =4). For many years MacDonnell wrote the chess column of *The Illustrated Sporting and Dramatic News* under the pseudonym of Mars. He died on 3 June 1899.

**Machine Gun Chess** a type of Fairy Chess in which every man that is attacked by a man is removed at the same time. When opposing men are mutually attacking each other they are both removed. Pieces that are sheltering behind other men remain on the board. Kings are treated like ordinary men; their removal does not end the game. The winner is the one who removes all of the opposing men. Machine Gun Chess was invented by J. E. H. Creed.

**Mackenzie, George Henry** (1837–1891) American chess player, born in Scotland; emigrated to the United States in 1863. He defeated the strongest players in national tournaments and was generally recognized as the American chess champion in 1880. Mackenzie came first at Frankfurt (1887). He died in New York, following a lingering heart disorder, on 14 April 1891.

**Magnus Smith trap** a trap arising in some variations of the Sicilian Defence. One example is: 1. P–K4, P–QB4 2. N–KB3, N–QB3 3. P–Q4, P×P 4. N×P, N–B3 5. N–QB3, P–KN3 6. B–QB4, P–Q3? 7. *N×N*, P×N 8. *P–K5*. White has the better position even after Black's best reply: 8 . . ., N–N5; while Black can lose his Queen if he plays carelessly: 8 . . ., P×P?? 9. B×Pch, K×B 10. Q×Q. Emanuel Lasker fell into this trap in his seventh game with Schlechter in their World Championship match, though not to the extent of losing his Queen, and eventually drew the game.

**Maiden's Game** a variant of chess in which a capture must be carried out whenever possible. It is mentioned in the Alfonso manuscript, written in the late thirteenth century, where it is stated that this game is named after the ladies of Ultramar (Morocco) who were believed to have invented it.

**majority** a group of pawns on one wing that outnumber the enemy pawns opposing them. If neither side has pieces, a healthy majority will always be able to create a passed pawn. However, if the majority contains one or more weaknesses in its pawn structure – such as backward, doubled, or hanging pawns – it may be impossible to force the creation of a passed pawn without the aid of pieces. This weak pawn majority is known as a crippled majority.

The importance of the majority steadily increases as the endgame is approached, but players often prepare for it from the opening. For instance, in the Exchange Variation of the Ruy Lopez, White swaps a Bishop for Knight on the fourth move to weaken Black's Queen-side pawn structure and obtain what is in effect a Queen-side majority. See **crippled majority**.

**major pieces** the Queens and the Rooks. A King and major piece can together checkmate a lone King while a King and minor piece cannot. Compare **minor pieces**. See also **relative value of pieces**.

**Makagonov System** an opening sequence arising out of the King's Indian Defence: 1. P–Q4, N–KB3 2. P–QB4, P–KN3 3. N–QB3, B–N2 4. P–K4, P–Q3 5. *P–KR3*. White prepares to play B–K3 without allowing . . . N–KN5, while also preparing to gain space on the King side with P–KN4. The system has never gained much popularity as it is believed to allow Black easy equality. Black's usual immediate reply: 5 . . ., O–O. This variation was devised by the Soviet International Master Vladimir Makagonov.

**Makagonov, Vladimir** (b. 27 August 1904) Soviet chess player; awarded the title International Master in 1950. His best results in the Soviet Championship were fourths in 1937 and 1939 and an equal fifth in 1944. He is a strong analyst and theoretician and acted in this capacity as Smyslov's second in the 1957 World Championship match against Botvinnik.

**Makarczyk, Kazimierz** (1901–1975) Polish chess player; awarded the title International Master in 1950. He was Polish Champion in 1948 and competed in the Chess Olympiads of 1928, 1930, 1931, 1933 and 1935.

**Makarichev, Sergei** (b. 17 November 1953) Soviet chess player; awarded the titles International Master in 1974 and International Grandmaster in 1976. (1976 Elo rating: 2495)

**Malich, Dr. Burkhard** (b. 29 November 1936) East German chess player; awarded the titles International Master in 1962 and International Grandmaster in 1975. He was East German Champion in 1958, played in the Student Olympiads of 1958, 1959 and 1960 and competed in every Chess Olympiad from 1962 to 1972. (1976 Elo rating: 2530)

**man** any chess unit, whether a piece or a pawn.

**'Mandarins of the Yellow Button'** a group of chess players who lived in Boston in the late nineteenth century. The original 'Yellow Button' was a yellow pin worn in a hat by Chinese imperial officials to indicate their high status in the civil service.

The Mandarins included C. F. Burille, F. H. Harlow, Dr E. M. Harris, C. F. Howard, Major O. E. Michaelis, General W. C. Paine, Dr H. Richardson, C. W. Snow, H. N. Stone, P. Ware Jr, and F. K. Young. This group formed the basis of the present Deschapelles Chess Club, Boston.

**Manhattan Variation** a defence arising out of the Queen's Gambit Declined: 1. P–Q4, P–Q4 2. P–QB4, P–K3 3. N–QB3, N–KB3 4. B–N5, QN–Q2 5. N–B3, *B–N5*. It was named after the Manhattan Chess Club, in New York City, where this variation became popular in the 1920s.

**Manila (1974)** a tournament held in the Philippines, won by Vasiukov (who scored 10½) ahead of Petrosian (9½) and Larsen (9).

**Mannheim (1914)** a tournament with eighteen competitors, interrupted by the outbreak of World War I. At the time it was terminated, Alekhine was leading (with 9½ out of 11 points) ahead of Vidmar, Spielmann, Breyer, Marshall, Réti, Tarrasch, etc.

**Mannheim Variation** an opening sequence arising out of the Queen's Gambit Accepted: 1. P–Q4, P–Q4 2. P–QB4, P×P 3. N–KB3, N–KB3 4. *Q–R4ch*. There are frequent possibilities of transposition into the Catalan Opening.

**Mansfield, Comins** (b. 14 June 1896) British problemist; awarded the titles International Judge of Chess Compositions in 1957, International Master for Chess Compositions in 1959 and International Grandmaster for Chess Compositions in 1972. He is a former president of the British Problem Chess Society and of the Permanent

Commission of FIDE for Chess Compositions. Mansfield is widely regarded as being one of the three greatest composers of chess problems of all time. In 1976 he was awarded the M.B.E. (Member of the Order of the British Empire) for his services to chess.

**Mao** a Fairy chesspiece that moves two squares at a time, the first orthogonally and the second diagonally. This means that it can move only to squares that a Knight could reach in the same position. Unlike a Knight, however, the Mao does not leap over other pieces and so can pin (and be blocked by) other pieces. It is often represented on diagrams by the symbol of a Knight that has been rotated one quarter-turn anti-clockwise. The Mao was introduced from Chinese chess by T. R. Dawson before World War I.

**Mar del Plata Variation** an opening sequence arising out of the King's Indian Defence: 1. P–Q4, N–KB3 2. P–QB4, P–KN3 3. N–QB3, B–N2 4. P–K4, P–Q3 5. N–B3, O–O 6. B–K2, P–K4 7. O–O, *N–B3*. After 8. P–Q5, this Knight will move to the King side via K2 to increase the force of an attack on that wing, while White will normally attempt to counterattack on the Queen side. This line of play is named after Mar del Plata (1953), where Gligorić adopted it in wins against Najdorf and Eliskases, although it had been played earlier by the Soviets (an example being the game between Taimanov and Bronstein in the 1952 Soviet Championship).

**Mariotti, Sergio** (b. 10 August 1946) Italian chess player; awarded the titles International Master in 1969 and International Grandmaster in 1974. He was Italian Champion in 1969 and 1971 and competed in the Chess Olympiads of 1972 and 1974 and the 1976 interzonal in Manila. Mariotti was born in Florence and was taught to play chess by Vincenzo Castaldi, an International Master. His first major success was winning the Italian Junior Championship in 1966; later results include firsts at Naples (1969), Reggio Emilia (1969), Hammersmith (1971) and Rome (1973), a second at Venice (1971) and a drawn match against Tatai in 1972 (+2 −2 =2). He is the first Italian to hold the GM title. (1976 Elo rating:2470)

**Maróczy bind** a pawn formation for White in the Sicilian Defence that allows a restraining control of the white squares of the fifth rank. It consists of pawns stationed on K4 and QB4, thus making Q5 a strong point. The strategic theme of the Maróczy bind is that of maintaining and increasing an advantage in space. It is named after Geza Maróczy, who demonstrated its force. Though the term was originally associated specifically with the variation: 1. P–K4, P–QB4 2. N–KB3, N–QB3 3. P–Q4, P×P 4. N×P, P–KN3 5. *P–QB4*, it is often now used to describe any similar pawn formation such as frequently arises from other Sicilian variations or from the English Opening.

**Maróczy, Geza** (1870–1951) Hungarian chess player; awarded the title International Grandmaster in 1950. He was born in Szeged, Hungary on 3 March 1870 and studied engineering at Zurich and Budapest before becoming a teacher of mathematics. Maróczy was one of the strongest players at the turn of the century with a record which included firsts at Monte Carlo (1902 and 1904), Ostend (1905), Bremen (1905) and Vienna (1908) and second places at Nuremberg (1896) and Carlsbad (1907). At this time he was one of the leading contenders for the World Championship and on 6 April 1906 an agreement for a World Championship match was signed between Lasker and Maróczy, but Maróczy later withdrew after negotiations over the choice of site for the match had broken down.

After World War I Maróczy emigrated to Holland where he drew a match with Euwe in 1921 (+2 −2 =0) and later moved to the United Kingdom. Although he still played tournament chess, and indeed played at New York (1924) and Carlsbad (1929), he concentrated increasingly upon his writing and upon training his pupils, who included Vera Menchik and Laszlo Szabo. He also acted as the controller of the two World Championship matches between Alekhine and Euwe.

Maróczy's style of play was defensive rather than aggressive and was characterized by patient positional manoeuvring. He was a supreme player of Queen and pawn endings and made several contributions to opening theory, including demonstrating the potential of the **Maróczy bind**. He died in Budapest on 29 May 1951.

**Maroćzy bind**

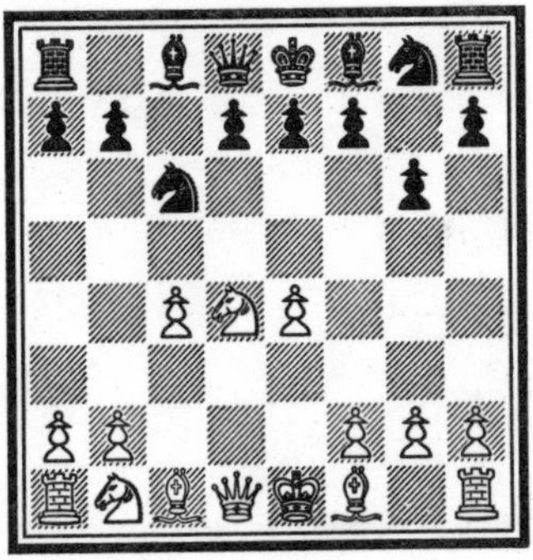

White has the Maroćzy bind (from a Sicilian Defence)

**Maróczy System (Four Knights' Game)** an opening sequence arising out of the Four Knight's Game: 1. P–K4, P–K4 2. N–KB3, N–QB3 3. N–B3, N–B3 4. B–N5, B–N5 5. O–O, O–O 6. P–Q3, P–Q3 7. *N–K2*. White avoids exchanging his Queen Knight. It is generally thought that Black can equalize easily. A common continuation is: 7 . . ., N–K2.

**Marović, Dražen** (b. 14 January 1938) Yugoslavian chess player; awarded the titles International Master in 1965 and International Grandmaster in 1975. Although he first played for Yugoslavia in the 1961 European Team Championship, he has never competed in a

Chess Olympiad. He is the editor of *Sahovski Glasnik*. (1976 Elo rating: 2485)

**Marseillaise Chess** a variant of chess in which each player makes two moves consecutively, either with the same or with different men. A check on the first move ends the turn. A player must move out of check on his first move or lose the game. This game was invented in 1925 and is also known as Marseilles Chess and Double-Move Chess.

**Marshall Attack** a defence arising out of the closed Ruy Lopez: 1. P–K4, P–K4 2. N–KB3, N–QB3 3. B–N5, P–QR3 4. B–R4, N–B3 5. O–O, B–K2 6. R–K1, P–QN4 7. B–N3, O–O 8. P–B3, *P–Q4*. Black sacrifices a pawn for open lines of attack on the King side and also often takes advantage of White's lack of development on the Queen side. Play normally continues: 9. P×P, N×P 10. N×P, N×N 11. R×N, when the modern 11. P–QB3 has replaced Marshall's original 11 . . . N–B3.

This variation was devised by Frank J. Marshall. In 1909 he had been decisively defeated in a match against Capablanca. As a result he avoided the Ruy Lopez for the next nine years and played instead Petroff's Defence; but in this period he discovered this variation, which he believed gave Black a winning position. In 1918 he met Capablanca in the first round of the Manhattan Chess Club tournament and played this attack, but Capablanca won in a sparkling game.

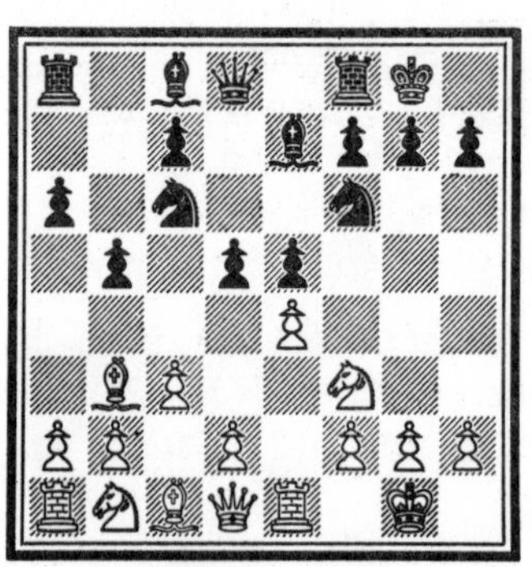

Position after 8 . . ., P–Q4

**Marshall Chess Club** one of the most famous chess clubs in the world. It was founded by Frank Marshall during World War I as the Chess Divan and changed to its present name in the 1930s. It is located at West 10th Street, New York.

**Marshall Defence** a defence occurring in the Queen's Gambit Declined: 1. P–Q4, P–Q4 2. P–QB4, *N–KB3*. This defence is generally considered unsatisfactory because Black abandons immediate control over the centre.

**Marshall, Frank James** (1877–1944) American chess player and one of the first International Grandmasters; born in New York. He was U.S. Champion from 1906 to 1936, when he voluntarily relinquished the title, and captained the American team in the Chess Olympics of 1930, 1931, 1933, 1935 and 1937. Marshall's first international tournament was Paris (1900) where he was equal third. Later results included firsts at Monte Carlo (1904), Cambridge Springs (1904), Scheveningen (1905), Nuremberg (1906), Dusseldorf (1908), New York (1911), Havana (1913) and Chicago (1926). In 1914 he came fifth at St Petersburg to receive the title of Grandmaster of Chess from Czar Nicholas. Marshall's results fluctuated more erratically than any other great player for he was always more concerned to create a beautiful game than to win. A true lover of chess, it is said that he played at least one game every day of his life and always took a pocket set to bed. Marshall's constant attempts to create brilliancies together with his natural optimism made him a weaker match than tournament player. He was easily defeated by Lasker in 1907 in a match for the World Championship (+0 −8 =7) and was also crushed by Capablanca two years later (+1 −8 =14). Yet even in the worst of troubles he was capable of finding some saving device and the term **Marshall swindle** became synonymous with a miraculous escape from apparently certain defeat.

***Marshall's Best Games*** an anthology of 100 games of Frank J. Marshall collected by P. Wenman. The book also contains a brief biography of Marshall and his tournament and match record. It was first published in 1948 and uses descriptive notation.

**Marshall swindle** another name for **swindle**. Marshall was notorious for discovering saving resources in otherwise hopeless positions. Indeed, a collection of some of his games was titled *Chess Swindles* for this reason.

**Marshall Variation** an opening sequence occurring in the Queen's Gambit Declined, arising out of the Slav Defence: 1. P–Q4, P–Q4 2. P–QB4, P–QB3 3. N–QB3, P–K3 4. P–K4, P×KP 5. N×P, B–N5ch 6. *B–Q2*, Q×P 7. B×B, Q×Nch 8. *B–K2*. Like the Marshall Defence, it was named after Frank J. Marshall, a U.S. champion and International Grandmaster. White sacrifices a pawn in return for better development. Black's best continuation is not to capture the KNP but to proceed with his development.

**Martinović, Slobodan** (b. 25 July 1945) Yugoslavian chess player; awarded the title International Master in 1976. (1976 Elo rating: 2420)

**Martz, William** (b. 21 March 1945) American chess player; awarded the title International Master in 1975. (1976 Elo rating: 2410)

**Mason Gambit** an opening sequence arising out of the King's Gambit: 1. P–K4, P–K4 2. P–KB4, P×P 3. *N–QB3*. It is generally believed to be inferior since Black can counterattack immediately by 3 . . ., Q–R5ch. It is named after the nineteenth-century player, James Mason. Also called **Keres Gambit**.

**Mason, James** (1849–1905) born in Kilkenny, Ireland on 19 November 1849 and brought to the United States while a child. There the family adopted the name of Mason to avoid anti-Irish prejudice and Mason's true name is still unknown today.

By the 1870s Mason had become the United States' leading player. In 1876 he defeated Bird, who was visiting the United States in a match (+11 −5 =4) and in the same year won both the Fourth American Congress and the New York Clipper Centennial Tournament.

Two years later admirers raised a subscription to send him to compete at Paris, but he did not manage to win a prize although he started well. Mason then settled in London and competed in numerous tournaments. He invariably began well and then deteriorated, losing to the weaker players after having defeated the stronger ones. In matches he was more successful. He defeated Blackburne in 1879 and Mackenzie in 1882 (both by +2 −1).

From 1893 Mason concentrated on writing such works as *Principles of Chess* (1893), *The Art of Chess* (1895), *Chess Openings* (1897), and *Social Chess* (1900). He died in London on 15 January 1905.

**Master** a title awarded by the national chess federations to their strongest players. Criteria for awarding the title vary among the countries. In the United Kingdom a player gains the title of British Master if he consistently achieves a B.C.F. grade of 216 (Elo rating: 2328) or if he gains an appropriate FIDE title. It is held for life. In the United States a player becomes a Master when he gains an Elo rating of 2200 (B.C.F. grade: 200). This is not held permanently, but can be retained only by consistently high performances. Compare **Candidate Master, International Master, International Grandmaster.**

***Master Prim*** a novel by James Whitfield Ellison which was published in 1968. It centres on the exploits of an uncouth American chess prodigy who is seen as a possible future World Champion. The book has been praised for its accuracy in conveying the cruelty in chess. Another pleasure is to try and identify the thinly disguised characters. Compare ***Dragon Variation, The***; ***Defence, The***; ***Royal Game, The*.**

***Masters of the Chess Board*** a book by Richard Réti, mainly composed of short biographies of seventeen of the strongest players of the nineteenth and twentieth centuries, together with analyses of their styles supplemented by scores of many of their games. It also contains an exposition of Réti's own system of play. It was first published in 1933, after Réti's death, and uses descriptive notation in the English edition.

**Master tournament** an international tournament held as a subsidiary event to a more important Grandmaster tournament. Often the winner of the Master group gains automatic qualification for the following year's Grandmaster group. Examples are the Masters tournaments at Cienfuegos, Netanya and Wijk aan Zee.

**Matanović, Alexander** (b. 23 May 1930) Yugoslavian chess player; awarded the titles International Master in 1951 and International Grandmaster in 1955. He is now the chief editor of *Chess Informant*. (1976 Elo rating: 2525)

**match** a contest consisting of a number of games played by the same contestants, whether the same players or the same teams. There are two varieties of match: the same players may contest a series of consecutive games over a period of time or the same teams may contest a series of games at the same time with several players competing. Individual matches impose different tensions than does playing in a tournament. A player who is decisively beaten in one game in a tournament sits down in the next round with a new opponent and a clean slate to some extent. If he is confronted by a player who has just beaten him he is at a psychological disadvantage. Some players are pre-eminently either tournament- or match-players: Steinitz was an outstanding match-player, while Lasker was just as obviously a tournament-player. Two contemporary examples are Petrosian as a match-player and Larsen as a tournament-player.

**match of the century** a description of the match between the U.S.S.R. and the rest of the world that was held in Belgrade, Yugoslavia in 1970. It was won by the Soviet team by the narrowest possible margin. See **U.S.S.R. v Rest of the World.**

**match-tournament** a chess competition combining elements of both match and tournament play. For example, six players might be grouped so that each plays four games against each of the other five – thus providing the elements of match play. Results of all the games of each player would then be used to determine the winner. The major match-tournaments have been St Petersburg (1895–1896) when Lasker, Pillsbury, Steinitz and Tchigorin competed; Ostend (1907); New York (1927); the Soviet Absolute Championship (1941); the World Championship (1948), when Botvinnik, Euwe, Keres, Reshevsky and Smyslov competed; and the Candidates' tournaments of 1959 and 1962.

**Mat du Berger, Le** *French for* Shepherd's Mate. English equivalent **Scholar's Mate.**

**mate** *short for* checkmate.

**Matera, Salvatore** (b. 5 February 1951) American chess player; awarded the title International Master in 1976. (1976 Elo rating: 2420)

**material** another name for **force.**

**mating attack** an attack upon the King that aims at checkmate. If successful, the game will end within a few moves and consequently objectives relevant for the ending (preservation of a sound pawn structure or maintenance of equality in material) may be discarded to help strengthen the attack. Such a policy is very risky and the player may find himself with a compromised game if the mating attack fails.

**Matulović, Milan** (b. 10 June 1935) Yugoslavian chess player; awarded the titles International Master in 1961 and International Grandmaster in 1965. He competed in the interzonal tournaments of 1967 (finishing 9th) and 1970 (18th). (1976 Elo rating: 2505)

**Maurian, Charles Amédée** (1838–1912) American amateur chess player of French descent; born in New Orleans, where he became a lifelong friend of Paul Morphy. Although Maurian never participated in public tournaments, he won first prize at the New Orleans Chess Club in 1858. According to Philip W. Sergeant, 'for thirty years he met in off-hand games, on level terms, Mackenzie, Steinitz, Tchigorin,

Zukertort, and other masters, and acquitted himself well'. Towards the end of his life, Morphy refused to play chess with anyone but Maurian.

**Maximummer** a problem in Fairy chess in which Black must always select the move that covers the greatest distance when measured from the centre to the centre of each square. QR1–K6 is a longer distance than QR1–QB7 and so would be preferred. Black has a choice only if two or more moves are both equal and the longest. The stipulation that Black must always play the longest move is sometimes relaxed for the 'capture' of the King – i.e. the move following checkmate. If this condition still applies the problem is described as a *consistent* Maximummer. Since its invention by T. R. Dawson in 1913, the Maximummer has grown in popularity until it is now recognized as being *customary* by the Piran Codex, which has published a table of the relative distances between all the squares of the chessboard.

**Max Lange Attack** an opening move arising out of the Two Knights' Defence or the Giuoco Piano. In the following typical progression, the characteristic or defining move of the Max Lange is in italics: 1. P–K4, P–K4 2. N–KB3, N–QB3 3. B–B4, N–B3 4. O–O, B–B4 5. P–Q4, P×P 6. *P–K5*. Black's usual immediate reply is: 6 . . ., P–Q4.

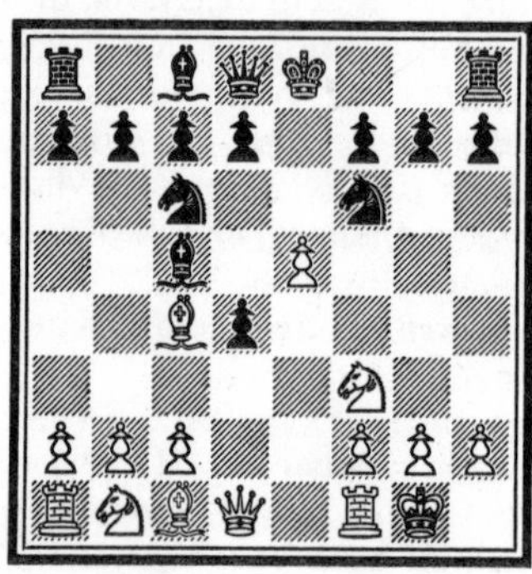

Position after 6. P–K5

**McConnell, James** (1829–1894) American amateur chess player; born in Louisiana. He engaged Paul Morphy in several friendly games when the quickly developing chess genius was not yet 12 years old (1849). On their first encounter, McConnell lost three of the four games played.

**McDonnell, Alexander** (1798–1835) leading London chess player of the early 1830s. The son of a Belfast physician, he became Secretary to the Committee of West India Merchants in London where he joined the Westminster Chess Club. By 1834 he had become recognized as the strongest player in London; in the summer of that year a series of matches was held in London between McDonnell and La Bourdonnais, France's strongest player. Over nearly four months 85 games were played and McDonnell was decisively defeated (+27 −45 =13), although he played many fine games. These matches were the first to be well documented and inspired many later players, especially Anderssen. The match was suspended in October to allow La Bourdonnais to return to Paris on business; before it could be resumed, McDonnell had contracted kidney disease. He died on 14 September 1835.

**M.C.O.** *abbrev. for Modern Chess Openings.*

**mechanical move** a move made automatically or with little conscious consideration other than the fact that it seems obvious or technically correct. The mechanical capture of a piece left *en prise*, for example, is usually made quickly by amateur players or beginners; at the Master level, a player will study the position more closely before capturing to check for possible traps or other complications that might follow too hasty a move.

**Mecking, Henrique** (b. 2 February 1952) Brazilian chess player; awarded the titles International Master in 1967 and International Grandmaster in 1972. Mecking qualified for the 1974 series of Candidates' matches by winning the Petropolis 1973 interzonal tournament, but was eliminated in the first round by Korchnoi. In the next series Mecking repeated his interzonal success by taking first place at Manila (1976). (1976 Elo rating: 2620)

**median system** a tie-breaking procedure based upon the opponents' scores. The tied players are ranked according to the total of their opponents' scores after the results of their highest and lowest opponents have been deducted. By excluding these extremes the chances of a freak result are reduced, but other tie-breaking methods are more popular – such as determining the result by using only the games played between the two players, or by the number of games each has won, or by the **Sonneborn-Berger system.**

**Medina, Garcia Antonio Angel José** (b. 2 October 1919) Spanish chess player; awarded the title International Master in 1950. He was Spanish Champion 1944–1946, 1947–1948, 1949–1950, 1952–1953 and 1963–1965. He was also Venezuelan Champion in 1955, 1956 and 1958 during a period when he lived in that country and represented Venezuela in the 1955 interzonal tournament where he finished equal 19th. He competed for Spain in the Chess Olympiads of 1964, 1966, 1968 and 1976. (1976 Elo rating: 2345)

**Mednis, Edmar** American chess player; awarded the title International Master in 1974. He is the author of several books including *How to beat Bobby Fischer* and *How Karpov Wins* and is a regular contributor to *Chess Life & Review*. (1976 Elo rating: 2435)

**melanpenia** (Kmoch's term) insufficient control of the dark squares. Compare **monochromy, leucopenia.** See ***Pawn Power in Chess.***

**memory** ability to recall past similar chess positions or even entire games is relatively common at the master level of play. For the beginner or intermediate level player, however, it is basically unwise to devote undue time to memorizing opening variations at the expense of attempting to understand the principles that underlie them. See **blindfold chess.**

**Menchik-Stevenson, Vera Francevna** (1906–1944) Woman World Champion from 1927 to 1944. She was born in Moscow on 16 February 1906 of an English mother and Czechoslovakian father and was brought to England in 1921.

In 1927 in London the first Women's World Championship was held and consisted of a twelve-player round-robin tournament with entrants from seven countries. Menchik entered as a representative of Russia (in later years she represented Czechoslovakia and England in this event) and was undefeated, winning all but her final game. She never lost her title, winning a further six tournaments as well as two matches against her great rival Sonja Graf. Among her other achievements was an equal second with Rubinstein at Ramsgate (1929) half a point behind Capablanca, third place at Maribor (1934) in front of Spielmann and Vidmar, and victory in a match against Mieses (+4 −1 =5). She is thought by many to have been the strongest female player of all time.

In 1937 she married R. H. S. Stevenson. He died in 1943 and a year later, on 27 June 1944, she was killed with her mother and sister in an air-raid on Kent. See **Vera Menchik Club**.

**Mephisto** ostensibly a chessplaying automaton that was constructed by Charles Godfrey Gumpel, a manufacturer of artificial limbs, in 1876. With **Isidor Gunsberg** inside it, Mephisto created considerable controversy when it entered and won the English Counties' Chess Association Handicap tournament (1878). One strong player, the Reverend George Alcock MacDonnell, withdrew in protest at the identity of Mephisto's operator being kept secret. Compare **Ajeeb, Turk**.

**Meran Defence** an opening sequence arising out of the Slav Defence to the Queen's Gambit Declined. A typical progression is as follows: 1. P–Q4, P–Q4 2. P–QB4, P–QB3 3. N–KB3, *N–B3* 4. N–B3, *P–K3* 5. P–K3, QN–Q2 6. B–Q3, *P × P* 7. B × BP, *P–QN4*. In the above progression, White often transposes moves 4 and 5. It was named after the Austrian resort of Meran, in which Akiba Rubinstein first played this variation during an international tournament in 1924. Also called **Meran Variation**. Compare **Accelerated Meran, Anti-Meran**

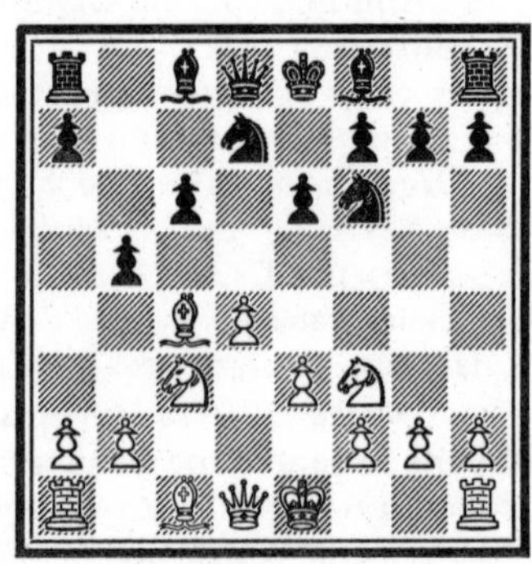

Position after 7 . . ., P–QN4

**Gambit, Blumenfeld Variation, Reynold's Variation, Romih Variation, Semi-Meran.**

**Meredith** any chess problem that contains from eight to twelve pieces. It is named after the 19th-century American problemist William Meredith.

**Mestel, A. Jonathan** (b. 13 March 1957) British chess player; awarded the title British Master in 1975. He was British Champion in 1976 (the youngest ever). Mestel was World Cadet Champion in 1974 and came third in the 1975 World Junior Championship. He represented England in the 1976 Olympiad. (1976 Elo rating: 2390)

**Metamorphosis** (or **Metamorphose**) a woodcut printed from 29 separate blocks, created by the famous Dutch design artist Maurits C. Escher. It measures 19.5 × 700 cm and consists of a mosaic of white and black squares that gradually change shape to reveal a wide variety of interrelated shapes and forms that constitute a progressive association of ideas. The final blocks in the design reveal chess pieces on the edge of a cuboidal chessboard, which finally resolves into a flat chessboard and the restated theme of the word 'metamorphose'. Escher created the woodcut in two parts (1939–40 and 1967–68). A reproduction of this interesting work forms the endpapers of Hugh Alexander's *A Book of Chess* (1973).

**Miagmasuren, Lhamsuren** (b. 10 August 1938) Mongolian chess player; awarded the title International Master in 1966. He came equal 19th in the 1967 interzonal and has won the Ulan Bator Championship on several occasions, including 1975. (1976 Elo rating: 2340)

**Miami Capablancas** a founding member of the **National Chess League**. In the league's first season the team came sixth under the leadership of Arnold Denker.

**Michel, Pablo** (b. 27 November 1905) Argentinian chess player; awarded the title International Master in 1956. Originally German, Michel was equal second in the 1935 German Championship and was a member of the German team in the 1939 Chess Olympiad, which was held in Argentina. On the outbreak of war he was granted asylum in Argentina. Later results included third places at Mar del Plata (1943, 1944 and 1946).

**middle-game** the phase of the game beginning after development has been completed and ending once material has been greatly reduced. Unlike the other sections of the game, there is little scope for memorized variations and the players must rely on their own ability and knowledge of general principles. It is in this phase of the game that tactical manoeuvres and attacks upon the King predominate. Compare **opening, ending.** See ***Art of the Middle Game***; ***Middle Game, The***.

***Middle Game, The*** a two-volume work by former World Champion M. Euwe and International Master H. Kramer. The first volume deals with the static conditions present in the game while the second deals with the dynamic conditions, as well as containing a survey of the styles of 38 Grandmasters and World Champions. It was first published in English in 1964 and uses descriptive notation.

**Mihaljčisin, Mihailo** (b. 23 February 1933) Yugoslavian chess player; awarded the title International Master in 1963. (1976 Elo rating: 2325)

**Mikenas, Vladas Ivanovich** (b. 17 April 1910) Soviet chess player; awarded the titles International Master in 1950 and International Judge in 1968. He was Lithuanian Champion in 1936 and represented that country in the Chess Olympiads of 1931, 1933, 1935, 1937 and 1939, in all of which he played on top board. Mikenas was Baltic Champion in 1945 and won the Championship of the Lithuanian Republic in 1947, 1948 and 1961.

**Milan (1975)** a round-robin tournament with twelve competitors, the first four of whom qualified for a match play-off. Portisch finished first in the tournament but lost the play-off to Karpov (3½ to 2½).

**Miles, Anthony J.** (b. 23 April 1955) British chess player; awarded the titles International Master in 1975 and International Grandmaster in 1976. Miles was second in the 1973 World Junior Championship, but won this event in 1974 to become automatically an International Master. He became the first British International Grandmaster by gaining grandmaster norms at the 'London Chess Fortnight' of August 1975 and at a tournament in Dubna, U.S.S.R. in February 1976. His other results include equal firsts in the 1976 U.S. National Open and in the 1976 I.B.M. tournament and an equal second at Lone Pine (1976). (1976 Elo rating: 2510)

**Milev, Zdravko** (b. 25 October 1929) Bulgarian chess player; awarded the title International Master in 1952. He was Bulgarian Champion in 1952, 1960 and 1961 and competed in the Chess Olympiads of 1954, 1956, 1958, 1960, 1962 and 1964. (1976 Elo rating: 2230)

**Milić, Borislav** (b. 20 October 1925) Yugoslavian chess player; awarded the title International Master in 1951. He competed in the Chess Olympiads of 1952 and 1956.

**Milner-Barry Gambit** a sharp variation in the French Defence, Advance Variation, in which White offers both his centre pawns for attacking chances. The characteristic moves are: 1. P–K4, P–K3 2. P–Q4, P–Q4 3. P–K5, P–QB4 4. P–QB3, N–QB3 5. N–B3, Q–N3 6. B–Q3, P×P 7. P×P, B–Q2 8. *O–O*, N×P 9. N×N, Q×N 10. *N–B3*. It was introduced by the British Master P. S. Milner-Barry.

**Minev, Nikolai Nikolaev** (b. 8 January 1931) Bulgarian chess player; awarded the title International Master in 1960. He was Bulgarian Champion in 1953, 1965 and 1966 and competed in the Chess Olympiads of 1954, 1956, 1958, 1960, 1962 and 1966. (1976 Elo rating: 2430)

**miniature** any chess problem that contains seven pieces or fewer.

**minor exchange** the swapping of a Bishop for a Knight. The player who has lost his Knight for a Bishop is said to have gained or won the minor exchange. This illustrates the change in the evaluation of the relative power of these pieces that has taken place in the past 100 years. Until the nineteenth century most players believed the Knight to be the stronger piece, because of the many tactical possibilities its move created. (As an example of this see **dice chess**, where the Bishop is ranked below the Knight).

However, the difference is very small and may be compensated for by other factors. In many openings, such as the Exchange Variation of the Ruy Lopez, a Bishop will be exchanged for a Knight (voluntarily losing the minor exchange) for the sake of damaging the opponent's pawn structure. See **exchange.**

**minority attack** an advance by one or more pawns towards a greater number of enemy pawns. The purpose of a minority attack is to create weaknesses in the opposing pawn structure that will negate the value of having a majority of pawns on that wing. For instance, a minority attack by two pawns against three will have been successful if doubled pawns that are unable to advance are created. The minority attack normally takes place on the wing on which the King has not castled and this is normally on the Queen side.

**minor pieces** the Bishops and the Knights. In general, these pieces are less powerful than the major pieces. For instance, on an open board at least two minor pieces and King are required to checkmate. Compare **major pieces**. See also **relative value of pieces.**

**minus score** a tournament or match score in which a player's losses outnumber his wins. If the same number were added or subtracted for a victory or defeat with draws being ignored, such a result would mean a negative score. However, under the normal scoring system one point is awarded for a win, half a point for a draw and no points for a loss. Under this system it is therefore impossible to get a minus score. Compare **plus score.**

**'mistake of the century'** a name given to the final move of a game between the Soviet Grandmaster Rafael Vaganian and the Yugoslavian International Master Rista Nicevski played at Skopje on 17 March 1976. Vaganian made a move completely overlooking the threat of a one-move checkmate against him. He resigned before it could be carried out.

**Modern Benoni** one of the sharpest variations of the Benoni Defence, popularized by Tal in the early 1960s. The characteristic moves are: 1. P–Q4, N–KB3 2. P–QB4, P–B4 3. P–Q5, *P–K3* 4. N–QB3, P×P 5. P×P, P–Q3.

***Modern Chess Openings (M.C.O.)*** an encyclopedia of the openings. It provides a concise analysis of the strategical aims behind each opening, together with extensive columns of the most important variations as well as detailed notes on uncommon divergencies. It was first published in the 1930s and is now in its 11th edition (1972) under the editorial direction of Walter Korn. It uses descriptive notation.

***Modern Chess Opening Theory*** a book by the Soviet Grandmaster Aleksei Suetin which deals with the strategical underpinnings of the openings. It also discusses how to teach opening theory and contains a programme for the study of the Ruy Lopez. This work is aimed at the advanced player. It was first published in English in 1965 and uses descriptive notation.

**Modern Defence** a defence to the King's pawn opening where Black responds to White's attempts to control the centre by a fianchetto of his King Bishop; its most direct line being: 1. P–K4, *P–KN3* 2. P–Q4, *B–N2*. It thus includes a wide variety of systems, but excludes major systems such as the Benoni, the Grünfeld, and the King's Indian. As with these hypermodern defences, Black allows White to build a strong centre which he then attempts to destroy. The name Modern Defence was coined by R. D. Keene and G. S. Botterill, who wrote a book solely about this opening. Compare **Pirc Defence.** Also called **Robatsch Defence,** and **Ufimtsev Defence.**

***Modern Ideas in Chess*** see ***Die Neuen Ideen im Schachspiel***.

***Modern Ideas in the Chess Openings*** a primer on eleven openings written by I. A. Horowitz. The major themes of each opening are explained, followed by move-by-move analysis of a main sequence in that opening and a game that begins in this manner. Finally, there is a compendium of 22 illustrative games. It was first published in 1953 and uses descriptive notation.

***Modern Openings in Theory and Practice, The*** a study of thirteen openings by A. P. Sokolsky. The main intention of the book is to show how the theme of each opening dominates the entire game and to this end there is a selection of illustrative games that feature each opening. Also set out are the principles and guidelines of correct play in the opening and middle-game. This book was translated by H. Golombek and E. Strauss and was first published in English in 1972. The English edition uses descriptive notation.

**Möhring, Gunter** East German chess player; awarded the title International Master in 1976. (1976 Elo rating: 2380)

**Möller Attack** an opening sequence arising out of the Giuoco Piano: 1. P–K4, P–K4 2. N–KB3, N–QB3 3. B–B4, B–B4 4. P–B3, N–B3 5. P–Q4, P×P 6. P×P, B–N5ch 7. N–B3, N×KP 8. O–O, B×N 9. *P–Q5*. This pawn sacrifice was known in Greco's time and was for many years thought to be refuted after Black's eighth move. However, according to Euwe the immediate advance of White's Queen pawn 'guarantees at least a draw'. The most common continuations are: 9 . . ., B–B3 and 9 . . ., N–K4. This variation was discovered by Möller in the late nineteenth century. Compare **Greco Variation.**

**monochromy** (Kmoch's term) insufficient control of squares of the same colour. If one of the players has a bad Bishop he is suffering from monochromy. See **leucopenia, melanpenia,** ***Pawn Power in Chess***.

**Monte Carlo** venue of an annual international tournament from 1901 to 1904. It was organized by a committee under the direction of Jules Arnous de Rivière, a former opponent of Morphy. The first tournament was won by Janowski, who apparently lost all his prize-money at the nearby casino. Later winners were Maróczy in 1902 and 1904 and Tarrasch in 1903. Unfortunately the tournament proved an insufficient attraction for visitors and in 1904 the main sponsor, Prince Dadian of Mingrelia, withdrew allowing the Ostend casino to hold a tournament in 1905. A unique feature of the Monte Carlo tournaments was the scoring used in the early events; to discourage draws a draw was only worth a quarter point to each player and had to be replayed. The winner of the second game would receive another half point, but if it too ended in a draw both players each received only another quarter point.

**Monticelli, Mario** (b. 16 March 1902) Italian chess player; awarded the title International Master in 1950. He was Italian Champion in 1929, 1934 and 1939 and competed in the Chess Olympiads of 1927, 1928, 1931, 1933 and 1935.

**Monticelli trap** a combination which gains material through a discovered attack on a piece together with a mating threat. It was discovered by the Italian International Master, Mario Monticelli.

From the diagrammed position play continues: 1. N–N5, B × N 2. B × QB, B × B 3. B × R, B–N4 4. R × P and White has won a pawn and the exchange.

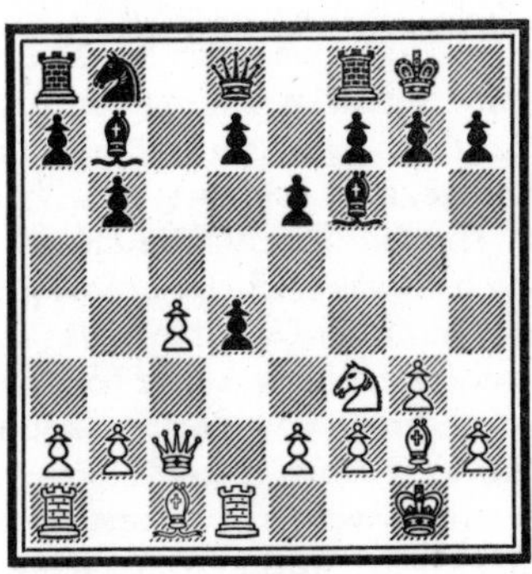

White threatens mate with 1. N–N5 and simultaneously attacks Black's Bishop

***Morals of Chess, The*** an essay on chess by Benjamin Franklin, written in 1779. In it Franklin discusses the merits of chess for improving the character of the players and lays down some rules of etiquette to observe during play.

**Morphy, Ernest** (1807–1874) American amateur chess player; uncle of Paul Morphy. According to Löwenthal, Ernest was 'generally considered the chess king of New Orleans.' He greatly encouraged his young nephew, Paul, and gave him many insights into the game.

**Morphy, Paul Charles** (1837–1884) American chess player; born in New Orleans on 22 June 1837, the son of a judge of the Supreme Court of Louisiana. He is generally considered to have been the foremost player in the world during his short but spectacular chess career, having defeated the strongest players in both America and Europe. Many authorities still rank him as the game's greatest natural master. One former World Champion (Euwe) called him 'the greatest chess phenomenon of all time'. Morphy excelled as a brilliant combinative player, and his Queen sacrifices, as an ominous prelude to checkmate, have continued to intrigue amateur and master players alike for well over one hundred years. But he was far more than a flashy master of the art of combinative play; even though Morphy is basically revered for his mastery of the open game (in which the principles of quick development, open lines and control of the centre play a decisive role), he was equally adept at exploiting any minor positional weaknesses of his opponents.

Morphy, who was trained in the legal profession and admitted to the bar at nineteen (on condition that he would not engage in practice until he came of age), was destined never to make a brilliant move in court – only over the chessboard. At about the age of six he learned the game from his father, although his serious chess career did not begin until 1857, when he came first (+14 −1 =3) at the first American Championship (New York). In 1858 he travelled to London and Paris, defeating all comers (even the strongest European player of the time, Adolf Anderssen); only Staunton refused to play a match with the young contender and Morphy was forced to return to America (May, 1859) without the satisfaction of beating the man who was formerly considered to be the strongest player in the world.

Upon his return home, after spending nearly a year in Europe, the 22-year-old Morphy temporarily edited a chess column in the New York *Ledger* (for which he was paid a fee of $3,000 a year) and was for a time on the staff of *Chess Monthly* (1859–60).

Morphy's serious chess career was over before he was 23. As Reinfeld comments: 'In only three years of active play he conquered the Old World as well as the New, gave the development of chess theory a mighty impetus, set new standards for accurate and elegant play, [and] enriched the chess world with many beautiful games.' Although Morphy often played against opponents of vastly inferior ability (whom he would insist on playing at the odds of a piece and move), he demonstrated the highest mastery of chess when playing against opponents such as Paulsen, Löwenthal and Anderssen. He was also an expert at endgames, a fact that escapes many chess lovers because of their belief that against most opponents this final stage of play was rarely reached – checkmate during the middle-game being a Morphy characteristic.

Back in New Orleans, Morphy attempted to establish himself in the legal profession but no one would take him seriously. He gradually entered a period of mental decline and developed a persecution mania; he was frequently seen strolling the streets of his home town quietly muttering to himself. This was the tragic aspect of his last days that gave rise to the descriptive phrase – 'The Pride and Sorrow of Chess' – by which Morphy is still identified. He died on 10 July 1884 after returning home from a long walk. His mother found him dead in the bath; the cause was reported as 'congestion of the brain, following the shock of cold water to an overheated body'.

**Morphy's Defence** a defence arising out of the Ruy Lopez: 1. P–K4, P–K4 2. N–KB3, N–QB3 3. B–N5, *P–QR3*. Since Black must eventually advance his Queen pawn, his Queen Knight will become pinned. Black's third move reduces the effect of the potential pin and allows Black to break it or prevent it in one move by the advance of the Queen Knight pawn. This defence is normally regarded as Black's strongest reply to the Ruy Lopez and was often played by Paul Morphy.

**Morra Gambit** an opening sequence arising out of the Sicilian Defence: 1. P–K4, P–QB4 2. *P–Q4*, P×P 3. *P–QB3*. White sacrifices a pawn for a gain in tempo and access of the Queen to her short diagonal. However, it is generally felt that Black can equalize while retaining the pawn. A common continuation is: 3. . . ., P×P 4. N×P, N–QB3 5. N–B3, P–Q3.

**Moscow (1925)** a tournament with 21 competitors, won by Bogoljubov (who scored 15½) ahead of Lasker (14) and Capablanca (13½).

**Moscow (1935)** a tournament with twenty competitors; Botvinnik and Flohr shared equal first place (with a score of 13 points each) ahead of Lasker (12½) and Capablanca (12).

**Moscow (1936)** a double-round tournament with ten competitors, won by Capablanca (13) ahead of Botvinnik (12) and Flohr (9½).

***Moscow Central Chess Club Bulletin*** one of the leading chess periodicals in the U.S.S.R. As well as featuring domestic and parochial news it publishes games and detailed analyses from all over the world. It is not available to the general public, but has a controlled circulation of 30,000. Compare ***64, Chess.***

***Most Instructive Games of Chess Ever Played, The*** a collection of 62 games compiled by Irving Chernev. Each illustrates some aspect of position play. The book was first published in 1966 and uses descriptive notation.

**Muffang, André** (b. 25 July 1897) French chess player; awarded the title International Master in 1951. He competed in the Chess Olympiads of 1927, 1928, 1935 and 1956.

**Mühring, Willem Jan** (b. 17 August 1913) Dutch chess player; awarded the title International Master in 1951. He competed in the Chess Olympiad of 1956.

**Mukhin, Mikhail** (1948–1977) Soviet chess player; awarded the title International Master in 1975. (1976 Elo rating: 2450)

**Müller, Hans,** (1896–1971) Austrian chess player; awarded the title International Master in 1950. He was born on 1 December 1896. Müller was joint Austrian Champion in 1947 and competed in the Chess Olympiads of 1928, 1930, 1933, 1935 and 1950. He was the author of more than twenty books and was also the compiler of one of the most comprehensive opening indexes in the world. He died on 28 February 1971.

**Munich International Junior Team Tournament (1972)** an international team tournament held in conjunction with the Olympic Games. It was organized under the Swiss System and play took place on four boards. The result was determined from match scores rather than from game scores.

The English team consisted of M. F. Stean, A. J. Miles, J. D. M. Nunn, and S. Saverymuttu with P. R. Markland as non-playing captain. It was undefeated in the competition and had assured itself of first place by the sixth and penultimate round.

**Murray, Harold James Ruthven** (1868–1955) chess historian; born in Camberwell, England on 24 June 1868. Murray was the eldest son of Dr James A. H. Murray, the first editor of the *Oxford English Dictionary*. He graduated from Balliol College, Oxford in 1890 and became teacher at Queen's College, Taunton where he learned to play chess. In 1896 he was appointed headmaster of Ormskirk Grammar School and soon afterwards began his researches into the history of chess with the encouragement of von der Lasa.

From 1901 to 1928 he was a Board of Education Inspector of Schools and had less opportunity to play chess. In this period he began to contribute articles to the *British Chess Monthly* and the *Deutsches Wochenschach*.

In 1913 his major work, *A History of Chess*, was published. This work took Murray over thirteen years to write, during which he learned Arabic to be able to read unpublished Arabic sources. As a work of scholarship it has never been surpassed; a new impression was published in 1962.

Following his retirement from the Board of Education, Murray served on his local council from 1931 to 1955. He died on 16 May 1955. His other books were *A History of Board Games Other than Chess* and *A Short History of Chess* (published posthumously, with additions by B. Goulding Brown and H. Golombek).

**Muse of Chess, The** another name for **Caïssa.**

**mutate** a term applied to certain chess problems by the problem composer Brian Harley (1883–1955); it describes 'a cumbrous-looking situation of many variations, in which the Key alters one or two commonplace mates.' See **key.**

**mute chain lever** (Kmoch's term) a chain lever in which neither side's base of the pawn chain is attacked. This means that a passed pawn is unlikely to result from pawn exchanges. Compare **double lever, lever.** See ***Pawn Power in Chess*****.**

**Muzio Gambit** an opening sequence arising in the King's Gambit: 1. P–K4, P–K4 2. P–KB4, P×P 3. N–KB3, P–KN4 4. B–B4, P–N5 5. *O–O*. White sacrifices his Knight in return for a large lead in development and an open King's Bishop file along which he can train his Rooks. After Black takes the Knight, White usually plays either 6. Q×P, or 6. B×Pch. Apparently this gambit is named after a seventeenth-century Italian named Mutio whose name was incorrectly transcribed.

***My Best Games of Chess 1908–1923*** a collection of 100 of Alekhine's best games compiled by Alekhine himself. Together with its companion volume, ***My Best Games of Chess 1924–1937***, it comprises what many believe to be the finest collection of games ever produced. It was first published in 1927 and uses descriptive notation. See ***My Best Games of Chess 1924–37*****,** ***Alekhine's Best Games of Chess 1938–45*****,** ***100 Instructive Games of Alekhine*****.**

***My Best Games of Chess 1924–37*** a collection of 140 of Alekhine's best games compiled by Alekhine himself. It is the second volume of the then World Champion's own annotated collection of games and is thought by many to be one of the finest collections of games ever to be produced. This volume covers all his World Championship matches. It was first published in 1939 and uses descriptive notation. See: ***My Best Games of Chess 1908–1923***, ***Alekhine's Best Games of Chess 1938–45***, ***100 Instructive Games of Alekhine***.

***My Chess Career*** some personal recollections of J. R. Capablanca. It records the author's chess career from its beginning to the Hastings Victory Congress (1919). Thirty-five games are given in full. The book was first published in 1920 and uses descriptive notation.

***My 60 Memorable Games*** an anthology compiled by Bobby Fischer of his most interesting games from 1957 to 1967. Each game also has a preface by Larry Evans explaining the reasons for course of play or the circumstances in which it was played. It is undoubtedly the best anthology of any player's games to appear since Alekhine's. It was first published in the U.K. in 1969 and uses descriptive notation.

***My System*** a work by Aron Nimzovitch expounding his theories on chess. It was (and is) one of the most influential books in the history of chess. It introduced completely new concepts such as the blockade and overprotection and displayed striking orginality when discussing standard subjects such as the art of manoeuvring, the power of Rooks on the seventh rank and pawn chains. *My System* was translated by Philip Hereford and was first published in English in 1929. It uses descriptive notation.

# N

**N** *abbrev. for* Knight. It is now preferred to the alternative abbreviation, **Kt**, because the latter is sometimes misread as **K** (the abbreviation for King).

**Najdorf, Miguel** (b. 15 April 1910) Argentinian chess player; awarded the title International Grandmaster in 1950. He was Argentinian Champion in 1950, 1951, 1955, 1960, 1966 and 1975. Najdorf was born in Warsaw and competed for Poland in the Chess Olympiads of 1935, 1937 and 1939. The 1939 Olympiad was interrupted by the outbreak of World War II and the whole Polish team decided to remain in the host country of Argentina with Najdorf himself becoming an Argentinian citizen in 1944. During the war years Najdorf won fifteen of the seventeen South American tournaments in which he competed and on a post-war tour of Europe came fourth at Groningen (1946) and first at Prague (1946) and Barcelona (1946). Encouraged by these results he announced his candidacy for the World Championship, but was not included in the 1948 World Championship match-tournament even when Fine dropped out. He did take part in the interzonals of 1948 and 1955 and in the Candidates' tournament of 1950, but never qualified for a World Championship match.

Najdorf played for Argentina in the Chess Olympiads of 1950 and 1952, scoring the best result on first board on both occasions, and in the Chess Olympiads of 1954, 1956, 1960, 1962, 1966, 1968, 1970, 1974 and 1976. He is also a strong blindfold player and in 1947 created a new world record by playing 45 games blindfold in 23½ hours (+39 −2 =4). (1976 Elo rating: 2510)

**Najdorf Variation** an opening sequence arising out of the Sicilian Defence: 1. P–K4, P–QB4 2. N–KB3, N–QB3 3. P–Q4, P×P 4. N×P, N–KB3 5. N–QB3, *P–QR3*. Black waits until White has revealed his intentions before committing his men. Other advantages of it are that it can form the base for a Queen-side pawn storm and indirectly allows the Queen to go to QB2 if necessary, since White cannot attack this square with a Knight on his QN5.

This opening is named after the Argentinian Grandmaster Miguel Najdorf, who pioneered it in the 1940s.

**Napier, William Ewart** (1881–1952) American chess player; born in Camberwell, England on 17 January 1881. Napier's family emigrated to the United States when he was five and he was brought up in New York. He was champion of the Brooklyn Chess Club by the age of 16; in the same year he defeated Steinitz in a game played in a New York tournament and won a match against Marshall.

At the beginning of the century, Napier returned to Europe with the intention of studying music; instead, he devoted most of his time to chess. He won the brilliancy prize at Hanover (1902) for his win over Bardeleben and in 1904 won the first British Championship to be organized by the B.C.F. Later in the year he came twelfth at Cambridge Springs (1904). In 1908 Napier became an American citizen and retired from tournament chess. He died in Washington on 6 September 1952.

**National Chess Day** a day in the United States (9 October 1976) officially declared by President Gerald R. Ford 'to give special recognition to a game that generates challenge, intellectual stimulation and enjoyment for citizens of all ages.'

**National Chess League** a round-robin tournament of U.S. chess teams that began in January 1976. Matches are played by telephone on six boards. If teams are tied for first place at the end of the season game-points are used as a tie-breaker.

The founding teams, which were drawn from every region of the U.S.C.F., were Boston, Chicago, Cleveland, Houston, Los Angeles, Miami, New York, San Francisco and Washington. The first season ended with the 'Washington Plumbers' as the champions, being placed first on game points.

**National Master** a title that is awarded by each nation rather than by FIDE. In the United Kingdom the title British Master (B.M.) is awarded to any Briton who consistently attains a grading of at least 216 (approximately 2328 on the Elo scale) or who is awarded a title by FIDE. The lower title of Candidate Master (C.M.) is awarded to any Briton who attains one grading of at least 225 (approximately 2400 on the Elo scale), or two gradings of at least 216 (approximately 2328 on the Elo scale) or who has two performances in tournaments of at least nine rounds that are evaluated at a minimum of 230 (approximately 2440 on the Elo scale). Both of these titles are awarded for life, unlike the titles awarded by many other countries.

**Navarovsky, Laszlo** (b. 3 April 1933) Hungarian chess player; awarded the title International Master in 1965. (1976 Elo rating: 2400)

**Nearest Man Mover** a type of Fairy Chess in which each player must move the man that is nearest to the settling-point of the last man to move. If two or more men satisfy this criterion the player may choose which one to move. As in orthodox chess the objective is to mate the opposing King.

**Nedeljković, Dr Serćko** (b. 4 December 1923) Yugoslavian chess player; awarded the title International Master in 1950. He has competed in the European Team Championship and has played in matches against the U.S.S.R. He is married to the International Woman Master Vera Nedeljković-Jovanović.

**Nedeljković-Jovanović, Vera** (b. 16 September 1929) Yugoslavian chess player; awarded the title International Woman Master in 1954. She was Yugoslavian Woman Champion from 1951–1953, and in 1958 and 1965. She competed in the 1963 Women's Chess Olympiad where she won all twelve of her games. She also competed in the Women's Candidates' tournaments of 1955, 1959, 1961 and 1964. She is married to Dr Serćko Nedeljković, who is also an International Master.

**Neikirch, Oleg Nikolaevich** (b. 8 March 1914) Bulgarian chess player; awarded the title International Master in 1952. He was Bulgarian Champion in 1937, 1938, 1940, 1948, 1953 and 1957. He competed in the Chess Olympiads of 1939, 1954, 1958 and 1960.

**Nemet, Ivan** (b. 14 April 1943) Yugoslavian chess player; awarded the title International Master in 1976. (1976 Elo rating: 2455)

**Neo-Catalan System** an opening sequence arising out of the Catalan Opening: 1. N–KB3, P–Q4  2. P–B4, P–K3  3. *P–KN3*. White avoids an early advance of his Queen pawn, unlike most variations of the Catalan Opening. This leads to positional rather than tactical play and can easily transpose into the Réti Opening.

**Neo-Grünfeld Defence** a variation of the Queen's pawn opening: 1. P–Q4, N–KB3  2. P–QB4, P–KN3  3. P–KN3, B–N2  4. B–N2, *P–Q4*. Black adopts the Grünfeld strategy of . . . P–Q4 despite White's King-side fianchetto in place of 3. N–QB3. The continuations most commonly found are: 5. P × P, N × P or 5. N–KB3, O–O. This defence is also sometimes known as the Kemeri Variation.

**Neo-Indian Defence** another name for the **Queen's Indian Defence**.

**Neo-Orthodox Variation** an opening sequence arising out of the Orthodox Defence to the Queen's Gambit Declined: 1. P–Q4, P–Q4  2. P–QB4, P–K3  3. N–QB3, N–KB3  4. B–N5, B–K2  5. P–K3, O–O  6. N–B3, *P–KR3*  7. *B–R4*. See **Lasker's Defence**. Compare **Anti-Neo-Orthodox Variation.**

**neo-romantic** a twentieth-century style of play that prefers ultra-aggressive attack to defence, but which has absorbed all the teachings of defence. There have been many neo-romantic players including Marshall, Spielmann, Larsen, Tal and (perhaps) Alekhine, yet they have not propounded a coherent body of principles as, for example, the **hypermodern** players did. It would seem that they share an emotional rather than intellectual committment to this style of play. Compare **romantic.**

**Neumann, Gustave Richard Ludwig** (1838–1881) German physician and amateur chess player; born in Gleiwitz, Germany on 15 December 1838. His results included a first at Dundee (1867) in front of Steinitz, a second at Altona (1872), an equal third at Baden-Baden (1870) and a fourth at Paris (1867). He died in Allenberg (then an Austro-Prussian province) on 16 February 1881.

**neutral piece** a Fairy chesspiece that can be used by either side. Neutral pawns may promote and then become neutral pieces. Unlike the Imitator, they can capture and check, but checks will normally be harmless since the attacked player will usually be able to move the neutral piece away.

***New Adventures of Puss-in-Boots, The*** Soviet fairytale film (1958) directed by A. Rou, in which chess pieces come to life and turn into human figures. The sets in the film are largely designed around chess motifs. The castle courtyard, for example, is a huge chessboard.

***New Traps in the Chess Opening*** a collection of 175 opening traps compiled by I. A. Horowitz. They are arranged by the openings in which they arise, which in turn are in alphabetical order. Each trap is accompanied by a diagram of the critical position; the moves of the variation in which it occurs are given in full until mate or a winning position has been established. The book was first published in the United Kingdom in 1966 and uses descriptive notation.

**New York (1857)** the first chess tournament (also called **American Championship** or **American Congress**) to be held in the United States to determine the national champion, to which all leading American players were invited. It was decisively won by Paul Morphy (+14 −1 =3) and virtually launched his short but spectacular chess career. See **First American Chess Congress, United States Championship.**

**New York (1924)** one of the strongest tournaments of all times. It was a double-round all-play-all event with ten contestants: Alekhine, Bogoljubov, Capablanca, Janowski, Edward Lasker, Emanuel Lasker, Maróczy, Marshall, Réti and Yates. It was won by Emanuel Lasker (+13 −1 =6) with Capablanca in second place (+10 −1 =9) and Alekhine in third (+6 −2 =12). This tournament was the occasion of Capablanca's first defeat in eight years – to Réti in the fifth round.

**New York (1927)** a match-tournament with six players. Each competitor met every other contestant four times, playing twenty games in all. The tournament was won by the World Champion Capablanca (+8 −0 =12) with Alekhine in second place (+5 −2 =13). The other players were (in the order that they finished) Nimzovitch, Vidmar,

Spielmann and Marshall. It seems probable that if Nimzovitch had finished above Alekhine in this tournament it would have been he who would have met Capablanca in the World Championship match later in the year. It was at this tournament that Nimzovitch was said to have protested that Vidmar, a heavy smoker, had an unlit cigarette in his mouth – on the grounds that the threat is stronger than the execution.

**New York Threats** a founding member of the **National Chess League**. In the league's first season the team came second. Members of the New York Threats included Robert Byrne, Leonid Shamkovich, Sal Matera, Andrew Soltis, Bernard Zuckerman, Pal Benkö, Edmar Mednis, Julio Kaplan and Arthur Bisguier.

**Nezhmetdinov, Rashid** (b. 15 December 1912) Soviet chess player; awarded the title International Master in 1954. He was schoolboy champion of Kazan in 1927 and became Kazan Champion of both chess and draughts in 1930. Nezhmetdinov won the Russian Federation Chess Championship in 1950, thus gaining the title of National Master, and is the only Soviet player to be a master in both chess and draughts. A book of his on chess theory and practice was published in 1953; it was the first chess book to be written in the Tatar language.

**Ničevski, Risto** (b. 28 June 1945) Yugoslavian chess player; awarded the title International Master in 1975. (1976 Elo rating: 2395)

**Nicholai, Nicholas de, Saint** see **Bonius Socius.**

**Nightrider** a Fairy chesspiece that can make several Knight-leaps in the same direction in its move. It is a type of Rider. This piece can cover a large distance but can attack at most only twelve squares, since it can make a maximum of only three jumps in any direction. For instance, a Nightrider on QB1, could only land on QR5, QN3, Q3, K2, K5, KB6, and KN3. It is represented on diagrams by an inverted Knight.

**Nikolac, Juraj** (b. 22 April 1932) Yugoslavian chess player; awarded the title International Master in 1975. (1976 Elo rating: 2485)

**Nikolić, Stanimir** (b. 26 January 1935) Yugoslavian chess player; awarded the title International Master in 1967.

**Nimzo-Indian Defence** a defence to the Queen pawn opening: 1. P–Q4, N–KB3 2. P–QB4, P–K3 3. N–QB3, *B–N5*. By this pin Black prevents an early P–K4 by White, but must be prepared to exchange his Bishop for the Knight in return for a weakening of White's pawn structure. This defence is more strategical and less tactical than its close relative the King's Indian Defence and is generally thought to be one of the strongest replies to the Queen pawn opening.

The name is a misnomer since the fianchetto of a Bishop, the characteristic of the Indian Defences, does not take place. With a transposition of moves it was played by Englisch against Steinitz at Vienna (1882) and by Blackburne against Englisch at London (1883). It was also played by Alekhine against Rubinstein at Leningrad (1914), but was first thoroughly analysed and played by Nimzovitch. (See illustration on p. 200).

Nimzo-Indian Defence

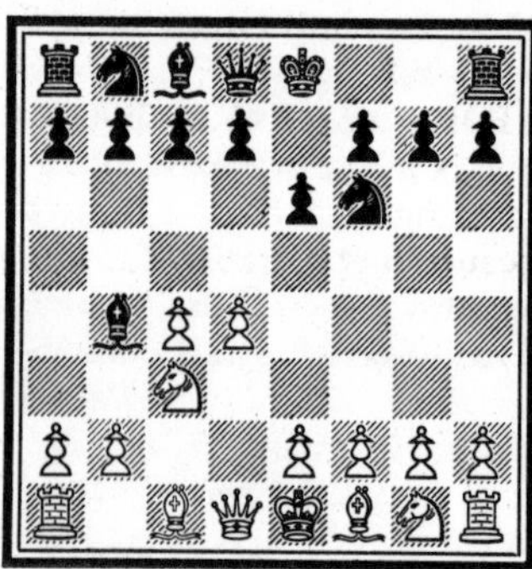

Position after 3 . . ., B–N5

**Nimzovitch, Aron** (1886–1935) leading chess player and theorist; born in Riga, Latvia on 7 November 1886. He was taught to play chess at the age of eight by his father, himself an expert player, yet became deeply interested only during his years at Berlin University. His pre-war tournament results were not outstanding and, perhaps motivated by disappointment, Nimzovitch evolved an original conception of chess that apparently contradicted the prevailing dogmas. His ideas included the concept of the blockade, overprotection, and a theory of pawn chains. He has been described as 'The Father of Modern Chess'.

Nimzovitch emigrated to Denmark after the Russian Revolution and in the 1920s scored many successes, of which his victory at Carlsbad (1929) was the greatest; in his post-war career he was first in thirteen of the 28 tournaments in which he participated. In this period he was one of the main contenders for the World Championship, but was never able to raise the $10,000 necessary to sponsor a challenge.

Nimzovitch was highly eccentric and nervous in temperament; this led to arrogant conduct with those whom he believed disagreed with his theories. Apparently he refused to speak to the Polish player Przepiorka for many years because Nimzovitch believed him to be a follower of Tarrasch. Nimzovitch died in Copenhagen on 16 March 1935. His major books in English are *Chess Praxis* and *My System*.

**Nimzovitch Attack** another name for **Larsen's Opening**.

**Nimzovitch Defence** a defence to the King pawn opening: 1. P–K4, *N–QB3*. Black's strategy of attacking White's Queen pawn with pieces has several weaknesses. His Queen Knight is awkwardly placed as it prevents the advance of the Queen Bishop pawn. A common continuation is: 2. P–Q4, P–Q4 3. N–QB3.

Only Nimzovitch, the inventor of this defence, played it regularly at top-class level.

**Nimzovitch Variation** another name for the **Winawer Variation**. This is its more common designation on the Continent due to the extensive contributions made to it by Nimzovitch.

**Noah's Ark Trap** a trap that can be set in the Ruy Lopez opening. White steps blindly into it on the tenth move. Typically it goes as follows: 1. P–K4, P–K4 2. N–KB3, N–QB3 3. B–N5, P–QR3 4. B–R4, N–B3 5. O–O, B–K2 6. R–K1, P–QN4 7. B–N3, P–Q3 8. *P–Q4?*, QN × P 9. N × N, P × N 10. *Q × P?*, P–B4 11. (White's Queen moves out of danger), P–B5 (winning White's Bishop). The trap is so named because it is apparently so ancient that Noah might well have used it. Another, equally fanciful, reason given for its name is the fact that the White Bishop is shut in an ark (or 'arc') of Black pawns.

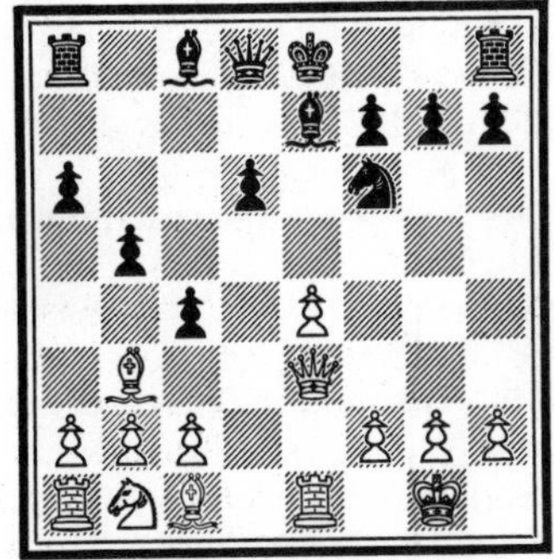

Position after 11 . . ., P–B5

***Noble Game of Chess, The*** a book by the Syrian chess player Philippe Stamma. In it he gives some information on the Syrian version of the game. For example, he mentions that castling was not allowed, that a promoted pawn could only become a Queen, and that the chessboard was commonly an unchequered piece of cloth marked with dividing lines.

**norm** the number of points a player must gain in a tournament to gain a qualification for the title International Master or International Grandmaster. Two norms must be achieved within three years of each other before the title is awarded by FIDE. The sizes of the norms will vary among tournaments according to the number of competitors and their overall strength. The latter factor is computed by FIDE through the International Rating List, which provides an estimate of the strength of the world's best players.

Each eligible tournament is placed into a category between 1 (where the tournament is the weakest) and 15 (which covers the strongest tournaments). The higher the category the lower the size of the norms as the opposition is consequently stronger. Certain tournaments cannot be assigned norms for the contestants to attempt to meet. The three main reasons for ineligibility are too few competitors, too low an average strength (so that the tournament would be below the minimum category) or too few foreign players (since only international tournaments are assigned norms). Category 5 is the lowest in which an IGM norm can be made.

**normal chess** the orthodox form of chess. See **traditional chess, variant forms of chess.**

**Normal Opening** formerly another name for the French Defence. It was named by Carl Andreyevich Jänisch, a leading Russian player of the nineteenth century who analysed it.

**Normal Position** an opening sequence arising out of the Evans Gambit: 1. P–K4, P–K4 2. N–KB3, N–QB3 3. B–B4, B–B4 4. P–QN4, B×NP 5. P–B3, B–R4 6. P–Q4, P×P 7. O–O, P–Q3 8. P×P, B–N3. In this position White has ample compensation for his sacrificed pawn in his strong pawn centre and well developed pieces, but Black's game is also sound. The most common continuations are: 9. N–B3 or 9. P–Q5. This is called the 'Normal Position' as it has been known and studied for nearly 150 years, i.e. almost as long as the Evans Gambit itself has been in existence.

**Nostalgic King** a Fairy chesspiece that must return to its K1 on its next move whenever it lands on a square that could be landed upon by a Queen on K1. It was invented by W. Hagemann of Braunschweig.

**notation** any method of recording the moves of a game by means of signs and symbols. The two most widely used systems are the algebraic and descriptive.

***Not Only Chess*** a collection of essays by Gerald Abrahams. Many topics are covered, but all deal with chess in some manner. It was first published in 1974 and uses descriptive notation.

**Nottingham (1936)** one of the strongest tournaments ever to be held in the United Kingdom. It was an all-play-all tournament and was jointly won by Botvinnik and Capablanca with ten points each. This was the first major international Soviet success and was also Emanuel Lasker's final tournament. His performance (seventh place with 7½ points) was very impressive considering the calibre of the opposition. Other competitors included Alekhine, Alexander, Bogoljubov, Euwe, Fine, Flohr, Reshevsky, Tartakover, Sir George Thomas, Vidmar and Winter.

**novice** see **beginner.**

**Novotelnov, Nikolai** (b. 9 December 1911) Soviet chess player; awarded the title International Master in 1950. He was Leningrad Champion in 1942, Champion of the Russian Federated Republic in 1947 and in the same year was first in the semi-final of the Soviet Championship.

**Nun, Josef** (b. 7 July 1933) Czechoslovakian chess player; awarded the title International Master in 1976. (1976 Elo rating: 2420)

**Nunn, John D. M.** (b. 25 April 1955) British chess player; awarded the titles International Master in 1975 and International Grandmaster in 1978. He was European Junior Champion in 1975, which gained him the title International Master. He came second at the I.B.M. Masters tournament (1975). (1976 Elo rating: 2435)

**Nuremberg (1896)** a tournament with nineteen competitors, won by Lasker (who scored 13½) ahead of Maróczy (12½), Pillsbury (12) and Tarrasch (12).

# O

**obtrusive piece** a piece in a chess problem that could only be a promoted piece. For instance, a Queen Bishop in the centre of the board must be an obtrusive piece if the Queen pawn and Queen Knight pawn have not moved. The presence of an obtrusive piece is considered to be a serious defect in a chess problem.

**O'Connell, Kevin J.** (b. 28 August 1949) British writer, editor and author of several books on chess. He is Assistant Editor of B.C.M. and Associate Editor of *The Chess Player*. His books include *The Games of Robert J. Fischer* and *The Complete Games of World Champion Anatoly Karpov*. He is the editor of *The Batsford Chess Yearbook*.

**odds** inequalities in the opening strengths of each player's forces. To give odds is to handicap yourself by reducing your material or forfeiting a tempo in order to offset any disparity in the ability of the two players. In descending order of importance, the most common types of odds are: 1) an agreement that all draws should be counted as a win for the weaker player, 2) sacrifice of a pawn and move, 3) sacrifice of pawn and two moves, 4) sacrifice of a minor piece, 5) sacrifice of a Rook, 6) sacrifice of a Rook, pawn and move, 7) sacrifice of two minor pieces, 8) sacrifice of Rook and minor piece, 9) sacrifice of a Queen. In the nineteenth century games at odds were commonplace. For instance, Morphy won a match against the Reverend John Owens after giving odds of a pawn and move. Today odds-playing is disliked, partly because it destroys the value of any memorized opening variations. Instead it is preferred to sacrifice time – the better player might play all his moves in five minutes while his opponent is allowed to take fifteen.

**offensive player** a player who is better at attacking manoeuvres than defensive manoeuvres.

**off-hand game** a friendly game that is not played in a tournament or official match and whose outcome does not affect the ratings of the players.

***Official Rules of Chess*** an official publication of FIDE that sets out the laws of chess. The latest revised edition in English was published in 1975 and also contains the relevant decisions of the 1974 FIDE Congress, which was held at Nice.

**Ogaard, Leif** (b. 5 January 1952) Norwegian chess player; awarded the title International Master in 1974. (1976 Elo rating: 2490)

**Ojanen, Kaarle Sakari** (b. 14 December 1918) Finnish chess player; awarded the title International Master in 1952. Ojanen was Finnish Champion 1950–1953, 1957–1962 and in 1967. He competed in the Chess Olympiads of 1937, 1950, 1952, 1956, 1958, 1960, 1966, 1968 and 1970.

**O'Kelly de Galway, Alberic** (b. 17 May 1911) Belgian chess player; awarded the titles International Grandmaster in 1956, International Correspondence Grandmaster in 1962, and International Judge in 1962. He has been Belgian Champion several times since 1936. His best performance over the board was first place at the 1947 zonal tournament. He became World Correspondence Chess Champion in 1964. O'Kelly de Galway was arbiter in the World Championship matches of 1963, 1966 and 1969.

In 1958 the Belgian government awarded him the decoration of the Golden Palm of the Order of the Crown for his achievements in chess. (1976 Elo rating: 2445)

**Olafsson, Fridrik** (b. 26 January 1935) Icelandic chess player; awarded the title International Master in 1956 and the title International Grandmaster in 1958. He was Iceland's first Grandmaster. (1976 Elo rating: 2550)

**oldest recorded game** this was played (according to H. J. R. Murray) in the first half of the tenth century between Abu-Bakr Muhammad b. Yaḫyā aṣ-Sūlī and his pupil Abū'l-Faraj al-Muzaffar b. Sa'īd al-Lajlāj. Murray discovered the game in a manuscript belonging to John G. White and deciphered and translated it. The rules of chess differed then in several instances. Pawns could advance only one square at a time and could promote only to a Queen. The Bishop could move only two squares diagonally and like the Knight could pass over an occupied square. The Queen could move only one square diagonally and there was no castling. The game went as follows: 1. P–KB3, P–KB3 2. P–KB4, P–KB4 3. N–KB3, N–KB3 4. P–KN3, P–KN3 5. R–N1, R–N1 6. P–KR3, P–KR3 7. P–K3, P–K3 8. P–KN4, P×P 9. P×P, P–KN4 10. P×P, P×P 11. P–Q3, P–Q3 12. P–K4, P–K4 13. B–K3, B–K3 14. N×NP, K–K2 15. P–B3, N×NP 16. K–K2, P–B3 17. P–Q4, P–Q4 18. P–N3, P–N3 19. N–Q2, N–Q2 20. Q–B2, Q–B2 21. Q–Q3, Q–Q3 22. N(Q2)–B3, N(Q2)–B3 23. B–R3, B–R3 24. B–KB5, B–KB5 25. QR–QB1, P–R3 26. P–B4, QR–B1 27. P–B5, P×BP 28. B×Pch, K–K1 29. P×KP, N(N5)×P 30. N×B, R×R 31. R×R, N×N 32. K×N and White has the superior position.

The oldest recorded game with the modern rules was played between Francisco de Castellni and Narcisco Vinoles, probably in Barcelona in 1485. The game went as follows: 1. P–K4, P–Q4 2. P×P, Q×P 3. N–QB3, Q–Q1 4. B–B4, N–KB3 5. N–B3, B–N5 6. P–KR3, B×N 7. Q×B, P–K3 8. Q×P, QN–Q2 9. N–N5, R–B1 10. N×RP, N–N3 11. N×R, N×N 12. P–Q4, N–Q3 13. B–N5ch, N×B 14. Q×Nch, N–Q2 15. P–Q5, P×P 16. B–K3, B–Q3 17. R–Q1, Q–B3 18. R×P, Q–N3 19. B–B4, B×B 20. Q×Nch, K–B1 21. Q–Q8mate.

**Old Indian Defence** a defence to the Queen pawn opening: 1. P–Q4, N–KB3 2. P–QB4, *P–Q3* 3. N–QB3, *P–K4*. The King Bishop is not fianchettoed in this defence although it is in most other Indian defences, but in formation and strategy this is otherwise typically Indian.

This opening was first played at Monte Carlo (1903) and became a favourite of Tchigorin. The ideas behind this opening were later refined to produce the King's Indian Defence, though the Old Indian is still occasionally seen today.

**Olympiad** see **Chess Olympiad.**

oldest recorded game

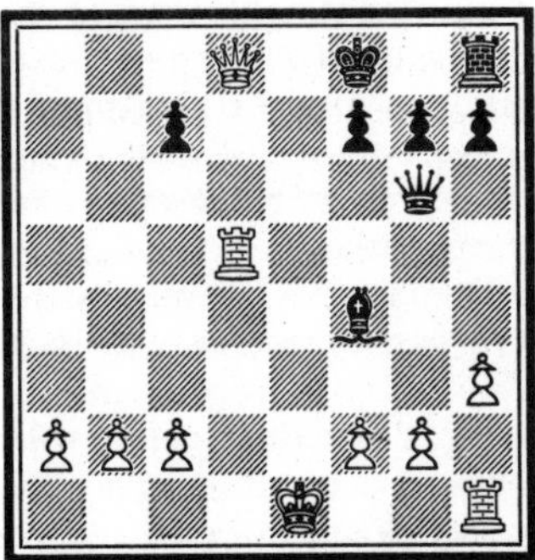

Position after 21. Q–Q8mate (1485)

**Olympiad for the Blind** another name for **IBCA Olympiad.**

**Onat, Ilhan** (b. 5 December 1929) Turkish chess player; awarded the title International Master in 1975. (1976 Elo rating: 2355)

***100 Instructive Games of Alekhine*** a collection of games played by Alekhine in his youth, compiled by Fred Reinfeld. The book consists of games played between 1905 and 1914. It was first published in 1949 under the title *The Unknown Alekhine* and renamed and republished in 1959. It uses descriptive notation. See ***My Best Games of Chess 1908–23, My Best Games of Chess 1924–37, Alekhine's Best Games of Chess 1938–45.***

**O–O** symbol for castles King side used in chess notation.

**O–O–O** symbol for castles Queen side used in chess notation.

**open board** a chessboard on which all or most of the pawns have been captured, leaving great freedom of movement for the remaining pieces.

**open file** one that has no pawns upon it. Open files are important as they provide paths for Rooks to penetrate into the opponent's position. For this reason, manoeuvring to gain control of (or prevent control by the opponent of) open files is a common feature of many games. See **file, half-open file.**

**open formation** (Kmoch's term) a pawn formation with one or more open files. See ***Pawn Power in Chess.***

**open game** a position where the pieces have plenty of room to manoeuvre, due to the presence of features such as open lines. The pieces will tend to be found in front of the pawns and so there will be more opportunities for exchanges and quick attacks. The King pawn opening will almost always lead to open games. Since the open game is characterized by the presence of room to manoeuvre, it can eventually develop from the closed game as men are exchanged off. Compare **closed game.**

**opening** the initial phase of the game. It is completed once all the pieces have been developed; this normally takes twelve moves or less. Like the endings, the openings have been extensively analysed and many variations have been studied that continue well into the middle-game. An opening is normally named after the player who invented or popularized it, after the tournament, town or area where it was first played, or after some characteristic feature of that opening. Most will have important variations which are also named.

Compare **middle-game, ending**. See ***Chess Openings, Theory and Practice***; ***How to Play the Opening in Chess***; ***Modern Chess Openings***; ***Modern Openings in Theory and Practice***.

**open line** any file or diagonal that has no pawns upon it. An open file can only be created by pawn captures. The most valuable use of an open line is to act as a path into the opponent's position. For example, control of an open file by the Rooks allows them to arrive on the seventh rank, thereby cordoning off the enemy King on the first rank and attacking the enemy pawns from the side and rear.

**open tournament** an event which players of any strength can enter. It thus provides opportunities for the weakest to compete against the strongest. Compare **congress**.

**Opočensky, Karel** (1892–1975) Czechoslovakian chess player; awarded the titles International Master in 1954 and International Judge in 1951. He was born on 7 November 1892 and died on 16 November 1975.

Opočensky was Czechoslovakian Champion in 1927, 1928, 1938 and 1944. His best result over-the-board was probably his performance on fourth board at the 1933 Olympiad, where he scored 11½/13. As an International Judge he was the arbiter of the World Championship matches of 1951 and 1954 and the Candidates' tournament of 1953.

**opposite-coloured Bishops** see **Bishops of opposite colours**.

**opposition** a situation that exists when a King must retreat, allowing the opposing King to gain ground. This can only occur when no other man can be moved and occurs almost exclusively in King and pawn endgames. In addition the Kings must be on the same rank, file or diagonal and be separated by an odd number of squares (so that they stand on squares of the same colour).

When only one square is separating the Kings, **direct opposition** is said to exist. The player who does not have the opposition, i.e. whose King is in **zugzwang**, must then retreat his King. The **distant opposition** exists when the Kings are on the same rank, file, or diagonal and are separated by three or five squares. The player who has the opposition can often convert this into direct opposition by advancing his King.

Gaining and taking advantage of the opposition is one of the commonest winning manoeuvres found in King and pawn endgames. For this reason manoeuvres to gain and lose tempi, such as triangulation of the King, are one of the prevalent characteristics of the endgame.

**Orang-Utan Opening** the original name of the Polish (or Sokolsky) Opening. It was coined in 1924 by Tartakover, who claimed that he thought of the opening while visiting New York Zoo, where an Orang-Utan recommended the move 1. P–QN4 to him. See also **Santasiere's Folly**.

opposition

Direct opposition and distant opposition

**organic weakness** any permanent defect in pawn structure. An organic weakness would be the presence of blocked doubled pawns. Its existence will normally lead to other disadvantages as the defender's freedom of action is limited because of the need to defend this weak-point. Unlike a functional weakness this is a static rather than a dynamic feature of the position. The term was coined by Euwe. Compare **functional weakness**.

**Ornstein, Axel** (b. 24 April 1952) Swedish chess player; awarded the title International Master in 1975. He was Swedish Champion in 1975. (1976 Elo rating: 2470)

**Orthodox Defence** an opening sequence arising out of the Queen's Gambit Declined. The classical position is arrived at as follows: 1. P–Q4, P–Q4 2. P–QB4, *P–K3* 3. N–QB3, N–KB3 4. B–N5, B–K2 5. P–K3, O–O 6. N–B3, QN–Q2 7. R–B1, P–B3. Black's second move defines this defence. The defence was named by Siegbert Tarrasch (1852–1934), who – according to I. A. Horowitz – 'poked fun at all systems except his own.' (See diagram on p. 208.) See **Alekhine Variation, Anti-Neo-Orthodox Variation, Canal's Variation, Classical Variation, Exchange Variation, Half-Classical Variation, Lasker's Defence, Neo-Orthodox Variation, Pillsbury Attack, Ragozin System.**

**orthodox problem** a **chess problem** in which White must checkmate Black in the stipulated number of moves and without infringing the laws of chess. Compare **Fairy Chess.**

**Oscar** see **Chess Oscar.**

**Osnos, Vialcheslav** (b. 24 July 1935) Soviet chess player; awarded the title International Master in 1965. (1976 Elo rating: 2490)

**Ostojić, Predrag** (b. 22 February 1938) Yugoslavian chess player; awarded the titles International Master in 1968 and International Grandmaster in 1975. He competed in the Student Olympiads of 1962, 1963 and 1964 and in the 1975 match against the U.S.S.R. Other results are equal first at the Hoogoven Masters tournament (1968), seconds at the Hoogoven Masters tournaments (1966 and 1967) and at Cleveland (1975) and a third at Olot (1974). (1976 Elo rating: 2495)

Orthodox Defence

Position after 2 . . ., P–K3

**O.T.B., OTB** *abbrevs. for* over the board. It refers to play that takes place face to face as opposed to correspondence chess (C.C.). Over-the-board play consumes more nervous energy and requires a greater degree of precise knowledge of chess theory.

**outer lever** (Kmoch's term) a **lever** that slopes away from the centre. Obviously what will be an outer lever for one player will not be for the other. Compare **inner lever, loose lever, tight lever.** See ***Pawn Power in Chess***.

**outerswap** (Kmoch's term) a type of **doubling** in which the pawn captures away from the centre. This normally weakens that player's position through the creation of doubled pawns and a decrease in control over the centre, but one major exception occurs in the Exchange Variation (Ruy Lopez) where: 4. . . ., QP × B is preferable to: 4. . . ., NP × B. Compare **centreswap, innerswap.** See ***Pawn Power in Chess***.

**outpost** a piece in the opponent's half of the board that stands on an open file and is supported by at least one pawn. Often it can be driven away only by a pawn, whose advance may create weaknesses elsewhere. The term was coined by Nimzovitch. Compare **support-point.**

**overprotection** the defence of an important square by more men than is strictly necessary. The concept was devised by Nimzovitch who stated that not only would the square be adequately protected but the defending pieces would 'find themselves well posted in every respect'.

**over the board** see **O.T.B.**

**overworked man** a man that has two or more tasks which it cannot perform simultaneously. For instance, a pawn might be protecting two pieces or a Rook might be guarding a piece as well as preventing a back-rank mate. If it is forced to fulfil one of its tasks a weakness is created elsewhere. For instance, in the position illustrated on p. 209, White won by 1. Q–K1!, and the Black Queen can no longer guard the Rook and prevent checkmate.

The winning variation is: 1. Q–K1!, Q–Q1 2. Q–K5, K–N1 3. Q–K6ch, K–R1 4. Q × R!.

**overworked man**

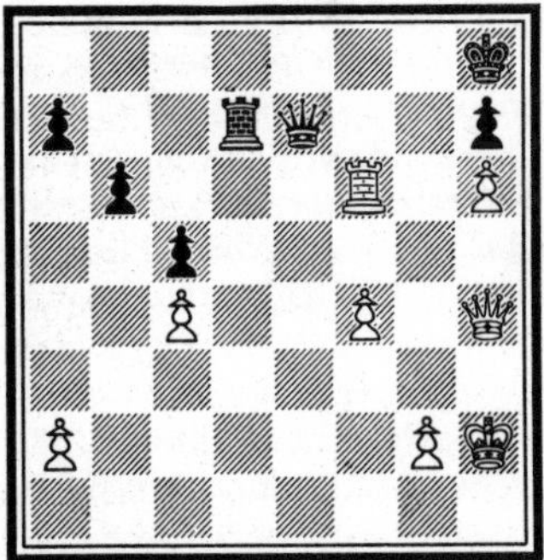

Wolfers vs. Koshnitzky (Australia, 1971)

**Owen, Rev. John** (1827–1901) British amateur chess player; born in Staffordshire. Owen was ordained in 1851 and became vicar of Hooton, Cheshire from 1862 to 1900. He was a member of the St George's Chess Club and was recognized to be one of London's strongest amateurs. In 1858 he played seven games with Morphy who gave him odds of pawn and move (+0 −5 =2). His best tournament result was third place at London (1862) ahead of Steinitz, Löwenthal, and Blackburne. Owen was also a popular chess columnist and wrote under the pseudonym of 'Alter'.

***Oxford Encyclopedia of Chess Games*** a major reference work that records all important chess games played since the introduction of modern rules in about 1485. Volume I (published in 1977) covers games up to the late nineteenth century. It is published by the Oxford University Press and edited by David Levy and Kevin O'Connell.

# P

**P** *abbrev. for* pawn.

**Pachman, Ludeck** (b. 11 May 1924) West German chess player; awarded the titles International Master in 1950 and International Grandmaster in 1954. He was Czechoslovakian Champion seven times and competed for Czechoslovakia in the Chess Olympiads of 1952, 1954, 1956, 1958, 1960, 1962, 1964 and 1966. He also participated in the interzonals of 1948, 1952, 1955, 1958, 1964 and 1976 (Manila).

Pachman was imprisoned following the Soviet invasion of Czechoslovakia in 1968, but was later allowed to emigrate to West Germany. For some years afterwards Soviet and other East European players boycotted any tournament in which he took part, causing a severe curtailment of his career. This boycott ended only with the 1976 interzonal when the FIDE qualifying cycle finally forced the Soviet players to compete again against Pachman. The same year he represented West Germany in the Chess Olympiad in Haifa.

Pachman is one of the leading opening theorists in the world. His publications include: *Complete Chess Strategy* (in three volumes) and *Pachman's Decisive Games*. (1976 Elo rating: 2520)

**Padevski, Nikola Botchev** (b. 29 May 1933) Bulgarian chess player; awarded the titles International Master and International Grandmaster in 1964. (1976 Elo rating: 2475)

***Palamède Français, Le*** a chess periodical that appeared in 1864 with Paul Journod as its editor. It lasted for less than a year. It had no links with *Le Palamède*.

***Palamède, Le*** the first chess periodical. It was founded in 1836 by La Bourdonnais, who also edited it until ill-health forced him to retire in 1839. *Le Palamède* then ceased publication, but was revived in 1841 by Saint-Amant and Joseph Méry, who became its joint-editors. It closed in 1847.

The periodical was named after Palamedes, an Ancient Greek who was believed to have made many inventions, including chess.

**Pan-American Championship** an international tournament held to discover the best player from the American continents. The first event was held in August 1974 in Winnipeg, Canada and was convincingly won by the American International Grandmaster Walter Browne (+12 −0 =3).

**Pan-American Team Championship** an event held to discover the strongest team from the American continents. The first championship, in which only the Latin American teams competed, was held in Tucuman, Argentina from 30 October to 9 November 1971. Eight teams competed in a round-robin tournament held on four boards. The event was decisively won by Argentina (25½ points), with Cuba second (17½ points) and Brazil and Chile joint third (16 points). Compare **European Team Championship.**

**Panno, Oscar** (b. 17 March 1935) Argentinian chess player; awarded the title International Master in 1954, after becoming World Junior Champion in 1953, and the title International Grandmaster in 1955. (1976 Elo rating: 2520)

**Panno Variation** an opening sequence arising out of the King's Indian Defence: 1. P–Q4, N–KB3 2. P–QB4, P–KN3 3. P–KN3, B–N2 4. B–N2, O–O 5. N–QB3, P–Q3 6. N–B3, *N–B3* 7. O–O, *P–QR3*. There are numerous continuations for both players. This variation was devised by Oscar Panno, an Argentinian Grandmaster, in 1955.

**Panov-Botvinnik Attack** an opening sequence arising out of the Caro-Kann Defence: 1. P–K4, P–QB3 2. P–Q4, P–Q4 3. P×P, P×P 4. *P–QB4*, N–KB3 5. *N–QB3*. White attempts to transpose into a favourable variation of the Queen's Gambit Accepted. Black's best immediate reply: 5 . . ., N–B3. This variation was devised and analysed by the Soviet players Vasily Panov and Mikhail Botvinnik in the 1930s and was believed for a long time to be one of White's strongest options against the Caro-Kann.

**Panov, Vasily** (1906–1973) Soviet chess player and theorist; awarded the title International Master in 1950. He was born in Kozelsk on 1

November 1906. In 1929 he won the Moscow Championship and competed in the finals of the Soviet Championship in 1934, 1937, 1939, 1940 and 1948. He was well-known for his researches into the openings, particularly the Caro-Kann, the Ruy Lopez and the King's Indian Defence. He was the author of numerous books including a collection of 300 of Alekhine's games and was chess correspondent for *Izvestia*. He died in January 1973.

**Pao** a Fairy chesspiece that moves like a normal Rook except when capturing. To capture a piece the Pao must jump over it, landing on any square that is directly on its path. Unlike the Locust, the Pao can move without capturing, when it moves like an orthodox Rook. The Pao, the Leo and the Vao were introduced from Chinese chess by T. R. Dawson.

**Paoli, Enrico** (b. 13 January 1908) Italian chess player; awarded the title International Master in 1951. He was Italian Champion in 1951, 1957 and 1968 and competed in the 1954 and 1976 Chess Olympiads. (1976 Elo rating: 2265)

**Paris (1867)** a double-round tournament with thirteen competitors, won by Kolisch (who scored 20) ahead of Winawer (19) and Steinitz (18).

**Paris (1900)** a tournament with seventeen competitors, won by Lasker (14½) ahead of Pillsbury (12½), Maróczy (12) and Marshall (12).

**Paris Gambit** an opening sequence arising out of the Paris Opening: 1. N–KR3, P–Q4 2. P–KN3, P–K4 3. *P–KB4*, B×N 4. B×B, P×P 5. O–O. White disrupts his pawns but attains the Bishop pair as well as an open King Bishop file. It is very rarely played.

**Paris Opening** an opening where White plays 1. *N–KR3*, partly for its shock value and partly to take Black out of the book. If it is not attacked, the Knight can support the advance of the King Bishop pawn attacking Black's pawn centre. The opening was given its name by its inventor – the (naturalized French) International Grandmaster, Tartakover.

**Parma, Bruno** (b. 30 December 1941) Yugoslavian chess player; awarded the titles International Master in 1961 and International Grandmaster in 1963. He was World Junior Champion in 1961. (1976 Elo rating: 2515)

**Paros, Dr Gyorgy** (1910–1975) Hungarian problem composer. He was born on 28 April 1910 and died on 17 December 1975. He was awarded the titles International Judge of Chess Compositions in 1956 and International Grandmaster for Chess Compositions in 1975.

Paros was the world's leading helpmate composer and won over 100 first prizes in his career. From 1933 until his death, he was editor of the problem section of the *Magyar Sakkelet*.

**parry a check** to interpose a man between the checking piece and the attacked King. Parrying a check is one of the three means of negating a check, the others are to capture the checking man and to move the King to an unattacked square. If none of these three methods is possible the King is checkmated.

**Parsloe's** the leading English chess club of the late eighteenth century. It was founded in 1792 and quickly attracted the cream of London life to its premises in St James's Street, among whom were a former prime minister, the Marquis of Rockingham, Charles James Fox, Edward Gibbon, the Ambassador of Saxony, Count Brühl (who was probably the strongest player), and the Rev. George Atwood, who recorded many of the games that were played at the club. The club's chief attraction was undoubtedly the visits of Philidor every spring. After 1793 Philidor lived in England in exile, and played at Parsloe's frequently until his death in 1795. This event marked the beginning of the decline of the club. Another French master, Verdoni, proved an unsuccessful replacement and membership decreased, with many former members transferring to the London Chess Club, which opened in 1807. Parsloe's struggled on for two more decades in relative obscurity until it eventually closed in the middle 1820s.

**partie** *French for* game. As France was undoubtedly the strongest chess-playing nation in the early nineteenth century, and had been for over a century, it became fashionable to use French terms. Steinitz originally called the famous game between Anderssen and Dufresne the 'Evergreen partie' rather than the 'Evergreen game'.

**Partos, Carol** (b. 10 August 1932) Romanian chess player; awarded the title International Master in 1975. (1976 Elo rating: 2410)

**passed pawn** a pawn that is not opposed by hostile pawns on its own file or the two adjacent files. Whenever such a pawn is created the strategy is to advance it whenever possible, as it increases in value with each move that it makes. Even when it does not promote it can often only be prevented by the sacrifice of a piece. See also **half-passed pawn, united passed pawns.**

**passer** (Kmoch's term) a **passed pawn.**

**passive** **1.** relating to a move that poses no threats. A passive move is thus purely defensive.

**2.** relating to a piece that has less mobility than its counterpart on the other side. Compare **active.**

**patzer** slang for an extremely weak player. The term is derived from the German verb *patzen* meaning to carry out badly or to blunder.

***Paul Morphy, the Chess Champion*** title of a book first published in 1859 by Morphy's friend and companion Frederick Milne Edge. It is currently (1977) available under the title *The Exploits and Triumphs in Europe of Paul Morphy, The Chess Champion.*

***Paul Morphy: The Pride and Sorrow of Chess*** a biography of Paul Morphy written by David Lawson, considered by some reviewers to be the best available. It was first published in 1976.

**Paulsen, Louis** (1833–1891) a leading chess player of the nineteenth century. He was born in Germany, but emigrated with his brother to the United States at the age of 21. He entered the First American Chess Congress (1857) and reached the final, but was decisively beaten by Morphy. Apparently Paulsen was such a slow player that Morphy refused ever to play him in a match.

The defeats against Morphy sharply exposed Paulsen's lack of opening theory. To remedy this he studied the openings thoroughly and made many innovations, although they were not all credited to him. For example, what are now known as the Göring Gambit and the Boleslavsky Variation of the Sicilian Defence were both discovered by Paulsen, who undoubtedly became one of the outstanding theorists of his era.

In 1860 Paulsen returned to Germany and became a professional chess player. His successes included firsts at Bristol (1861), Leipzig (1877), Frankfurt (1878) and Brunswick (1880). He also played three matches against Anderssen, drawing the first in 1862 (+3 −3 =2) and winning in 1876 (+5 −4 =1) and 1877 (+5 −3 =1). Paulsen was also an excellent blindfold player, creating a world record in 1859 when he played fifteen simultaneous blindfold games.

**pawn** a chessman that moves forward one square at a time with the option of advancing two squares on its first move. It can capture only on the two diagonally adjacent squares in front of it. If it reaches the eighth rank it can be promoted into any piece except the King. Each side begins with eight pawns which initially occupy the second rank. Theoretically the pawn is the least valuable of the chessmen; three are approximately as valuable as one minor piece.

The pawn's move has remained almost unchanged throughout the history of chess. The only alterations have been the introduction of the first-move option to move two squares and the formulation of the **en passant** rule.

Pawns advance one square at a time (except on their first move, when they have the option of two moves) and capture diagonally

In Arabic this man was called the *baidaq* (foot-soldier) and this name was translated when chess was introduced into Europe. Its English name is ultimately derived from the Latin *pedes* (foot-soldier). In the nineteenth century the name for peasant was substituted in several languages, examples being *bonde* in Danish and *Bauer* in German. Abbrev. **P.** See **pawn promotion.**

**pawn chain** a group of pawns on adjacent files that support each other, but cannot advance either by reason of a blockade or because of the threat of capture. A pawn chain is a static feature while a **pawn roller** is dynamic. Almost by definition pawn chains will be found most often in closed games. According to Nimzovitch, a pawn chain should be attacked at its weakest point, which is its base.

**pawn-cross** (Kmoch's term) a grid system to determine a pawn's location on the chessboard. The number of squares on the rank on either side of the pawn are called the lee and luff. The number of squares on the file that are in front of and behind the pawn are called the frontspan and rearspan. See ***Pawn Power in Chess***.

**pawn island** any pawn or group of pawns that cannot be defended by other pawns. The largest possible pawn island consists of eight pawns while the smallest consists of only one. The fewer pawn islands a player has (assuming each side to have an equal number of pawns) the less likely are there to be weaknesses in his position. The term was coined by Capablanca.

***Pawn Power in Chess*** an analysis by Hans Kmoch of the use of pawns in chess. It is especially notable for the immense amount of jargon that the author created in it, such as quartgrip, ram, sealer and telestop. These terms are not in general use.

**pawn promotion** the transmutation of a pawn into any piece except the King upon reaching the eighth rank. Although the pawn will normally be exchanged for a Queen, it is sometimes tactically justifiable to turn it into a lesser piece (see **underpromotion**).

The law governing pawn promotion varied widely throughout mediaeval Europe. In some countries a pawn could only promote into a piece that had previously been captured and if no capture of a piece had been made the pawn remained inert on the eighth rank until one took place. A common variation was a ban on the presence of two Queens of the same colour on the board at the same time as this might seem to encourage bigamy! A much rarer rule decreed that a pawn could only promote into the piece whose file it stood on. Here, a pawn on the King file would promote into a Queen.

**pawn push** another name for **pawn roller**.

**pawn roller** a steady concerted advance of two or more united pawns. This can have a wide variety of purposes, perhaps to promote a pawn, perhaps to disrupt a castled King's defences, or perhaps to tie down some of the opponent's forces, so weakening him elsewhere. Pawn rollers that cannot be blockaded are exceptionally dangerous as they usually can only be halted by the sacrifice of a piece. Also called **pawn storm, steamroller**.

**pawn storm** another name for **pawn roller**.

**pawn structure** a pawn formation of one colour or the joint pawn formation of both sides. A pawn structure will either be static or dynamic depending upon whether the pawns are blocked or are free to advance.

Pawn structures consist of unit pawns (see **pawn chain**) or isolated groups known as pawn islands. Strong features that they can contain are passed pawns and pawn majorities, while characteristically weak features are backward pawns, doubled pawns, hanging pawns, and isolated pawns.

The pawn structure after the opening is the predominant factor in determining the correct middle-game strategies of both players.

**Pearl of Zandvoort** the name given to the twenty-sixth game of the first world championship match between Alekhine and Euwe, played in Zandvoort, Holland in December, 1937. It has been unanimously described as the best game in the match and was the winning blow for Euwe. Euwe was White: 1. P–Q4, P–K3 2. P–QB4, P–KB4 3. P–KN3, B–N5ch 4. B–Q2, B–K2 5. B–N2, N–KB3 6. N–QB3, O–O 7. N–B3, N–K5 8. O–O, P–QN3 9. Q–B2, B–N2 10. n–K5, N×N 11. B×N, B×B 12. K×B, Q–B1 13. P–Q5, P–Q3 14. N–Q3, P–K4 15. K–R1, P–B3 16. Q–N3, K–R1 17. P–B4, P–K5 18. N–N4!, P–B4 19. N–B2, N–Q2 20. N–K3, B–B3 21. N×P!, B×B 22. N×QP, Q–N1 23. N×P, B–B3 24. N–Q2, P–KN4 25. P–K4, P×P 26. P×P, B–Q5 27. P–K5, Q–K1 28. P–K6, R–KN1 29. N–B3, Q–N3 30. R–KN1!, B×R 31. R×B, Q–B3 32. N–N5, R–N2 33. P×N, R×P? 34. Q–K3, R–K2 35. N–K6, R–KB1 36. Q–K5, Q×Q 37. P×Q, R–B4 38. R–K1, P–KR3 39. N–Q8, R–B7 40. P–K6, R–Q7 41. N–B6, R–K1 42. P–K7, P–N4 43. N–Q8, K–N2 44. N–N7, K–B3 45. R–K6ch, K–N4 46. N–Q6, R×KP 47. N–KPch, Resigns.

**Peasants' Revolt** a variant of chess in which White has only a King and eight pawns while Black has only a King, King pawn and four Knights. The extra Knights initially stand on KB1 and QB1 while all other men begin the game on their original squares. As in orthodox chess, the objective is to checkmate the opponent's King.

Initial position for Peasants' Revolt

***Penguin Book of Chess Positions, The*** a collection of 100 chess puzzles compiled by C. H. O'D. Alexander. By attempting to solve them the reader can gain an estimate of his strength. There is also an introductory section on the elements of combination. The book was first published in 1973 and uses descriptive notation.

**Penrose, Jonathan** (b. 7 October 1933) British chess player; awarded the title International Master in 1961. He was British Champion in 1958, 1959, 1960, 1961, 1962, 1963, 1966, 1967, 1968 and 1969. He competed in every Chess Olympiad from 1952 to 1962 and in the Chess Olympiads of 1968 and 1970. His best results in these events were in 1962 (+9 −1 =7) and in 1968 (+10 −0 =5). In the final round of the 1960 event, he became the first player to defeat Tal after the latter won the World Championship. Dr Penrose was undoubtedly the best British chess player of the 1950s and 1960s, but unfortunately his work as a psychologist prevented him playing the game professionally. (1976 Elo rating: 2415)

**Perez Perez, Francisco José** (b. 8 September 1920) Cuban chess player; awarded the title International Master in 1959. Perez Perez was Spanish Champion in 1946, 1948, 1954, and 1960. He also played for Spain in the Chess Olympiads of 1958 and 1960 as well as in the European Team Championship of 1961. Perez Perez has now become a naturalized Cuban and played for Cuba in the 1964 Chess Olympiad. (1976 Elo rating: 2325)

**perfect score** the result for a competitor who plays and wins all of his games in a particular tournament. Lajos Steiner achieved a perfect score in winning the 1950 New South Wales Championship (11 wins). Although Capablanca obtained 13 points out of 13 in winning the 1913 Rice Chess Club tournament, this technically was not a perfect score since two of his opponents (Beihoff and Stapfer) defaulted their games.

**Permanent Rules Commission of FIDE** a committee of FIDE that meets at irregular intervals to settle disputes about the laws of chess that are submitted to them by the national chess federations. The interpretations and opinions of the commission are later included in annual supplements to the *Official Rules of Chess*. The commission consists of seven members, each nominated by their own national federation. Elections to the commission are held every four years.

**perp** *abbrev. for* perpetual check.

**perpetual check** an endless series of checks that do not lead to checkmate. Achieving perpetual check is one way of drawing a game.

**Petran, Pal** (b. 15 September 1945) Hungarian chess player; awarded the title International Master in 1976. (1976 Elo rating: 2415)

**Petroff, Alexander Dmitrievitch** (1794–1867) Russia's first great player. He was born in Viserovo on 12 February 1794 and learned to play chess when only four.

Petroff, who was a civil servant, had little opportunity to play against the top European masters and is remembered for his writings and his researches. In 1824 he published a primer on chess, which contained Philidor's games with Petroff's annotations, and also wrote short stories with chess as a motif as well a work on draughts. His most significant piece of research was with Jänisch on the opening now named after him (see **Petroff's Defence**).

In 1840 the government transferred him to Warsaw where he married and lived for the rest of his life. He visited Western Europe twice; once in the 1850s and once in 1863, but entered no tournaments. He died in Warsaw on 22 April 1867.

**Petroff's Defence** a defence to the King pawn opening: 1. P–K4, P–K4 2. N–KB3, *N–KB3*. Black develops symmetrically while White maintains the pressure through simple development. Common continuations are: 3. N × P, and 3. P–Q4.

This opening appears in the Göttingen manuscript, but was first extensively analysed by Petroff and Jänisch in the 1830s and after. It was regularly played by both Pillsbury and Marshall. It is also known, particularly in Europe, as the **Russian Defence**.

**Petrosian, Tigran** (b. 17 June 1929) Soviet chess player; World Champion from 1963 to 1969; awarded the titles International Master and International Grandmaster in 1952. He was Soviet Champion in 1959 and 1961 and competed in every Chess Olympiad from 1958 to 1974. He has competed in five interzonals, four Candidates' tournaments, two series of Candidates' matches and three World Championship matches.

He was born in Tbilisi, Georgia (U.S.S.R.) and moved to Armenia when young. Petrosian learned to play at eight and defeated Flohr in a simultaneous display five years later. He won the Soviet Junior Championship in 1946 and in 1947 became a Soviet Master. Over the next few years he concentrated upon expanding his theoretical knowledge and in 1951 won the Moscow Championship. In 1952 he became an International Grandmaster by coming second in the Soviet Championship and by coming fifth in the 1952 interzonal, where he did not lose a game. (This performance was repeated in the 1955 interzonal.)

Throughout the 1950s Petrosian steadily grew in strength until finally his victory in the 1962 Candidates' tournament led to a match with Botvinnik for the World Championship. In the match, Petrosian successfully imposed his own style and forced the games into positions uncongenial to Botvinnik (+5 −2 =15). Botvinnik's right as World Champion to a return match had recently been abolished and Petrosian's next opponent was Spassky in 1966. (In this match, also, the games were close manoeuvring struggles that suited Petrosian better than Spassky and Petrosian was the victor (+4 −3 =17); but in the 1969 final Spassky, the challenger again, defeated Petrosian (+4 −6 =13.)

After this match Petrosian announced his intention not to seek the title again, but changed his mind and entered the eighth Candidates' series of matches. In the quarter finals he outsat Hübner, who forfeited the match in protest at the playing conditions (+1 −0 =6) and defeated Korchnoi in the semi-finals (+1 −0 =9). In the finals of the Candidates' matches he was matched against Fischer and was defeated after nine games, after being equal after five (+1 −5 =3).

In the next series of Candidates' matches he defeated Portisch in the quarter-finals (+3 −2 =8), but was defeated by Korchnoi in the semi-finals (+1 −3 =1).

Petrosian obtains a higher percentage of draws than most players and this tends to reduce his tournament successes. However, he has scored the highest percentage on his board in five Chess Olympiads and has won several tournaments, among which was Lone Pine (1976).

Petrosian's style of play is to reduce his opponent's attacking opportunities rather than take direct action himself. Once his opponent has been reduced to passivity, he probes the position until weaknesses have been induced and only then goes on to the attack. This highly original conception leads to games in which Petrosian makes obscure moves that destroy the enemy position almost by magic. However, if the opponent plays well the chance of the game ending in a draw is increased. Whether Petrosian's style foreshadows the chess of the future is impossible to say. It is, at any rate, one way in which it might develop. (1976 Elo rating: 2635)

**Petrov** a variant spelling of **Petroff**.

**Petrov, Vladimir** (1907–1945) Latvian chess player; Latvian Champion in 1935 and 1937 (co-Champion in 1934). He was equal first at Kemeri (1937) with Flohr and Reshevsky, ahead of Alekhine and Keres. He died in a prison camp in 1945.

**Pfeiffer, Gerhard** (b. 14 June 1923) West German chess player; awarded the title International Master in 1957. He was joint West German Champion in 1964 and competed in the Chess Olympiads of 1950, 1952, 1954, 1956, 1958 and 1960. He is also a composer of endgame studies and problems.

**Pfleger, Helmut** (b. 6 August 1943) West German chess player; awarded the titles International Master in 1965 and International Grandmaster in 1975. He was joint West German Champion in 1965 and competed in the Chess Olympiads of 1964, 1968 and 1970. By profession he is a doctor of psychology, and is one of the few non-professional players to have earned the title International Grandmaster. (1976 Elo rating: 2545)

**pfuscher** *German for* **1.** a blunderer.
**2.** an extremely weak move.

**Philidor, François André Danican** (1726–1795) French chess player and theorist; born in Dreux near Versailles. Philidor came from a family of professional musicians and became a chorister at the Chapel Royal, Versailles at the age of six. When he moved to Paris in 1740 he soon became known as a strong chess player (in 1744 he created a sensation at the Café de la Régence by playing two games blindfold), but was still primarily a musician. In 1745 the failure of a musical engagement stranded Philidor in Amsterdam and forced him to support himself by playing chess. His reputation as a player grew and in 1747 Philidor visited England where he defeated Stamma (+8 −1 =1) despite giving odds of draw and move. In the following year he published **Analyse du Jeu des Échecs**, one of the most important books in chess history. In it the importance of the pawns was stressed for the first time (Philidor's famous dictum: 'The pawns are the soul of chess'.) and the weaknesses of backward, doubled or isolated pawns were illustrated with great clarity.

In 1750 Philidor began a tour of Germany and England by visiting Berlin to give an exhibition before Frederick the Great. He returned to France in 1754 and concentrated upon his music for the next eighteen years, composing many highly successful operas. In 1772 he again visited London and returned in each succeeding year to work at Parsloe's by giving exhibitions and lessons. When war broke out in 1793 between England and Revolutionary France he was in London and found it impossible to return home. He died in London 31 August 1795.

***Philidorean, The*** one of the first chess periodicals. It was published in England in 1837 under the editorship of George Walker and ceased publication in 1838 after six editions.

**Philidor Gambit** an opening sequence arising out of the King's Gambit: 1. P–K4, P–K4  2. P–KB4, P × P  3. N–KB3, P–KN4  4. B–B4, B–N2  5. *P–KR4*. White attempts to destroy Black's pawn chain. Black's commonest continuations: 5 . . ., P–KR3 and 5 . . ., P–N5. Also called **Greco-Philidor Gambit**.

**Philidor's Defence** a defence to the King's pawn opening: 1. P–K4, P–K4  2. N–KB3, *P–Q3*. Black strengthens his centre at the cost of walling-in his King Bishop. White's best immediate reply: 3. P–Q4. The defence was analyzed in the Göttingen manuscript, but is named after François Philidor, who developed it. Curiously, though, Philidor never played this defence in any of his recorded games.

**Philidor's Legacy** a type of smothered mate that was ascribed to Philidor in Thomas Pruen's *Introduction to the History and Study of Chess* (1804). From the diagram play continues: 1. Q–Q5ch, K–R1  2. N–B7ch, K–N1  3. N–R6dbl ch, K–R1  4. Q–N8ch, R × Q  5. N–B7mate.

**Phillips, Alan** British chess player; British Champion in 1954 (with L. Barden).

**Piasetski, Leon** (b. 24 December 1951) Canadian chess player; awarded the title International Master in 1975. (1976 Elo rating: 2390)

**Piatigorsky Cup Tournament** a double-round, round-robin tournament held in the United States in 1963 and 1966. Its competitors were all Grandmasters. The tournaments were sponsored and organized by Mrs Jacqueline Piatigorsky (nee Rothschild; wife of the cellist Gregor Piatigorsky), who has competed in several U.S. Women's Championships.

In 1963 the event was won by Keres and Petrosian, who each scored 8½ out of 14 points. The 1966 tournament was won by Spassky with 11½ points out of 18 followed by Fischer with 11.

**piece** **1.** any chessman except the pawn. Pieces can be sorted into three categories: the Kings, the major pieces (Queens and Rooks), and the minor pieces (Bishops and Knights).

**2.** (loosely) any chessman, including the pawn.

**piece play** manoeuvring by the pieces. This occurs either when the pawns are on their best squares or when the pawn position is completely blocked.

**Pietzsch, Wolfgang** (b. 21 December 1930) East German chess player; awarded the titles International Master in 1961 and International Grandmaster in 1965. He was East German Champion in 1949, 1959, 1962 and 1967. He competed in the Chess Olympiads of 1952, 1958, 1960, 1962, 1966, 1968 and 1970.

**Pillsbury Attack** a sequence of moves arising out of the Orthodox Defence to the Queen's Gambit Declined. The characteristic attacking development is made by White in the four moves in italics: 1. P–Q4, P–Q4 2. P–QB4, P–K3 3. N–QB3, N–KB3 4. B–N5, B–K2 5. P–K3, O–O 6. N–B3, QN–Q2 7. Q–B2, P–QN3 8. P×P, P×P 9. *B–Q3*, B–N2 10. *O–O*, P–QR3 11. *N–K5*, P–B4 12. *P–B4*. It was named after Harry Nelson Pillsbury. See **Orthodox Defence.**

**Pillsbury Defence** another name for the **Cambridge Springs Defence.**

**Pillsbury, Harry Nelson** (1872–1906) a leading American chess player; U.S. Champion 1897–1906. Pillsbury learned to play at 16 and was one of the strongest American players by the age of 20, when he became a professional chess player. Nevertheless, he was still comparatively unknown when invited to play at Hastings (1895). He won this extremely strong event with Lasker, Steinitz, Tarrasch, and Tchigorin sharing second place. Later results included third place at St Petersburg (1895), Nuremberg (1896), and Budapest (1896); second place at Vienna (1898), London (1899), and Paris (1900); and first place at Munich (1900).

His most unusual occupation as a professional chess player was as the operator of **Ajeeb** (a chess-playing automaton) from 1898 to 1904. He was also an outstanding blindfold chess player, breaking Zukertort's world record in 1900 by playing sixteen games blindfold (+11 −1 =4); eventually he set a new record by playing 22 games (+17 −1 =4). A frequent feat he performed was to play a number of games of chess and draughts blindfold while playing whist and at the end to call out a list of 30 unrelated words selected by the audience at the beginning.

In his final years Pillbury's health began to deteriorate seriously. He could finish only eighth at Cambridge Springs (1904) and a visit to Bermuda in the following year did no good. On 17 June 1906 he died of syphilis (general paresis of the insane).

**Pillsbury Variation** an opening sequence arising out of the Four Knights' Game: 1. P–K4, P–K4 2. N–KB3, N–QB3 3. N–B3, N–B3; 4. B–N5, B–N5 5. O–O, O–O 6. P–Q3, P–Q3 7. B–N5, *N–K2*. Black gives his opponent the opportunity to create black doubled pawns on the King Bishop file, but it seems best for White to refrain from capturing the Knight. The most common continuation is: 8. N–KR4. This variation was created by the American player Harold Nelson Pillsbury.

**Pilnik, Hermann** (b. 8 January 1914) Argentinian chess player; awarded the title International Master in 1950 and the title International Grandmaster in 1952. (1976 Elo rating: 2435)

**pin** A method of immobilizing a man by attacking it in such a manner that its moving away would expose a more important piece to attack along the same line. The pinned piece must frequently be given up to avoid greater loss. Compare **skewer**.

A pin on White's Knight and a half-pin on Black's Rook

**pincer lever** (Kmoch's term) two **levers** which together attack a pawn chain at two points, its base included. A pincer lever exists when one side has pawns on his Q5 and KN6 while the other has pawns on his Q3, K3 and KB2. Exchanges in this type of situation should give both sides passed pawns. Compare **chain lever**. See ***Pawn Power in Chess***.

**pinned piece** one that parries a check or whose move would uncover an enemy attack on a more important piece. It thus loses its immediate freedom of movement. See **parry a check**.

**Pinter, Jozsef** (b. 9 November 1953) Hungarian chess player; awarded the title International Master in 1976. (1976 Elo rating: 2420)

**pion coiffé** *French for* **capped pawn**.

**Piran Codex** a code of rules for all types of chess problem drawn up at the Congress of Problemists, held in Piran, Yugoslavia, in 1958. Its comprehensiveness and coverage of all aspects of the chess problem have enabled a high degree of uniformity to be created throughout the world.

**Pirc Defence** a defence to either the King pawn or the Queen pawn opening: 1. P–K4, *P–Q3* 2. P–Q4, *N–KB3*. (White's moves are interchangeable.) Black attempts to close the game and assault the centre with long-range attacks by the pieces followed by undermining pawn advances on the wings. Thus the strategy of Black in this defence is almost identical to that in the Modern Defence into which it can transpose at many points.

This opening is named after the Yugoslavian player Vasja Pirc who first played it in the 1940s. Also called **Ufimtsev Defence, Yugoslav Defence.** Compare **Modern Defence, Robatsch Defence.**

**Pirc Variation** an opening sequence arising out of the Classical Variation of the Nimzo-Indian Defence: 1. P–Q4, N–KB3 2. P–QB4, P–K3 3. N–QB3, B–N5 4. Q–B2, *P–B4* 5. P×P, *O–O*. Black quickly completes his development in this variation, which is generally felt to provide equality for Black. This opening is named after the Yugoslavian player Vasja Pirc, who devised it.

**Pirc, Vasja** (b. 19 December 1907) Yugoslavian chess player; awarded the titles International Master in 1950 and International Grandmaster in 1953. He was Yugoslavian Champion in 1935, 1936, 1937, 1949 and 1953 and competed in the Chess Olympiads of 1931, 1935, 1937, 1950, 1952 and 1954. Pirc also took part in the 1948 interzonal in which he was joint eleventh.

**Pistyan (1912)** a tournament with eighteen competitors, won by Rubinstein (who scored 14) ahead of Spielmann (11½) and Marshall (10½).

**Pistyan (1922)** a tournament with nineteen competitors, won by Bogoljubov (who scored 15) ahead of Alekhine (14½) and Spielmann (14½).

**Plachutta theme** a theme in chess problems in which an initial sacrifice by White causes two defenders that can move on the same squares (Rook and Rook or Queen and Rook or Bishop) to hinder each other. It is normally found in three-movers and uses the concept **interference** in a more complex manner than does the **Grimshaw theme.** The idea was developed by the nineteenth-century problem composer J. Plachutta.

**Planinc, Albin** (b. 18 April 1944) Yugoslavian chess player; awarded the titles International Master in 1970 and International Grandmaster in 1972. (1976 Elo rating: 2485)

**Plater, Kazimierz** (b. 3 March 1915) Polish chess player; awarded the title International Master in 1950. He was Polish Champion in 1949, 1956 and 1957 and competed in the Chess Olympiads of 1952, 1956 and 1960.

**playing the board** attempting to make the best or at least the technically correct moves in a game, without concern for the personal quirks or psychological propensities of the opponent.

**playing the man** attempting to confront an opponent not only by making strong or technically correct moves but also by making moves designed to worry or perplex him, especially moves chosen after study and analysis of the adversary's personal quirks, playing style or basic offensive and defensive repertoire. See **psychology**.

**Pleiades** a group of seven visible stars in the constellation of Taurus. This became the nickname of seven influential German players of the nineteenth century. See **Berlin Pleiades**.

**plus-flight theme** a theme in chess problems where the King can escape from the initial threat only by moving to any of the four orthogonally adjacent squares. In the common two-move chess problem this means that the two moves must both check the King and cover its square of origin. Compare **star-flight theme**.

**plus score** a tournament or match score in which a player's wins outnumber his losses. If the same number were added or subtracted for a victory or defeat with draws being ignored, such as result would mean a positive score. However, under the normal scoring system of one point for a win, half a point for a draw and no points for a loss it is possible to obtain a positive score without winning any games, but merely by drawing one or more games. Compare **minus score**.

***Pocket Guide to Chess Endgames*** a compendium of the endgames that occur most frequently in actual play, compiled by David Hooper. It covers approximately 800 possibilities, was first published in 1970 and uses the descriptive notation. Compare ***Basic Chess Endings***.

**Pocket Knight Chess** a variant of chess in which each player has an extra Knight, which can be placed wherever desired upon the board at any stage of the game instead of making a move. It then functions as an ordinary Knight.

**point count** a simplistic method of evaluating the strengths and weaknesses of chess positions in which estimates are made by assigning positive and negative values for material and positional features. For example, an extra pawn is worth three points and a Rook on the seventh rank is worth one point. This method is similar to the point-count system used in bridge and was devised by I. A. Horowitz and G. Mott-Smith.

**poisoned pawn** a pawn that appears to be undefended and free for the taking, but whose capture often results in loss of the capturing piece several moves later. The apparently free pawn is most often the Queen Knight pawn, and the capturing piece the adversary's Queen.

**poisoned pawn variation** a line in the Sicilian defence, Najdorf variation, in which White sacrifices his Queen Knight pawn. The characteristic moves are: 1. P–K4, P–QB4 2. N–KB3, P–Q3 3. P–Q4, P×P 4. N×P, N–KB3 5. N–QB3, P–QR3 6. B–N5, P–K3 7. P–B4, *Q–N3* 8. Q–Q2, *Q×P*. Though theory considers the line quite playable for Black, great accuracy is required, as was shown in the eleventh game of the 1972 World Championship match: Bobby Fischer lost his Queen at move 25 after adopting this line.

**Polerio, Giulio Cesare** Italian chess player, one of the strongest of the late sixteenth and early seventeenth centuries. Little is known of his early life. In 1574 he visited Spain as the servant of Giovanni **Leonardo**, but returned to Italy in the following year and settled in Rome under the patronage of Giucomo Buoncompagno, Duke of Sora. Several manuscripts written by him have survived. They record contemporary games and analyse many openings including most variations of the King's Gambit, the Queen's Gambit Declined, the Caro-Kann Defence, the Sicilian Defence, the Two Knights' Defence, the Four Knights' Game and various fianchetto defences.

**Polerio's Gambit** another name for the **Fegatello Attack.**

**Polish Defence** a defence to the Queen pawn opening: 1. P–Q4, *P–QN4*. It can also arise by transposition from the Réti Defence. The ideas behind this defence are those of the Polish Opening, but Black has one tempo less to carry out his plans. It was first played by A. Wagner in Stanislau in 1912.

**Polish Gambit** another name for the **Zukertort Gambit.**

**Polish Immortal** the name given to a game played between Glucksberg and Najdorf in Warsaw in 1935. Glucksberg was White: 1. P–Q4, P–KB4 2. P–QB4, N–KB3 3. N–QB3, P–K3 4. N–B3, P–Q4 5. P–K3, P–B3 6. B–Q3, B–Q3 7. O–O, O–O 8. N–K2, QN–Q2 9. N–N5, B × Pch 10. K–R1, N–N5 11. P–B4, Q–K1 12. P–KN3, Q–R4 13. K–N2, B–N8! 14. N × B, Q–R7ch 15. K–B3, P–K4! 16. QP × P, QN × Pch 17. P × N, N × Pch 18. K–B4, N–N3ch 19. K–B3, P–B5! 20. KP × P, B–N5ch 21. K × B, N–K4ch 22. P × N, P–R4mate. Compare **Immortal Game.**

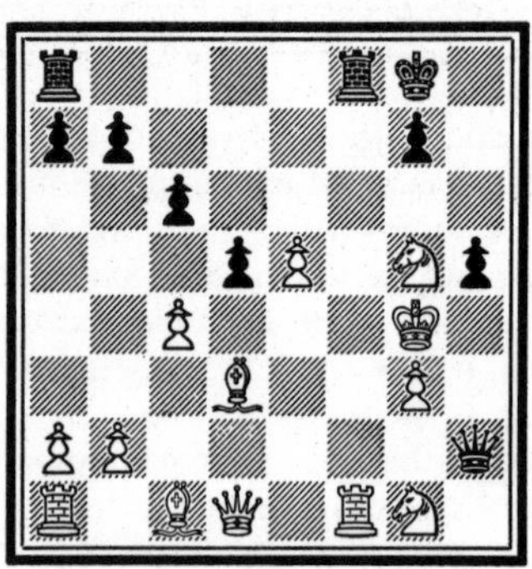

Position after 22 . . ., P–R4mate

**Polish Opening** or **Attack** an opening where White plays 1. *P–QN4*. This inhibits the advance of Black's Queen Bishop pawn should he decide to play a Queen-side opening and allows a fianchetto of the Queen Bishop on the second move to gain control of the long diagonal. It was originally analysed by the Viennese player Berthold Englisch and has since been played by Tartakover, Sokolsky, and Pachman. Also called **Orang-Utan Opening, Sokolsky Opening**. See **Santasiere's Folly.**

**Polugayevsky, Lev** (b. 20 November 1934) Soviet chess player;

awarded the titles International Master in 1961 and International Grandmaster in 1962. Polugayevsky is one of the foremost Soviet chess players as shown by his success in qualifying for the quarter-final of the Candidates' matches in 1974 where he was defeated by Karpov and his win over Mecking in the 1977 quarter-final of the Candidates' matches (+1 −0 =11). (1976 Elo rating: 2635)

**Pomar, Arturo Salamanca** (b. 1 September 1931) Spanish chess player; awarded the titles International Master in 1950 and International Grandmaster in 1962. Pomar was one of the outstanding chess prodigies; he was champion of the Balearic Isles at the age of 11. (1976 Elo rating: 2430)

**Ponziani, Domenico Lorenzo** (1719–1792) major Italian theorist and chess writer. Born in Modena, Ponziani graduated from the University of San Carlo in 1742 and was Professor of Civil Law there from 1742 to 1772. He became a priest in 1764 and a canon at Modena Cathedral in 1766. In 1784 he became Vicar General and was appointed Capitular Vicar one year later.

His main work on chess, *Il giuoco incomparabile degli scacchi*, was published in Modena in 1769. In a later edition (published in 1782) he described the principles of the Italian school. In contrast to the beliefs of Philidor, emphasis was laid on the need for full mobility of the pieces. The pawn structure was considered unimportant except for denying the enemy pieces their best squares.

**Ponziani's Opening** an opening sequence: 1. P–K4, P–K4 2. N–KB3, N–QB3 3. *P–B3*. White attempts to create a strong centre, but his lack of development allows Black to equalize swiftly. The opening appeared in the Göttingen manuscript (1490), but was first thoroughly analyzed by Domenico Ponziani of Italy in his work, *Il giuco incomparabile degli scacchi*.

**Porat, Josef** (b. 7 June 1909) Israeli chess player; awarded the title International Master in 1952. He was Champion of Palestine in 1937 and Israeli Champion in 1953, 1957, 1959 and 1963. He competed for Germany in the 1928 Chess Olympiad, for Palestine in the Chess Olympiads of 1935 and 1939 and for Israel in the Chess Olympiads from 1952 onwards. In 1964 he qualified for the interzonal, where he came twenty-first. (1976 Elo rating: 2335)

**Porreca, Georgio** (b. 30 August 1927) Italian chess player; awarded the title International Master in 1957. He was Italian Champion in 1950 and 1956 and competed in the Chess Olympiads of 1950, 1952 and 1954. (1976 Elo rating: 2285)

**Portisch, Ferenc** (b. 4 September 1939) Hungarian chess player; awarded the title International Master in 1975. (1976 Elo rating: 2425)

**Portisch, Lajos** (b. 4 April 1937) Hungarian chess player; awarded the titles International Master in 1958 and International Grandmaster in 1961. He has been Hungarian Champion on numerous occasions since 1957 and competed in every Chess Olympiad from 1956 to 1974. One of the world's leading players, he has qualified for the Candidates' matches four times – the last occasion being in 1976, when he qualified with Petrosian from a three-way play-off (Tal being eliminated) after these three had tied in the 1976 Biel interzonal. (1976 Elo rating: 2625)

**positional** relating to a move, manoeuvre or style of play governed by strategic rather than tactical considerations. Thus a positional move is also likely to be a **quiet move.**

**positionally won game** see **winning position.**

**Pospisil, Joseph** (1861–1916) Bohemian composer of chess problems, born in what is now part of Czechoslovakia. In his *Ceske Melodie* (1908) he discussed the philosophy behind the problems composed by the so-called Bohemian School (which basically involve three-movers): 'The Bohemian composer is concerned mainly with three points. He wants to render two or more variations with great economy and unity; he wants to secure model mates for his main variations; and he wants to present an attractive initial setting, suggestive of freedom, without overcrowding or obviously unnatural arrangements.'

**postal chess** another name for **correspondence chess.**

**postalite** (informal) a person who plays **postal chess.**

**Poutiainen, Pertti** (1952–1978) Finnish chess player; awarded the title International Master in 1976. He was Finnish Champion in 1974. (1976 Elo rating: 2425)

***Practical Chess Endings*** a book on endgame play by Paul Keres; generally considered to be one of the best works available on the subject. It was first published in 1974.

**Praeceptor Germaniae** *Latin for* Germany's teacher; *nickname of* Siegbert Tarrasch.

**Prague Variation** a variation occurring in the Queen's Gambit Declined, arising out of the Tarrasch Defence. The typical progression is as follows: 1. P–Q4, P–Q4 2. P–QB4, P–K3 3. N–QB3, P–QB4 4. P–QP, KP × P 5. N–B3, N–QB3 6. P–KN3, N–B3 7. B–N2. See **Tarrasch Defence.**

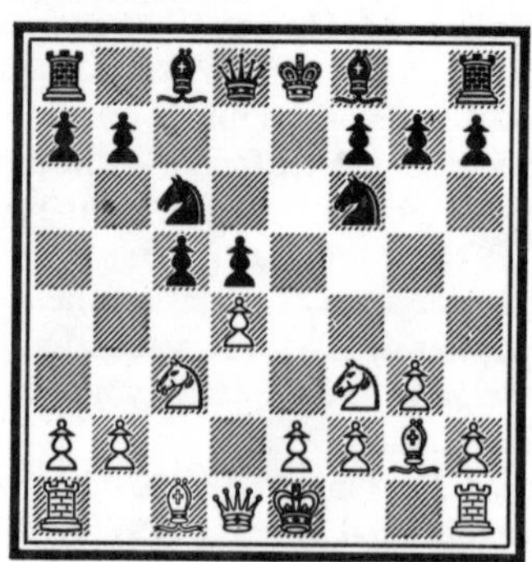

Position after 7. B–N2

**praxis** *German for* practice. *Chess Praxis* was the title of a book by Nimzovitch in which the concepts elucidated in *My System* were further explained and developed. It was also the title of a book by Howard Staunton, written as a sequel to his *Chessplayer's Handbook.*

**prepared variation** an improved sequence of moves in an opening devised in analysis rather than over the board. It can be used as much for its surprise value as for its objective merit. In international chess many choices of openings are conditioned by fear of the possible existence of a prepared variation.

**Pride and Sorrow of Chess, The** a descriptive phrase often applied to Paul Morphy: *pride*, because of his brilliant contributions to chess; *sorrow*, because of his tragic decline mentally following his short meteor-like burst across the chess world.

**Pride of the Family, The** a descriptive phrase given by Nimzovitch to his win at Riga (1913) against Alapin. Nimzovitch played White: 1. P–K4, P–K3 2. P–Q4, P–Q4 3. N–QB3, N–KB3 4. P × P, N × P 5. N–B3, P–QB4 6. N × N, Q × N 7. B–K3, P × P 8. N × P, P–QR3 9. B–K2, Q × NP 10. B–B3, Q–N3 11. Q–Q2, P–K4 12. O–O–O!, P × N 13. B × QP, N–B3 14. B–B6!, Q × B 15. KR–K1ch, B–K2 16. B × Nch, K–B1 17. Q–Q8ch, B × Q 18. R–K8mate.

**Princess** a Fairy chesspiece that possesses the powers of both the Bishop and the Knight. It is thus a type of combined chessman.

***Principles of Chess, The*** a book by the American master James Mason. It teaches the elements of chess, discusses general principles and contains a section on master games. This book was first published in 1893, immediately becoming a best-seller, and has been reissued many times. In 1946 it was extensively revised by Fred Reinfeld, who discarded all the original games and replaced them with more modern examples. The book uses descriptive notation. See ***Art of Chess***.

**Prins, Lodewijk** (b. 27 January 1913) Dutch chess player; awarded the titles International Master in 1950 and International Judge in 1960. He was Dutch Champion 1965–1967 and has competed in numerous Chess Olympiads since 1937. In 1952 he qualified for the interzonal where he finished equal twentieth. (1976 Elo rating: 2265)

**priority of check** to get out of check takes precedence over all other objectives, since if the King cannot extricate himself from check in one move it is checkmate and the game is over.

**Prism** a Fairy chesspiece that bends the moves of Bishops, Rooks, and Queens through an angle of 90°. A player may move his Prism to any vacant square on the board on his move.

**Pritchett, Craig** (b. 15 January 1949) Scottish chess player; awarded the title International Master in 1976. (1976 Elo rating: 2410)

**problem chess** see **chess problem**.

**problem child** Black's Queen Bishop, which is often hemmed in by its own pawns. This occurs particularly often in the French Defence and the Queen's Gambit. See **French Bishop**.

***Problemist, The*** the journal of the **British Chess Problem Society**. It was first published in 1926 and appears monthly.

**professional** any player whose principal occupation is playing chess. This will frequently be supplemented by closely-related activities, such as writing on chess and giving exhibitions. However, in the

Western world only the most successful players can support themselves and their families solely by chess, despite the recent upsurge in interest in the game and the consequent increase in prize-money. This means that many professional players have other occupations, which somewhat blurs the distinction between the amateur and the professional; Larsen has said that he drifted into becoming a chess professional. In the Communist states there might appear to be more amateur players at the highest level since most have other occupations. For instance, Geller is an economist, Polugayevsky is a railway engineer, and Spassky is a journalist. In practice they are full-time professional players. Compare **amateur.**

**Professor of Chess** *nickname of* J. H. Sarratt.

***Profile of a Prodigy*** a biography of Bobby Fischer, written by Frank Brady. It was first published in 1965.

**Progressive Chess** a variant of chess in which each player has successively one more move; White plays one move, Black two, White three, Black four, etc. A check ends a move; a player must move out of check immediately or lose the game. This game, which was a favourite of C. H. O'D. Alexander, never lasts for very long. Also called **Scotch Chess, Blitz.**

**Prohibition Chess** a variant of Chess in which no checks can be made until checkmate is delivered.

**promotion** see **pawn promotion.**

**Prompt Corner** one of the few cafés in London where chess can be played. Situated in Hampstead, Prompt Corner is always crammed with players who come from all over London to meet, eat, and play chess.

**prophylaxis** action to negate a possible threat before it can arise. The term was taken from medicine by Nimzovitch and the idea is now a regular feature of modern play. A common example is the move: P–KR3, to prevent a pinning of the Knight on KB3 by a Bishop on KN4.

**Protean man** a Fairy chesspiece or pawn that assumes the power of the last man it captures. If (for example) a Protean King captures a Rook, Bishop and Knight in three consecutive moves, it would move successively like a King, Rook, Bishop and then Knight.

**protected passed pawn** a passed pawn that is defended by a pawn of the same colour, which may not be a passed pawn itself.

**PRU** an alternative acronym for the **Modern Defence.** It arises from the fact that the Modern Defence is a generic term covering the Pirc Defence, the *R*obatsch Defence, and the *U*fimtsev Defence.

**psychology** chess played above the intermediate level usually involves more than merely choosing what seems to be the best move in a particular position (see **playing the board**); it also involves trying to understand something about the psychological make-up of the opponent (see **playing the man**). Many masters who enter important tournaments or matches spend considerable time in advance analyzing the style of play and characteristics of their intended opponents. Some

International Grandmasters, and others, maintain a file on their potential adversaries in which all the scores and results of their important games are entered or cross-referenced, with notes on openings, defences and variations they have used recently, and their propensity for attacking, defensive, or positional play under set circumstances.

***Psychology of the Chess Player, The*** a short book by Reuben Fine (who is both an International Grandmaster and a psychoanalyst) which attempts to analyze the game of chess and its peculiar fascination for players at the master level. Fine reviews the psychoses, mental aberrations and eccentricities of several players, including Morphy and Steinitz. Some of his psychoanalytic overlays have been criticized, however, such as his explanation of the hidden significance of the King: 'First of all, it stands for the boy's penis in the phallic stage, and hence re-arouses the castration anxiety characteristic of that period.' One wit has suggested that when Fine abandoned serious chess to devote his life to psychology 'it was a great loss for chess and at best a draw for psychology.' Nevertheless, the book makes amusing reading and is occasionally informative (at least about the way a psychologist-grandmaster's mind works). It was first published in 1956, and was formerly entitled *On Chess and Chess Masters: Psychoanalytic Observations*.

**Puc, Stojan** (b. 9 April 1921) Yugoslavian chess player; awarded the title International Master in 1950. He competed in the Chess Olympiad of 1950. (1976 Elo rating: 2370)

**Pudovkin, Vsevolod Ilarionovich** (1893–1953) Soviet film producer and director. One of his first films was the surprisingly successful realistic comedy *Chess Fever* (1925).

**pull** (colloquial) a slight advantage in a game of chess.

**Purdy, Cecil John Seddon** (b. 27 March 1907) Australian chess player and writer; awarded the titles International Master in 1951 and International Correspondence Chess Grandmaster in 1953. He was Australian Champion in 1935, 1937, 1949 and 1951 and was New Zealand Champion in 1924. He was Australian Correspondence Champion 1938–1953 and was World Correspondence Champion 1953–1958. In 1976 he was made a Member of the Order of Australia for services to chess.

In 1929 he founded and edited the *Australasian Chess Review*, which changed its name in 1946 to *Chess World* with Purdy still as its editor. He has written several books, including *How Euwe Won*, *The Return of Alekhine* and *A Guide to Good Chess*.

**Puttino, il** *Italian for* the youth; *nickname of* Giovanni Leonardo.

**Pytel, Krzystof** (b. 15 May 1945) Polish chess player; awarded the title International Master in 1975. (1976 Elo rating: 2420)

# Q

**Q** *abbrev. for* Queen.

**QB** *abbrev. for* Queen Bishop.

**QBP** *abbrev. for* Queen Bishop pawn.
**QGA** *abbrev. for* Queen's Gambit Accepted.
**QGD** *abbrev. for* Queen's Gambit Declined.
**QKt** *abbrev. for* Queen Knight.
**QKtP** *abbrev. for* Queen Knight pawn. See also **QNP**.
**QN** *abbrev. for* Queen Knight. See also **QKt**.
**QNP** *abbrev. for* Queen Knight pawn.
**QP** *abbrev. for* Queen pawn.
**QR** *abbrev. for* Queen Rook.
**QRP** *abbrev. for* Queen Rook pawn.
**quadruplets** (Kmoch's term) four pawns of the same colour that are on the same file. They have all the weaknesses of **doubled pawns**, but to a much greater degree. Naturally, quadruplets are seen very rarely in actual play, but one example can be found in the game played between Alekhine and Nenerakov in 1907. See ***Pawn Power in Chess***.

Alekhine vs. Nenerakov (Moscow, 1907)

**quality** a translation of the term used for the *exchange* in many parts of Europe, including France, Italy, and Germany.
**quart** (Kmoch's term) four horizontally adjacent friendly pawns. Compare **duo, trio**. See ***Pawn Power in Chess***.
**quartgrip** (Kmoch's term) a formation in which four pawns are confronted by four opposing pawns. A typical arrangement exists when each has pawns on his KR4, KN3, KB3 and K4. The major feature of the quartgrip is the advantage it gives to the player with the more advanced pawns, since if passed pawns are created through exchanges he will be able to promote his first. In the above example the chances are equal. See ***Pawn Power in Chess***.
**Queen** **1.** a chessman that moves in a straight line in any direction over any number of unoccupied squares. It is the most powerful piece in the game; its approximate value is equal to that of three minor pieces. Each side begins with one Queen which initially occupies the square between the King and Bishop.

The Queen has undergone the most radical transformation of all the pieces in the history of chess. In Arabic it was known as the *firzān* or *firz* (counsellor) and could move only one square diagonally. On its introduction into Europe its name was either corrupted or replaced by a word for Queen, since this name was suggested by the otherwise symmetrical arrangement of the pieces and its location beside the King. This caused some problems. For instance, the promotion of a pawn to a Queen while the original piece was still on the board surely signified bigamy! This was solved by various means, including restrictions on promotion and a renaming of the promoted pawn. The modern move of the Queen was introduced in the late fifteenth century and soon was accepted throughout Europe. Its significance was very great; it immeasurably speeded up the game, made analysis of the opening necessary for the first time and increased the value of the pawns (as pawn promotion would normally be decisive). *Abbrev.* Q.

**2.** (lower case) to promote a pawn to a Queen when it reaches the eighth rank.

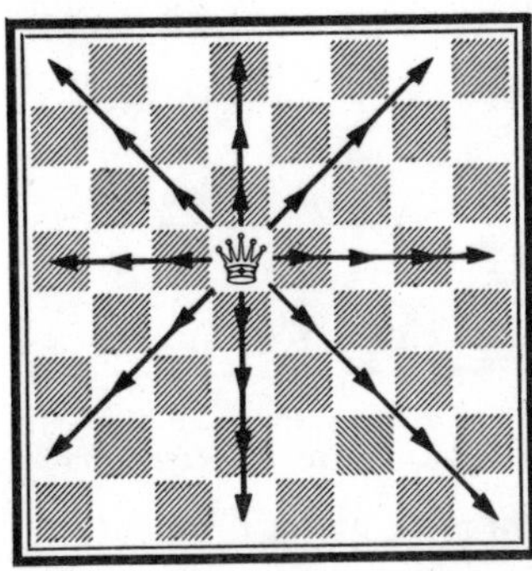

Potential moves of the Queen over unobstructed squares

**queening a pawn** promoting a pawn that reaches the eighth rank into a Queen. See **pawn promotion**.

**Queen Knight Opening** another name for the **Dunst Opening**.

**Queen's Fianchetto Defence** **1.** any opening where Black plays 1 . . ., P–QN3. Frequently played with success against 1. P–K4 by the Rev J. Owen last century, this defence has, however, never gained general respectability.

**2.** an opening sequence arising out of the French Defence: 1. P–K4, P–K3 2. P–Q4, *P–QN3*. The most common continuations are: 3. N–QB3, B–N2 and 3. P–QB4, B–N2.

**Queen's Fianchetto Opening** another name for **Larsen's Opening**.

**Queen's Gambit** a Queen's pawn opening: 1. P–Q4, P–Q4 2. *P–QB4*.

**Queen's Gambit Accepted** an opening sequence in which Black immediately captures the pawn offered by White in the Queen's Gambit: 1. P–Q4, P–Q4 2. P–QB4, *P×P*.

**Queen's Gambit Declined** any opening sequence in which Black declines the immediate offer of White's pawn in the Queen's Gambit.

Black has various means of declining the Queen's Gambit. See **Albin Counter Gambit, Argentine Variation, Cambridge Springs Defence, Manhattan Variation, Marshall Defence, Meran Defence, Orthodox Defence, Slav Defence, Symmetrical Defence, Tarrasch Defence,** and **Tchigorin Defence.**

**Queen side** the files originally occupied by the Queen, Queen Bishop, Queen Knight, and Queen Rook. Also called **Queen's wing.**

**Queen's Indian Defence** a defence to the Queen pawn opening: 1. P–Q4, N–KB3 2. P–QB4, P–K3 3. N–KB3, *P–QN3*. Black plans to control his K5 with pieces, thus taking advantage of White's unaggressive third move. Also called **Neo-Indian Defence.**

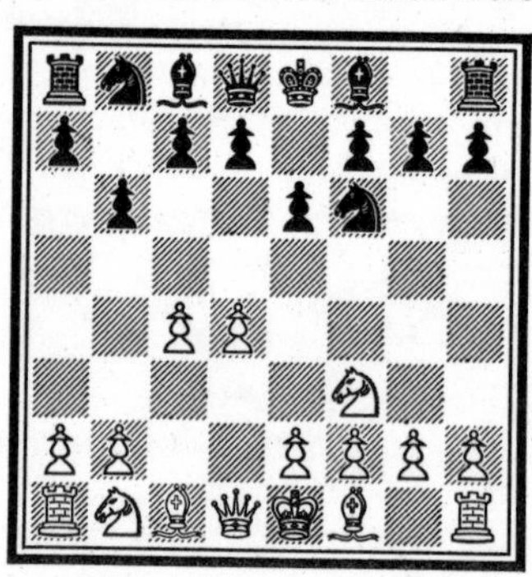

Position after 3 . . ., P–QN3
(Black is prepared on his next move to develop his Bishop on QN–2)

**Queen's Pawn Counter Gambit** a defence to the Queen pawn opening: 1. P–K4, P–K4 2. N–KB3, *P–Q4*. The most common continuation is: 3. P×P. Compare **Greco Counter Gambit.**

**Queen's Pawn Game** any opening where White plays 1. *P–Q4*. Strictly speaking, this name is not given to openings where White continues with the Queen's Gambit.

**Queen's Pawn Opening** any opening where White plays: 1. *P–Q4*. Compare **Queen's Pawn Game.**

**Queen's wing** another name for **Queen side.**

**queue method** (Kmoch's term) the alignment of the major pieces behind a pawn which is then exchanged once control of the file is assured. This can only be undertaken if there is sufficient space for the pieces to mass behind the pawn, if they are safe from the attacks of minor pieces or pawns and if there are no counterthreats to meet elsewhere. An attack by the queue method against a King is especially dangerous if there are enough attackers, but in these situations the King itself is a strong defensive piece. See ***Pawn Power in Chess.***

**quiet move** a move that neither checks nor captures and which does not contain any direct threats. In chess problems the best key aesthetically is generally considered to be some kind of quiet move since this apparently gives Black the greatest freedom of action.

**Quinones, Oscar Carrillo** (b. 14 January 1941) Peruvian chess player; awarded the title International Master in 1963. He competed in the

Chess Olympiads of 1964, 1970 and 1972. He also took part in the 1964 interzonal where he came twentieth. (1976 Elo rating: 2350)

**Quinteros, Miguel Angel** (b. 28 December 1947) Argentinian chess player; awarded the titles International Master in 1970 and International Grandmaster in 1973. He competed in the 1973 Leningrad interzonal and the 1976 Manila interzonal. His tournament results include a first at Arrecife de Lanzarote (1974) and an equal first in the Brazilian Open (1976). (1976 Elo rating: 2540)

# R

**R** *abbrev. for* Rook.

**Rabar, Braslav** (1919–1973) Yugoslavian chess player; awarded the title International Master in 1950. He was Yugoslav Champion in 1951 and played in the Chess Olympiads of 1950, 1952, and 1954. He also competed in the European Team Championship of 1957.

**Radashkovich, Itzhak** (b. 4 July 1947) Israeli chess player; awarded the title International Master in 1976. (1976 Elo rating: 2445)

**Radev, N.** Bulgarian chess player; awarded the title International Master in 1976. (1976 Elo rating: 2370)

**radio match** a match played by radio. The initial radio match between the United States and the U.S.S.R. was played in 1945 and was the first post-war international sports event. The crushing victory of the U.S.S.R. by 15½ points to 4½ was totally unexpected, as the United States had been the leading chess nation of the 1930s. In fact this event presaged the future domination of the Soviet school of chess. Soviet teams later played radio matches against the United Kingdom (1946, 1947 and 1954) and again against the United States (1954 and 1955), winning all of them. Compare **correspondence chess, cable match, telex match.**

**Radulov, Ivan** (b. 7 January 1939) Bulgarian chess player; awarded the titles International Master in 1968 and International Grandmaster in 1972. He competed in the 1973 Leningrad interzonal. Radulov's tournament results include firsts at Montilla-Moriles (1974) and Torremolinos (1975) and an equal first in the 1974 Bulgarian Championship. (1976 Elo rating: 2515)

**Ragozin, Viatcheslav** (1908–1962) Russian chess player; awarded the title International Grandmaster in 1950. Noted mainly for his contribution to opening theory in the Queen's Gambit Declined. See **Ragozin System.**

**Ragozin System** an opening sequence arising out of the Orthodox Defence to the Queen's Gambit Declined: 1. P–Q4, P–Q4 2. P–QB4, P–K3 3. N–QB3, N–KB3 4. N–B3, *B–N5*. It was named after the Soviet chess player Viatcheslav Ragozin. Also called **Ragozin Variation.** See **Orthodox Defence.**

**Raičević, Vladimir** (b. 2 May 1949) Yugoslavian chess player; awarded the titles International Master in 1975 and International Grandmaster in 1976. (1976 Elo rating: 2465)

**Rajković, Dusan** (b. 17 June 1942) Yugoslavian chess player; awarded the title International Master in 1974. (1976 Elo rating: 2420)

**ram** (Kmoch's term) a pawn formation composed of two opposing pawns that are vertically adjacent, thus blocking each other's advance. It resembles two fighting rams that are deadlocked. The existence of rams favours the defender, because they cause immobility, separate the two forces, hamper a possible pawn roller and keep lines closed. See ***Pawn Power in Chess***.

**ram attack** (Kmoch's term) an attack whose main objective is the establishment of a pawn on Q6 while the opposing pawn is still standing on its Q2. (This specific pawn formation is termed the **ram** by Kmoch.) The Queen pawn may also sometimes be exchanged so as to gain control of the newly created half-open Queen file. The ram attack can be seen in some sequences in the **Greco Variation**. See ***Pawn Power in Chess***.

**ram formation** (Kmoch's term) a **half-open formation** of pawns where the opposing pawn structures are connected by at least one **ram**. See ***Pawn Power in Chess***.

**ram system** (Kmoch's term) the **Boleslavsky Variation**. See ***Pawn Power in Chess***.

**Randomized Chess** a variant of chess in which White's pieces are arranged on the back rank at random, the only stipulation being that the Bishops must be on different-coloured squares. Black then arranges his pieces in exact imitation and the game is then played as in a normal game. There are 1440 unique arrangements of the pieces that are possible so that variety is assured. Compare **Baseline Chess**.

**rangers** (Kmoch's term) the pawns on the flank on which the King has not castled. While the **centre pawns** and **home pawns** have some defensive duties with respect to the King, the rangers do not and may advance, according to Kmoch, 'with gusto'.

**ranger side** (Kmoch's term) the flank on which the King has not castled. Compare **home side**. See ***Pawn Power in Chess***.

**rank** one of the eight columns of squares that run horizontally across the chessboard. They are numbered outwards from each player's side of the board; thus the row on which the pieces originally stand is the first rank, the row on which the pawns stand is the second rank, and so on up to the rows on which the opponent's pawns and pieces originally stand, which are the seventh and eighth ranks respectively. Thus each rank has a different name for each player. Compare **file**.

**rapid transit** another name (especially in the United States) for **lightning chess**.

**Rashkovsky, Naum** (b. 18 April 1946) Soviet chess player; awarded the title International Master in 1976. (1976 Elo rating: 2485)

**Rat** another name for the **Modern Defence**. The name was first used in the nineteenth century and was revived by a group of Canadian players, including Duncan Suttles, who have analysed the opening. According to R. D. Keene and G. S. Botterill it has acquired its name because the opening possesses a rat-like cunning.

**rating** another name for **grading**.

**Razuvayev, Yuri** (b. 10 October 1945) Soviet chess player; awarded the titles International Master in 1973 and International Grandmaster in 1976. (1976 Elo rating: 2495)

**rearspan** (Kmoch's term) the squares of a file that are behind a pawn. As the rearspan increases the freedom of that pawn's pieces is usually increased. Compare **frontspan, interspan.** See ***Pawn Power in Chess*.**

**rear-twin** (Kmoch's term) the less advanced member of a pair of **doubled pawns.** Compare **front-twin, loose twin, sham twin, tight twin, twin.** See ***Pawn Power in Chess*.**

**recording of games** in competitive chess each player must write down all the moves of a game. If a player is in extreme time trouble he may postpone this until the time trouble is over, but should keep a record of the number of moves made. If moves were not accurately recorded it would be impossible to claim a **draw** by **repetition of position** or by the **fifty-move rule** since such claims could not be verified.

**rectangular power** the ability to move orthogonally in all directions. This especially applies to the Rooks, which can move in no other way, but also belongs to the King and Queen. Compare **diagonal power.**

**Red-Cross Man** a Fairy chesspiece that belongs to neither side, and can neither capture nor be captured. Its purpose is to interpose between any checks by the quickest route. It was invented by J. G. Ingram.

**Ree, Hans** (b. 15 September 1944) Dutch chess player; awarded the title International Master in 1968. Ree was Dutch Champion in 1967, and has regularly played in the Chess Olympiads. (1976 Elo rating: 2420)

**Reflex-mate** a problem in Fairy Chess in which each player attempts to compel the other to mate him. If a player can mate on the move he must do so. In chess problems these constraints mean that if the solver selects an incorrect continuation he is forced to checkmate Black rather than solve the problem. This is a type of Selfmate and was invented by the British problemist Benjamin G. Laws.

**refutation** a demonstration that proves a previously accepted move, variation or opening to be inadequate, given best play on both sides. In the cycle of innovation and supposed refutation there may be no final judgements – the supposed refutation may itself be refuted. For instance, the main variation of the Giuoco Piano has been known since the time of Greco but for many generations was felt to be refuted by an exchange of Bishop for Knight at the proper point. However, the Möller Attack re-established the line and it is now thought to lead to equality. A second example is that of the Muzio Gambit, which was frequently claimed to have been refuted in the early years of this century, but which theory now believes to result in an equal game.

**refute** to prove that a previously accepted move, variation, or opening is inadequate, given best play by both sides.

**Reinfeld, Fred** (1910–1964) American writer on chess. He was twice New York State Champion and was also Champion of the Manhattan and Marshall Chess Clubs at various times. He was a prolific author on all aspects of chess with nearly 100 titles published.

**Rejfir, Josef** (1909–1962) Czechoslovakian chess player; awarded the title International Master in 1956. He played in the Chess Olympiads of 1928, 1930, 1931, 1933, 1935, 1956 and 1958.

**relative value of pieces** the relative values of pieces is not stable, but fluctuates throughout the game. For instance, a Knight is more valuable than a Bishop in a closed position and less valuable in an open position. A pawn steadily grows in value as the game continues, so that while a pawn may be sacrificed in an opening gambit eventually a piece might be gladly sacrificed to prevent it queening. All cases of under-promotion are examples of unexpected relative values of pieces. Nevertheless, there is common agreement on the basic relative value of pieces before allowing for any specific circumstances. As a rough guide the Euratom Committee on computer chess, under the chairmanship of Dr Max Euwe, assigned the following values: pawn = 10, Bishop = 30, Knight = 30, Rook = 45, Queen = 85, King = 1000. Obviously, the King is more important than everything else put together; a lower nominal value for it might encourage a computer to win material rather than mate the opposing King or (even worse) to sacrifice its own King in a bid to win material!

**Relay Chess** a type of Fairy Chess in which pieces and pawns can move in the same manner as any men protecting them. Thus a Rook guarded by a Knight could move both like a Rook and Knight. Two exceptions are the King (which can only move normally) and the pawns (which cannot use Relay power to reach the eighth rank). Relay Chess was devised by Mannis Charosh, who also invented **U-Chess**.

**Rellstab, Ludwig** (b. 23 November 1904) West German chess player; awarded the titles International Master in 1950 and International Judge in 1951. He competed in the Chess Olympiads of 1950, 1952 and 1954. (1976 Elo rating: 2265)

**repetition of position** a game may be claimed as a draw if the same position occurs three times with the same player to move. In this case the draw may only be claimed by the player whose move it is. He must inform the tournament or match official that the position will have occurred three times after he had made his move or that the position on the board is itself occurring for the third time. No draw may be claimed when it is the opponent's turn to move. If a claim that the game is a draw is disputed by the opponent, the official plays the game through and the claim is examined. If it is correct, the game is declared a draw. If it is incorrect, the game is continued and the elapsed time spent in looking into the claim is counted against the claimant. This type of draw is uncommon and it is easy to make errors when claiming it. In the twentieth game of the Spassky-Fischer match, Fischer incorrectly claimed a draw through repetition of position. Although the position had occurred three times, it had not been repeated with the same player to move each time. However, Spassky did not dispute the claim.

**Reshevsky, Samuel (Sammy)** (b. 26 November 1911) American chess player; awarded the title International Grandmaster in 1950. He was American Champion in 1936, 1938, 1940, 1942, 1946 and 1969 and competed in the Chess Olympiads of 1937, 1950, 1952, 1958, 1964, 1968, 1970 and 1974. He took part in the 1948 World Championship match-tournament as well as in four interzonals, one Candidates' tournament and one series of Candidates' matches.

Reshevsky, who was born in Ozierkow, Poland, was the greatest of all child chess prodigies. He learned to play at the age of four and by the age of eight was touring Europe and America giving simultaneous exhibitions. He first defeated an International Grandmaster, Janowski, at the age of 11 and 'retired' a year later to concentrate upon his education. He returned to chess after graduating from Chicago University in 1932 and obtained a number of important victories, among which were firsts at New York (1934), Margate (1935), Kemeri (1937) and Hastings (1937); a third at Nottingham (1936) and a fourth at Avro (1938).

In 1948 he was one of the five competitors who took part in the World Championship match-tournament and finished equal third. He was refused permission by the State Department to compete in the 1950 Candidates' tournament, which was held in Budapest; but after defeating Najdorf in matches in 1952 (+8 −4 =6) and 1953 (+5 −4 =9) for the 'Championship of the Western World' unsuccessfully challenged Botvinnik to a match. His best result in the World Championship qualifying cycle was an equal second in the 1953 Candidates tournament. In 1961 a match was held between him and Fischer, but was forfeited by Fischer after a dispute with the organizers (+2 −2 =7).

Reshevsky spends comparatively little time studying opening theory and often consumes an inordinate amount of time during this phase of the game with the result that he is frequently in severe time trouble. However, he is a brilliant lightning player and normally manages to beat the clock. He prefers closed positions in which his talent for tactical complications can be shown. (1976 Elo rating: 2515)

**resign** to concede the game. There are many ways to resign a game, the best undoubtedly being with a brave smile. More colourful methods have been used though. Nimzovitch's example is not recommended; after losing in the final round of a rapid transit tournament in Berlin (so failing to come first) he stood on the table and shouted, *Gegen diesen Idioten muss ich verlieren?* ('I have to lose to this idiot?'). A much quieter way was adopted by von Bardeleben at Hastings (1895). At the point when defeat became inevitable in his game with Steinitz (see **Steinitz's Gem**) von Bardeleben quietly put on his hat and left the hall, so losing on time. At Kecskemet (1927) H. Mueller used a more novel ploy. At the adjournment Mueller sealed his next move and handed it to the official. He had not turned up when play resumed the next day, which was hardly surprising as his sealed move was *aufgegeben* (resign). Alekhine was famed for throwing his King across the playing hall, which could have been risky for innocent bystanders. To have to resign can be a galling experience and it may be preferable to do it when the victor is not there. It has been alleged that in the eleventh game of the Spassky-Fischer match Fischer played on after losing his Queen until he could resign when Spassky was out of the room. Perhaps for the same reason Spassky resigned the final game and thus the title over the phone; a perfectly legal method, as Lothar Schmid was at pains to point out.

**Réti Gambit** an opening sequence arising out of the Réti Opening: 1.

**Réti Opening**

N–KB3, P–Q4 *2. P–B4*. This opening was used by Réti, its inventor, at New York (1924) to defeat Capablanca in his first loss in eight years.

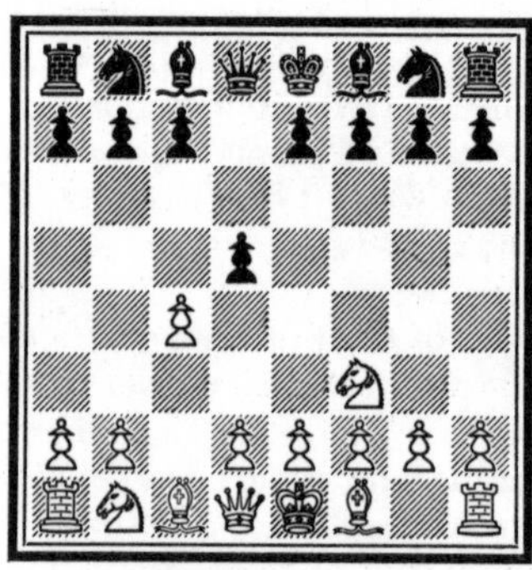

Position after 2. P–B4

**Réti Opening** an opening sequence introduced by 1. N–KB3.

**Réti, Richard** (1889–1929) Czechoslovakian chess player, theoretician and writer, born in Pezzinok, near Bratislava, on 28 May 1889 and brought to Vienna as a child. There he joined the renowned Vienna Chess Club and, after an uncompleted course at the university, became a chess professional.

His tournament successes included firsts in the Charousek Memorial Tournament (1918), at Gothenburg (1922), and at Teplitz-Schonau (1922), and fifth place at New York (1924).

Réti was also a noted composer of endgame studies and problems, as well as being an excellent blindfold player. In 1919 he broke the blindfold simultaneous display record by playing twenty-four games in Haarlem, the Netherlands (+12 −3 =9). This record was soon broken by Breyer, but Réti regained his title by playing twenty-nine games at São Paulo (+21 −2 =6).

Réti's main claim to fame lay in his development and exposition of the **hypermodern** principles of the new era. Although only two of his books were published during his lifetime, they became enormously influential (see ***Die Neuen Ideen im Schachspiel***). In them he expressed the beliefs of the hypermodern school.

He died of scarlet fever in Prague on 6 June 1929.

**retrograde analysis** a type of Fairy Chess problem in which the preceding moves of each player must be reconstructed. Typical problems are to have to deduce whose turn it is to move, whether either side can castle, and if capturing en passant is possible. A common task in retrograde analysis is to discover the shortest game that could lead to the diagrammed position. By convention the diagrammed position must be legal, although it can be improbable. For instance, White can only have three Bishops if it is certain that one of them could be an underpromoted pawn.

**reverse opening** see **inverted opening.**

**Reynolds' Variation** an opening sequence arising out of the Meran Defence: 1. P–Q4, P–Q4 2. P–QB4, P–QB3 3. N–KB3, N–B3 4. N–B3, P–K3 5. P–K3, QN–Q2 6. B–Q3, P×P 7. B×BP, P–QN4 8. B–Q3, P–QR3 9. P–K4, P–B4 10. *P–Q5*. The most common continuation is: 10 . . ., P–K4 11. P–QN3, B–Q3.

**Ribli, Zoltan** (b. 6 September 1951) Hungarian chess player; awarded the titles International Master in 1970 and International Grandmaster in 1973. He came second in the 1971 World Junior Championship and competed in the 1976 Manila interzonal, where he was equal fifth. Ribli was Hungarian Champion in 1973 and 1974; his other results include firsts at the Reykjavik zonal (1975) and Budapest (1975). (1976 Elo rating: 2575)

**Rice Gambit** an opening sequence arising out of the Kieseritzky Gambit: 1. P–K4, P–K4 2. P–KB4, P×P 3. N–KB3, P–KN4 4. P–KR4, P–N5 5. N–K5, N–KB3 6. B–B4, P–Q4 7. P×P, B–Q3 8. *O–O*. Black's best immediate reply: 8 . . ., B×N. This opening is rarely seen despite the efforts that an American professor, Isaac L. Rice, made at the beginning of this century to popularize it. Not only did he sponsor tournaments where this gambit was exclusively played – e.g., Ostend and Monte Carlo (1904) and Monte Carlo (1905) – but he also founded the Rice Gambit Association in 1906 with the world champion Emanuel Lasker as secretary. The Association's primary purpose was to investigate the Rice Gambit, although it did undertake other tasks.

**Rice, John M.** (b. 19 July 1937) British composer of chess problems. He is the author of several books, including *An ABC of Chess Problems, Chess Problems: Introduction to an Art* (with Michael Lipton and R. C. O. Matthews) and *The Two-Move Chess Problem: Tradition and Development* (with Michael Lipton and Barry P. Barnes).

**Richardson, Keith B.** (b. 2 April 1942) awarded the title International Grandmaster of Correspondence Chess in 1975, becoming the first British player to be awarded the title of Grandmaster for chessplaying. He was British Junior Champion in 1962, winner of the British Universities' Championship in 1963 (jointly) and in 1964, and was twice captain of the British Universities' Student Olympiad team. Richardson first competed in the World Correspondence Chess semi-final in 1965–1967 when he came second. He competed again in the 1968–1971 event and came first and also represented the United Kingdom in the 1972–1975 event.

**Richter, Emil** (1894–1971) Czechoslovakian chess player; awarded the title International Master in 1951. He was Czechoslovakian Champion in 1948.

**Richter, Kurt** (1900–1969) East German chess player; awarded the title International Master in 1950. He was born on 24 November 1900 and died on 29 December 1969. Richter competed in the Chess Olympiads of 1930 and 1931 and also wrote several books about chess. It was after him and not Emil Richter that the Richter-Rauzer Attack was named.

**Richter-Rauzer Attack** an opening sequence arising out of the Sicilian Defence: 1. P–K4, P–QB4 2. N–KB3, N–QB3 3. P–Q4, P×P 4. N×P, N–B3 5. N–QB3, P–Q3 6. *B–KN5*. This line is probably the most popular continuation in the Sicilian Defence. It was originally devised in the 1930s by Kurt Richter and was later developed by Rauzer.

**Rider** one of the three main types of Fairy chesspiece. It moves along straight lines and so may pin and be blocked by other pieces. Orthodox riders are the Rook and the Bishop; heterodox riders are the Nightrider and the Edgehog. Compare **Hopper, Leaper.**

**Rifle Chess** a type of Fairy Chess in which captures are made by removing the attacked man from the board while the capturing piece or pawn remains stationary. Each capture counts as one move; the pieces and pawns otherwise move normally. Rifle Chess was devised by W. J. Seabrook in 1921.

**rimpawn** (Kmoch's term) a pawn on a Rook file. Rimpawns create many exceptional situations in the ending and in many cases properly played endings with a rimpawn end in stalemate whereas with any other pawn there would be a clear win. Compare **innerpawn.** See ***Pawn Power in Chess*.**

**risk** the danger inherent in a move. Any move carries a degree of risk if only because development is delayed elsewhere, but it is usually applied only to moves that seriously increase the chances of defeat if unsuccessful. In annotations a risky move is followed by [!?] if the annotator believes it to be justified and by [?!] if he considers the move unsound. See **wild.**

**Robatsch Defence** a defence to either the King pawn or the Queen pawn opening: 1. P–K4, *P–KN3* 2. P–Q4, *B–N2*. (White's moves are interchangeable.) Black develops while avoiding an early attack or dispute for the centre. The main advantage of this defence over its close relative the Pirc Defence is its greater degree of flexibility. For instance, the King Knight may be developed at K2 rather than KB3.

This opening is now named after the Austrian player Karl Robatsch who popularized it. Also called **Fianchetto del Rey, King's Fianchetto Defence.** Compare **Pirc Defence, Modern Defence.**

Position after 2 . . ., B–N2

**Robatsch, Karl** (b. 14 October 1928) Austrian chess player; awarded the titles International Master in 1957 and International Grandmaster in 1961. He is best known for the defence: 1. P–K4, *P–KN3* 2. P–Q4, *B–N2*, which he pioneered as an alternative to the Pirc Defence. (1976 Elo rating: 2445). See **Modern Defence.**

**Rödl, Dr Ludwig** (1907–1970) West German chess player; awarded the title International Master in 1953; born on 30 April 1907. He was second in the German Championships of 1931 and 1933.

**Rodriguez, Amador** (b. 18 October 1957) Cuban chess player; awarded the title International Master in 1975. He came equal first in the Cienfuegos Masters tournament (1975) and in the same year won the first Central American Junior Championship. (1976 Elo rating: 2405)

**Roget's Knight's tour** a type of **Knight's tour** that was discovered in the middle of the nineteenth century. The board is divided into quarters and the Knight lands on every square of one quarter of the board before proceeding to the next segment.

**Rogoff, Kenneth** (b. 22 March 1953) American chess player; awarded the title International Master in 1974. (1976 Elo rating: 2480)

**Romanishin, Oleg** (b. 5 January 1952) Soviet chess player; awarded the title International Master in 1973. His results include firsts at Novi Sad (1975), Dortmund (1976) and Hastings (1976–7), and an equal second in the 1975 Soviet Championship. (1976 Elo rating: 2560)

**Romanovsky, Pyotr** (1892–1964) Soviet chess player; Soviet Champion in 1923 and (jointly) in 1927; awarded the title International Master in 1950. In later life he concentrated upon teaching chess and among his pupils were Alatortsev, Antoshin, and Chekhover.

**romantic** a style of play that favoured sacrifices, brilliancies, double-edged mating attacks and preferred a counterattack to a passive defence. In modern times it evolved in the eighteenth century with the Italian school of players, who stressed the paramount importance of swift attack and piece-play in contrast to the teachings of Philidor. Romantic play dominated the early nineteenth century and reached its apex with Morphy, who can also be regarded as the first classical player. With the example of his play and the teachings of Steinitz the romantic school merged into the **classical** school, which also favoured attack but only after proper preparation by swift development, occupation of the centre with pawns, creation and seizure of open lines, etc. Romantic players still exist, however, but are usually described as **neo-romantic.**

**Romih Variation** an opening sequence arising out of the Semi-Meran: 1. P–Q4, P–Q4 2. P–QB4, P–QB3 3. N–KB3, N–B3 4. N–B3, P–K3 5. P–K3, QN–Q2 6. B–Q3, *B–N5*. Instead of the pawn advance characteristic of the **Meran Defence,** Black opts for piece play, temporarily restraining the advance of White's King pawn. The most common continuation is: 7. P–QR3, B–R4 8. Q–B2.

**Rook** a chessman that moves in a straight line vertically or horizontally over any number of unoccupied squares. Each side begins with two Rooks which initially occupy the corner squares.

The Rooks play little part in the opening and are often the final pieces to be moved. They are most effective in the middle-game and ending when they can seize and operate along open files.

The piece originally represented a chariot and was known in Arabic as the *rukhkh*. When chess was introduced into Europe the meaning of this name was forgotten and either the word was corrupted, as in English, or a new name was substituted based upon the piece's appearance. For example, this piece is known in Dutch as the *Kasteel*, in French as the *tour*, and in German as the *Turm* – which all mean castle or tower. In contrast to the radical changes undergone by the piece's name, its move has remained unchanged throughout the history of chess. Also called **castle**. Abbrev. **R**.

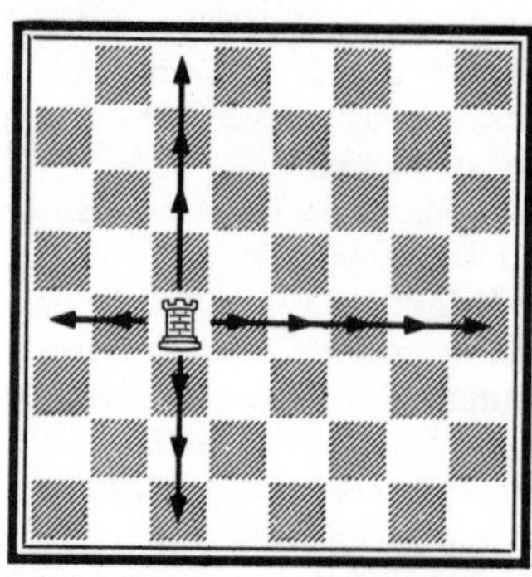

Potential moves of the Rook over unobstructed squares

**Rook lift** (Kmoch's term) a manoeuvre through which a Rook moves in front of its own pawns. It can then operate along closed or half-open files as if they were half-open or open files respectively. However, this is a dangerous action in the opening and middle-game as it exposes the Rook to attacks from pawns and minor pieces. See ***Pawn Power in Chess***.

**Rossetto, Hector Decio** (b. 8 September 1922) Argentinian chess player; awarded the titles International Master in 1950 and International Grandmaster in 1960. (1976 Elo rating: 2420)

**Rossolimo, Nicolas** (1910–1975) Franco-American chess player; awarded the titles International Master in 1950 and International Grandmaster in 1953. He was born in Kiev on 28 February 1910 and emigrated to France with his mother in 1929, becoming a French citizen. There he won the Paris Championship ten times and was French Champion in 1948; he competed for France in the Chess Olympiads of 1950 and 1952. In 1953 Rossolimo moved to the United States, where he became a citizen. He won the U.S. Open Championship in 1955 and competed for the United States in the Chess Olympiads of 1958, 1960 and 1966. He died on 24 July 1975.

**Rossolimo's Chess Studio** a chess meeting house in Thompson Street, New York, run by Nicolas Rossolimo until his death.

**round-robin** a tournament in which each competitor plays every other competitor at least once. Generally this is only practicable when the number of competitors is limited. The first round-robin tournament took place in London in 1851 soon after the famous tournament. It was organized by the London Chess Club, which had disassociated itself from the major tournament, and was open to foreigners only. The entrants were Anderssen (who won), Harrwitz, Horwitz, Meirhofer, Szabo, Löwenthal, and Kling. The last two dropped out and were replaced by Ehrmann and Kieseritzky. Also called **all-play-all** or **American**. Compare **Swiss System**.

**Royal Game, The** *descriptive phrase for* chess. The first record of its use is found in *Reson and Sensuallyte*, a fifteenth-century translation by John Lydgate of an anonymous French poem. Here chess is described as 'that playe most Royal'. This description does not appear in the French original. In the seventeenth century it was included in the titles of two important books: *Le Royal Jeu des Eschecs*, a translation of the work by Lopez which was published in Paris in 1615; and *The Royall Game of Chesse-play*, a translation by F. Beale of Greco's work which was published in London in 1656.

***Royal Game, The*** the last completed work of Stefan Zweig before his suicide in 1944. It describes the confrontation between Dr B., a cultured Austrian refugee who had been tortured by the Nazis, and Czentovic, a boorish idiot-savant whose sole talent had made him chess champion of the world. Dr B. had withstood his torturers by mentally playing through an anthology of games stolen from a captor. This had made him a world-class player, but the strains of constantly trying to defeat himself had finally led to a nervous breakdown. He recovered and was allowed to go into exile, but was warned by his doctors that he must never play chess again. On board the ship taking him to South America he discovered that Czentovic was giving a consultation game. Tempted, Dr B. played and revealed his astonishing ability. He won an individual game against Czentovic that was hastily arranged, but was driven to the verge of collapse in a second game and retired from the game forever, leaving Czentovic triumphant. Compare ***Defence, The***; ***Dragon Variation, The***; ***Master Prim***.

**Royal Piece** a Fairy chesspiece that moves and has the powers of an orthodox piece, but is also considered to be a King for checks, checkmates, stalemates, etc. Royal pieces date back to at least 1878.

**Rubinstein, Akiba** (1882–1961) Polish chess player; born in Stawiski, Russian Poland on 12 December 1882. Like Steinitz, Rubinstein was a Talmudic scholar and turned to chess after learning to play at 16. Within a few years of his international debut at Kiev (1903) he was in the front rank of chess players with victories that included Ostend (1907), Carlsbad (1907), St Petersburg (1909), San Sebastian (1912), Pistyan (1912) and Breslau (1912). Altogether he won thirteen of the 23 major tournaments in which he competed before World War I – an unparalleled record. Rubinstein was also a successful match-player and defeated Marshall (twice), Salwe, Teichmann, Mieses and Bogoljubov, although usually by small margins.

In these years Rubinstein was the logical contender for the World Championship, but could not raise the financial backing for a match with Lasker. The War blighted his hopes. By 1919, Capablanca had become the main challenger and Rubinstein was in decline.

In this period Rubinstein's mental illness began. He was still capable of playing superb chess, but was unpredictably erratic. His post-war record included firsts at Vienna (1922), Meran (1924), Marienbad (1925) and the highest percentage in the 1930 Chess Olympiad where he played on first board, yet these results alternated with times when he would play extremely poorly and often commit inexplicable blunders.

Throughout the years his mental illness worsened. He was troubled by an imaginary fly which accompanied him everywhere; his feelings of paranoia grew and he feared attempts on his life by Alekhine and others. He grew steadily more uncommunicative. In 1932 he retired from chess completely and lived quietly in Brussels.

Rubinstein's capacity for work on chess was immense. He claimed to study six hours a day for 300 days a year and play in tournaments for another 60 days. This effort was distilled into creations that have won praise for their unsurpassed elegance and beauty. Réti described them as 'the most perfect demonstrations of Steinitz's teachings', while Fine has written that 'Better chess cannot be played by mortal man'. They were characterized by the constant presence of an overriding strategy and an almost incredible refinement of technique. Rubinstein was limited in his openings and always advanced the Queen pawn as White. (Once he sat down to play and touched his Queen pawn only to discover that a prankster had nailed it to the board.) Yet his contributions to opening theory were important, even though confined to a narrow area (see **Rubinstein Variation**). His métier lay in the endings – as shown by Euwe's comment that 'he possessed an almost supernatural feeling for the endgame and for Rook endings in particular'. It was said that to enter a level ending against Rubinstein was a certain way to lose. Rubinstein was, perhaps, the strongest player never to become World Champion. He died on 14 March 1961.

**Rubinstein trap** a combination which wins an apparently protected pawn as recapture would lose the Queen to an attack by a Bishop.

The trap is named after Rubinstein, who fell into versions of it twice in two years! The first instance took place in a game against Euwe at Bad Kissingen (1928) and is shown in the diagram on p.245. Euwe played: 1. N × P, and Rubinstein could not take the Knight because of: 2. B–B7. The second occasion on which he fell into the trap was against Alekhine at San Remo (1930).

**Rubinstein Variation** **1.** an opening sequence arising out of the Four Knights' Game: 1. P–K4, P–K4 2. N–KB3, N–QB3 3. N–B3, N–B3 4. B–N5, *N–Q5*. Although this piece moves twice in the opening, this variation has never been refuted. An exchange of Knights often leads to a draw, but capture of the King pawn by White gives Black a potentially dangerous attack.

**2.** an opening sequence arising out of the French Defence: 1. P–K4,

P–K3 2. P–Q4, P–Q4 3. N–QB3, *P×P*. This capture relaxes the tension in the centre and allows White a freer hand. It is rarely played. The most common continuation is: 4. N×P.

**3.** an opening sequence arising out of the Nimzo-Indian Defence: 1. P–Q4, N–KB3 2. P–QB4, P–K3 3. N–QB3, B–N5 4. *P–K3*. White ignores the pin and develops simply. Common continuations are: 4 . . ., P–QN3 and 4 . . ., O–O. This variation is the most popular response to the Nimzo-Indian Defence.

**4.** an opening sequence arising out of the Tarrasch Defence to the Queen's Gambit Declined: 1. P–Q4, P–Q4 2. P–QB4, P–K3 3. N–QB3, P–QB4 4. BP×P, KP×P 5. N–B3, N–QB3 6. *P–KN3*. White intends to fianchetto his King Bishop and attack the isolated Queen pawn. The most common continuation is: 6 . . ., N–B3.

All four variations are named after their inventor, Akiba Rubinstein.

**Rubinstein trap**

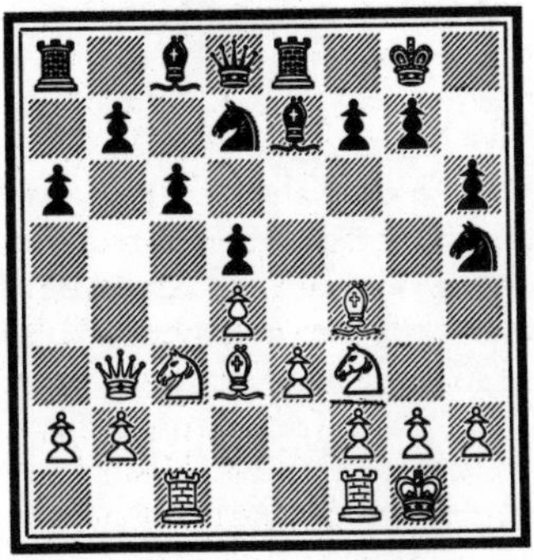

Rubinstein vs. Euwe (Bad Kissingen, 1928)

**Rubtsova, Olga Nikolayevna** (b. 1909) Soviet female chess player; Women's World Champion from 1956 to 1958. She first won the Soviet Women's Championship in 1927 and won it again in 1931, 1937 and 1949. She became Women's World Champion by defeating both Bykova and Rudenko in a triangular match, but lost the title to Bykova two years later (+4 −7 =3).

**Rudenko, Ludmila** (b. 1904) Soviet female chess player; Women's World Champion from 1949 to 1953. She won the title in a tournament organized by FIDE, but lost it to Bykova four years later (+5 −7 =2).

**rules of chess** see ***Laws of Chess, The***.

**Russian Defence** formerly another name for **Slav Defence**. Another name for **Petroff's Defence**.

**Russian System** a variation occurring in the Grünfeld Defence. It usually arises as follows: 1. P–Q4, N–KB3 2. P–QB4, P–KN3 3. N–QB3, P–Q4 4. *Q–N3* (or 4. N–B3, B–N2 5. *Q–N3*). White prepares to create a powerful centre with P–K4 as well as hampering

Black's natural counterstrike, . . . P–QB4. It is called the Russian System because of the extensive analysis that Soviet players have devoted to this opening.

**Russia's chess teacher** *descriptive phrase for* Emmanuel Shiffers.

**Ruy Lopez (Opening)** one of the oldest and most popular of the King's pawn openings: 1. P–K4, P–K4 2. N–KB3, N–QB3 3. *B–N5*. It is named after a sixteenth-century Spanish clergyman, Ruy Lopez, who edited a book on chess openings. The first record of this ancient opening was in the late fifteenth century in the anonymous Göttingen Manuscript. It was not until the middle of the nineteenth century, however, that the Ruy Lopez received serious critical attention, much of it from the pen of the Russian chess analyst, Carl Andreyvich Jänisch (1813–1872). It is one of the most deeply analysed of all openings, and entire books have been devoted to its complex possibilities.

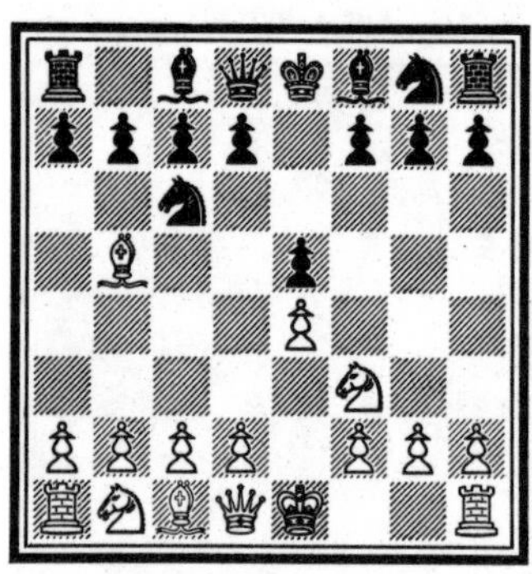

Position after 3. B–N5

# S

**Saavedra, Fernando** (1847–1922) a monk whose sole claim to fame in chess was the discovery of a single move! The problem illustrated on p.247 appeared in the *Weekly Citizen* of Glasgow on 18 May 1895. It was adjudged a draw after: 1. P–B7, R–Q3ch 2. K–N5, R–Q4ch 3. K–N4, R–Q5ch 4. K–N3, R–Q6ch 5. K–B2, R–Q5 6. P–B8=Q, R–B5ch 7. Q×R stalemate. Saavedra pointed out that 6. P–B8=R! wins after 6 . . ., R–QR5 7. K–N3.

**sac** *abbrev. for* **sacrifice.**

**Sacconi, Comte Antonio** (1895–1963) Italian chess player; awarded the title International Master in 1951. He was born on 5 October 1895 and became a National Master in 1921. Italian Champion in 1935, Sacconi competed in the Chess Olympiads of 1927, 1928, 1933 and 1935. He died on 22 December 1963.

**sacrifice** to give up (deliberately) material in return for some advantage, such as a gain in tempo, greater control of the board, disruption of the opponent's defence, attacking prospects, etc. If the sacrifice occurs in the opening it is known as a gambit. A sacrifice that succeeds with best play on both sides is said to be sound; if it does not it is said to be unsound. In practice the soundness of a sacrifice is of less importance than the question of whether it provides good chances of success. A sacrifice against a timid opponent could be the best choice even if it is unsound. This policy of playing the man rather than the board was one of the strategies of Lasker. Some players are naturally aggressive: Tal has said that he does not attempt to prove that a sacrifice that he is considering in a game is sound, merely that it is not unsound. The onus of proof is on the defender. Nevertheless, sacrifices have declined in number since the days before Steinitz. Now it is realised that sacrifices that are made without adequate development of pieces are practically certain to fail; defensive ability has increased markedly. It is still true, though, that a player who doesn't disclose when he has blundered can gain an admirable reputation as an attacking player. As Koltanowski told Sir George Thomas when asked if he had lost or sacrificed the exchange: 'If I lose, it was a mistake. If I win, then it was a sacrifice!'

**Saavedra, Fernando**

Saavedra problem

**Sahović, Dragutin** (b. 8 August 1940) Yugoslavian chess player; awarded the title International Master in 1976. (1976 Elo rating: 2420)

**Saidy, Anthony** (b. 16 May 1937) American chess player; awarded the title International Master in 1969. He was Canadian Open Champion in 1960, American Open Champion in 1967 and competed in the 1964 Chess Olympiad. Saidy is a regular writer on chess; his works include *The Battle of Chess Ideas* and (with Norman Lessing) *The World of Chess*. (1976 Elo rating: 2435)

**Saint-Amant, Pierre Charles Fournier** (1800–1872) the strongest French chess player of his era. Saint-Amant was born on 2 September 1800 at Montflanquin. Entering the government service, he was sent as a clerk to French Guinea in 1819. In 1821 he returned to France and began to frequent the Café de la Régence, learning the game from Deschappelles. Although talented, he did not become a chess professional and entered the wine trade. His reputation grew in 1836 when he visited England on business and in passing defeated some of the best English players. After the death of La Bourdonnais in 1840, Saint-Amant was undoubtedly the strongest player in France – the strongest chess nation in the world. In 1843 he again visited England, where he defeated Staunton in a match of six games, winning three and losing two. Several months later a return match was held in Paris where he was decisively beaten, losing eleven, winning six and drawing four. After this, Saint-Amant played less frequently, concentrating instead of reviving and editing *Le Palamède*, the chess journal founded by La Bourdonnais, until it closed down in 1847. In 1848 he re-entered the government service and distinguished himself in the Revolution as a captain of the National Guard by protecting the Tuileries from the mob. For this he was made its Governor and later the French Consul in California in 1851–1852, after which he played no serious chess. He died on 25 October 1872 after being thrown from a carriage.

**Šajtar, Jaroslav** (b. 3 December 1921) Czechoslovakian chess player; awarded the titles International Master in 1950 and International Judge in 1955. He competed in the Chess Olympiads of 1952 and 1954 and played in the 1947 radio match against the United Kingdom. In 1956 he was appointed a vice-president of FIDE and is now the FIDE zonal president responsible for the administration of the East European zone.

**Sämisch, Friedrich** (b. 20 September 1896) West German chess player; awarded the title International Grandmaster in 1950. Sämisch became a National Master after winning the 1920 Berlin Hauptturnier and played in many tournaments over the next twenty years as well as playing on second board in the 1930 Chess Olympiad. However, he is especially remembered for his researches into opening theory.

**Sämisch Variation** **1.** an opening sequence arising out of the King's Indian Defence: 1. P–Q4, N–KB3 2. P–QB4, P–KN3 3. N–QB3, B–N2 4. *P–K4*, P–Q3 5. *P–B3*. White constructs a strong pawn-centre either eventually to launch a King-side pawn storm or gradually to suffocate Black. This opening was known in the 1890s, but it was not until 1925 that Friedrich Sämisch developed it.

**2.** an opening sequence arising out of the Nimzo-Indian Defence: 1. P–Q4, N–KB3 2. P–QB4, P–K3 3. N–QB3, B–N5 4. *P–QR3*. White actually forces Black to carry out his strategy of doubling White's pawns in the belief that they will reinforce the centre rather than weaken it. Black's best immediate reply: 4 . . ., B × Nch. It is said that this variation was confused with that in the King's Defence and received its name by mistake – having nothing to do with Sämisch!

**Sanchez, Luis** (b. 1917) Colombian chess player; awarded the title International Master in 1951. He played in the Chess Olympiads of 1954, 1956 and 1958. (1976 Elo rating: 2385)

**Sämisch Variation**

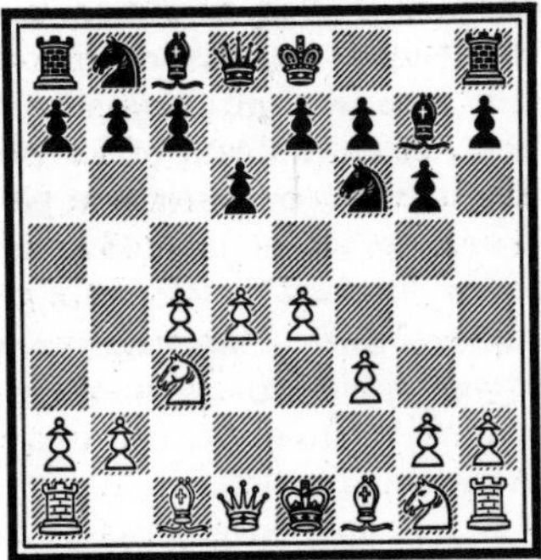

Position (def. 1) after 5. P–B3

**sandglass** a device for recording the time taken by each player, used before the perfection of the chess clock. By the middle of the nineteenth century the slowness of many games caused reforms to be proposed. One of the most popular was for each player to have a sandglass to record the total time taken. When it was that player's turn his sandglass would be upended allowing the sand to fall into the lower chamber and when it was the opponent's move the sandglass would be set horizontally, so stopping the flow of sand. If each player had a three-hour sandglass the game could last no more than six hours. An advantage of this arrangement was that it set a time limit for the whole game, whereas previous reforms had attempted to set a time limit for each move; this was not only inadequate for some moves but it did little to prevent excessively long games.

Sandglasses were first tried in the match between Anderssen and Kolisch in 1860 and were used frequently from that date. After the introduction of the chess clock at London (1883), they were slowly replaced. Also called **hourglass**.

**San Francisco Dragons** a founding member of the **National Chess League**. In the league's first season the team came fourth. The two strongest members of the team were James Tarjan and John Grefe.

**Sanguinetti, Raul** (b. 3 February 1933) Argentinian chess player; awarded the title International Master in 1957. He was Champion of Argentina in 1956, 1957, 1962 and 1965. Sanguinetti has participated in several Chess Olympiads since 1956 and was also a competitor in the 1958 and 1976 (Biel) interzonals. (1976 Elo rating: 2480)

**San Sebastian (1911)** an international all-play-all tournament with fifteen competitors, held in San Sebastian, Spain. To qualify for the tournament a player had to have achieved at least two third places in other major international tournaments, but an exception was made for Capablanca who was invited to compete (his first international tournament) because of his victory in his match with Marshall. Bernstein and some of the other players objected to his inclusion, but Capablanca silenced the criticism by defeating Bernstein in the first round in a game that won the Rothschild brilliancy prize.

The tournament was won by Capablanca (+6 −1 =7) in the most sensational debut since Pillsbury at Hastings (1895). He was defeated only by Rubinstein who came equal second with Vidmar, while Marshall was fourth. The other competitors were (in order of finishing): Nimzovitch, Schlechter, Tarrasch, Bernstein, Spielmann, Teichmann, Janowski, Maróczy, Burn, Duras and Leonhardt.

**San Sebastian (1912)** a double-round tournament with eleven competitors, narrowly won by Rubinstein (who scored 12½) ahead of Nimzovitch (12) and Spielmann (12).

**Santasiere's Folly** an opening sequence: 1. N–KB3, P–Q4 2. *P–QN4*. White prevents the advance of Black's Queen Bishop pawn, so hampering Black's normal development in the Queen pawn opening. It has only been consistently played by the American player Anthony Santasiere.

**Saragossa Opening** one where White plays 1. *P–QB3*, deliberately inviting Black to take the initiative. It can develop into an inverted Caro-Kann Defence. This opening was played by Louis Paulsen at Nuremberg (1883) and Dresden (1892), but was first seriously analysed in the 1920s by the members of the Saragossa Chess Club, especially José Juncosa.

**Sarratt, J. H.** (?–1820) British chess player and writer. Sarratt's origins are unknown, but by the early nineteenth century he had become a leading member of the London Chess Club. A former pupil of Verdoni, he played in the Italian, not the Philidorean style, and strongly influenced English style. Sarratt was the first English translator of Damiano, Lopez and Salvio and styled himself the 'Professor of Chess'. His most important original works were the *Treatise* (1808) and the *New Treatise* (1821).

**Savon, Vladimir** (b. 26 September 1940) Soviet chess player; awarded the titles International Master in 1967 and International Grandmaster in 1973. He was Soviet Champion in 1972 and competed in the 1972 Chess Olympiad. (1976 Elo rating: 2545)

**saw** (Kmoch's term) a zig-zag formation of pawns. The **Stonewall Formation** is one of the commonest examples. See ***Pawn Power in Chess***.

**Sax, Gyula** (b. 18 June 1951) Hungarian chess player; awarded the titles International Master in 1972 and International Grandmaster in 1976. His tournament results include firsts at Reggio Emilia, Madonna di Campiglio, Vrnjačka Banja (all in 1974) and Rovinj/Zagreb (1975). (1976 Elo rating: 2530)

***Scacchia Ludus*** *Latin for* the game of chess; a Latin poem on chess written in the sixteenth century by the Bishop of Alba, Marcus (Antonius) Hieronymus Vida. Its subject is a game of chess played between Apollo and Mercury in front of the other gods; in it, the moves of the men are described and the course of the game is vaguely outlined.

The poem was composed in 1513, but was not published by its author until 1527; it attained immediate popularity and was reprinted and translated many times in the sixteenth century. The best-known English translation of the poem was made by the eighteenth-century poet Oliver Goldsmith, but was not published until 1854.

**Scafarelli, Francesco** (b. 23 October 1933) Italian chess player; awarded the title International Master in 1957. He competed in the Chess Olympiads of 1952 and 1954. Scafarelli also represented Italy in the 1953 World Junior Championship, in which he was ninth.

**Scandinavian Defence** another name for **Centre Counter Defence**.

***Schachzeitung*** see ***Deutsche Schachzeitung***.

**Scheveningen (1913)** a tournament with thirteen competitors, won by Alekhine (who scored 11½) ahead of Janowski (11).

**Scheveningen Variation** an opening sequence arising out of the Sicilian Defence: 1. P–K4, P–QB4 2. N–KB3, P–K3 3. P–Q4, P×P 4. N×P, N–KB3 5. N–QB3, *P–Q3*. The limited advance of his centre pawns creates a cramped position for Black, but if White's customary King-side attack is repulsed then Black can play P–Q4 more easily than in most other variations of the Sicilian Defence. Common continuations for White are: 6. B–K2 or 6. P–KN4. This system was first played by Euwe at Scheveningen (1923).

**Schiffers** a variant spelling of **Shiffers**.

**Schlechter, Carl** (1874–1918) a leading Austrian player at the beginning of the twentieth century; born in Vienna on 2 March 1874. His first international tournament was Leipzig (1894); from then he competed regularly in tournaments until the outbreak of World War I, drawing over fifty per cent of his games – as much through his tendency to agree to draws in advantageous positions as through drawish play. As a result he was nicknamed 'the Drawing Master' by Tarrasch. Ironically, when he played Lasker in a World Championship match in 1910 he merely needed to draw the last game to gain the title and had a winning position, but unfortunately he missed several opportunities to draw and eventually lost – consequently drawing the match (+1 −1 =8) and allowing Lasker to retain the title. Other results included firsts at Munich (1900), Ostend (1906, 1907), Prague (1908), and Carlsbad (1911); he also defeated Janowski in a match in 1902 (+6 −1 =3) and drew a match with Tarrasch in 1911 (+3 −3 =10).

From 1899 until his death, Schlechter was the editor of the *Deutsche Schachzeitung* and was also responsible for the 1916 revision of Bilguer's *Handbuch des Schachspiels*. He died of starvation in Budapest on 27 December 1918.

**Schlechter Variation** a variation occurring in the Queen's Gambit Declined, arising out of the Slav Defence: 1. P–Q4, P–Q4 2. P–QB4, *P–QB3* 3. N–KB3, N–B3 4. P–K3, *P–KN3* 5. N–B3. It was named after Carl Schlechter. See illustration on p. 252.

**Schliemann Defence** a defence to the Ruy Lopez: 1. P–K4, P–K4 2. N–KB3, N–QB3 3. B–N5, *P–B4*. Black attempts to seize the initiative by an early pawn-advance, obtaining a superior centre and an open

King Bishop file. White has several good replies. Since he is ahead in development his game is generally thought to be superior. The opening is named after Schliemann, who first played it in Europe. On the Continent it is known as the **Jänisch Defence** after the Russian who played it before Schliemann.

**Schlechter Variation**

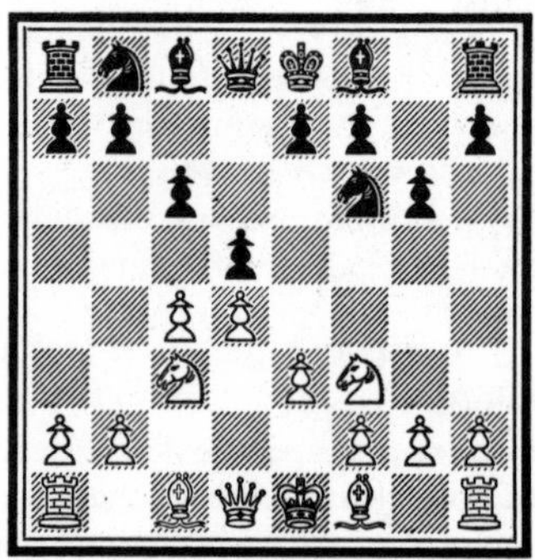

Position after 5. N–B3

**Schmid, Lothar** (b. 10 May 1928) West German chess player; awarded the titles International Master in 1951, International Grandmaster in 1959, International Correspondence Chess Grandmaster in 1959 and International Judge in 1974. He competed in the Chess Olympiads of 1950, 1952, 1954, 1956, 1958, 1960, 1962, 1964, 1968, 1970 and 1974. An outstanding correspondence player, Schmid was equal second with L. Endzelins in the second Correspondence World Championship with 10½ points out of 15. In 1972 he was the Chief Arbiter for the World Championship match between Spassky and Fischer. (1976 Elo rating: 2520)

**Schmidt, Paul** (b. 20 August 1916) West German chess player; awarded the title International Master in 1950. He was Estonian Champion in 1935 and 1937 and German Champion in 1941.

**Schmidt, Wladzimierz** (b. 10 April 1943) Polish chess player; awarded the titles International Master in 1968 and International Grandmaster in 1976. He was Polish Champion in 1974 and 1975. (1976 Elo rating: 2485)

**Schneider, Lars-Ake** (b. 10 July 1955) Swedish chess player; awarded the title International Master in 1976. (1976 Elo rating: 2365)

**schodra** a game similar to chess that is played by the Soyotas and other semi-primitive peoples of Russian Asia. Like chess, it appears to be derived from **chaturanga**.

**Scholar's Mate** a mate in four moves: 1. P–K4, P–K4 2. B–B4, B–B4 3. Q–R5, N–KB3 4. Q×BPmate. It has been known for centuries and was mentioned in the second edition of Arthur Saul's *Famous Game of Chesse Play*, published in 1640. It is often erroneously referred to as Fool's Mate. See **Fool's Mate**.

Scholar's Mate

Position after 4. Q × BPmate

**Schwalbe, Die** *German for* the swallow. A German periodical for chess problems, regarded by many as the finest in the world. It is named after a famous chess problem by J. Kohtz and C. Kockelhorn, which was published in 1911. The full title of this problem, 'Eine Schwalbe macht noch keinen Sommer' (one swallow doesn't make a summer), was an allusion to the sparsity of output of the composers at that time.

**Schweber, Samuel** (b. 16 July 1936) Argentinian chess player; awarded the title International Master in 1961. He competed in the 1955 World Junior Championship when he was ninth and has represented his country in several Chess Olympiads. (1976 Elo rating: 2455)

**score** **1.** the written moves of a game, by which it can be reconstructed by other players. A legible score must be kept by each player in FIDE games; if this is not done the game may be lost by forfeit.

**2.** the result of a game, match or tournament.

**score sheet** a sheet on which the score of a game is written down. In FIDE events this will be provided by the organizers. Games may be forfeited if the moves on the score sheet are illegible or if the score sheet of each player is not sealed in an envelope provided by the organizers, should the game be adjourned.

**scoring** (in tournaments) usually this is one point for a win, half a point for a draw and nought for a loss. This system was first adopted at Dundee (1867), but has occasionally been discarded in favour of other systems. At Monte Carlo (1901 and 1902) players who drew were awarded a quarter point each and asked to replay the game. The winner of the replay received another half point; if the replay also ended in a draw, both players each received another quarter point. Emanuel Lasker was another who believed that the normal system of scoring was inadequate. He proposed a system where the players would split ten points per game in the ratio: five–five for a draw, six–four for baring a King, eight–two for achieving stalemate and ten–nil for achieving checkmate or resignation.

**Scotch Chess** another name for **Progressive Chess**.

**Scotch Four Knights' Game** an opening sequence arising out of the Four Knights' Game: 1. P–K4, P–K4 2. N–KB3, N–QB3 3. N–B3, N–B3 4. *P–Q4*. White attempts to open lines for his pieces, but wholesale exchanges tend to diminish the advantage of having the first move. Black's best immediate reply: 4 . . ., P×P. This opening can easily transpose into the Scotch Opening.

**Scotch Gambit** an opening sequence arising out of the Scotch Opening: 1. P–K4, P–K4 2. N–KB3, N–QB3 3. P–Q4, P×P 4. *B–QB4*. White develops his pieces naturally, but Black faces few problems. Black's usual immediate replies: 4 . . ., B–B4, or 4 . . ., N–B3.

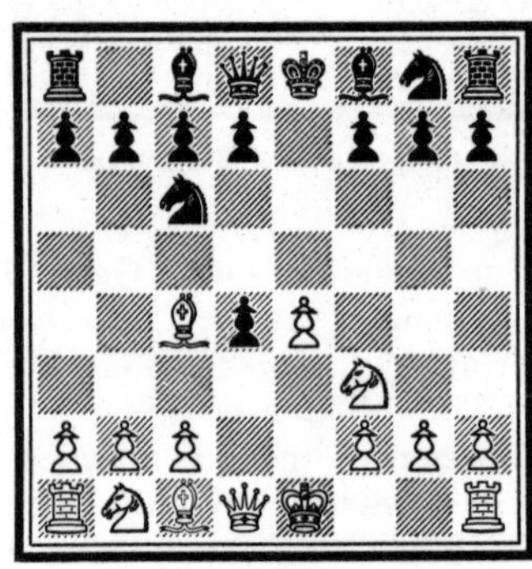

Position after 4. B–QB4

**Scotch Opening** an opening sequence: 1. P–K4, P–K4 2. N–KB3, N–QB3 3. *P–Q4*. White opens lines for his pieces, but Black can equalize easily. Black's best immediate reply: 3 . . ., P×P. The opening was discussed by Ercole del Rio in 1750 and analyzed by Giambattista Lolli in 1763, but derives its name from its use in the correspondence match between the Edinburgh Chess Club and the London Chess Club in 1824. Also called **Scotch Game.**

**Scott, R. H. V.** (1889–1953) British chess player; British Champion in 1920. He died on 10 January 1953.

**sealed move** the final move made before the adjournment of a game. The player whose move it is must write it unambiguously on his score sheet, and must then include it with the score sheet of his opponent in an envelope, seal the envelope and only then stop his clock. On the envelope must be written the players' names, the position immediately before the sealed move, the time taken by each player, and the name of the player sealing the move as well as the number of this sealed move. The envelope must then be handed to the arbiter or other appropriate official. If any of these conditions are not fulfilled the game can be lost by forfeit. See also **adjournment**.

**sealer** (Kmoch's term) a pawn that cannot move and which hinders the movement of its own pieces. In endings a bad Bishop is often the result of the presence of numerous sealers. Compare **sweeper**. See ***Pawn Power in Chess***.

**second** someone who assists the competing player by helping to devise opening variations, analyze adjourned games, pinpoint the strengths and weaknesses of opponents, etc. The first World Championship in which they were officially allowed was in the Alekhine-Euwe match (1935). They have been around for much longer though; both Staunton and Saint-Amant had two seconds each in their match (1843).

Many believe that seconds should be banned since they remove the element of personal combat, as they transform games into battles between teams rather than individuals. Indeed, a player without a second is effectively penalized although he has committed no crime. However, in contradiction to this, some Grandmasters refuse to have seconds, notably Fischer and Larsen. Larsen has criticized them on the grounds that 'The typical second tends to become something like a compromise politician: when he has a difficult problem (opening or adjournment) he will be satisfied with a solution which will not be criticized, though it may not be absolutely best.'

**seeding** a procedure adopted in certain of the later Chess Olympiads when the number of entrants was too large for a single round-robin tournament. Instead, preliminary tournaments were adopted from which the teams qualified for finals of different strengths.

For this to be fair, the preliminary tournaments had to be of approximately equal strength to prevent the strongest teams clashing in them and thus distorting the composition of the finals. Thus, the teams were seeded in presumed order of strength by a committee of team captains and then assigned to the preliminary groups.

This was done in the following manner. The teams were seeded and the team names written down in columns, the number of which corresponded to the preliminary groups. The composition of each group was found by reading down each column. For example, if there were sixty-three teams and eight preliminary groups, the first group would consist of teams 1, 16, 17, 32, 33, 48, and 49.

Unfortunately, it was extremely difficult to estimate the relative strengths of the teams, especially those with several young players, and an incorrect seeding could markedly affect a team's chance of qualifying for a high final.

In 1976 this procedure was replaced by the **Swiss System**.

**self-block** a **flight square** on which one of the King's defenders has been stationed. Fatal examples of self-blocks may be observed in any **epaulet mate, Guéridon** or **smothered mate,** but they may also be seen in the overwhelming majority of checkmates that occur in the middle game.

**Selfmate** a problem in Fairy Chess in which White forces Black to mate him. It is one of the oldest forms of unorthodox problem. Also called **Sui-mate.**

**Semi-Meran** any opening sequence arising out of the Meran Defence in which Black deviates from the orthodox sequence of moves by *not* playing: 6 . . ., P × P. The three most popular choices are: 6 . . ., B–K2, 6 . . ., B–Q3 and 6 . . ., B–N5. After the first two choices the most common continuation for White is: 7. P–K4, establishing a strong centre. The third choice is known as the **Romih Variation.**

**semi-open game** a position where most of one side's pieces stand in front of their own pawns while most of the other side's pieces stand behind their pawns. Semi-open games normally arise from the King pawn opening when Black has not replied with: 1 . . ., P–K4, an example being the French Defence. Compare **closed game, open game.**

**Semi-Slav** an opening sequence occurring in the Queen's Gambit Declined, characterized by Black playing an early . . . P–K3 in addition to the . . . P–QB3 of the Slav Defence: 1. P–Q4, P–Q4 2. P–QB4, *P–K3* 3. N–QB3, *P–QB3*. See **Meran Variation, Romih Variation, Anti-Meran Gambit.**

**Semmering (1926)** a tournament with eighteen competitors, narrowly won by Spielmann (who scored 13) ahead of Alekhine (12½), Vidmar (12), Nimzovitch (11½) and Tartakover (11½).

**Semmering-Baden (1937)** a double-round tournament with eight competitors, won by Keres (who scored 9) ahead of Fine (8), Capablanca (7½) and Reshevsky (7½).

**sentry** (Kmoch's term) an enemy pawn on a file adjacent to that occupied by the pawn. The Rook pawns will only be faced by one sentry each, but every other pawn will be opposed by two. Thus, three pawns (the **counterpawn** and the two sentries) must normally be captured, diverted or passed before the pawn becomes a **passed pawn**. See ***Pawn Power in Chess*.**

**Sergievsky, Vladimir** (b. 3 October 1936) Soviet chess player; awarded the title International Master in 1966.

**series-helpmate** a type of Fairy Chess problem in which Black plays a series of moves without interruption until at the end of this series White checkmates in one move. Compare **helpmate.**

**Seven Stars of Berlin** a descriptive term sometimes applied to the German chess players who were known as the **Berlin Pleiades.**

**seventh rank** the rank on which an opponent's pawns are originally stationed. A Rook on the seventh rank is usually a powerful piece, especially when the enemy King is on the eighth rank. Not only will it be able to attack the enemy pawns laterally, forcing them to be defended by pieces or to advance (since they cannot be protected by pawns), but it will also be able to cordon off the King from the centre of the board.

Two Rooks on the seventh rank can often decide the outcome of the game. They can not only attack enemy pawns laterally and cordon off a King on the eighth rank, but also often harrass the King with a series of checks, which frequently leads to perpetual check or checkmate if the King is hampered in any way.

***Seventh Seal, The*** Swedish dramatic film (1957) written and directed by Ingmar Bergman. The main character, The Knight (Antonius Blok), plays a fearful game of chess against the personification of Death to secure his own life and the lives of all mankind.

***Shakhmatny Bulletin*** one of the leading chess periodicals in the U.S.S.R. It appears once a month and has a circulation of 20,000. Compare ***Shakmatny U.S.S.R.***, **64**, ***Chess***, ***Moscow Central Chess Club Bulletin***.

***Shakhmatny U.S.S.R.*** one of the leading chess periodicals in the U.S.S.R. It appears once a month and has a circulation of 55,000. Compare ***64***, ***Chess***, ***Moscow Central Chess Club Bulletin***, ***Shakhmatny Bulletin***.

**Shamkovich, Leonid** (b. 1 June 1923) Israeli chess player; awarded the titles International Master in 1962 and International Grandmaster in 1965. He was originally from the U.S.S.R., but emigrated to Israel in 1974 where he stayed for two years before moving first to Canada and then to the United States. (1976 Elo rating: 2485)

**sham sacrifice** an offer of material which if accepted will lead either to a forced gain of equal or greater material or to checkmate. See **sacrifice**.

**sham twin** (Kmoch's term) a doubled pawn that is certain to be undoubled by a capture. Compare **loose twin, tight twin, twin**. See **undoubling**, ***Pawn Power in Chess***.

**Sharif, Mehrshad** (b. 11 July 1952) Iranian chess player; awarded the title International Master in 1975. (1976 Elo rating: 2355)

**sharp** relating to a move, manoeuvre or style of play that carries a high degree of risk. Sharp play jeopardizes the chances of a draw and so will lead to defeat if unsuccessful.

**shatranj** *Arabic for* chess. It is a corruption of the Persian word *chatrang* (chess) and was adopted when chess was introduced from Persia, probably in the eighth century A.D. As *ash-shatranj* (the chess), the word was itself corrupted into *ajedrez* in Spain and *xadrez* in Portugal. Everywhere else in Europe the name for the game was derived from the Arabic name for the King (*shah*).

**Sherwin, James** (b. 25 October 1933) American chess player; awarded the title International Master in 1958. He was equal fifth in the 1953 World Junior Championship and competed in the 1958 interzonal where he finished in seventeenth place.

**Shiffers, Emmanuel** (1850–1904) Russian player and popularizer of chess. He was known as 'Russia's chess teacher' and was the first Russian to give talks on the game. His lectures were held in the hall of the St Petersburg Chess Association in 1889. Shiffers also wrote numerous articles as well as a textbook, *Chess Self-Taught*, and trained many pupils, notably Tchigorin, who defeated him in a match in 1880 (+1 −7 =3).

**Shogi** a Japanese game played on a board of 9×9 squares with both sides having twenty men represented by flat counters differentiated by symbols inscribed on their faces. Each side has the equivalent of one King, ten minor pieces and nine pawns. As in chess, the purpose of the game is to checkmate the enemy King, i.e., the Gyoku. There are several important differences, however. Each pawn (Fu) can only move forward one square in each turn and has no special move for capturing, so that they can capture any man immediately in front of them, but cannot capture on the diagonals as pawns in chess do. This prevents the creation of fixed pawn chains and leads to a more fluid game than occurs in chess. In Shogi captured men do not remain off the board, but change sides and re-enter the game on any vacant square on the board at the cost of a move. Most of the men can be promoted upon reaching the back three ranks of the opponent's territory, although none is transformed into a piece as powerful as the Queen in chess. All these factors ensure that Shogi is a much more tactical game than chess since there are fewer permanent weaknesses that can be exploited. In fact, it is less worthwhile to try to do so: a cleverly-placed re-entry of a new piece is always likely to be more profitable. Indeed, Shogi has been described as being one vast middle-game with a very abbreviated opening and no endgame. Also called **Japanese Chess.** See **Fu, Gin, Gyoku, Hisha, Kaku, Kei, Kin, Kyo.**

**short castling** castling on the King side. The Rook moves only two squares, one fewer than when castling on the Queen side. Symbol **O–O.** Compare **long castling.**

**Shortest game** the quickest mate (Fool's Mate) takes two moves, but games have ended before that. Playing in the New York Championship, Frank Marshall once faced an opponent who opened: 1. P–K4. Jocularly Marshall offered his resignation and was held to it despite his protests. According to the *British Chess Magazine* (1891) a similar incident happened in the London chess club, Purssell's. Playing in a casual game, Blackburne opened: 1. P–K3, and joked, 'Ah, now I resign'. His opponent also held him to it. In the Luton Chess Congress of February 1974 S. Reuben and A. J. Miles agreed to a draw without making any moves at all. This has created a great deal of controversy as to whether it was or was not legal. Compare **longest game.**

**shot** (colloquial) an unexpected move that has become extremely strong only as a result of the opponent's previous move.

**Showalter, Jackson Whipps** (1860–1935) American chess player and U.S. Champion 1894, 1895–1897, 1906–1909; born in Minerva, Kentucky. Showalter competed in the first matches for the U.S. Championship when he lost title matches to Lipschütz and Hodges (both of whom then retired from chess). Showalter finally won a match for the title in 1895 and held it until his defeat by Pillsbury in 1897 (+8 −10 =4). Upon Pillsbury's death Showalter again became U.S. Champion until his defeat by Marshall in 1909. Although Showalter rarely finished high in tournaments, he was able to defeat the best players and twice won matches against Janowski (+4 −2 =1, +4 −2 =0). He was nicknamed 'the Kentucky Lion' because of his great mane of hair. Showalter died on 6 February 1935.

**Sicilian Attack** another name for **English Opening.**

**Sicilian Defence** a defence to the King pawn opening: 1. P–K4, *P–QB4*. It was introduced in 1594 by Polerio. Since the middle of the nineteenth century it has become increasingly popular as one of the most dynamic and aggressive responses to 1. P–K4. See **Accelerated Fianchetto, Boleslavsky System, Dragon Variation, Maróczy bind, Morra**

**Gambit, Nimzovitch Variation, Richter-Rauzer Attack, Scheveningen Variation, Sozin Attack.**

**Sicilian Defence**

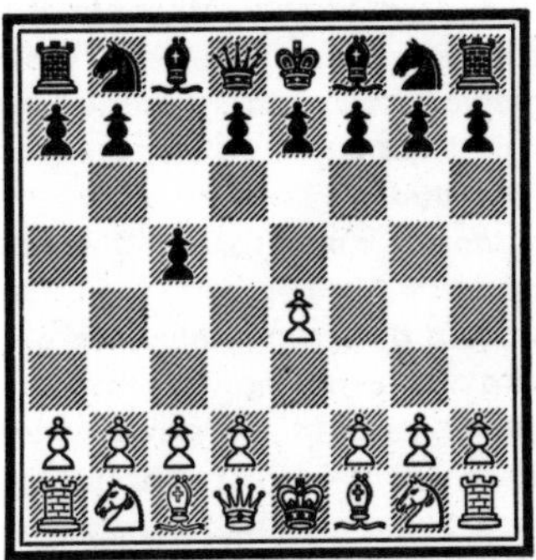

Position after 2 . . ., P–QB4

**Sicilian Dragon** see **Dragon Variation.**

**Siege Game, The** another name for **wei-chi**, ancient Chinese board game based on the seizure and trapping of the opponent's forces (counters or men).

**Sigurjonsson, Gudmundur** (b. 25 September 1947) Icelandic chess player; awarded the titles International Master in 1970 and International Grandmaster in 1975. He played in the 1967 World Junior Championship and has competed in several Chess Olympiads, including that of 1972 when he was team captain. Among his other results are a second at Hastings (1974), a fourth at Oslo (1974) and an eighth at Tblisi (1974). (1976 Elo rating: 2530)

**Silva, Fernando** Portuguese chess player; awarded the title International Master in 1975. (1976 Elo rating: 2340)

**Simagin's Improved Variation** a variation occurring in the Grünfeld Defence, arising out of the Non-classical Exchange Variation: 1. P–Q4, N–KB3 2. P–QB4, P–KN3 3. N–QB3, P–Q4 4. P×P, N×P 5. P–K4, N×N 6. P×N, B–N2 7. B–QB4, O–O 8. N–K2, *N–B3*. This is thought to be an improvement on Simagin's Lesser Variation.

**Simagin's Lesser Variation** a variation occurring in the Grünfeld Defence, arising out of the Non-classical Exchange Variation: 1. P–Q4, N–KB3 2. P–QB4, P–KN3 3. N–QB3, P–Q4 4. P×P, N×P 5. P–K4, N×N 6. P×N, B–N2 7. B–QB4, O–O 8. N–K2, *P–N3*. It was created by the Russian International Grandmaster V. P. Simagin (1919–1968). Black intends to make a fianchetto with his Queen Bishop and complete his development before intensifying the pressure on White's centre by P–QB4. If White plays 9. O–O, this is a possible plan. However, 9. P–KR4 is regarded by many as being a complete refutation. Compare **Simagin's Improved Variation.**

**Simagin, Vladimir Pavlovich** (1919–1968) Soviet chess player; awarded the titles International Master in 1950 and International Grandmaster in 1962. His main triumphs in play were his victories in the Moscow Championship (1947 and 1959), but his main achievements were in the field of opening theory.

**simplify** to exchange pieces in order to lessen the opponent's attack or to minimize the likelihood of tactical complications arising in a winning position. A player with a clearly superior game will often simplify to a won ending in order to avoid any chance of a swindle by the opponent. See **liquidation.**

**Simpson's Divan** another name for the **Divan.**

**simul** *short for* simultaneous display.

**simultaneous blindfold chess** see **blindfold chess.**

**simultaneous display** an exhibition in which a very good player plays several games at once, usually at least twenty. Boards are normally arranged in a circle inside which the master stands. He will usually have White on each board and will start the display by making an opening move at each board. When he returns to his starting point that opponent will make his first move and the master will quickly make his second move, before passing on to the next board, where this process will be repeated. In effect this means that the chessmaster is playing 20 or more games at odds, since each of his opponents will have much more time than he to consider his next move. Often the master will allow the opponents to take more time by passing on to the next board if asked. Despite the advantage in time that each opponent has, the master will usually achieve a score of 90 per cent or more. The greatest simultaneous display was undertaken by G. J. Martin in London in 1957. He played 142 opponents, defeating 130, drawing eleven and losing to one in less than four hours forty minutes. The Swedish Grandmaster Gideon Stahlberg played 400 opponents on a replacement basis in Buenos Aires in 1940 and defeated 379 in 36 hours. Abbrev. **simul.**

**singleton** (Kmoch's term) an **isolated pawn.** See ***Pawn Power in Chess.***

**sitzfleisch** *German for* sitting flesh. Before the introduction of time limits the term was used to describe games where players took an inordinately long time over moves, often in the hope that the opponent would blunder or resign from boredom or, perhaps, die before the end of the game. McDonnell often took one and a half hours or more over a single move in his match with La Bourdonnais. In the London tournament (1851) sitzfleisch was so prevalent that some moves took two and a half hours or more. In the American Congress (1857) Paul Morphy met Louis Paulsen in the final; Paulsen played so slowly that Morphy was reported to have shed tears of frustration while he waited for Paulsen to move. This is hardly surprising since Paulsen once took eleven hours to make one move! It is interesting to note that when Morphy returned from his triumphant tour of Europe Paulsen challenged him to a match. Morphy politely but firmly declined. Another example of sitzfleisch that seems almost reasonable in comparison occurred in the second match between Staunton and Saint-Amant when the final game of 66 moves lasted 14½ hours. Sitzfleisch was the main reason for the introduction of time limits.

**64** one of the leading chess periodicals in the U.S.S.R. It was founded in 1919 and now appears weekly in newspaper format under the editorship of the ex-world champion Petrosian. It has a circulation of 100,000. Its name refers to the 64 squares of the chessboard.

**skewer** a tactical manoeuvre in which a piece is attacked and forced to move out of the way to protect itself, allowing a second and less valuable piece to be captured. The skewer is the opposite of the pin. In the former a valuable piece shields a less valuable piece and so moves out of the line of the attack. In the latter a less valuable piece shields a more valuable piece and so is captured since it cannot move out of the line of the attack. A Knight can neither skewer nor pin pieces. Also called **x-ray**.

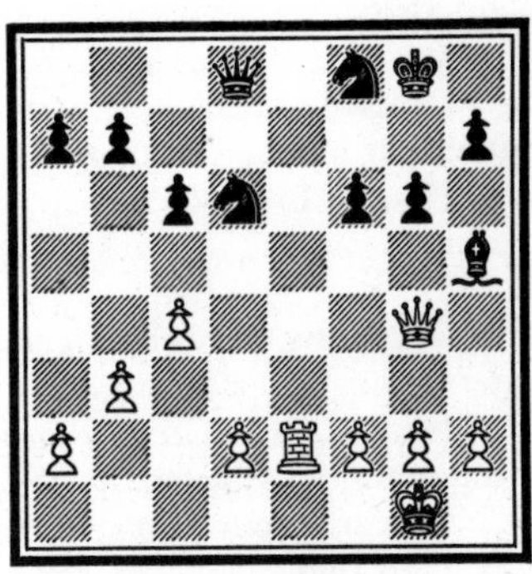

When White's Queen moves, the Black Bishop captures the Rook (which was skewered)

**skittles** a casual chessgame played for no stakes. The term is used more commonly in the United States than in the United Kingdom.

**Skopje** town in Yugoslavia; host to several chess events, of which the 1972 Chess Olympiad was undoubtedly the most important.

**Slater, James Derrick** (b. 13 March 1929) British financier and chess patron. Principally known to the chess world as the contributor of £50,000 which saved the 1972 World Championship match in Reykjavik, he has also been a steadfast supporter of British chess. He offered a prize of £5,000 to the first Briton to become an International Grandmaster (won by A. J. Miles in 1976) and has donated generously to many tournaments (including £20,000 to Hastings and £3,000 to Teesside, 1973).

**Slav Accepted** an opening sequence arising out of the Slav Defence to the Queen's Gambit Declined. A typical progression is as follows: 1. P–Q4, P–Q4 2. P–QB4, P–QB3 3. N–KB3, N–B3 4. N–B3, *P×P* 5. P–QR4, B–B4 6. P–K3. See **Slav Defence**.

**Slav Declined** an opening sequence arising out of the Slav Defence to the Queen's Gambit Declined: 1. P–Q4, P–Q4 2. P–QB4, P–QB3 3. N–KB3, N–B3 4. *P–K3*. See **Slav Defence**.

**Slav Defence** a defence occurring in the Queen's Gambit Declined: 1 P–Q4, P–Q4 2. P–QB4, *P–QB3*. As in all defences, the Slav has both its advantages (not obstructing the Queen Bishop) and disadvantages (prohibiting early P–QB4). This method of defending the pawn immediately attacked by White has been known since the late sixteenth century, although it was not until about 1920 that it became a popular and deeply analysed line of play. See also **Marshall Variation, Meran Defence, Schlechter Variation, Semi-Slav, Slav Accepted, Slav Declined, Winawer Counter Gambit.**

**Sliwa, Bogdan** (b. 4 February 1922) Polish chess player; awarded the title International Master in 1953. He was Polish Champion in 1946, 1951, 1952, 1953, 1954 and 1960. He competed in the Chess Olympiads of 1952, 1956, 1958, 1960, 1962, 1964 and 1966.

**slon** *Russian for* elephant. English equivalent: Bishop. See **Bishop.**

**Slous, F. L.** (1802–1892) British amateur chess player; Chairman of the Stock Exchange (London). He was considered by at least one close friend (a Mr George Walker) to have been a potentially stronger player than Howard Staunton, but for the fact that ill health forced him to abandon serious play. He met Paul Morphy in 1859 in London; the result of their one recorded game (13 April) was abandoned as a draw after 30-odd moves.

**Smederevac, Petar** (b. 26 August 1922) Yugoslavian chess player; awarded the title International Master in 1965.

**Smejkal, Jan** (b. 22 March 1946) Czechoslovakian chess player; awarded the titles International Master in 1970 and International Grandmaster in 1972. He came fourth in the 1973 Leningrad interzonal and 12th in the 1976 Biel interzonal. (1976 Elo rating: 2615)

**smothered mate** a mate delivered by a Knight when the enemy King is completely blocked by adjacent men. The diagram on p. 263 illustrates the first smothered mate that was published in England, appearing in the *Royall Game of Chesse Playe* (1656) by Beale. From the diagram play continues: 1 . . ., Q×BPch 2. K–R1, Q–N8ch 3. R×Q, N–B7 mate. See **Philidor's Legacy.**

**Smyslov System** a variation occurring in the Grünfeld Defence, arising out of the Russian System: 1. P–Q4, N–KB3 2. P–QB4, P–KN3 3. N–QB3, P–Q4 4. N–B3, B–N2 5. Q–N3, P×P 6. Q×BP, O–O 7. P–K4, *B–N5*. Black follows this with KN–Q2–N3 and N–B3, opening the long diagonal and increasing the pressure on White's centre. This opening was named after Vasily Vasilevich Smyslov, who first played it in Groningen in 1946. There are several other Smyslov systems (variations) including at least two in the Ruy Lopez.

**Smyslov, Vasily Vasilevich** (b. 24 March 1921) Soviet chess player; awarded the title International Grandmaster in 1950; World Champion from 1957 to 1958. He was joint Soviet Champion (with Bronstein) in 1949 and competed in the Chess Olympiads of 1952, 1954, 1956, 1958, 1960, 1964, 1968, 1970 and 1972. Smyslov played in the interzonals of 1964 (in which he was equal first), 1970, 1973 (in Leningrad) and 1976 (in Biel). He also competed in the Candidates' tournaments of 1950, 1953, 1956 (winning the last two) and 1959; in the 1965 Candidates' matches; in the 1948 World Championship match-tournament and in three World Championship matches.

Smyslov was born in Moscow and taught to play chess at the age of six by his father. At the age of 17 he tied for first place in the 1938 Moscow Championship to gain the title of Master; two years later he came third in the 1940 Soviet Championship, behind Bondarevsky and Lilienthal. In the subsequent 1941 Soviet Absolute Championship he was third. During the war Smyslov won the Moscow Championship three times, was third at Groningen (1946) and second at Warsaw (1947). Because of these results, he was included in the 1948 World Championship match-tournament, in which he came second.

Even at this stage he was not fully committed to life as a chess professional, for he possesses a fine baritone voice and at one time hoped to become a singer with the Bolshoi Opera. The decision to concentrate upon chess must have been reached by 1953, when he won the 1953 Candidates' tournament and qualified for the 1954 World Championship match against Botvinnik. Unfortunately, he could only draw it (+7 −7 =10), allowing Botvinnik to retain his title; but undaunted, Smyslov won the next Candidates' tournament and again was matched against Botvinnik in the 1957 World Championship match. Smyslov won (+6 −3 =13) to become World Champion.

Botvinnik, as ex-champion, exercised his prerogative to a return match in the following year. Smyslov was the favourite to win; not only was he ten years younger, but he also had a big plus score against Botvinnik in their games since 1954. In fact, Botvinnik won the first three games and hung on to regain the title (+5 −7 =11).

In 1965 Smyslov qualified for the Candidates' matches, but was defeated in the quarter-finals by Geller (+0 −3 =5). Although he is no longer the force that he was in the 1950s, he remains one of the best players in the world. His style is positional and involves subtle manoeuvring rather than violent combinations. At endings he is preeminent. (1976 Elo rating: 2580)

**Smothered mate**

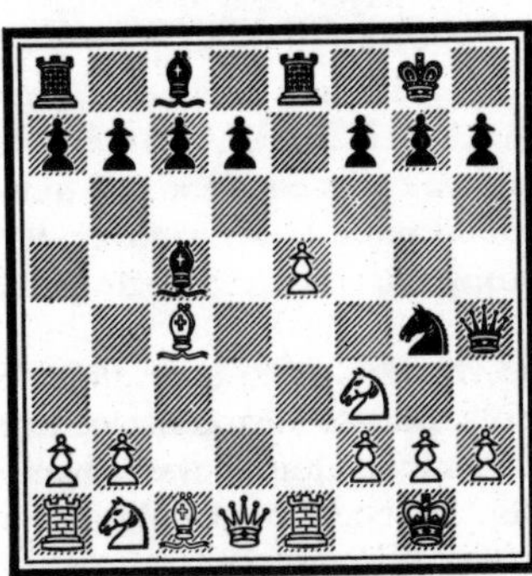

The first smothered mate to be published in England. (Black to mate in three moves)

**sneaker** (Kmoch's term) a pawn that was originally opposed by an enemy pawn, but has become a passed pawn through a sacrificial combination. Sneakers will normally be found on the sixth or seventh ranks or otherwise the defender normally manages to reach them in time to stop them promoting. See ***Pawn Power in Chess***.

**Sokolsky Opening** another name for the **Polish Opening.** It is so named because of the analysis devoted to it by the Soviet theoretician, A. P. Sokolsky. See **Orang-Utan Opening.**

**Soltis, Andrew E.** American chess player; awarded the title International Master in 1974. He competed in the 1970 Student Olympiad; other results include a first at Reggio Emilia (1972) and a fourth at Cleveland (1975). (1976 Elo rating: 2450)

**Sonneborn-Berger system** a tie-breaking procedure in which each player concerned receives the sum of the scores of his defeated opponents plus half the scores of those players with whom he has drawn. The player with the highest resulting total is the winner.

The idea for the system was suggested in 1873 by Oscar Gelbfuhs, a Viennese chess player, and was independently created by William Sonneborn of London in 1886 and Johann Berger of Graz in 1887. The system was first used at London (1889) to divide the prize money.

**Soos, Bela** (b. 6 February 1930) West German chess player; awarded the title International Master in 1967. Soos was born in Romania and represented that country in the Chess Olympiads of 1956, 1962, 1966 and 1968, but emigrated in 1972. (1976 Elo rating: 2340)

**Sosonko, Gennadi** (b. 18 May 1943) Soviet-born chess player and one-time second of Korchnoi, now living in and playing for Holland; awarded the titles International Master in 1974 and International Grandmaster in 1976. He won the 1975 Barcelona zonal to qualify for the 1976 Biel interzonal, in which he came 12th. (1976 Elo rating: 2505)

**soul of chess** a descriptive phrase for the pawns; coined by Philidor in his *Analyse du Jeu des Echecs* (Analysis of Chess).

***Soviet School of Chess, The*** a survey of chess in the U.S.S.R. written by A. Kotov and M. Yudovich. In it they attempt to set down the philosophy of the Soviet players and to this end they write about the history of chess in Russia and the biographies of Russia's greatest players, including Tchigorin and Alekhine. The bulk of the book is taken up by biographies and analyses of the styles of the U.S.S.R.'s leading players. The book also contains 128 games. It was first published in English in 1958 and uses descriptive notation in this edition.

**Sozin Attack** an opening sequence arising out of the Sicilian Defence: 1. P–K4, P–QB4 2. N–KB3, P–Q3 3. P–Q4, P×P 4. N×P, N–KB3 5. N–QB3, N–B3 6. *B–QB4*. White develops naturally, aiming for Black's KB2. Black's most common immediate reply: 6 . . ., P–K3. The opening is named after the Soviet master Sozin, who played it in the 1920s, but it became popular only after its adoption by Fischer.

**space** the squares on the chessboard controlled by the player. An increase in the space controlled by one player results in a decrease in the space controlled by the other, with a concomitant congestion of his men. Space is the third of the three basic elements in which each player tries to gain an advantage, the others being force and tempo or time. Although players will often voluntarily relinquish space as in the Modern Defence, this is only in the belief that the space can be regained in the middle-game with an increased advantage.

**span** (Kmoch's term) all the squares in front of and behind a pawn. See **frontspan, interspan, rearspan,** ***Pawn Power in Chess***.

**span control** (Kmoch's term) the number of squares of a half-open file that are controlled by a player. For instance, if White has a pawn on his QB3 and no pawn on the Queen file while Black has a pawn on his Queen Bishop file and a pawn on his Q4, White's span control is two on the Queen Bishop file and four on the Queen file. Together the two players' span controls are 2:5 and 4:3 so that Black has a slight superiority in space. See ***Pawn Power in Chess***.

**Spanish Game** another name for the **Ruy Lopez**.

**span-minus** (Kmoch's term) a minority of the squares controlled on a half-open file. Compare **span-plus**. See ***Pawn Power in Chess***.

**span-plus** (Kmoch's term) an advantage in the number of squares controlled on a half-open file. With only one pawn on a half-open file one side must always have a span-plus whether it is in the ratio of 6:1, 5:2 or 4:3, although this may be compensated for by the opponent's greater control of a second half-open file. See ***Pawn Power in Chess***.

**Spassky, Boris** (b. 30 January 1937) Soviet chess player; World Champion from 1969 to 1972; awarded the titles International Master in 1953 and International Grandmaster in 1955. He was World Junior Champion in 1955 and competed in the Student Olympiads of 1955, 1957, 1958, 1960 and 1962. He was Soviet Champion in 1961 and 1973 and competed in the Chess Olympiads of 1962, 1964, 1966, 1968, 1970 and 1974. Spassky has competed in three interzonals (winning one), one Candidates' tournament, three series of Candidates' matches (winning two) and three World Championship matches.

Spassky was born in Leningrad and in 1941 was evacuated to a Kirov childrens' home, where he learned to play chess. On his return to Leningrad in 1946, he joined the local Young Pioneers' chess club and won the schoolboy championship of Leningrad in 1949. He came second in the 1952 Leningrad Championship and in the following year came equal fourth in his first international tournament, Bucharest (1953), for which he was awarded the title of International Master. His victory in the World Junior Championship two years later resulted in his being awarded the title International Grandmaster – the youngest player to win the title up to that time. In the same year, he played in his first interzonal and qualified for the subsequent Candidates' tournament (in which he was equal third).

From 1958 to 1961 Spassky was comparatively unsuccessful and experienced severe conflicts with his trainer Alexander Tolush as well as personal troubles; he became divorced in 1961. In 1961 he began his come-back by winning the Soviet Championship and in 1964 came equal first in the Amsterdam interzonal to qualify for the 1965 Candidates' matches, which he won by successively defeating Keres (+4 −2 =4), Geller (+3 −0 =5) and Tal (+4 −1 =6) to meet Petrosian in the 1966 World Championship match. In this event, Spassky attempted to fight Petrosian with his own weapons by playing long manoeuvring games, but lost after a severe battle (+3 −4 =17).

The next series of Candidates' matches was again won by Spassky, who defeated Geller (+3 −0 =5), Larsen (+4 −1 =3) and Korchnoi (+4 −1 =5) to qualify to meet Petrosian in 1969. This match was played in a more aggressive style than their previous encounter and was won by Spassky (+6 −4 =13), who became the tenth official World Chess Champion.

Spassky had generally been expected to retain the title for several years. He had met and defeated almost all of his most powerful opponents in matches and had won in decisive style. However, his results as World Champion were unimpressive and in 1970 Fischer came out of retirement.

In the 1972 title defence against Fischer, Spassky was completely outplayed. After half the match had been completed he was three points behind and was unable to make up the deficit (+3 −7 =11). He was severely criticized in the U.S.S.R. for the poor form shown in this match, but partially redeemed himself by winning the 1973 Soviet Championship. In the 1974 series of Candidates' matches he defeated Robert Byrne (+3 −0 =3), but then lost to Anatoly Karpov (+1 −4 =6). Spassky's decline continued in 1976 when he finished equal tenth at the Manila interzonal. In 1976 he was granted permission to live in France for one year, accompanied by his French wife, but was not allowed to compete in any tournaments.

Spassky excels in the middle game, where his tactical ability has full scope. In this he most resembles Alekhine, especially in a liking for complex positions. This is coupled with a chameleon-like ability to adapt his style to the type that most discomforts his opponent. (1976 Elo rating: 2630)

**Spassky Variation** an opening sequence arising out of the Nimzo-Indian Defence: 1. P–Q4, N–KB3 2. P–QB4, P–K3 3. N–QB5, B–N5 4. *B–N5*. White pins the opposing Bishop in his turn. The most common continuation is: 4 . . ., P–KR3 5. B–R4, P–B4! This variation was devised in the late 1950s by a group of Leningrad players and was popularized by the future World Champion Boris Spassky. Also called **Leningrad Variation**.

**speculative** relating to any move or sequence of moves whose outcome cannot be foreseen. Many sacrifices are speculative, being made from nebulous positional or strategic considerations and not as a result of computing forced variations.

**Spielmann, Rudolf** (1883–1942) Austrian chess player; born in Vienna on 5 May 1883. Spielmann learned to play while very young and was exhibited as a child prodigy. He matured into a combinative and aggressive player with an affection for the romantic style of play of Anderssen and Tchigorin; his persistent efforts to revive the popularity of gambits caused Tartakover to nickname him, 'The Last Knight of the King's Gambit', which was the opening upon which Spielmann devoted most of his energies. His philosophy of play is illustrated by his book *The Art of Sacrifice in Chess*, which discusses and classifies the various types of sacrifice.

Spielmann's results included firsts at Stockholm (1909 and 1919), Baden (1911), the Gambit Tournament Baden (1914), Semmering (1926) and Magdeburg (1927) and second places at San Sebastian (1912) and Pistyan (1922).

In his later years, political upheavals forced Spielmann into exile in Sweden where he died on 20 August 1942 at the age of 59.

**Spielmann Variation** an opening sequence arising out of the Nimzo-Indian Defence: 1. P–Q4, N–KB3 2. P–QB4, P–K3 3. N–QB3, B–N5 4. *Q–N3*. Black's commonest continuation: 4 . . ., P–B4. White attacks the pinning Bishop at the cost of making his Queen much more vulnerable. This variation was played first by Rudolf Spielmann at Carlsbad (1929).

**Spike, The** an opening where White plays: 1. *P–KN4*. It discourages an early development of Black's KN to KB3 and allows an early fianchetto of the KB, with pressure on the long diagonal. Its main value, though, is surprise.

Its name is an allusion to the position of the KNP which sticks into the centre. Also called **Grob's Attack, Kolibri Opening.**

**spite check** a meaningless check by the defender that delays a forced mating sequence, but does not prevent it.

**Spraggett, Kevin** (b. 10 November 1954) Canadian chess player; awarded the title International Master in 1975. (1976 Elo rating: 2450)

**Square** a square area of the chessboard visualized by the players to discover if an unaided King could capture an unsupported pawn before or immediately after it reached the eighth rank.

The length of one side of the Square is measured by the number of squares on the file between the pawn and the eighth rank including those squares. If the King is inside this Square before the pawn's turn to move then it can catch the pawn. See illustration on p. 268.

**Stahlberg, Gideon** (1908–1967) Swedish chess player; awarded the titles International Grandmaster in 1950 and International Judge in 1951. He was born on 26 January 1908 and by his late teens was regarded as one of Sweden's strongest players. He was Swedish Champion in 1927, 1929, and 1939 and competed in thirteen Chess Olympiads between 1930 and 1964 playing a record number of 200 games that has since been exceeded only by Najdorf.

Stahlberg was playing in Argentina in the 1939 Chess Olympiad when World War II began and he decided to remain in South America. During his stay there he won or came second in practically every tournament in which he competed and after a major victory at Mar del Plata (1947) asked the Swedish chess federation to back his bid for the

World Championship. However, although he competed in the interzonals of 1948, 1952 and 1955 Stahlberg never qualified for a Candidates' tournament. In 1951 he acted as the arbiter in the World Championship match between Botvinnik and Bronstein and fulfilled this function in several later matches. As well as being a strong chess player, Stahlberg was a bridge player of almost international standard. He died in Leningrad on 26 May 1967.

**Square**

White to move promotes the pawn; Black to move enters the square and draws

**stalemate** a type of draw that exists when the player whose turn it is to move is not in check, but has no legal move available. Stalemates are commonly found in many types of endgames. There is, however, no unarguable logical justification for regarding stalemate as a draw and its treatment has differed at different times and in different countries. In Shogi and Indian chess stalemate is illegal. In England, until the eighteenth century, the player delivering the stalemate lost the game. There have been many proposals to alter the rule yet again. Lasker once proposed that the player delivering the stalemate should be regarded as having made an inferior form of win.

Lazdies vs. Zenita (Riga, 1936)
White drew by: 1. Q–B8ch, K–B3 2. Q–R8ch, K–B4 3. P–N4ch, P×P 4. R–Q5ch!, P×R 5. Q–B8ch!, Q×Qstalemate

**Stamma, Philippe** eighteenth-century Syrian chess player and writer; at one time interpreter of oriental languages for George II. He wrote *The Noble Game of Chess* (1745), published in London. See **Aleppo Gambit.**

**star-flight theme** a theme in chess problems where the King can escape from the initial threat only by moving to any of the four diagonally adjacent squares. Since in the common two-move chess problem two squares must be covered that are not covered initially (the King's final square as well as his starting point) checkmate is often delivered by a Bishop. Compare **plus-flight theme.**

**Statham tournament** see **Louis D. Statham Masters-Plus Tournament.**

**Staunton chessmen** the only style of chessmen officially permitted for use in FIDE events. They were designed in 1835 by Nathaniel Cook who (in 1852) persuaded Howard Staunton that they should be called 'Staunton' chessmen and sold with a facsimile of his signature on the box of each set. In 1900 Cook's firm was taken over by John Jacques & Son Ltd., who still market Staunton sets.

Contemporary Staunton chessmen are essentially unchanged from the original sets. The first King Knights and King Bishops had small crowns imprinted upon them to distinguish them, but this is no longer done. The coronet of the Queen originally had eight points to signify the eight directions in which she could travel, but modern Queens can have any number of points on their coronets.

**Staunton Defence** another (antiquated) name for the **Benoni Counter Gambit.** The name is erroneous in that, although it was played in the match between Staunton and Saint-Amant in 1843, it was played by Saint-Amant, not Staunton.

**Staunton Gambit** an opening sequence arising out of the Dutch Defence: 1. P–Q4, P–KB4 2. P–K4. Black's first move does not develop a piece, so that White can afford to react aggressively by offering a pawn in return for increased mobility for his pieces. However, it is generally believed that the gambit will only provide equality given best play. Black's best immediate reply: 2 . . ., P×P.

**Staunton, Howard** (1810–1874) British chess player; generally considered the world's best player from 1843 to 1851. He was allegedly the illegitimate son of Frederick Howard, fifth Earl of Carlisle, and was brought up in poverty with little education; eventually Staunton established himself as an eminent Shakespearean scholar. He learned to play chess in his early 20s and became London's strongest player within a few years. In 1836 he lost some games to Saint-Amant, France's strongest player, on a visit by the latter to London; he had his revenge in 1843 by defeating Saint-Amant decisively in a match held in Paris (+11 −6 =4). Staunton was then recognized as the world's best player, but was at the peak of his form for a very brief time. Within a year he suffered an attack of pneumonia that permanently weakened his health. Nevertheless, Staunton still managed to play; in 1846 he defeated both Horwitz (+14 −7 =3) and Harrwitz (+7 −0 =0). Staunton's style of play seems curiously modern in that he preferred closed games, as shown by his preference for the English Opening and Sicilian Defence.

In 1840 he founded and edited the monthly *Chess Players' Chronicle* and used this and his chess column in the *Illustrated London News* (which he wrote from 1844 until his death) to indulge in heated polemics with his contemporaries. In 1847 his book *The Chess Players' Handbook* (based on the *Handbuch des Schachspiels*) was published and became the standard English guide to chess for several generations. It was followed in 1849 by *The Chess Players' Companion*, and in 1860 by *Chess Praxis*.

Staunton dominated and enlivened the British chess scene; his irascibility constantly led to disputes with his fellow players, while his vitality led to new ventures such as the first telegraph match. In 1851 he organized the first modern chess tournament (see **Great Exhibition tournament**). Although the members of the City of London Chess Club refused to participate, there were many strong entrants from abroad. Staunton expected to win, but was knocked-out in the semi-finals by Anderssen, who won the tournament and became recognized as the world's strongest player.

From this point Staunton played less chess. In 1854 he sold the *Chess Players' Chronicle* to concentrate upon his Shakespearean researches. It was upon these that he was working when he was challenged to a match by Morphy. Staunton gave the impression that he was willing to play a match eventually, but constantly delayed meeting Morphy and finally backed out. He should undoubtedly have stated earlier that he was unwilling to play.

Throughout the rest of his life Staunton continued in this manner, engaging in bitter feuds and promoting chess. By the time of his death, Britain was the leading chess nation and this must largely have been due to him. He died on 22 June 1874.

***Staunton the English World Chess Champion*** a biography of Howard Staunton by R. D. Keene and R. N. Coles. In addition to a 25-page biography it contains 60 annotated games and positions. It was first published in 1976 and uses descriptive notation.

**steamroller** another name for a **pawn roller**.

**Stean, Michael F.** (b. 4 September 1953) British chess player; awarded the title International Master in 1975. He was equal first in the 1974 British Championship (but only shared fourth place in the play-off) and competed in the Chess Olympiads of 1974 and 1976. In the former Olympiad he won the $1,000 Turover brilliancy prize for the best game played in the A-final. (1976 Elo rating: 2420)

**Stein, Leonid Zakharovich** (1935–1973) one of the foremost Soviet players of the post-war era. Stein was a relatively late developer since, although he made his debut in the Ukraine Junior Championship at the age of sixteen, he did not become a Soviet Master until 1959. This delay was made up for in the 1960s when Stein won the U.S.S.R. Championship three times (1963, 1965, and 1970) as well as winning numerous strong tournaments, of which Moscow (1967), Kecskemet (1968), Hastings (1968), Talinn (1969), and the Alekhine Memorial Tournament (1971) are examples. However, these victories did not compensate Stein for his failure to achieve his remaining ambition – to compete in the World Championship. Twice (Stockholm, 1962 and Amsterdam, 1964) he qualified for the Candidates' series, but was barred on the now discarded rule limiting the number of nationals allowed to qualify. In both tournaments he had a sufficiently high position but was surpassed by three Soviet players who took the U.S.S.R.'s quota of places. This three-player limit rule was abolished for the Sousse interzonal (1967), but here Stein merely tied for the bottom qualifying place and lost the playoff after refusing a draw that, as it subsequently turned out, would have given him the final qualifying place. Stein qualified to compete in the Brazil interzonal (1973) and was optimistic about his prospects, but collapsed and died a month before the tournament – bringing to a tragic end the life of one of the most attacking and romantic players of his generation.

**Steiner, Herman** (1905–1955) U.S. chess player born in Hungary; awarded the title International Master in 1950. He was U.S. Open Champion in 1942 (with Yanofsky) and 1946 and U.S. Champion in 1948. He competed in the Chess Olympiads of 1930, 1931 and 1950 and played for the United States against the U.S.S.R. in the ten-player double-round radio match of 1945. His score of 1½ against Bondarevsky was a third of the U.S. total.

**Steiner, Lajos** (b. 14 March 1903) Australian chess player; awarded the title International Master in 1950. He was Hungarian Champion in 1936 and Australian Champion 1945–1949, 1953–1955 and 1959–1960. Steiner was originally Hungarian and played for that country in the Chess Olympiads of 1931, 1933 and 1935. Other results included second places at Kecskemet (1927) and Hastings (1927) and firsts at Vienna (1935 and 1938). He also won a match against Lilienthal in 1934 (+3 −1 =2) and another against Grob in 1935 (+3 −1 =0). In the late 1930s he emigrated to Australia and in 1948 he represented that country in the interzonal where he came nineteenth.

**Steinitz Gambit** an opening sequence arising out of the Vienna Game: 1. P–K4, P–K4 2. N–QB3, N–QB3 3. P–B4, P×P 4. *P–Q4*. White has two central pawns and a Bishop trained on the advanced Black pawn, but contemporary opinion believes this gambit to be suicidal. Black's best immediate reply: 4 . . ., Q–R5ch. This opening was introduced by Steinitz at Dundee (1867) and was played regularly – for example, in the last game of his world championship match with Zukertort.

**Steinitz position** a position where a player has numerous pieces arranged on the back rank. Steinitz's policy of refuting gambits by accepting gambit pawns and incurring the inevitable pressure often led to such positions. For this reason Steinitz described his style as 'trigger chess' – pulling his pieces backwards in order the better to spring.

**Steinitz, Wilhelm** (1836–1900) Austrian chess player, born in Prague; World Champion from 1866 to 1894. His mathematical aptitude persuaded his family to send him to the Vienna Polytechnic in 1857, but he left without completing his studies and became a chess professional in the cafés of the city. In 1861 he won the championship of the Vienna Chess Club and, as part of the prize, was sponsored to take part in the London (1862) tournament. Steinitz came only sixth, but remained in England to enter more tournaments and matches of which the most important was his victory over Blackburne (+7 −1 =2). In 1866 a match was arranged between him and Anderssen, to the surprise of all, but the result was even more astonishing: Steinitz won (+8 −6). Steinitz then proclaimed himself to be the world's best player, but his claim was not generally accepted as long as Morphy lived. He followed this by a series of tournament results which proved him to be fallible, coming third at Paris (1872), second at Dundee (1867) and Baden-Baden (1870), and first at London (1872) and Vienna (1873).

From 1873 to 1882, Steinitz withdrew from active chess to perfect his theories, returning only to defeat Zukertort and Blackburne in matches in 1874 and 1876 (both by the score of 7 games to 0). Steinitz returned to active play in 1882, when he came first at Vienna. In 1883 he went to the United States, where he played a match against Zukertort (1883) and won decisively (+10 −5 =5). This was officially described as a match for the World Championship. Steinitz, who was a much better match than tournament player, played three more matches in the next six years (defeating Tchigorin twice and Gunsberg once). Finally, in 1894, he was defeated by the relatively unknown Emanuel Lasker (+5 −10 =4). This was Steinitz's first defeat in a match in 32 years. A rematch two years later resulted in an even more crushing defeat. Poverty forced him to keep playing, but his sanity and health were breaking down. In 1890 he was committed to an asylum in New York, where he died on 12 August 1900.

Steinitz's style in his early career was conventionally romantic and sacrificial. This changed as he developed, until it became revolutionary in concept. He was the originator of the technique of playing in closed positions and so forms a counterpart to Morphy, who developed the techniques of play in open positions. For instance, the concepts of weak squares, the importance of the centre, and the importance of the two Bishops were all developed by Steinitz.

**Steinitz's Gem** the name given to a game played between Wilhelm Steinitz and Kurt von Bardeleben at Hastings (1895). It was described by Reuben Fine as being 'A game with a combination which ranks amongst the most profound ever made'. It went as follows: 1. P–K4, P–K4 2. N–KB3, N–QB3 3. B–B4, B–B4 4. P–B3, N–B3 5. P–Q4, P×P 6. P×P, B–N5ch 7. N–B3, P–Q4 8. P×P, KN×P 9. O–O, B–K3 10. B–KN5, B–K2 11. B×N, QB×B 12. N×B, Q×N 13. B×B, N×B 14. R–K1, P–KB3 15. Q–K2, Q–Q2 16. QR–B1, P–B3 17. P–Q5, P×P 18. N–Q4, K–B2 19. N–K6, KR–QB1 20. Q–N4, P–KN3 21. N–N5ch, K–K1 22. R×Nch, K–B1 23. R–B7ch, K–N1 24. R–N7ch, K–R1, 25. R×Pch. At this point von Bardeleben deliberately forfeited the game by leaving the room, so losing on time, since mate is now inevitable.

**St George attack** (Kmoch's term) an attack on the pawn structure characteristic of the **Dragon Variation**. The King Rook pawn is advanced and exchanged for one of the pawns in front of the castled King; this is followed up by the alignment of the major pieces on the open King Rook file. In this attack White must castle on the Queen side and strive to keep the centre closed or otherwise the Rook will be diverted to contest any open files that come into being there. See ***Pawn Power in Chess***.

**Stoltz, Gösta** (1904–1963) Swedish chess player; awarded the titles International Master in 1950 and International Grandmaster in 1954. He was Swedish champion in 1951, 1952, and 1953.

**Stonewall Formation** a pawn formation with pawns on QR2, QN2, QB3, Q4, K3, KB4, KN2, and KR2. It is named the Stonewall because of its structural stability.

The Stonewall strategy is a King-side attack with the opponent countering in the centre or on the Queen side.

This pawn structure has been known since the last century, when it was played by Zukertort, and crops up in several openings, including Bird's Opening, the Dutch Defence, the Slav Defence, and the Queen's Gambit Declined.

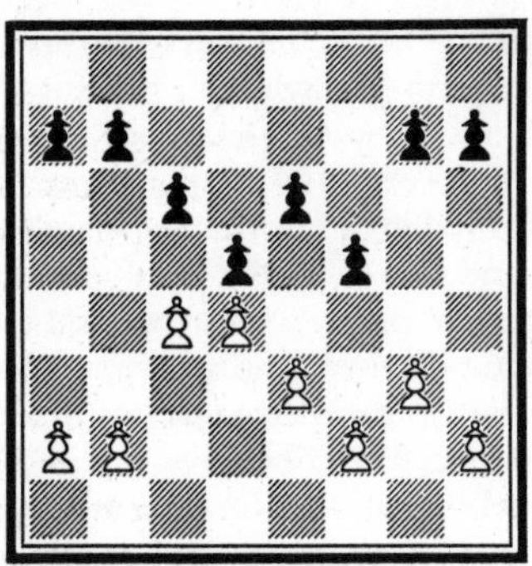

Stonewall formation

**stop proper** (Kmoch's term) the square immediately in front of a pawn. See **blockade, stop squares, telestop, *Pawn Power in Chess***.

**stop squares** (Kmoch's term) the squares of a pawn's **frontspan**. Any man that occupies one of the stop squares will be able to 'stop' the pawn's advance. See **blockade, stop proper, telestop, *Pawn Power in Chess***.

**St Petersburg (1895–1896)** a match-tournament in which the four competitors played six games against each of the others. It was won by Lasker (who scored 11½) ahead of Steinitz (9½), Pillsbury (8) and Tchigorin (7).

**St Petersburg (1909)** a tournament with nineteen competitors. Lasker and Rubinstein shared equal first place (scoring 14½ each) ahead of Duras (11) and Spielmann (11).

**St Petersburg (1914)** one of the strongest-ever tournaments, with Alekhine, Bernstein, Blackburne, Capablanca, Gunsberg, Janowski, Lasker, Marshall, Nimzovitch, Rubinstein and Tarrasch competing. The tournament was organized in two phases. In the first leg the eleven competitors played each other once; the five highest scorers then entered the second leg where they played each other twice. The scores from both legs were then aggregated. The tournament was won by Lasker, who overtook the frontrunner, Capablanca, in the eighteenth round. Capablanca was second, followed by Alekhine, Tarrasch and Marshall respectively. These five were awarded the title of **Grandmasters of Chess** by Czar Nicholas II to commemorate their performances and, in fact, are regarded as the first Grandmasters.

**straggler** (Kmoch's term) a **backward pawn.** See ***Pawn Power in Chess.***

**strategy** the overall objectives of a player, which he will attempt to carry out throughout the game. One player's strategy might be to castle on one side and carry out a minority attack on the other. The extent to which this overall plan will be carried out will depend upon the strength of the resistance and the existence of any opportunities arising in the short term. Compare **tactics.**

**Ströbeck** a village in the German Democratic Republic where reputedly every inhabitant is able to play chess. Allegedly the game was introduced to the village in 1068 when Duke Guncelin, a Slav nobleman, taught his guards to play while a prisoner of war there. By 1600 the village had become famous throughout Europe and in the eighteenth and nineteenth centuries it was visited by several masters including Ludwig, Bledow, Max Lange, and William Lewis.

There are many indications of the popularity of chess in Ströbeck. For more than a century chess has been an official subject at the local school and the Young Pioneers can gain chess badges. Every official village document bears a seal with a chessboard inscribed upon it and the church's weathervane is a chessboard. Traditionally, displays of living chess were held at coronation ceremonies, and these pageants are still held regularly.

**strong square** a square on the board that cannot be attacked by enemy pawns, that cannot be effectively attacked by pieces, and from which the opposing player's men can be hampered and one's own men securely established.

**Student Olympiad** an annual international event in which teams of students aged 27 or less compete against each other. Each team consists of four players and up to two reserves. The Olympiads are organized by the International Student Union under the auspices of FIDE and are held in a different country each year. Initially the number of entrants was low enough to allow a round-robin tournament, but the event has now grown too large and teams must now compete to qualify for the *A*, *B*, or *C* finals as in the Chess Olympiads.

The first Olympiad was held in Oslo, Norway in 1954. The U.S.S.R. has won the majority of the Olympiads, but has not dominated them as it has the Chess Olympiads or the Women's Chess Olympiads.

In the early years of this event there was no age qualification, only an unclear definition of what constituted a student. This resulted in some surprisingly old students competing, and the age limit was brought in to maintain the spirit of the competition. Also called **World Student Team Championship.**

**study** see **endgame study.**

**Suba, Mihai** (b. 1 June 1947) Romanian chess player; awarded the title International Master in 1975. (1976 Elo rating: 2450)

**Suer, Nevzat** (b. 1925) Turkish chess player; awarded the title International Master in 1975. (1976 Elo rating: 2285)

**Suetin, Aleksei** (b. 16 November 1926) Soviet chess player and leading writer and theoretician. He was awarded the title International Master in 1961 and the title International Grandmaster in 1965. (1976 Elo rating: 2525)

**Sui-mate** another name for **Selfmate**. Sui is Latin for 'of himself' or 'of herself'.

**Sultan Khan, Mir** (1905–1966) Indian chess player, born in the Punjab; British Champion in 1929, 1932 and 1933. An illiterate peasant, he visited the U.K. in 1929 as a servant in the entourage of Sir Umar Hayat Khan and (after becoming familiar with European chess) was soon recognized as a natural chess genius. At Hastings (1930–1931) he defeated Capablanca in their single encounter, and came third in the tournament (behind Euwe and Capablanca). In Prague (1931) he drew against Alekhine and Bogoljubov and defeated Rubinstein and Flohr, with a total score of 11½ out of 17. Sultan Kan returned with his master to India in December 1933, and thereafter he seemed to vanish into chess obscurity. He died in Pakistan in 1966 from tuberculosis.

**Sunnucks, Patricia Anne** (b. 21 February 1927) British chess player; awarded the title International Woman Master in 1954. She was British Ladies' Champion in 1957, 1958 and 1964. Sunnucks compiled and edited *The Encyclopaedia of Chess* (1970; 2nd ed. 1976).

**Superpawn** a Fairy pawn that moves and captures normally, but over an indefinite range. An orthodox pawn can move one or two squares forward on its first move and one square thereafter, provided that it is not blocked, while a Superpawn can always advance to the edge of the board provided that it, too, is not blocked. An orthodox pawn can capture any man that is one square away diagonally, while a Superpawn can capture at any distance diagonally. It was invented by a German problemist, Dr W. Speckmann, in 1967.

**support-point** a square on which a piece can be established, which can be protected by at least one pawn, and which cannot be attacked by an enemy pawn. For example, after 1. P–Q4, P–Q4 2. B–B4, the square K5 is not a support-point (although it can be protected by a pawn) since it can be attacked by Black's King Bishop pawn. However, after 2 . . ., P–KB4? the square K5 becomes a support-point.

The most important support-points are those in the centre or in the opponent's half of the board, because minor pieces stationed there can disrupt the defence.

The term was devised by Euwe and Kramer.

**Suradiradja, Herman** Indonesian chess player; awarded the title International Master in 1976. (1976 Elo rating: 2345)

**surrendering the centre** voluntarily ceding control of the middle of the board. This is the feature of many of the hypermodern defences, such as the Grünfeld Defence and the King's Indian Defence. In these defences Black encourages White to construct a classical pawn centre in the belief that it contains inherent weaknesses which can be seized upon.

**Suttles, Duncan** (b. 21 December 1945) Canadian chess player; awarded the titles International Master in 1967 and International Grandmaster in 1973. He competed in the 1965 World Junior Championship to win the B-final and also played in the 1967 interzonal. (1976 Elo rating: 2470)

**Sveshnikov, Evgenny** (b. 11 February 1956) Soviet chess player; awarded the title International Master in 1975. He was first at Decin (1974). (1976 Elo rating: 2510)

**Swedish Variation** a variation occurring in the Queen's Gambit Declined, arising out of the Tarrasch Defence. The typical progression is as follows: 1. P–Q4, P–Q4 2. P–QB4, P–K3 3. N–QB3, P–QB4 4. P×QP, KP×P 5. N–B3, N–QB3 6. P–KN3, *P–B5* 7. B–N2, B–QN5 8. O–O, KN–K2. See **Tarrasch Defence.**

**sweeper** (Kmoch's term) a pawn that is sacrificed by being advanced in order to open lines for the pieces. Compare **sealer.** See ***Pawn Power in Chess.***

**swindle** an avoidable combination that converts a lost position into a draw or a win. It is almost invariably some type of trap into which the opponent has carelessly stepped.

The game between Evans and Reshevsky in the U.S. Championship (1964) ended in what is now an infamous swindle.

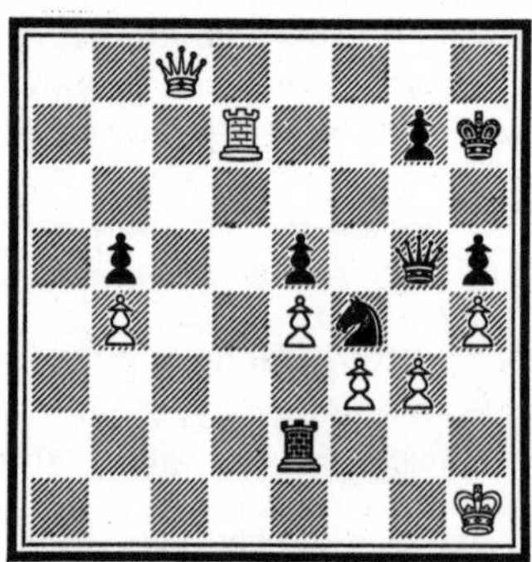

Evans vs. Reshevsky (New York, 1964)

Here Reshevsky could have avoided the trap by: 48 . . ., Q–B3 but was careless through overconfidence and played instead: 48 . . ., Q×P?? There followed: 49. Q–N8ch!, K×P 50. R×Pch!, and the game is drawn either through perpetual check or stalemate.

This is also often known as a **Marshall swindle** since Frank J. Marshall was famed for extricating himself from hopeless positions by such means. Indeed Marshall was so notorious for this characteristic that he chose *Marshall Swindle* as the title of one of his books.

**Swiss King** *nickname of* Walter Shawn Browne.

**Swiss System** a method of pairing competitors in a tournament, often used when it is impossible for each person to play everyone else. In the first round players may be paired either at random or according to some criterion such as their grades, but from then on each player will be matched against players with scores equal to his own wherever possible, unless an accelerated pairing system is being used. This means that in the second round a winner will meet another winner, a loser will meet a loser and a player who drew will meet another who drew. In the third round those who have scored two points will play among themselves, as will those with 1½ points, 1 point, ½ point and no points. In this way players will tend to gravitate towards other players of approximately equal strength as the tournament continues, with the stronger players rising to the top and the weaker players dropping to the bottom. Two constraints on the system are that players will play each other no more than once during the tournament and that, wherever possible, players will play with alternate colours in successive rounds, and take equal numbers of whites and blacks throughout the tournament.

The main advantage of the Swiss System over a knockout competition is that it allows each person to play a fixed number of games, so that an exceptionally bad game is less disastrous. Its main advantage compared to an all-play-all competition is that the number of rounds played in it is almost unrelated to the number of competitors.

**switchback** any variation in chess problems in which the key-move piece returns to the square it stood on at the beginning of the problem.

**symbols** various symbols are used in modern chess notation to save space and, in many cases, to overcome language barriers. The following table lists those in common use.

| *Symbol* | *Meaning* |
|---|---|
| – | moves to |
| × | captures |
| : | captures (in algebraic notation) |
| O–O | castles King side |
| O–O–O | castles Queen side |
| + | check |
| ++ | double check or (sometimes) mate |
| ‡ | mate |
| = | even position |
| ± | slight advantage for White |
| ∓ | slight advantage for Black |

| | |
|---|---|
| ± | definite advantage for White |
| ∓ | definite advantage for Black |
| ±± | White has a won position |
| ∓∓ | Black has a won position |
| ! | good move |
| !! | excellent move |
| ? | poor move |
| ?? | very bad or losing move |
| !? | interesting (and probably good) move creating complications |
| ?! | interesting (but probably poor) move creating complications |
| 1–O | Black resigns |
| ½–½ | Draw agreed |
| O–1 | White resigns |

**Symmetrical Defence** (Queen's Gambit) a defence occurring in the Queen's Gambit Declined, characterized by the symmetrical move in italics: 1. P–Q4, P–Q4 2. P–QB4, *P–QB4*. With proper play, White is generally considered to have a slight advantage if Black adopts this line.

**symmetrical exchange** a capture of a man at the cost of a man of the same type. Thus, the exchange of a Knight for a Knight would be a symmetrical exchange.

**symmetrical pawn structure** a position in which the pawn structure of one player exactly reflects the pawn structure of the other. Such a balanced position will tend to reduce the prospects of a decisive result; this is one reason why assymetrical defences have grown in popularity in the twentieth century.

**symmetry** the identical positioning of both sides' men, so that each side confronts a mirror image of itself. The initial position on the chessboard is an example of symmetry, while the Four Knights' Game and Petroff's Defence are examples of symmetrical openings. Prolonging the imitation of moves can be dangerous for Black, as White has a lead of one tempo in development and eventually will be able advantageously to break the symmetry.

**Szabados, Eugenio** (b. 3 July 1898) Italian chess player; awarded the titles International Master and International Judge, both in 1951.

**Szabó, Laśzló** (b. 19 March 1917) Hungarian chess player; awarded the titles International Grandmaster in 1950 and International Judge in 1954. He was Hungarian Champion in 1937, 1946, 1950, 1952, 1954, 1959 and 1968. Szabó competed in the Chess Olympiads of 1935, 1937 and in every Chess Olympiad from 1952 to 1968. He also took part in the interzonals of 1948, 1952 and 1955 and competed in the Candidates' tournaments of 1950, 1953 and 1956. Szabó is also the author of several books on chess. (1976 Elo rating: 2525)

**Szekely, Peter** (b. 8 February 1955) Hungarian chess player; awarded the title International Master in 1976. (1976 Elo rating: 2460)

**Szen, Josef** (1805–1857) Austro-Hungarian chess player. He founded the Budapest Chess Club in 1839 and played for it in its famous correspondence match with the Paris Chess Club (November 1842 to February 1846). Budapest's surprising victory, by winning both games played, raised the prestige of the team's members (the other two were Szen's former schoolfriend Löwenthal and Vicenz Grimm) and in 1851 Szen was invited to play in the Great Exhibition tournament, where he was eliminated in the second round by Anderssen.

**Szen's Position** a chess problem composed by Josef Szen in which White has pawns on his QR2, QN2 and QB2 and the King on Q1, while Black has pawns on KR2, KN2 and KB2 and the King on K1. The position can be used to demonstrate some principles of pawn endings such as how the Kings should move in front of the pawns and how in this type of symmetrical position the result will depend upon whose turn it is to move.

**Szilagyi, György** (b. 4 July 1921) Hungarian chess player; awarded the title International Master in 1956, the year in which he also represented Hungary in the Chess Olympiad. (1976 Elo rating: 2380)

**Szily, Dr Jozsef** (1913–1976) Hungarian chess player; awarded the title International Master in 1950. He competed in the 1952 Chess Olympiad and in the 1961 European Team Championship.

**Szmetan, Jorge** Argentinian chess player; awarded the title International Master in 1976. (1976 Elo rating: 2450)

**Szymczak, Zbigniew** Polish chess player; awarded the title International Master in 1976. (1976 Elo rating: 2400)

# T

**tactical complication** a move made deliberately to complicate a relatively clear position. It is usually a defensive measure adopted to pressurize the opponent who otherwise has an obvious and satisfactory line of play. Although it may be objectively unsound it can give the opponent opportunities to go wrong. This ploy can work at all levels – Emanuel Lasker was notorious for successfully introducing tactical complications into otherwise lost positions. Compare **Marshall swindle, swindle.**

**tactical finesse** a quiet move based upon a hidden resource in the position.

**tactics** manoeuvres to take advantage of opportunities arising in the short term. Tactics take priority over the general strategy of the player since they gain immediate advantage if correct. Compare **strategy.**

**Taimanov, Mark** (b. 7 February 1926) Soviet chess player; awarded the titles International Master in 1951 and International Grandmaster in 1952. He was Soviet Champion in 1956 and competed in the 1955 Student Olympiad and the 1956 Chess Olympiad. He has competed in three interzonals, one Candidates' tournament and one series of Candidates' matches.

Taimanov learned chess at eight when he began to play in tournaments at his music school. (He is a gifted pianist.) By the age of 11 he was one of a group of children who received special coaching from Botvinnik. He became a Soviet Master in 1944; won the Leningrad Championship in 1948 and 1950; and came equal second in the 1952 interzonal and equal ninth in the following year's Candidates' tournament.

He qualified for the 1970 interzonal by coming fifth, but was eliminated in the quarter-finals of the Candidates' matches by Fischer (+0 −6 =0). In the 1973 Leningrad interzonal he came equal eighth.

Taimanov has been responsible for many original and important contributions to opening theory, particularly in the Sicilian, King's Indian, Nimzo-Indian and Grünfeld defences. His ideas have significantly added to the understanding and interpretation of all these openings. His book on the Nimzo-Indian (first published in 1956) is one of the classics of opening theory literature. (1976 Elo rating: 2540)

**Taimanov Variation** an opening sequence arising out of the Sicilian Defence: 1. P–K4, P–QB4 2. N–KB3, N–QB3 3. P–Q4, P×P 4. N×P, *P–K3* 5. N–QB3, *Q–B2*. As is usual in the Sicilian Defence, Black attempts not only to obtain counterplay on the Queen side (especially on the Queen Bishop file), but also to develop the King Bishop more actively than occurs in most other variations. Common continuations for White are: 6. B–K2 or 6. P–KN3. This variation was often played in the late nineteenth century, but is named after Mark Taimanov, who developed it extensively in the 1960s (other important contributors were Isaac Boleslavsky and Ilya Kan).

**Tal, Mikhail** (b. 9 November 1936) Soviet chess player; World Champion from 1960 to 1961; awarded the title International Grandmaster in 1957. He was Soviet Champion in 1957, 1958, 1967 (with Polugayevsky) and 1972 and competed in the Chess Olympiads of 1958, 1960, 1962, 1966, 1972 and 1974. He has competed in four interzonals, two Candidates' tournaments and two series of Candidates' matches.

Tal learned to play when aged eight and became a Soviet Master at 16. In 1957 he graduated in history and philology from Riga University (with a dissertation on Russian humorists) and in the same year began a meteoric rise by winning the Soviet Championship – the youngest player to do so since Botvinnik. He won the 1958 interzonal with the greatest number of points ever scored in this event and also triumphed in the 1959 Candidates' tournament to meet Botvinnik in the subsequent World Championship match. Botvinnik was generally expected to repulse Tal's sacrificial attacks and win, but Tal was unbeatable and handed Botvinnik his worst-ever defeat (+6 −2 =13). In the return match the experts favoured Tal who had won so convincingly and had youth on his side, but again were proved wrong. Tal had spent some time in hospital following an operation and was in poor health, while Botvinnik had prepared thoroughly. Botvinnik forced the games into balanced positions unsuited to Tal's style and Tal suffered an even more crushing defeat than Botvinnik had (+5 −10 =6).

Since then Tal's form has been erratic. Periods when he has been invincible (such as in 1972) have alternated by times when his kidney illness has severely handicapped him. In the 1962 Candidates' tournament he was forced to withdraw after three rounds and enter hospital. A revival was seen in the 1965 series of Candidates' Matches in which he defeated Portisch in the quarter-finals (+4 −1 =3) and Larsen in the semi-finals (+3 −2 =5), but lost to Spassky in the finals (+1 −4 =6). In the 1968 series Tal defeated Gligorić in the quarter-finals (+3 −1 =5), but lost to Korchnoi in the semi-finals (+1 −2 =7). Tal returned to the peak of his form in 1972 and seemed invincible, winning five major tournaments and going over 60 games without defeat, but failed in the 1973 Leningrad interzonal, coming only eighth. Another revival occurred in 1976 when he came equal second at the Biel interzonal, but was subsequently eliminated in the play-off with Portisch and Petrosian to decide the Candidates' qualifiers.

According to Euwe, 'In powers of combination [Tal] perhaps outdoes even Alekhine. Sacrifice is second nature to him.' While other players only make sacrifices that they are convinced are sound, Tal will make sacrifices if he cannot prove them to be unsound. He admitted making dubious moves in his first match with Botvinnik to put him under pressure. This pressure is increased by the fact that Tal is one of the fastest players in the world so that the opponent often finds himself in time trouble. In such situations the refutation of an unsound sacrifice may be discovered only after the game, giving the impression that Tal was lucky. Tal has himself joked about this by saying that there are two kinds of sacrifices: Tal sacrifices and correct ones. For him the ultimate soundness of a move is relatively unimportant; like Lasker he chooses the moves that cause the most problems for his opponents.

As well as being an active player, Tal is a chess journalist and is the editor of the Latvian periodical *Chess*. (1976 Elo rating: 2615)

**Tan, Lian Ann** (b. 8 September 1947) Singapore chess player; awarded the title International Master in 1973 after he qualified for the interzonal tournament at Petropolis. (1976 Elo rating: 2365)

**Tank** a Fairy chesspiece that moves like a King and can move other men in turn. It captures enemy men in the normal manner and can also move on to any adjacent square occupied by a man of its own colour. This is pushed to the adjacent square that is directly in line and any man there is either captured or pushed forward in turn, etc. This process will continue until the edge of the board is reached and any man on the edge will be pushed off (except for the King). Pawns may be pushed back to their original squares, when they will be allowed to advance two squares initially again. If they are pushed to the first or the eighth ranks they will promote as usual. The Tank was invented by K. J. Goodare.

**Tarjan, James E.** (b. 22 February 1952) American chess player; awarded the titles International Master in 1974 and International Grandmaster in 1976. He was first at Subbotica (1975). (1976 Elo rating: 2490)

**Tarrasch Defence** an opening sequence arising out of the Queen's

Gambit Declined: 1. P–Q4, P–Q4 2. P–QB4, P–K3 3. N–QB3, *P–QB4*. It is named after Siegbert Tarrasch who considered that it provided Black room to develop his pieces. Its major drawback is a weakened pawn structure, characterized by Black's isolated Queen pawn. See **Closed Variation, Prague Variation, Swedish Variation.**

**Tarrasch, Siegbert** (1862–1934) German chess player and one of the first International Grandmasters; born in Breslau on 5 March 1862. Tarrasch was a doctor of medicine and practised in Nuremberg and Berlin for many years, playing chess only as a hobby; nevertheless, he was one of the strongest players of the late nineteenth century. His tournament victories were numerous and included firsts at Breslau (1889), Manchester (1890), Dresden (1892), Leipzig (1894), Vienna (1898), Monte Carlo (1903) and Ostend (1907), a second at Hastings (1895), and a fourth at St Petersburg (1914).

He finally played a match for the World Championship in 1908, but was past his prime and lost easily to Lasker (+3 −8 =5) despite having winning positions in several games. Results of other matches included victories against Marshall, Mieses, and Wahlbrodt; draws against Tchigorin and Schlechter; and another loss to Lasker in 1916.

Tarrasch was also a supreme, chess teacher. He took Steinitz's concepts, purged them of their creator's eccentricities, and presented them clearly and succinctly in books such as *The Game of Chess* and *Three Hundred Chess Games*. He was undoubtedly one of the most influential writers on chess and was known as 'Praeceptor Germaniae' (Germany's teacher), but as a corollary had a dogmatic tendency which led to lively and witty clashes with the hypermoderns. He died in Munich on 17 February 1934.

**Tarrasch trap** as a source of endless confusion, two variations have both been called the *Tarrasch trap* and both arise in the Ruy Lopez. The first was played by Tarrasch in Frankfurt in 1887, with Zukertort as Black. The game went as follows: 1. P–K4, P–K4 2. N–KB3, N–QB3 3. B–N5, P–QR3 4. B–R4, N–B3 5. O–O, N×P 6. P–Q4, P–QN4 7. B–N3, P–Q4 8. P×P, B–K3 9. P–B3, B–K2, 10. R–K1, O–O 11. N–Q4, Q–Q2? 12. *N×B!*, P×N 13. R×N, Resigns. The second was played in Dresden in 1892 with Marco as Black. The game went as follows: 1. P–K4, P–K4 2. N–KB3, N–QB3 3. B–N5, P–Q3 4. P–Q4, B–Q2 5. N–B3, B–K2 6. O–O, N–B3 7. R–K1, O–O? 8. B×N, B×B 9. P×P, P×P 10. Q×Q, QR×Q 11. N×P, B×P 12. N×B, N×N 13. N–Q3, P–KB4 14. P–KB3, B–B4ch 15. N×B, N×N 16. B–N5, R–Q4 17. B–K7, Resigns (If 17 . . ., R–K1 18. P–QB4!). In this game Marco walked into a prepared variation: Tarrasch had published the whole game as analysis in the *Deutsche Schachzeitung* eighteen months earlier.

**Tartakover, Savielly Grigorievitch** (1887–1956) Polish chess player; awarded the title International Grandmaster in 1950. He was born in Rostov-on-Don on 9 February 1887, but left Russia in 1899 following the death of his parents in a pogrom. Tartakover studied law at Geneva and Vienna but, after serving as an officer in the Austrian army during

World War I, became a chess professional in the 1920s. His many tournament successes included firsts at Vienna (1905, 1922 and 1923), Nuremberg (1906), Hastings (1926, 1927 and 1945), London (1927), Paris (1929), Liege (1930) and Lodz (1935). He also competed for Poland in every Chess Olympiad from 1930 to 1939 and (after taking French citizenship) in the 1950 Chess Olympiad. In addition he wrote several valuable books, including *A Breviary of Chess*, *Die Hypermoderne Schachpartie* and *500 Master Games of Modern Chess*, which display his wit and talent for epigrams (known as 'Tartakoverisms') – such as, 'It's always better to sacrifice your opponent's men.' In style, Tartakover linked the classical players and the new school, which he named the 'hypermoderns'.

Tartakover's other occupations included work as a scriptwriter and as a translator of Russian poetry into French and German. He was competing in the Argentinian Chess Olympiads when World War II began, but returned to Europe and fought in the Free French army under De Gaulle. He died in Paris on 5 February 1956.

**Tatai, Stefano** (b. 23 March 1938) Italian chess player; awarded the title International Master in 1966. He was Italian Champion in 1962, 1965 and 1967. Tatai competed in the Chess Olympiads of 1966, 1968, 1970 and 1976. (1976 Elo rating: 2465)

**Tchigorin Defence** a defence occurring in the Queen's Gambit Declined: 1. P–Q4, P–Q4 2. P–QB4, *N–QB3*. It was named after the Russian chess player Mikhail Ivanovich Tchigorin, who often played this line of immediate counterattack. With proper play by White, it is generally considered to be an unfavourable system of defence.

**Tchigorin Indian** another name for the **Old Indian Defence**.

**Tchigorin, Mikhail Ivanovich** (1850–1908) strongest Russian chess player of the nineteenth century. He learned the game when aged 16, but only became seriously interested seven years later when he began visiting the Café Dominika in St Petersburg. There in 1875 he met Winawer who greatly encouraged him and in 1879 he won the Russian Congress tournament and defeated Shiffers in a match a year later (+7 −1 =3). His first international tournament was Berlin (1881) where he was equal third with Winawer. Later results included an equal first at New York (1889), first at Budapest (1896), and second at Hastings (1895). He met Steinitz in World Championship matches in 1889 and 1892 and narrowly lost both (+6 −10 =1, +8 −10 =5) and also successfully played two games by telegraph against Steinitz in 1890 and 1891.

Tchigorin worked hard to establish chess in Russia; in 1880 in St Petersburg he organized the first Russian chess club. Tchigorin also edited a monthly chess periodical, *Shakmatny Listok* and when this was losing money he supported it himself. His style of play contrasted sharply with that of Steinitz; instead of focusing on the static strengths and weaknesses of a position he preferred a dynamic approach, accepting weaknesses for advantages elsewhere. He is regarded in the U.S.S.R. as being the founder of the Soviet school of chess.

**T.D.** *abbrev. for* tournament director. This is most common in the United States.

**Team Championship of the European Economic Community** an annual international team tournament inaugurated in 1975 to commemorate the enlargement of the E.E.C. One team from each member-state of the E.E.C. competes in the tournament, which is a round-robin event. The first such event was held in Ostend, Belgium and was won by the Dutch team (Sosonko, Ree, Kuijpers, Logterink and Boersma).

**technique** the knowledge and experience that enables a player to achieve a win mechanically and without undue exertion. The possession of technique is one of the fundamental differences between the expert and the amateur.

***Technique in Chess*** a book by Gerald Abrahams. It analyses the operation in chess of technique, which is defined as 'the awareness of the functions of the pieces and of their peculiar resources . . . and methods of exploiting these things in recurring situations.' It was first published in 1961 and uses descriptive notation.

**telepower** (Kmoch's term) the long range of the Bishop. See ***Pawn Power in Chess***.

**telestop** (Kmoch's term) all the squares of a pawn's frontspan except the first. Thus, if a pawn is on KB4 its telestop will be KB6, KB7 and KB8. See **blockade, stop proper, stop squares, *Pawn Power in Chess***.

**telex match** a series of chess games played by means of telex. The first inter-city match to involve a team from the United Kingdom took place on 3 April 1976 and was contested by London and Belgrade. After adjudication London emerged the winners by 4½ points to 3½ points. A similar event took place on 11 September 1976 between teams representing London and New York and was decisively won by the latter. Compare **cable match, radio match.**

**tempo** *Italian for* time. It means a gain of time in that a player who has gained or lost tempi, perhaps in the opening, has achieved his objectives more quickly or slowly than his opponent. Tempo is one of the three basic elements in which each player attempts to gain an advantage, the others being force and space. The maxim that each piece should be moved once only in the opening was formulated to avoid a waste of tempi. It is sometimes stated that a gain of a pawn is worth the loss of three tempi, but this will clearly depend on the situation. In certain cases occurring in the endgame it might be desirable to lose a tempo. Examples of such situations are when **zugzwang** exists or when the opposition cannot be maintained. A common manoeuvre to lose a tempo is triangulation of the King.

**tempo-stroll variation** any move or sequence of moves without direct tactical or strategic implications, made to mark time and encourage one's opponent to declare his plans.

**ten-second chess** chess played at the rate of ten seconds per move. Also called **Blitz.**

**Teschner, Rudolf** (b. 1922) German chess player. He was born on 16

February 1922. Teschner was West German Champion in 1951 and was awarded the title International Master in 1957. He played in the 1952 and 1956 Chess Olympiads, but has concentrated mainly on journalism rather than play. For many years he has been the editor of the *Deutsche Schachzeitung*.

***Test Your Chess*** an anthology of chess problems compiled by Gerald Abrahams. By attempting to solve them the reader is able to obtain an estimate of his strength. This book was first published in 1963 and uses descriptive notation.

**text** the moves of the main line of a piece of analysis or a game, as opposed to the variations analysed in the notes.

**text move** the move that is offered in written analysis as the main line of a variation in preference to the (perhaps equally valid) alternatives.

**thematic move** a move that is in harmony with the strategic ideas inherent in the opening selected. For instance, in the King's Gambit thematic moves for White would involve the transfer of the pieces to the King side and not the Queen side, since the main justification of the pawn sacrifice is to open lines on that flank.

**Theresa of Avila, Saint** (1515–1582) a Spanish Carmelite nun who wrote a devotional work, *The Way of Perfection*, using chess in allegory. In Spain she is considered to be the patron saint of chess players. She is also known as Saint Theresa de Jesus.

***Think Like a Grandmaster*** a book by Alexander Kotov. It attempts to convey how a Grandmaster thinks when playing chess and to this end he explains how he himself analyses variations, formulates a plan and first inculcated in himself a sense of positional judgment. In this book the author describes how Botvinnik, Tal, Petrosian and other Grandmasters studied chess and trained themselves in its complexities. The book was translated by Bernard Cafferty and was first published in English in 1971 using descriptive notation.

**Thomas, Sir George Alan** (1881–1972) British chess player; awarded the titles International Master in 1950 and International Judge in 1952. He was British Champion in 1923 and 1934 and competed in the Chess Olympiads of 1927, 1930, 1931, 1933, 1935, 1937 and 1939. In the 1931 event he had the best result of any player on third board. He was born in Constantinople on 14 June 1881 and was taught to play chess by his mother, herself a chess champion. His best tournament result was equal first with Euwe and Flohr at Hastings (1934) in front of Botvinnik and Capablanca, both of whom he had defeated. As well as being skilled at chess, Thomas was an expert badminton player and was several times All England Badminton Champion, including 1923 when he was also British Chess Champion; the Thomas Cup (badminton's counterpart to the Davis Cup) was presented by him.

Sir George remained interested in chess after his playing days were over and worked especially hard in encouraging chess among the young. He died on 23 July 1972.

**three-dimensional chess** chess played on more than one board with men able to move from one board to another. Since the boards could be superimposed on top of each other this means that men can move in three dimensions. A well-known type of three-dimensional chess is **Total Chess.**

**three-handed chess** a variant form of chess for three players, invented by Marinelli in 1722 (Murray, *A History of Chess*, p. 859). See **four-handed chess, variant forms of chess.**

**Three Knights' Game** a defence to the King pawn opening: 1. P–K4, P–K4 2. N–KB3, N–QB3 3. N–B3, or *B–N5*, or *P–KN3*. Black attempts to avoid the Four Knights' Game which would arise after 3 . . ., N–B3.

**three-mover** an orthodox **chess problem** in which White must checkmate Black in three moves. Together with the **two-mover**, this type of problem forms the bulk of orthodox problems.

***Through the Looking Glass*** a book written by Lewis Carroll as a sequel to his *Alice's Adventures in Wonderland*. It was first published in 1872 and relates the dream-sequence tale of Alice's adventures when she climbs over the fireplace mantel and through the mirror above it. In the world beyond the glass ('looking-glass country'), Alice first spots several living chessmen in the hearth among the cinders, including the Red King and Red Queen. She discovers that the countryside in this strange land is laid out like a gigantic chessboard, and soon finds herself involved as a white pawn in a whimsical and fantastic game of chess – a plot feature that constitutes the bulk of the story. On reaching the eighth rank. Alice finally becomes a Queen. See **Carroll, Lewis.**

**Tietz system** a method of apportioning the prize money of a tournament. One share of the total prize money is distributed proportionately among the competitors according to the number of games each has won, while a second share is distributed proportionately among those competitors who have won over fifty per cent of their games. The Tietz system was employed at Ostend (1906). It was devised by Viktor Tietz.

**tight duo** (Kmoch's term) a **duo** where at least one of the vertically adjacent squares is occupied by an enemy pawn. Compare **buffer duo, loose duo.** See ***Pawn Power in Chess.***

**tight lever** (Kmoch's term) a **lever** where one pawn is also directly opposed by an enemy pawn. This means that only the player with the two pawns has the choice of capturing or bypassing the enemy pawn; his opponent can only capture if he wishes to alter the status quo. Compare **inner lever, loose lever, outer lever.** See ***Pawn Power in Chess.***

**tight twin** (Kmoch's term) a doubled pawn that cannot be undoubled by force. Compare **sham twin, tight twin, twin.** See ***Pawn Power in Chess.***

**time** **1.** the period in which each player must make a certain number of moves. This will be 2½ hours for 40 moves in master tournaments, 1½ hours for 30 or 36 moves (or even faster) in weekend tournaments or club matches.

**2.** the number of moves needed to achieve an objective, such as development of all the pieces. See **tempo.**

**time control** the move that marks the last of the number of moves that must be played within the stated time. In master play moves must be made at the rate of 16 per hour and the time controls are at move 40 (after 2½ hours per player), at move 56 (after another hour), at move 72 (after a further hour), etc. In less important events, games are played at a quicker rate and different time controls are set, e.g. in club matches play usually takes place at the rate of 24 moves per hour with a time limit of 1½ hours for each player and a time control at move 36. If the time control is not reached within the time limit the game is lost.

**time limit** a specified amount of time in which a player must carry out a fixed number of moves. In international chess the time limit is normally two and a half hours for a player to make 40 moves followed by a time limit of one hour for each extra set of 16 moves. If the time limit is exceeded the offending player loses the game.

Time limits were introduced in the second half of the nineteenth century to prevent games lasting an inordinately long time due to **sitzfleisch.**

**time trouble** a situation arising when a player has insufficient time in which to reach the time control. Time trouble is a classic reason for blunders. It is a well-known fact that every game lost on time would have been a win but for that! Some players are notorious for consistently getting into time trouble; Reshevsky must be the outstanding example.

**Timman, Jan** (b. 14 December 1951) Dutch chess player; awarded the titles International Master in 1971 and International Grandmaster in 1974. His tournament results include firsts at Sombor (1974) and Neyanya (1975). (1976 Elo rating: 2550)

**Timoshchenko, Gennadi** (b. 27 April 1949) Soviet chess player; awarded the title International Master in 1976. (1976 Elo rating: 2470)

**title inflation** a derogatory term that describes the effects of what many experts believe to be a growing trend – the awarding of FIDE titles, especially International Master and International Grandmaster, to players who are not really as strong as those titles imply. It is generally agreed that of the approximately 140 IGMs living today, for example, few could equal or even approach the playing strength of the five players originally awarded the title Grandmaster of Chess (Alekhine, Capablanca, Lasker, Marshall and Tarrasch).

It is alleged that the FIDE representatives of small countries always vote to keep the title qualifications as easy as possible in order that their players may gain unmerited titles; also, the accusation has been made that fraudulent practices exist, such as the buying and selling of points to ease title-getting.

**titles** the highest are awarded by FIDE, with lesser titles awarded by the national chess federations. This is a fairly recent development, for until 1950 the only title awarded by FIDE was that of World Champion. The title *master* was applied unofficially to any player of international standard, while the title *grandmaster* was popularly and loosely applied to those players who were contenders for the World Championship.

However, FIDE was much stronger in the post-war era than it had been in the pre-war period, and in 1950 began to award titles to those who fulfilled certain standard criteria. This practice still continues.

FIDE awards the titles of **International Grandmaster, International Master, International Woman Master** and **International Woman Grandmaster** to the world's strongest players. From 1951 it has awarded the title of **International Judge** to arbiters of international experience. On the recommendations of the relevant bodies, FIDE also awards the titles of: **Correspondence World Champion, International Correspondence Chess Grandmaster, International Correspondence Chess Master, International Grandmaster for Chess Compositions, International Master for Chess Compositions, International Arbiter for Chess Compositions,** and **Correspondence Grandmaster for the Blind.** See **St Petersburg (1914).**

**TN** *abbrev. for* theoretical novelty. The term is used in chess publications to indicate an innovation in a standard variation. It first appeared in ***Informator*** and is now widely used.

**Tolush, Alexander** (1910–1969) Soviet chess player. He was born on 1 May 1910 and died on 3 March 1969. Tolush was awarded the titles International Master in 1950 and International Grandmaster in 1953 and also became an International Correspondence Chess Master in 1962.

Tolush's best results over the board were victories in the Leningrad Championship in 1938, 1946, and 1947; a second-place in the U.S.S.R. Championship in 1950; and his victory at Bucharest (1953). He never represented the U.S.S.R. in the Chess Olympiads, but competed several times in the European Team Championships.

Tolush has been described as brilliant but erratic. He was, however, a noted trainer and among his pupils were Keres and Spassky.

**top board** the player in a team who must meet the strongest opponents in a match, tournament, or other event. In events such as the Chess Olympiads each player is assigned to a board or designated first or second reserve. It is then impossible to play on a lower board during the event. Consequently the player on top board will play on it throughout the event except when he has a rest day.

**Toran Albero, Román** (b. 8 October 1931) Spanish chess player; awarded the titles International Master in 1954 and International Judge in 1957. Toran Albero was Spanish Champion in 1951 and 1953 and has competed in the Chess Olympiads several times. He is also the editor of the chess periodical *Ajedrez Español* (Spanish Chess). (1976 Elo rating: 2445)

**Torre Attack** an opening sequence arising out of the Queen pawn opening: 1. P–Q4, N–KB3 2. *N–KB3*, P–K3 3. *B–N5*. The most common continuations are: 3 . . ., P–KR3 and 3 . . ., P–B4. This opening may also be played against the King's Indian Defence. It was devised by the Mexican chess player Carlos Torre.

**Torre, Carlos** (1904–1978) Mexican chess player; awarded the title International Grandmaster in 1977. Torre's tournament career lasted barely three years before it was cut short by mental illness. During that period he won the Louisiana Championship (1923), came equal third at Marianske-Lazne (1925) and was equal fifth at Moscow (1925) where he defeated Emanuel Lasker. He later competed at Leningrad (1925) and also in Chicago (1926), coming equal second at both events.

**Torre, Eugenio** (b. 4 November 1951) Philippine chess player; awarded the titles International Master in 1972 and International Grandmaster in 1974. Torre is the first Asian Grandmaster outside the U.S.S.R. His first major international competition was the 1969 World Junior Championship, in which he came thirteenth by winning the B Final (the A Final was won by Karpov). He has since participated in the Chess Olympiads of 1970, 1972, 1974 and 1976 and has competed in the 1973 Leningrad interzonal and the 1976 Manila interzonal. (1976 Elo rating: 2505)

**Torres y Quevedo, Leonardo** (1852–1939) Spanish mathematician and scientist. Perhaps the most brilliant Spanish scientist of his time, his contribution to chess was the creation of Ajedrecista (chess player), a chess automaton capable of delivering mate with King and Rook against King. It was able to recognize illegal moves by its opponent and would end the game if three illegal moves were played. In 1955 Spain commemorated Torres y Quevedo with a special postage stamp issue.

**Total Chess** a type of **three-dimensional** chess which is played on four superimposed boards. A man can move to any square vertical to that which could be occupied normally, but may not move into or across the vertical projection of a pawn. The men are initially arrayed on the lowest board.

The game was created in 1946 by Charles Beatty.

**Toth, Bela** (b. 19 April 1943) Italian chess player; awarded the title International Master in 1974. (1976 Elo rating: 2405)

**touch-move** a law of chess stipulating that a man that is touched without adequate warning must be moved on the next turn (if it belongs to the forces of the player who touched it) or must be taken on the next move (if it does not belong to the man who touched it). If these conditions are legally impossible to satisfy no penalty is exacted. See **J'adoube.**

***Tournament, The*** Polish animated cartoon film (1960) made by Wladyslaw Nehrebecki, featuring a world inhabited entirely by chessmen.

**tournament book** a record of all the games played in a tournament with annotations of the most interesting ones, the results of the entrants and background information about the event. Two of the best tournament books are that for New York (1924) by Alekhine and *Championship Chess* by Botvinnik, which records the 1941 Soviet Championship match-tournament.

**tournament director (TD)** an organizer and arbiter of a tournament. His functions include enforcing the rules impartially and arranging the pairings for each round. In the most important tournaments he will be complemented by an appeals committee, usually composed of competing players, to which competitors can refer decisions with which they disagree. So great are the power and responsibility of the TD that the U.S.C.F. operates a certification system. It also stipulates that any tournament that is intended to be rated by the U.S.C.F. must have at least one Certified Tournament Director. Usually the responsibilities of a Tournament Director differ from those of a chief arbiter in that the former is responsible for the pre-tournament organization, including invitations to participants, while the arbiter is only concerned with upholding the laws of chess during the event.

**Tournament of Nations** one of the official titles of the **Chess Olympiad**.

**traditional chess** the standard or orthodox form of chess, played according to the official rules of the game as outlined by FIDE. See **variant forms of chess**.

***Traité du Jeu des Echecs*** a seventeenth-century book on chess written by Gioachino Greco. It is generally considered to be the outstanding work of its period.

**transition** a phase in the game when the opening merges into the middle-game or when the middle-game merges into the ending.

**Transparent Piece** a Fairy chesspiece through which any other chesspiece can pass. It was invented by C. D. Locock.

**transpose** to play the standard moves of an opening or defence in an irregular order, or to reach a common position by an unusual sequence of moves.

**transposition** the reaching of a standard position in the opening by an unusual sequence of moves. This can occur either by playing the normal moves in a non-standard order (e.g. 1. P–QB4, P–K3 2. P–Q4, P–Q4 is a transposition to the Queen's Gambit Declined) or by more extravagant means (e.g. 1. P–Q4, P–QB4 2. P–QB3, P×P 3. P×P, P–Q4 is a transposition to the Slav Defence).

Sometimes the deliberate adoption of an opening transposition may be used to avoid certain variations which could occur with standard move orders.

**trap** a disguised threat which the victim activates by unwarily playing a superficially tempting move. The success of a trap is usually based upon the opponent's disregard of strategic or tactical principles, and so traps are most commonly found in the games of weak players. Although the overwhelming majority of traps are nameless, certain of them are based upon positions that crop up frequently and some of these have received titles; examples are the **Blackburne trap, Lasker trap, Monticelli trap, Rubinstein trap** and **Noah's Ark trap**. In complete contrast, others have been named because they have arisen only once, but in important games (for example, the **Tarrasch trap**).

**trappy move** a move that creates tactical complications leading to checkmate or a gain in material, space or tempo if met incorrectly. The term is usually derogatory, implying that the move is weak if the opponent does not overlook the threats it poses and defends correctly.

In annotations it will be followed by the symbol [!?] if the annotator believes it to be sound or the best move in that position and by [?!] if he considers it unsound or if there were stronger alternative moves available.

***Treasury of Chess Lore, The*** an anthology of articles, stories, and quotations compiled by Fred Reinfeld. It was first published in 1951.

**Trébuchet** *French for* trap, siege weapon; an elementary form of zugzwang that most players have met. As shown in the diagram, both players are defending their pawns with their Kings. Thus whoever moves first must desert his pawn and so lose it. The trébuchet occurs regularly in the endgame and is, perhaps, the commonest zugzwang.

The first to move loses a pawn

**triad** (Kmoch's term) a group composed of a pair of doubled pawns and an adjacent friendly pawn. If its possessor attempts to create a passed pawn from this formation Kmoch advises always advancing the leading doubled pawn first. However, like all doubled pawn formations the triad has inherent weaknesses. Compare **trio.** See ***Pawn Power in Chess***.

**triangulation** a manoeuvre in which a King takes two moves to arrive on a square that it could have reached in one. The three squares on which it stands during this process thus form the three points of a triangle. Triangulation is almost exclusively found in the ending where a player may often need to lose a move in order to put his opponent in **zugzwang.**

**Trifunović, Dr Petar** (b. 31 December 1910) Yugoslavian chess player; awarded the titles International Master in 1950 and International Grandmaster in 1953. He was Yugoslavian Champion in 1945, 1946, 1947, 1952 and 1961. Trifunović competed in the Chess Olympiads of 1935, 1937, 1950, 1952, 1954, 1958 and 1962 and in the 1950 Olympiad had the best score of any player (+8 −1 =4) although other players had higher percentages. He competed in the 1948 interzonal and finished only in tenth place, but seemed to have qualified for the subsequent Candidates' tournament due to the withdrawal of eligible players such as Euwe, Reshevsky and Fine. However, at the last moment the event was reduced in size and Trifunović was excluded.

**Tringov, Georgi Petrov** (b. 7 March 1937) Bulgarian chess player; awarded the titles International Master in 1962 and International Grandmaster in 1963. Tringov competed in the 1955 World Junior Championship and later played in all the Student Olympiads from 1957 to 1960. He represented Bulgaria in the Chess Olympiads of 1956, 1958, 1962, 1966, 1968, 1970, 1972 and 1974. His best performance in this event was in the 1968 Olympiad in which he had the best result on second board (+8 −0 =6). Tringov has appeared in an interzonal on one occasion, when he participated in the 1964 tournament, coming fourteenth. (1976 Elo rating: 2490)

**trio** (Kmoch's term) three horizontally adjacent friendly pawns. Compare **duo, quart.** See ***Pawn Power in Chess.***

**triplets** (Kmoch's term) three pawns of the same colour that are on the same file. They have all the weaknesses of **doubled pawns,** but to a much greater degree. See ***Pawn Power in Chess.***

**Troianescu, Octav** (b. 4 February 1916) Romanian chess player; awarded the title International Master in 1950. He was Romanian Champion in 1946, 1954, 1956, and 1957 and competed in the Chess Olympiads of 1956 and 1960. (1976 Elo rating: 2300)

**Troitzky mate** a Bishop mate that was discovered by the famous Russian problem composer A. A. Troitzky and first published in *Nova Vremia* in 1895. From the diagrammed position play continues: 1. B–R6ch, K–N1 2. P–N7, K–B2 3. P–N8=Qch, K×Q 4. K–K6, K–R1 5. K–B7, P–K4 6. B–N7mate.

White to play and win

**Tseshkovsky, Vitaly** (b. 25 September 1944) Soviet chess player; awarded the titles International Master in 1973 and International Grandmaster in 1975. His results include firsts at Bucharest (1974) and Leipzig (1975) and an equal second at Rovinj/Zagreb (1975). (1976 Elo rating: 2550)

**Tsvetkov, Alexandre** (b. 7 October 1914) Bulgarian chess player; awarded the title International Master in 1950. He was Bulgarian Champion in 1938, 1940, 1945, 1948, 1950 and 1951. He competed in the Chess Olympiads of 1939, 1954 and 1956.

**Tukmakov, Vladimir** (b. 25 March 1946) Soviet chess player; awarded the titles International Master in 1970 and International Grandmaster in 1972. He competed in the 1965 World Junior Championship and the 1973 Leningrad interzonal. (1976 Elo rating: 2490)

**Turk, The** ostensibly a chessplaying automaton. It appeared to consist of a cabinet filled with machinery to which was attached a chessboard and the torso and head of a dummy of a Turk. After the audience had satisfied itself that there was no room for anyone to hide within the cabinet a game would commence. Upon its turn to move, the Turk's head would slowly rotate from side to side while its left hand grasped and moved a chessman – to the accompaniment of the rattling of clockwork from within the cabinet. It almost invariably won.

The Turk was invented by Baron Wolfgang von Kempelen and was first displayed in 1770, when it was shown to the Austrian Court. It was hugely successful and was subsequently exhibited in Germany, France, and England. On von Kempelen's death in 1804, it was sold to Johann Nepomuk Maelzel, a Bavarian musician, who also toured Europe with it where it played many celebrities including Napoleon. In 1825 Maelzel took the Turk to the United States. The ownership of the Turk changed several times following Maelzel's death (1837) before it was finally bought by the Chinese Museum, Philadelphia. There it remained until its destruction by fire in 1854.

The Turk's secrets were never completely discovered despite investigation by many cynics. Popular theories were that somehow a child, dwarf, or legless man was concealed inside. In fact a normal man of small stature controlled the Turk behind an intricate arrangement of movable partitions and telescopic drawers. The machinery that appeared to pack the inside of the cabinet was bogus and could be folded away easily once the cabinet's doors were closed. Many, including Edgar Allen Poe, believed that the hidden player must be able to see the chessboard through a concealed hole in the Turk's chest. The truth was much more ingenious. The opponent's chessmen were magnetized and the squares of the chessboard were made of thin pieces of metal beneath which were suspended metallic discs. When an opponent's man landed on a square the disc was attracted to the underneath of the chessboard. When it was removed the disc fell away. The player operating the Turk could reconstruct his opponent's move by watching the rise and fall of these discs. He would then make his move by manipulating the Turk's arm, probably through a system of levers. The success of the Turk was immense, partly because its operators were all strong players (including among others the Austrian, Allgaier, the Englishman, Lewis and the Frenchman, Mouret). Compare **Ajeeb**, **Mephisto**.

**twin** 1. a chess problem in two parts in which the position in the second half of the problem is similar but not identical to the position in the first half of the problem. Common means of changing the position include rotating the board, adding or removing one piece or pawn, and substituting one man for another. Normally White will have to mate the Black King in both of the two parts of the twin.

**2.** (Kmoch's term) one of a pair of doubled pawns. See ***Pawn Power in Chess***.

**Two Bishops Sacrifice** a sacrifice of both Bishops for two of the pawns protecting a castled King. It was first seen in the game between Lasker and Bauer at Amsterdam (1889). From the diagram Lasker continued: 1. N–R5, N×N 2. B×Pch!, K×B 3. Q×Nch, K–N1 4. B×P!, K×B 5. Q–N4ch, K–R2 6. R–B3, P–K4 7. R–R3ch, Q–R3 8. R×Qch, K×R 9. Q–Q7!, and soon won since one of the Bishops must be captured.

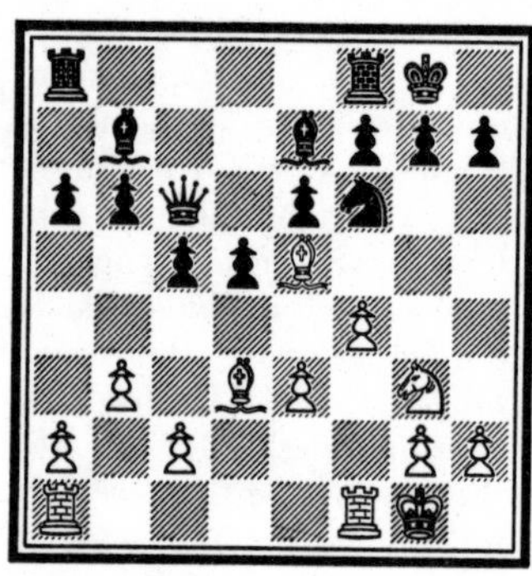

Lasker vs. Bauer (Amsterdam, 1889)

**Two Knights' Defence** a defence to the King's Pawn Opening: 1. P–K4, P–K4 2. N–KB3, N–QB3 3. B–B4, N–B3. Black develops quickly, but is exposed to complications following an attack on his King Bishop pawn by 4. N–N5. This opening appeared in Polerio as well as the treatise by Gianutio, which was published at approximately the same time (1597). In 1839 Bilguer wrote a pamphlet on this opening alone and it has since been deeply analyzed. It forms the subject of a monograph by Petrosian and Suetin.

**two-mover** an orthodox **chess problem** in which White must checkmate Black in two moves. The correct first move is the **key**; it will either maintain or create zugzwang for Black, in which case the problem is known as a **block problem**, or will create new threats to replace the ones that are destroyed by the move.

**Two Pawns Game** another (unusual) name for **Russian System**.

# U

**U-Chess** *abbrev. for* Unambiguous Three-symbol Chess. A type of Fairy Chess in which no move may be made unless it can be expressed unambiguously in three symbols or less in descriptive notation. This means that PK4 (P–K4) is permissible as is P×N (provided that it is unambiguous), but PB4 may be ambiguous in the opening and if so is disallowed. It was invented by M. Charosh and is based upon an idea of Irving Chernev's.

**Udemann Code** a method of notation designed for the transmission of moves by telegraph. As is shown in the diagram each square is designated by two letters.

Each move is represented by the two letters of the initial square and the two letters of the square of arrival. For example, the opening: 1. P–K4, P–Q4 2. P×P, is represented in the Udemann Code as: 1. GEGO, RERO 2. GORO. Castling is shown by the movement of the King alone: if White castled on the King side this is written down as GAKA.

The code is named after its inventor Louis Udemann (1854–1912). Udemann was born in Westphalia, Germany but was taken to the United States by his parents at the age of 12. He was the chess editor of the *Chicago Tribune*.

**Udovčić, Mijo** (b. 11 September 1920) Yugoslavian chess player; awarded the titles International Master in 1957 and International Grandmaster in 1962. He competed in the 1964 Chess Olympiad.

**Ufimtsev Defence** another name for the **Pirc Defence.** It is named after the Soviet theorist Ufimtsev, who was analysing it in the 1940s at approximately the same time as Vasja Pirc.

**Uhlmann, Wolfgang** (b. 29 March 1935) East German chess player; awarded the titles International Master in 1956 and International Grandmaster in 1959. He shared fifth place in the 1970 interzonal to qualify for the 1971 series of Candidates' matches, where he lost in the first round (5½–3½) against Larsen. (1976 Elo rating: 2555)

**Uitumen, Tudev** (b. 27 August 1939) Mongolian chess player; awarded the title International Master in 1965. He came equal 20th in the 1970 interzonal. (1976 Elo rating: 2385)

**Ujtelky,** Dr Maximillian Samuel Rudolf (b. 20 April 1915) a Czechoslovakian who is a lawyer by profession; awarded the title International Master in 1961. (1976 Elo rating: 2305)

**Unambiguous Three-symbol Chess** see **U-Chess.**

**underdevelop** to develop insufficiently because of unwise positioning of men or through a loss of a tempo or more.

**underdevelopment** insufficient development caused through unwise positioning of men or a loss of one tempo or more. At the very least it will cause a cramped game and may even result in a lost game. A common reason for underdevelopment is the movement of a piece more than once in the opening; another is the over-timid placing of the men. While underdevelopment is less likely to be fatal in closed than in open games, it is always serious.

**underpass** a manoeuvre in an endgame of King and pawn versus King that is used to gain the opposition. The attacking King does not move towards the other King, but instead moves away from it behind the pawn (the underpass). When the defending King advances the attacking King moves in front of the pawn and gains the opposition.

**underpromote** to promote a pawn that reaches the eighth rank into a piece that is inferior to a Queen.

**underpromotion** the promotion of a pawn that reaches the eighth rank to a piece that is less powerful than a Queen. This is invariably carried out to take advantage of, or guard against, some decisive short-range tactical threat. For example, in the following position promotion to a Queen would not win for White in view of the threat of mate.

The solution is: 1. R–B8ch, R×R 2. Q–R7ch!, K×Q 3. P×R=Nch!, and White wins by capturing the Queen followed by the pawns.

For a famous example of underpromotion to a piece other than a Knight see **Saavedra, Fernando**.

**undoubling** moving one of a pair of **doubled pawns** on to another file where no friendly pawns stand. This can only occur through a capture.

**unfree** (Kmoch's term) relating to a pawn that is opposed by an enemy pawn on the same file. At the beginning of the game every pawn is unfree. See **counterpawn**, ***Pawn Power in Chess***.

**unite** to place men of the same type and colour on squares where they can mutually support each other. The strongest united pieces are the Rooks, which can move without surrendering their mutual defence. Pawns that are united are also strong, as they need less support from pieces.

**united passed pawns** passed pawns of the same colour that are on adjacent files and able to support each other. Because they can defend one another their value is proportionately greater than two separate passed pawns. For instance, when the Kings are too far away to affect the issue, two united passed pawns on the fifth and sixth ranks opposed by a Rook can force the promotion of one of them if they have the move. Also called **connected passed pawns.** See **passed pawn.**

**united pawns** pawns of the same colour that are on adjacent files and are able to support each other. Compare **isolated pawn.**

**United States Championship** an invitational tournament held to determine the U.S. Champion; entrants are chosen on the basis of their current U.S.C.F. ratings. It was first held officially in 1890, but has been an annual event only since 1957. See **New York (1857).**

**United States Chess Federation** the governing organization of chess in the United States. It was created in 1939 by the amalgamation of the American Chess Federation, the National Chess Federation, and the Western Chess Federation and now has several thousand members. It exists to promote chess within the United States and as an affiliate of FIDE is responsible for all American participation in FIDE events. The official publication of the federation is *Chess Life & Review* which appears monthly. Its address is 479 Broadway, Newburgh, New York 12550. Abbrev **U.S.C.F.** or **USCF.**

**United States Open Championship** an annual chess tournament that has been held in the United States since 1900. It adopted the Swiss System of pairing in 1947.

***Unknown Alekhine, The*** formerly the title of *100 Games of Alekhine*, by Fred Reinfeld.

**Unzicker, Wolfgang** (b. 26 June 1925) West German chess player (a lawyer by profession); awarded the titles International Master in 1950 and International Grandmaster in 1954. He has been West German Champion on numerous occasions.

Unzicker qualified for the interzonals in 1952 and 1955, when he came ninth and sixteenth respectively. He has also competed in the Chess Olympiads of 1956, 1958, 1960, 1962, 1964, 1968, 1970, 1974 and 1976. (1976 Elo rating: 2530)

**U.S.C.F.** or **USCF** *abbrev. for* United States Chess Federation.

**U.S.S.R. v Rest of the World** a match between teams representing the U.S.S.R. and the rest of the world, held in Belgrade, Yugoslavia during March and April 1970. Each team consisted of ten players plus reserves and there were four games on each board.

The U.S.S.R. won very narrowly (20½ to 19½); the result depended on the last game to finish, which was won by Smyslov over Olafsson. A worrying feature for the Soviets was the performance of their players on the top four boards, where only 5½ points were scored out of a possible 16. This match was the scene of a successful return to international chess by Fischer, who defeated Petrosian on second board (+2 −0 =2). Also known as **Match of the Century.**

See **World Blitz Championship.**

# V

**Vadasz, László** (b. 27 January 1948) Hungarian chess player; awarded the title International Master in 1975. (1976 Elo rating: 2465)

**Vaganian, Rafael** (b. 15 October 1951) Soviet chess player; awarded the title International Grandmaster in 1971. He competed in the 1971 World Junior Championship. Vaganian's results include a first at Kragujevac (1974). (1976 Elo rating: 2550)

**Vaisman, Volodea** (b. 25 December 1937) Romanian chess player; awarded the title International Master in 1975. His tournament results include firsts at Wroclaw (1974) and Iasi (1975). (1976 Elo rating: 2485)

**Vaitonis, Pavilas** (b. 15 August 1911) Canadian chess player; awarded the title International Master in 1952. He was Lithuanian Champion in 1934, 1937, 1942, 1943 and 1944 and Canadian Champion in 1951 and 1957. He emigrated to Canada in 1949. Vaitonis competed for Lithuania in the Chess Olympiads of 1933, 1935, 1936, 1937 and 1939.

**Vajda, Dr Arpad** (1896–1967) Hungarian chess player; awarded the titles International Master in 1950 and International Judge in 1954. He was born on 2 May 1896 and competed in the Chess Olympiads of 1927, 1928, 1930, 1931 and 1933. He died on 25 October 1967.

**value of pieces** see **relative value of pieces.**

**Van den Berg, Carel Benjamin** (1924–1971) Dutch chess player, awarded the title International Master in 1963. He was born on 12 February 1924 and graduated in law and philosophy before becoming a chess professional. Although he competed in the 1958 Chess Olympiad, he was primarily a chess writer rather than an active player and collaborated with Euwe on a number of works. He died on 30 June 1971.

**Van Scheltinga, Tjeerd Daniel** (b. 6 March 1914) Dutch chess player, awarded the title International Master in 1965. He competed in the Chess Olympiads of 1937, 1939, 1950, 1952 and 1954. (1976 Elo rating: 2325)

**Van't Kruys Opening** an opening where White plays: 1. P–K3, deliberately inviting Black to take the initiative. It can develop into an inverted French Defence, but is rarely played. The opening is named after a Dutch player who used it in a number of games against Anderssen in the 1860s.

**Vao** a Fairy chesspiece that moves like a normal Bishop except when capturing. To capture a piece the Vao must jump over it, landing on any square that is directly on its path. Unlike the Locust, the Vao can move without capturing, when it moves like an orthodox Bishop. The Vao, the Leo, and the Pao were introduced from Chinese chess by T. R. Dawson.

**variant forms of chess** any form of chess that deviates from the orthodox game in one or more specific ways, such as by modification of the official rules, increase in the normal number of pieces, creation of new types of pieces, change in the way pieces move, etc. See **Atomic Chess, Cylinder Chess, Fairy Chess, four-handed chess, Hexagon**

**Chess, Losing Chess, Machine Gun Chess, Pocket Knight Chess, Randomized Chess, three-dimensional chess, three-handed chess.**

**variation** **1.** any opening sequence.
**2.** any sequence of moves that deviates from those actually played.

**Vasyukov, Eveni** (b. 5 March 1933) Soviet chess player; awarded the titles International Master in 1958 and International Grandmaster in 1961. His greatest international success was taking first place in the strong tournament at Manila (1974). (1976 Elo rating: 2580)

**Velikov, Petar** (b. 30 March 1951) Bulgarian chess player; awarded the title International Master in 1975. (1976 Elo rating: 2385)

**Velimirović Attack** an opening sequence arising out of the **Sozin Attack** in the **Sicilian Defence**: 1. P–K4, P–QB4 2. N–KB3, N–QB3 3. P–Q4, P×P 4. N×P, N–B3 5. N–QB3, P–Q3 6. B–QB4, P–K3 7. *B–K3*. White will continue with the moves: Q–K2, O–O–O and P–KN4, beginning a King-side pawn roller which will normally be backed up by the advance of either the King Bishop pawn or King Rook pawn. Black's best defences are either to attack in the centre by eventually playing P–Q4, or by counterpunching on the Queen side.

This variation was devised by the Yugoslavian International Grandmaster Dragoljub Velimirović and is regarded as one of White's most aggressive and dangerous continuations.

**Velimirović, Dragoljub** (b. 12 May 1942) Yugoslavian chess player; awarded the titles International Master in 1972 and International Grandmaster in 1973. He was Yugoslavian Champion in 1975. (1976 Elo rating: 2525)

**Vera Menchik Club** a mythical club consisting of all those masters who were defeated by Vera Menchik-Stevenson (née Menchik). In 1929 a great deal of controversy was caused when she was invited to compete at Carlsbad. The Viennese master, Albert Becker was one of several who felt she was too weak a player and he sarcastically suggested that the few masters she did manage to beat should be forced to join the Vera Menchik Club. Later in the tournament he became the founding member.

Other members of the Vera Menchik Club included: Alexander, Colle, Euwe, Golombek, Milner- Barry, Reshevsky, Sämisch, Lajos, Steiner, Sultan Khan, Sir George Thomas, and Yates. See **Menchik-Stevenson, Vera Francevna.**

**Verduga, Dennis** Ecuadorian chess player; awarded the title International Master in 1975. (1976 Elo rating: 2265)

**Veresov System** an opening sequence where White develops his Queen side before his King side. It generally arises in the following manner: 1. P–Q4, N–KB3 2. N–QB3, P–Q4 3. *B–N5*. This opening was first played regularly by Kurt Richter in the 1920s, but is named after Gavrill Veresov, a Russian master who has been playing and studying the opening since the 1930s.

**Verlinsky, Boris** (1887–1950) Soviet chess player; awarded the title International Master in 1950. He was Champion of Moscow in 1928 and Soviet Champion in 1929. Although strong tactically, he competed in only one international tournament – Moscow (1925).

**Verney, G. H.** a nineteenth-century British author of books on chess, including *Chess Eccentricities* (1885) and *Four-Handed Chess* (1881). One of the two basic variants of four-handed chess is known as the **Verney Game**. (For details of the rules of the game, see Sunnucks' *Encyclopaedia of Chess*.) See **four-handed chess.**

**vertical cylinder** a type of Fairy chessboard which has its Rook files joined. It can be imagined as a board wrapped around a bottle. This means that a Rook on QR3 can move directly to KR3 without crossing the centre of the board, while a Bishop can move from Q1 via KR5 to QB8. The vertical cylinder is the most commonly used type of Fairy chessboard and is normally shown as an ordinary diagram without borders at the sides. See **Cylinder Chess.** Compare **anchor-ring, horizontal cylinder.**

**Vicentz Treatise** the first known work on chess to appear in print. It was published in Vicentz, Spain in 1495 and dealt with the openings. No copies of it are known to exist today.

**Vidmar, Dr Milan** (1885–1962) Yugoslavian chess player; awarded the title International Grandmaster in 1950. He was born in Ljubljana on 22 June 1885. Vidmar studied electro-engineering at Vienna University and lectured in it at Ljubljana University. An academic rather than a professional chess player, he only competed in tournaments when free of university commitments; indeed, there were several periods of some years when he played no serious chess at all. Yet, despite his lack of practice, Vidmar was a strong player as shown by his results. He competed in the Chess Olympiads of 1931 and 1935 and his results included firsts at the Coburg **Hauptturnier** (1904), Vienna (1917), Berlin (1918), Hastings (1925), Bad Sliac (1932) and Basle (1952) and second places at San Sebastian (1911) and Hastings (1929). He died in Ljubljana on 10 October 1962.

**Vidmar, Milan** (b. 16 December 1909) Yugoslavian chess player; awarded the title International Master in 1950. He competed in the 1950 Chess Olympiad; his best tournament results are equal second with his father, Dr Milan Vidmar, at Ljubljana (1945) and fifth at Belgrade (1948).

**Vienna (1873)** a tournament with twelve competitors, each playing a three-game match against each of the others, won by Steinitz (who beat Blackburne in a play-off match).

**Vienna (1882)** a double-round tournament, one of the longest ever held, with eighteen competitors. Wenawer and Steinitz tied for first place (with a score of 24 each) ahead of Mason (23).

**Vienna (1898)** a double-round tournament with nineteen competitors, won by Tarrasch (who scored 27½) ahead of Janowski (25½) and Steinitz (23½). It was the longest tournament ever held.

**Vienna Game** an opening sequence: 1. P–K4, P–K4 2. *N–QB3*. White develops a piece and prepares to advance his King Bishop pawn, transposing into the King's Gambit. Black's most common immediate reply: 2 . . ., N–KB3. This opening was analyzed by Hamppe, a Viennese player, in the late 1840s and was first seen in tournament play in

Vienna Game

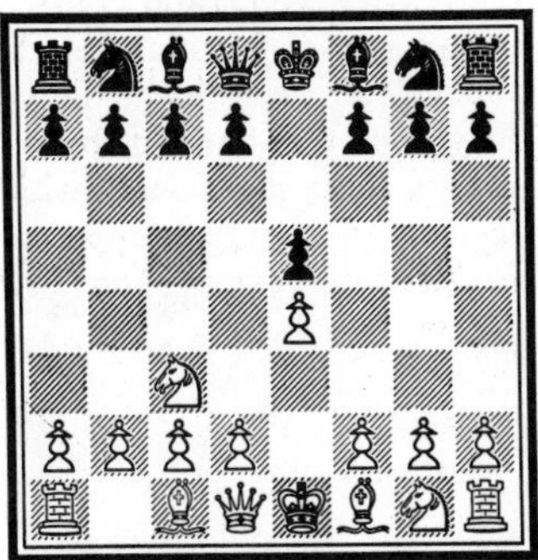

Position after 2. N–QB3

the Vienna Congress (1873).

**Vizantiades, Lazaros** (b. 2 April 1938) Greek chess player; awarded the title International Master in 1968. (1976 Elo rating: 2280)

**Vladimirov, Boris** (b. 17 May 1929) Soviet chess player; awarded the title International Master in 1963. (1976 Elo rating: 2445)

**Vogt, Lothar** (b. 17 January 1952) East German chess player; awarded the titles International Master in 1973 and International Grandmaster in 1976. (1976 Elo rating: 2480)

**Volga Gambit** the prototype of the Benkö Gambit. After: 1. P–Q4, N–KB3 2. P–QB4, P–B4 3. P–Q5, P–QN4, Black would meet 4. P × P, with 4 . . ., P–K3 rather than with Benkö's recommendation of 4 . . ., P–QR3 followed eventually by . . ., P–KN3.

**Von der Lasa** see **Lasa, Baron Tassilo von Heydebrand und der.**

**Vukić, Milan** (b. 1 April 1942) Yugoslavian chess player; awarded the titles International Master in 1967 and International Grandmaster in 1975. He was Yugoslavian Champion in 1974. Other results include firsts at Banjaluka (1974) and Varna (1975) and seconds at Vinkovci (1974) and Bajmok (1975). (1976 Elo rating: 2510)

**Vuković, Vladimir** (1898–1975) Yugoslavian chess player, arbiter, and author; awarded the titles International Master in 1951 and International Judge in 1952.

For many years Vuković edited *Sahovsky Glasnik*, the official periodical of the Yugoslavian chess federation. Among the books he wrote are *The Art of Attack* and *The Chess Sacrifice*.

# W

**Wade, Robert G.** (b. 10 April 1921) British chess player; awarded the titles International Master in 1950 and International Judge in 1958. Born in New Zealand, he was New Zealand Champion three times and was British Champion in 1952 and 1970. He competed for England in the Chess Olympiads of 1954, 1956, 1958, 1960, 1962 and 1972. (1976 Elo rating: 2360)

**Wagner, Heinrich** (1888–1959) German chess player; awarded the title International Master in 1953. He was born on 9 August 1888. Wagner competed in the Chess Olympiads of 1927, 1928, 1930 where he had the second highest score for a reserve player (+8 −1 =5) and 1931. He retired from competitive chess in the 1930s and died in Hamburg on 24 June 1959.

**Walker, George** (1803–1879) leading English chess player and writer on chess; born on 13 March 1803. After his teacher, William Lewis, retired in 1827 Walker was regarded as one of the strongest players in England. In 1831 he was one of the founders of the Westminster Club and eight years later he founded the St George's Club. A prolific author, he was also the chess columnist of *Bell's Life* from 1834 to 1873. Walker was one of the first players to record systematically the games that he played or witnessed. He was present at all the games of the matches between La Bourdonnais and McDonnell and recorded each of them; if he had not, most of the 85 games would undoubtedly have been lost to posterity. He died on 23 April 1879.

**Ware, Preston, Jr** (1820–1890) American chess player. He was an influential member of the '*Mandarins of the Yellow Button*' of Boston. In 1882 he visited Europe and played at Vienna (1882). Here he provided Steinitz with his first defeat in nine years, but finished last of those who completed the tournament.

**war game** any type of game, especially a board game, in which the capture or immobilization of pieces plays a significant role. Many such games, including chess, are loosely based on military-type tactics and strategy. See **Kriegspiel.**

**Washington Plumbers** a founding member of the **National Chess League** and the league's first champions. It tied with the New York Threats on match points (+7 −0 =2), but was placed first on game points (+24 −6 =18). The team consisted of Lubomir Kavalek, Larry Gilden, Mark Diesen, Charles Powell, John Meyer, Robert Eberlein, Sam Greenlaw and Bill Hook.

**weak square** another name for **hole.**

***Wedding With Obstacles*** Czechoslovakian comedy film (1950) produced by Miroslaw Cikan. It features a young mechanical engineer (played by Wladimir Raz) whose principal hobby is solving chess problems.

**wedge** (Kmoch's term) a group of pawns arranged in an inverted V-shape. It can thus drive itself like a wedge into the opponent's half of the board. See ***Pawn Power in Chess*.**

**wei-chi** (or **Wei-k'i**) an ancient Chinese board game using counters of glass, stone or other materials. It has been traced back as far as the reign of the emperor Kieh Kwei (1818–1767 B.C.).

**Weinstein, Norman** American chess player; awarded the title International Master in 1975. (1976 Elo rating: 2430)

**Weinstein, Raymond** (b. 1941) American chess player; awarded the title International Master in 1961. He competed in the 1960 Chess Olympiad as second reserve, scoring 84 per cent, and also played in the

Student Olympiads of 1960 and 1961, with the best score on second board on both occasions. Weinstein qualified for the 1962 interzonal, but decided not to play and in the late 1960s increasingly withdrew from chess.

**Westerinen, Markku Heikki Julius** (b. 28 April 1944) Finnish chess player; awarded the titles International Master in 1967 and International Grandmaster in 1975. Westerinen was Finnish Champion in 1965, 1966 and 1968 and competed in the Chess Olympiads of 1962, 1964, 1966, 1968, 1970, 1972, 1974 and 1976. (1976 Elo rating: 2485)

**Westphalia Defence** an opening sequence arising out of the Queen's Gambit Declined: 1. P–Q4, P–Q4 2. P–QB4, P–K3 3. N–QB3, N–KB3 4. B–N5, QN–Q2 5. N–B3, *B–N5* 6. P×P, P×P 7. P–K3, *P–B4*. Black intends to attack on the Queen side. This defence was devised by a group of European masters while travelling to the New York tournament of 1927 on the S.S. *Westphalia*. Compare **Cambridge Springs Defence.**

**Wexler, Francisco José Bernardo** (b. 1 April 1925) Argentinian chess player; awarded the title International Master in 1959. He was Argentinian Champion in 1959 and competed in the Chess Olympiads of 1956, 1960 and 1964.

**White** the player who moves first, i.e. the one who has the light-coloured chessmen. In fact, the chessmen are unlikely to be white in colour while their counterparts are unlikely to be black as the harsh contrast would be uncomfortable to look at for long periods of time. Compare **Black.**

**White, John Griswold** (1845–1928) founder of the largest chess library in the world. White was a prominent attorney from Cleveland, Ohio who was also an avid bibliophile. Upon his death his collection of works on folklore, orientalia, and chess was left to the Cleveland Public Library of which he had been president. This bequest formed the nucleus of what is now the John G. White Collection, which contains over 20,000 books, magazines, manuscripts, town records etc. on chess, as well as more than 25,000 duplicates in other languages.

**white-square weakness** inability to control the light squares of the chessboard. This normally arises when the white-square Bishop (White's King Bishop or Black's Queen Bishop) has been captured or when too many pawns have been placed on black squares. White-square weakness allows the opponent to station his men on the light squares, where they are relatively immune from attack, and often provides undefended open lines for the opponent's pieces to penetrate the defences. For instance, when the fianchettoed Bishop of a castled King is captured the enemy Queen can often move along the unguarded long diagonal to deliver checkmate.

The discovery of white and black square weaknesses was one of Steinitz's most important contributions to chess theory. Compare **black-square weakness.** See **hole.**

**White to play and win** the most common task in problems and studies. By convention, it is White that carries out checkmate in the two- and three-move problems rather than Black.

**wild** relating to a move that carries a high degree of risk. In annotations it will be followed by the symbol [!?] when the annotator believes it to be dangerous but good and by [?!] when he believes it to be unsound. See **risk.**

**Wilkes Barre variation** an opening sequence arising out of the Two Knight's Defence: 1. P–K4, P–K4 2. N–KB3; N–QB3 3. B–B4, N–B3 4. N–N5, *B–B4!?* Black sacrifices his King Bishop pawn in return for swift development and a dangerous counterattack. White's usual immediate replies: 5. P–Q4 5. N×BP or 5. B×Pch. It was devised by the Wilkes Barre Club, an American (Pennsylvania) club that used it in correspondence games in the 1920s and 1930s.

**Wilson, Thomas Bright** (1843–1915) British amateur chess player; member of the Manchester Chess Club and inventor of the first mechanical chess clock (first used in London in 1883). See **chess clock.**

**Winawer Variation** an opening sequence arising out of the French Defence: 1. P–K4, P–K3 2. P–Q4, P–Q4 3. N–QB3, *B–N5*. With this pin Black begins a strong Queen-side attack, while White normally counterattacks on the opposite wing. The most common continuation is: 4. P–K5. This variation, which is one of the strongest continuations of the French Defence, is named after the nineteenth-century Polish player Simon Winawer.

**wing** another name for **flank.** The King's wing comprises the files of the King Bishop, King Knight and the King Rook while the Queen's wing comprises the files of the Queen Bishop, Queen Knight and Queen Rook.

***Winning Chess*** a book by Irving Chernev and Fred Reinfeld. Its purpose is to improve the reader's attacking play by familiarizing him with combinations. Each basic attacking theme – e.g., the discovered attack, pin or attack on a vulnerable back rank – is described with the aid of numerous diagrams. After each theme has been described the reader can test himself with a quiz to discover his grasp of that combination. The book was first published in 1949 and uses descriptive notation.

***Winning Chess Traps*** 300 traps in the openings collected by Irving Chernev. The traps are grouped together by their openings, which are given space in relation to their popularity. Thus 52 winning combinations are shown in the Ruy Lopez and only one in the Greco Counter Gambit. This book was first published in 1947 and uses descriptive notation.

**winning move** a move that brings about a position from which victory can be achieved through a **forced sequence** of moves. In chess problems the winning move is known as the **key.**

**winning position** a position where correct play ensures a win, either of a decisive amount of material or of the game. It has been said that while ordinary players are concerned with trying to win from a winning position, experts are merely concerned with gaining one, as the technique necessary for success is taken for granted.

**winning the exchange** swapping a Bishop or Knight for a Rook. See **exchange.**

**Winter, William** (1898–1955) British chess player; British Champion in 1935 and 1936. He was born on 11 September 1898 and died on 18 December 1955.

**Wisker, John** (1846–1884) British chess player; born in Hull. He was British Champion in 1870 and 1872 and was Secretary of the British Chess Association from 1872 to 1877. Wisker went to London in 1866 to become a reporter for the *City Press* and was befriended by Staunton. He won the British Championship twice in succession, so winning the challenge cup outright. In 1872, Wisker became co-editor of the *Chess Players' Chronicle*. In 1877 he emigrated to Australia in an attempt to contain the tuberculosis from which he suffered and there became the editor of the *Australasian*. He died on 18 January 1884 from the combined effects of bronchitis and tuberculosis.

**Women's Chess Olympiad** a triennial event, held under the auspices of FIDE, in which teams of female players compete.

The first Olympiad took place in 1957, when 21 teams competed at Emmen, Holland. There was then a lapse of six years until the second Olympiad was held at Split, Yugoslavia. The Olympiads have been held regularly since 1963.

The organization of the event is similar to that of the Chess Olympiads, but the smaller number of teams that enter means that preliminary rounds do not always have to be held. A second difference is that the teams themselves are smaller, consisting of only two players and a reserve. This number was enlarged to three players plus reserve at Haifa (1976). Also called **Women's World Team Championship.**

**Women's World Championship** this was first held in London in 1927, to coincide with the fourth congress of FIDE and the first Chess Olympiad. The event, which was a round-robin tournament with twelve competitors from eight countries, was won by Vera Menchik with 10½ points out of 11. She successfully defended her title in six later championships and two matches up to the outbreak of World War II. Her death in an air-raid in 1944 left the title vacant and in 1949 FIDE organized a sixteen-player round-robin tournament to find her successor. This was the first Women's World Championship in which Soviet players competed; it was won by one of their representatives, Ludmila Rudenko.

In 1953, zonal and Candidates' tournaments were introduced and have been retained for every subsequent championship. The final has always been a match between the World Champion and the winner of the Candidates' tournament, with the exception of 1956 when there was a match-tournament with the World Champion, the ex-champion, and the winner of the Candidates' tournament competing.

The outstanding female player of the post-war era is undoubtedly the fifth World Champion, Nona Gaprindashvili, who won the title in 1962. She has successfully defended it in five matches.

In the 50 years since the title Women's World Champion was created, there have been only six holders:

1927–1944 Vera Menchik
1944–1949 (Vacant)
1949–1953 Ludmila Rudenko
1953–1956 Elizaveta Bykova
1956–1958 Olga Rubstova
1958–1962 Elizaveta Bykova
1962–1978 Nona Gaprindashvili
1978– Maya Chiburdanidze

**Women's World Team Championship** another name for **Women's Chess Olympiad.**

***Wonders and Curiosities of Chess*** an anthology of odd chess facts compiled by Irving Chernev. For instance, it tells which World Champion was once arrested as a spy, gives the score of a game where Capablanca received odds of a Queen and reveals which player had the worst-ever tournament performance (+0 −26 =0). This book is a revised and enlarged version of a book, *Curious Chess Facts*, which was published in 1937. In its new format it was first published in 1974 and uses descriptive notation.

**won ending** an ending where winning is purely a matter of technique and book knowledge. From it, a win can be demonstrated through some sequence of forced moves which can often be found in textbooks on the endings. See **winning position.**

**Wood, Baruch H.** (b. 13 July 1909) British chess player; founder, publisher and editor of the periodical *Chess* and chess correspondent of *The Daily Telegraph* and *The Illustrated London News*. He played for the British Chess Federation in the Olympiad at Buenos Aires (1939) and has represented the United Kingdom in several international tournaments. Wood is a former British Correspondence Chess Champion (1944–1945).

**woodpusher** a very weak player who has no plans and little perception of the plans of his opponent. He simply 'pushes' his men, often made of wood, around the board. Also called **woodthumper.**

**woodthumper** another name for a **woodpusher.**

**World Blitz Championship** an international tournament that was held in Herceg Novi, Yugoslavia in 1970 immediately after the 'match of the century' between the U.S.S.R. and the rest of the world. It was a double-round tournament of twelve players in which each had only five minutes to make all his moves of a game.

The tournament was won by Fischer with 19 points out of 22 followed by Tal (14½), Korchnoi (14), and Petrosian (13½). The size of Fischer's victory highlighted his phenomenally good form following his return to international chess, but was slightly unexpected as Petrosian and Tal were previously considered to be the world's best blitz players. See: **U.S.S.R. v Rest of the World.**

**World Cadet Championship** an unofficial international tournament held annually to discover the world's best player under 18 years of age. It was inaugurated in 1975, when it was won by the British player

Jonathan Mestel and remained in British possession the following year through the victory of David Goodman. The event is run under the Swiss System.

**World Champion** the chess title of World Champion was not considered to be official prior to Wilhelm Steinitz, although there is no doubt that several players before him (notably Anderssen and Morphy) were in fact the leading players of their day and most certainly deserve to be considered world champions. Since 1948, awarding of the title World Champion has been under the direct control of FIDE. Prior to then, the winner of championship matches could determine whom he would next play to defend the title and was able to name his own terms and accept or reject the suggested venue. The world title was formerly considered to be the personal property of the holder. This led to abuses in which the champion might refuse to play his strongest potential opponent or even refuse to defend his title at all for periods of several years. Lasker, for example, did not defend his title for nearly ten years (1898–1907).

The following table lists the official World Champions and the inclusive years of their reigns:

| | |
|---|---|
| Wilhelm Steinitz | 1866–1894 |
| Emanuel Lasker | 1894–1921 |
| José Raoúl Capablanca | 1921–1927 |
| Alexander Alekhine | 1927–1935 |
| Max Euwe | 1935–1937 |
| Alexander Alekhine | 1937–1946 |
| Mikhail M. Botvinnik | 1948–1957 |
| Vasily Smyslov | 1957–1958 |
| Mikhail M. Botvinnik | 1958–1960 |
| Mikhail Tal | 1960–1961 |
| Mikhail M. Botvinnik | 1961–1963 |
| Tigran Petrosian | 1963–1969 |
| Boris Spassky | 1969–1972 |
| Robert J. Fischer | 1972–1975 |
| Anatoly E. Karpov | 1975– |

**World Championship qualifying cycle** the three-year process to determine the challenger for the next World Championship match. Since 1948 the stages in this cycle have been the **zonal tournaments,** the **interzonal tournaments** and the **Candidates' tournaments** or **Candidates' matches.**

At present the world is divided into ten zones, which all hold triennial zonal tournaments in the same year as the World Championship match of the previous cycle. Each nation is allocated a number of places based upon the strength of its chess players and selects its representatives by its own criteria. The leading players in the zonals then qualify for the interzonal tournaments with other players who have been nominated by FIDE. Until 1970 only one interzonal was held in each qualifying cycle; since 1973 two interzonals have been held. The leading players in the interzonals then proceed to the next stage, which was a Candidates' tournament until 1962; since 1965 it has been a series of Candidates' matches. There they are joined by the loser of the previous World Championship match and the player who was second in the previous series of Candidates' matches; all compete in a series of knock-out matches. The final winner becomes the challenger for the next World Championship match. This whole sifting process takes four years, but as the cycles overlap there are only three years between each zonal, interzonal, etc.

***World Chess Championship 1957*** an account of the 1957 World Championship match by H. Golombek. The author was the Chief Arbiter of this match and provides a brief history of the World Championship, biographies of the two contestants (Botvinnik and Smyslov) and comprehensive annotations and commentaries on the games. There is a brief section on the theoretical value of the openings used plus contributions by Botvinnik and Smyslov. The book was first published in 1957 and uses descriptive notation.

**World Chess Federation** another name for the **Fédération Internationale des Échecs** (International Chess Federation).

**World Correspondence Chess Championship** another name for **Correspondence World Championship.**

**World Junior Championship** an annual international tournament held to discover the world's best young player. Each member-nation of FIDE may nominate one player aged under 20 by 20 September of that year, except for the host nation which may nominate two competitors. The winner of the tournament automatically becomes an International Master. Past winners include Boris Spassky (1955), Florin Gheorghiu (1963), Anatoly Karpov (1969), and Tony Miles (1974).

The first World Junior Championship was held in Coventry and Birmingham, England in 1951 and the event was repeated biennially until 1973. Initially the tournament was either a round-robin or consisted of preliminaries and graded finals. Since 1975 the tournament has been run under the Swiss System.

*World Junior Champions*

| | | |
|---|---|---|
| 1951 | Boris Ivkov | (Yugoslavia) |
| 1953 | Oscar Panno | (Argentina) |
| 1955 | Boris Spassky | (U.S.S.R) |
| 1957 | William Lombardy | (United States) |
| 1959 | Carlos Bielicki | (Argentina) |
| 1961 | Bruno Parma | (Yugoslavia) |
| 1963 | Florin Gheorghiu | (Romania) |
| 1965 | Bojan Kurajica | (Yugoslavia) |
| 1967 | Julio Kaplan | (Puerto Rico) |
| 1969 | Antoly Karpov | (U.S.S.R.) |
| 1971 | Werner Hug | (Switzerland) |
| 1973 | Alexander Belyavsky | (U.S.S.R.) |
| 1974 | Anthony Miles | (England) |
| 1975 | Valery Chekhov | (U.S.S.R.) |
| 1976 | Mark Diesen | (United States) |

***World of Chess, The*** an extensive survey of the history of chess and the contemporary chess scene written by Anthony Saidy and Norman Lessing. As well as exploring the relatively unknown areas of chess, they analyse a large number of games and examine the interaction between the styles and the temperaments of the world's greatest players. The book was first published in 1974 and uses descriptive notation.

**World Student Team Championship** the official title of the **Student Olympiad.**

**World Team Championship** one of the official titles of the **Chess Olympiad.**

**Wurzburger trap** a trap that arises in the Vienna Game: 1. P–K4, P–K4 2. N–QB3, N–KB3 3. P–KB4, P–Q4 4. BP×P, N×P 5. *P–Q3*, Q–R5ch? 6. P–N3, N×P 7. N–B3, Q–R4 8. *N×P!* For instance, Black quickly loses after: 8 . . ., N–R3 9. N–B4, Q–R3 10. N–R3, Q moves 11. P×N, while his alternatives also lead to a good game for White.

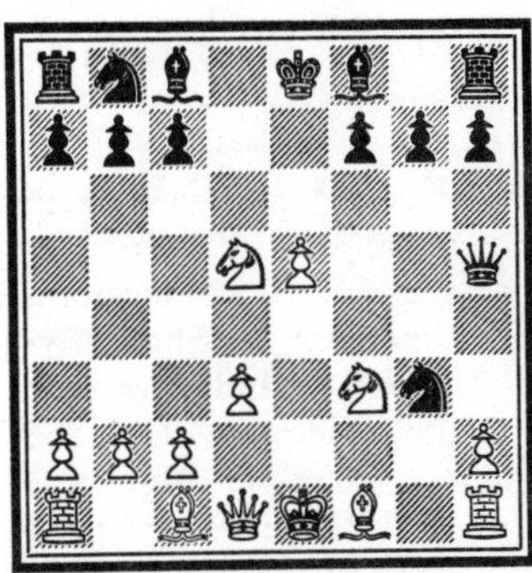

Position after 8. N×P! (threatening 9. N×Pch, winning the Rook)

**Wyvill formation** a pawn formation that favours Black.

White has a crippling weakness in his doubled pawns and consequently is able to attack only on the King side. Strategically Black's best plan is to castle on the Queen side and anchor a Knight at QB4, eventually opening the Queen Bishop file by advancing the pawn on that file.

This formation was named after the English player Wyvill by Euwe and Kramer, who believe him to be the first to analyse it systematically.

# X

**X** *symbol for* captures. It is used in both algebraic notation and descriptive notation, although algebraic notation also uses the symbol ':' to represent this. For example, e4×f5 (algebraic notation) and P×P (descriptive notation) both mean pawn captures pawn. This symbol was only widely adopted as recently as the second half of the nineteenth century. Previously, moves had been written out in full. See **algebraic notation, descriptive notation.**

**x-ray** another name for a **skewer.**

# Y

**Yanofsky, Daniel Abraham** (b. 26 March 1925) Canadian chess player; awarded the title International Master in 1964 and the title International Grandmaster in the same year. (1976 Elo rating: 2430)

**Yates, Frederick Dewhurst** (1884–1932) British chess player; born in Birstall, Yorkshire on 16 January 1884. He was British Champion in 1913, 1914, 1921, 1926, 1928 and 1931 and competed in the Chess Olympiads of 1927 and 1930. Although trained as an accountant, Yates became a professional chess player at a time when this was extremely rare. To support himself he was for many years the chess columnist of the *Manchester Guardian* and was the author (with Winter) of *Modern Master Play* as well as the writer of accounts of the World Championship matches between Alekhine and Capablanca and Alekhine and Bogoljubov.

Yates performed indifferently in international tournaments, often dropping points against the weaker players after having defeated the best. At his best, however, he was capable of defeating anyone. His entry to the tournament at Hamburg (1910) was criticized by Tarrasch on the grounds that Yates was too weak a player – and, indeed, Yates won only one game in the whole tournament, but that was against Tarrasch in 33 moves! Other notable wins were a victory at Carlsbad (1923) over Alekhine after an 18-move combination that won the game a brilliancy prize and a win at San Remo (1930) in a game against Vidmar that was described by Alekhine as being the finest played since the war.

Yates died in London 11 November 1932 as the result of a defective gas meter in his bedroom.

**Young, Franklin Knowles** (1857–1931) American chess player and writer. In his largely abstruse books on the game (including *Field Book of Chess Generalship* and *Major and Minor Tactics of Chess*), he applied military terms to chess.

**Yudovich, Mikhail** (b. 8 June 1911) Soviet chess player; awarded the title International Master in 1950. He is a member of the Praesidium of the Soviet chess federation. Yudovich is a professional journalist and has written several books on chess, notably *The Soviet School of Chess* which he wrote in collaboration with Alexander Kotov.

**Yugoslav Attack** an opening sequence arising out of the Dragon Variation of the Sicilian Defence: 1. P–K4, P–QB4 2. N–KB3, P–Q3 3. P–Q4, P×P 4. N×P, N–KB3 5. N–QB3, P–KN3 6. B–K3, B–N2 7. *P–B3*. White defends both his King pawn and his KN4 square with this move and prepares for a King-side attack, usually after playing Q–Q2, B–QB4, O–O–O and advancing the King-side pawns.

This variation was devised in the 1950s by a group of Yugoslavian players and since that time has firmly established itself as White's greatest threat to the Dragon Variation.

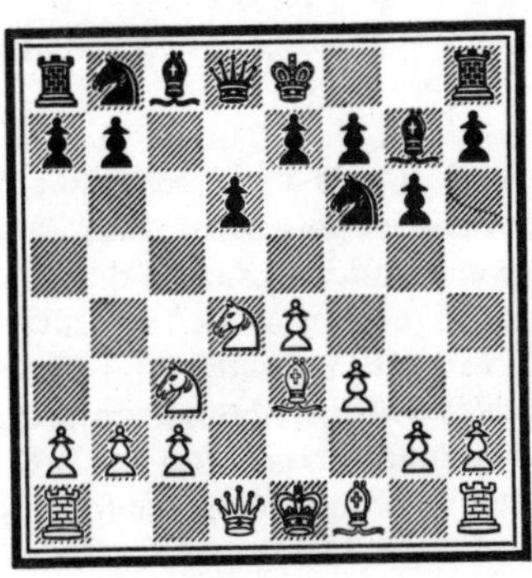

Position after 7. P–B3

**Yugoslav Defence** another name for the **Pirc Defence.**

**Yugoslav Variation** an opening sequence arising out of the King's Indian Defence: 1. P–Q4, N–KB3 2. P–QB4, P–KN3 3. P–KN3, B–N2 4. B–N2, O–O 5. N–QB3, P–Q3 6. N–B3, *P–B4*. Black intends attacking on the Queen side. The most common continuation is: 7. O–O.

This system was invented in the 1950s by a group of Yugoslavian players including Gligorić.

# Z

**Zagorovsky, Vladimir P.** (b. 1925) Soviet chess player; winner of the fourth Correspondence World Championship (1 February 1962 to 1 March 1965), in which he did not lose a single game. As a result, he was awarded the title International Grandmaster of Correspondence Chess.

**Zaitsev, Alexander** (b. 15 June 1935) Soviet chess player; awarded the titles International Master in 1965 and International Grandmaster in 1967.

**Zaitsev, Igor** (b. 27 May 1939) Soviet chess player; awarded the titles International Master in 1970 and International Grandmaster in 1976. (1976 Elo rating: 2435)

**Zak, Vladimir** (b. 1913) Soviet chess player; the first trainer of Boris Spassky. He co-authored a book on the King's Gambit (with Victor Korchnoi).

**Zatulovskaya, Tatyana Yakovlevna** (b. 8 December 1935) Soviet chess player; awarded the title International Woman Master in 1961. She was Soviet Woman Champion in 1962, competed in the Women's Chess Olympiads of 1963 and 1966, and qualified for the Women's Candidates' tournaments of 1964 and 1967, and Candidates' matches in 1971.

**Zebra** a Fairy chesspiece that moves like a Knight, but has a longer range. It is a type of Leaper. While a Knight moves 1 × 2 squares, a Zebra moves 2 × 3 squares. A Zebra on QB1 could thus move to KB3, K4, or QR4. Compare **Camel, Giraffe.**

**Zinnowitz Variation** an opening sequence arising out of the King's Indian Defence: 1. P–Q4, N–KB3 2. P–QB4, P–KN3 3. N–QB3, B–N2 4. P–K4, P–Q3 5. *N–B3, O–O* 6. *B–N5*. White indirectly prevents the advance of Black's King pawn, forcing him to come to a decision as to his pawn formation. Black's best immediate reply: 6 . . ., P–KR3. This variation became popular in the late 1960s after the East German Grandmaster Burkhard Malich had successfully deployed it at Zinnowitz (1966) in East Germany.

**Zita, František** (b. 29 November 1909) Czechoslovakian chess player; awarded the title International Master in 1961. He was Czechoslovakian Champion in 1943 and competed in the Chess Olympiads of 1937, 1939, 1952 and 1954. He also took part in the first European Team Championship, which was held in 1957.

**Znosko-Borovsky, Eugène Alexandrovitch** (1884–1954) Russian emigré chess player and writer; born in St Petersburg on 16 August 1884 and educated at the Lyceum of Alexander I.

He fought and was wounded both in the Russo-Japanese War and in World War I. In the Russian Revolution he fought in the White forces and was evacuated to France in 1920; he lived there until his death.

His first international tournament was Ostend (1906), where he received a brilliancy prize for his victory over Burn. Although he had tournament successes, such as first at Paris (1930), and victories over leading players, such as Capablanca, Euwe, Janowski, Rubinstein and Tarrasch, he is primarily remembered for his publications. They include *The Art of Chess Combinations*, *Capablanca and Alekhine*, *The Middle Game in Chess*, and *How Not to Play Chess*.

Znosko-Borovsky was also a noted blindfold player. He died on 31 December 1954.

**zonal tournament** the initial stage in the three-year qualifying cycle to select a challenger in the subsequent match against the World Champion.

Zonal tournaments began in 1947, when two were held in Europe.

Since then they have changed slightly. FIDE has divided the world into a number of zones (at present ten) and each holds a zonal tournament on a round-robin basis. The competitors are selected by their national chess federations; the number of competitors each country has in the zonal tournament depends on its strength in chess at that time. The highest-placed players in each zonal tournament qualify for the interzonal tournaments of the succeeding year. The number of qualifiers from each zonal depends on the strength of the zone. Also called **zonal**.

**Zook the book** *nickname of* **Bernard Zuckerman.**

**Zuckerman, Bernard** (b. 31 March 1943) American chess player; awarded the title International Master in 1970. He was equal first in the 1976 World Open. Zuckerman has an enormous knowledge of opening theory and is nicknamed 'Zook the book'. (1976 Elo rating: 2450)

**zugzwang** *German for* move compulsion. A player is said to be in zugzwang when any move he makes will result in the loss of a piece or otherwise seriously weaken his position, though the opponent presents no concrete threat. In the diagrammed position, Sämisch (White) resigned for he had no good moves: he was completely in zugzwang. If he played 26. P–R3 or P–N3, then 26 . . ., P–QR4; if 26. K–R2 or P–N4, then 26 . . ., R(B4); if 26. QR moves, then 26 . . ., R–K7; if 26. B–QB1, then 26 . . ., B × N!.

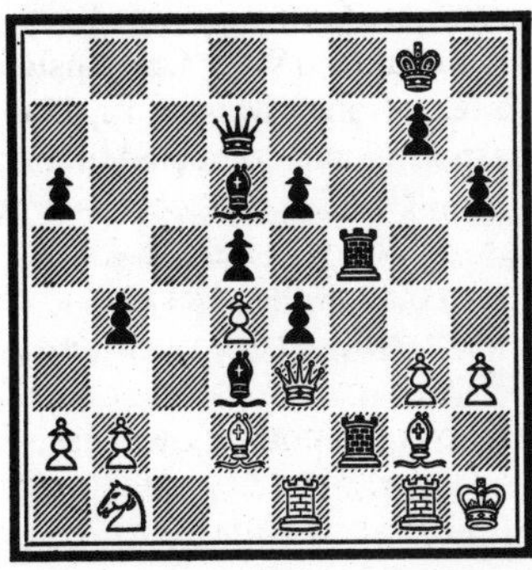

Sämisch vs. Nimzovitch (Copenhagen, 1923)

**Zuidema, Coenraad** (b. 29 August 1942) Dutch chess player; awarded the title International Master in 1964. He competed in the Chess Olympiads of 1964, 1966 and 1968. (1976 Elo rating: 2445)

**Zukertort Gambit** an opening sequence: 1. N–KB3, P–Q4 2. *P–K4*. Although rarely played, it has a plethora of names: according to the *Dictionaire des Echecs* (as reported in the May 1976 issue of B.C.M.), it is also known as the **Abonyi Gambit, Budapest Gambit** (with colours reversed), **Lemberg Gambit, Lvov Gambit, Polish Gambit** and the **Tennyson Gambit.**

**Zukertort, Johannes Hermann** (1842–1888) World Championship contender; born in Riga. He graduated with a doctorate of medicine from

Breslau University in 1865 and served with the Prussian Army in the campaigns against Austria and France, receiving decorations for gallantry. He was fluent in eleven languages and was a skilled swordsman and marksman as well as being a talented pianist.

He first became well-known through his skill in blindfold chess and in 1876 he set a world record of sixteen games (+12 −1 =3) which lasted for 24 years. From 1867 to 1871 he co-edited the *Neue Berliner Schachzeitung* with Anderssen, his former chess teacher, and played two matches against him, losing in 1868 (+3 −8 =1) and winning in 1872 (+5 −2 =0). He was invited to compete at London (1872) because of this victory, but only finished third. Shortly afterwards he played Steinitz in a match and was decisively beaten (+1 −7 =4). Zukertort remained in Britain (becoming a citizen in 1878) and founded the *Chess Monthly* in which he carried out fierce polemics with Steinitz, who wrote in *The Field*.

Later results included a second place at Leipzig (1877), and a first at Paris (1878) and London (1883) where he finished three points ahead of Steinitz. He also won matches against the French Champion Rosenthal in 1880 (+7 −2 =5) and Blackburne in 1881 (+7 −2 =5). By this time many considered him the world's strongest player.

In 1886, after two years of negotiations, a match between Steinitz and Zukertort was held successively in New York, St Louis, and New Orleans (since Steinitz had emigrated to America in 1883). Interest was heightened by the contrast between the revolutionary play of Steinitz and Zukertort's romanticism and by the acrimony between the two. At a New York banquet the speaker proposed a toast to 'the World Champion' and both Steinitz and Zukertort stood up in acknowledgement. Zukertort built up a large lead in New York, but Steinitz drew even in St Louis and won in New Orleans where Zukertort's health broke down (+5 −10 =5). According to Lasker, 'The one who was the greater thinker won the day from the one who had the greater talent'.

Zukertort returned to London where he died on 20 June 1888.

**Zurich Variation** an opening sequence arising out of the Nimzo-Indian Defence: 1. P–Q4, N–KB3 2. P–QB4, P–K3 3. N–QB3, B–N5 4. Q–B2, *N–B3*. Although this move blocks the Queen Bishop pawn, the invariable follow-up of P–Q3 and P–K4 should provide equality. The most common continuation is: 5. N–B3, P–Q3 6. P–QR3.

This variation was first used at Zurich (1934), and is also known as the Milner-Barry Variation, after the English master who pioneered it.

**Zvorikina, Kira Alekseyevna** (b. 29 September 1920) Soviet chess player; awarded the title International Woman Master in 1952. She was Soviet Woman Champion in 1951, 1953, 1956, 1957 and 1958. She also competed in the Women's Chess Olympiads of 1957 and 1963. Zvorikina took part in the Women's Candidates' tournaments of 1952, 1955, 1959, 1961 and 1964. She won this event in 1959 which qualified her to meet the World Champion Elizaveta Bikova in a match for the title in 1959. However she was defeated by Bikova (+2 −6 =5).

**Zwaig, Arne** (b. 6 February 1947) Norwegian chess player; awarded the

Zurich Variation

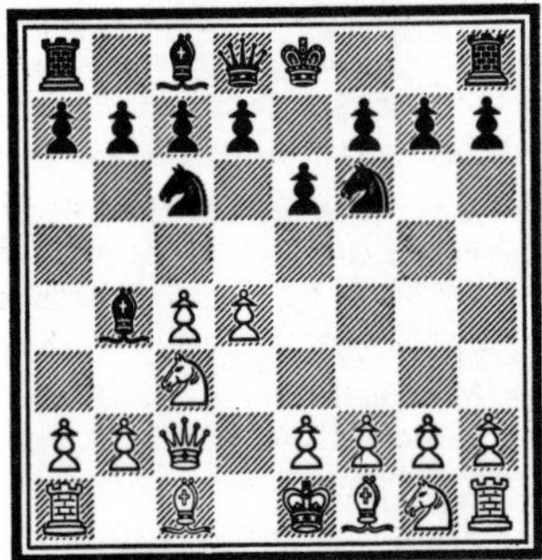

Position after 4 . . ., N–B3

title International Master in 1975. Zwaig came first at Hamar (1975) and won the Norwegian Championship in the same year. (1976 Elo rating: 2475)

**zwischenzug** *German for* intermediate move. A move which interrupts an apparently forced sequence. A common example is when a player delivers check before capturing a man that he had left en prise.

# Appendix

## 1977 Elo Ratings (⩾ 2400)

| Elo Rating | Name and Title | Country |
|---|---|---|
| 2780 | Fischer (IGM) | U.S. |
| 2690 | Karpov (IGM) | U.S.S.R. |
| 2645 | Korchnoi (IGM) | (stateless) |
| 2645 | Petrosian (IGM) | U.S.S.R. |
| 2635 | Mecking (IGM) | Brazil |
| 2630 | Botvinnik (IGM) | U.S.S.R. |
| 2625 | L. Portisch (IGM) | Hungary |
| 2620 | Hort (IGM) | Czechoslovakia |
| 2620 | Polugayevsky (IGM) | U.S.S.R. |
| 2620 | Tal (IGM) | U.S.S.R. |
| 2615 | Larsen (IGM) | Denmark |
| 2615 | Ljubojević (IGM) | Yugoslavia |
| 2610 | Spassky (IGM) | U.S.S.R. |
| 2600 | Hübner (IGM) | West Germany |
| 2595 | Ribli (IGM) | Hungary |
| 2595 | Romanishin (IGM) | U.S.S.R. |
| 2595 | Smyslov (IGM) | U.S.S.R. |
| 2590 | Geller (IGM) | U.S.S.R. |
| 2590 | Timman (IGM) | Netherlands |
| 2590 | Tseshkovsky (IGM) | U.S.S.R. |
| 2585 | Gulko (IGM) | U.S.S.R. |
| 2580 | R. Byrne (IGM) | U.S. |
| 2575 | Smejkal (IGM) | Czechoslovakia |
| 2570 | Gufeld (IGM) | U.S.S.R. |
| 2565 | Andersson (IGM) | Sweden |
| 2565 | Balashov (IGM) | U.S.S.R. |
| 2565 | Gligorić (IGM) | Yugoslavia |
| 2565 | Sax (IGM) | Hungary |
| 2565 | Vasyukov (IGM) | U.S.S.R. |
| 2560 | Bronstein (IGM) | U.S.S.R. |
| 2560 | Olafsson (IGM) | Iceland |
| 2555 | Belyavsky (IGM) | U.S.S.R. |
| 2555 | Evans (IGM) | U.S. |
| 2555 | Kholmov (IGM) | U.S.S.R. |
| 2555 | Miles (IGM) | U.K. |
| 2555 | Quinteros (IGM) | Argentina |
| 2555 | Uhlmann (IGM) | East Germany |
| 2550 | Kuzmin (IGM) | U.S.S.R. |
| 2550 | Liberson (IGM) | Israel |
| 2550 | Panno (IGM) | Argentina |
| 2550 | Torre (IGM) | Philippines |
| 2545 | Browne (IGM) | U.S. |
| 2545 | Gheorghiu (IGM) | Romania |
| 2545 | Kavalek (IGM) | U.S. |
| 2545 | Krogius (IGM) | U.S.S.R. |
| 2545 | Vaganian (IGM) | U.S.S.R. |
| 2540 | Lutikov (IGM) | U.S.S.R. |
| 2540 | Pfleger (IGM) | West Germany |
| 2540 | Savon (IGM) | U.S.S.R. |
| 2540 | Tukmakov (IGM) | U.S.S.R. |
| 2535 | Csom (IGM) | Hungary |
| 2535 | Dzhindzhikhashvili (IM) | Israel |
| 2535 | Furman (IGM) | U.S.S.R. |
| 2535 | Gipslis (IGM) | U.S.S.R. |
| 2535 | Malich (IGM) | East Germany |

| Elo Rating | Name and Title | Country |
|---|---|---|
| 2530 | Adorjan (IGM) | Hungary |
| 2530 | Euwe (IGM) | Netherlands |
| 2530 | Kurajica (IGM) | Yugoslavia |
| 2530 | Lombardy (IGM) | U.S. |
| 2530 | Parma (IGM) | Yugoslavia |
| 2530 | Sosonko (IGM) | Netherlands |
| 2530 | Szabó (IGM) | Hungary |
| 2530 | Taimanov (IGM) | U.S.S.R. |
| 2525 | Dvoretsky (IM) | U.S.S.R. |
| 2525 | Hulak (IGM) | Yugoslavia |
| 2525 | Lein (IGM) | (stateless) |
| 2525 | Najdorf (IGM) | Argentina |
| 2525 | Suetin (IGM) | U.S.S.R. |
| 2525 | Unzicker (IGM) | West Germany |
| 2525 | Velimirović (IGM) | Yugoslavia |
| 2520 | Averbakh (IGM) | U.S.S.R. |
| 2520 | Chekhov (IM) | U.S.S.R. |
| 2520 | Rogoff (IM) | U.S. |
| 2520 | Schmid (IGM) | West Germany |
| 2520 | Sigurjonsson (IGM) | Iceland |
| 2520 | Sveshnikov (IM) | U.S.S.R. |
| 2515 | Karasev (IM) | U.S.S.R. |
| 2515 | Makarichev (IGM) | U.S.S.R. |
| 2510 | Darga (IGM) | West Germany |
| 2510 | Gurgenidze (IGM) | U.S.S.R. |
| 2510 | Ivkov (IGM) | Yugoslavia |
| 2510 | Keene (IGM) | U.K. |
| 2510 | Matulović (IGM) | Yugoslavia |
| 2510 | Nei (IM) | U.S.S.R. |
| 2510 | Rashkovsky (IM) | U.S.S.R. |
| 2510 | Razuvayev (IGM) | U.S.S.R. |
| 2505 | Alburt (IM) | U.S.S.R. |
| 2505 | Matanović (IGM) | Yugoslavia |
| 2505 | Sanguinetti (IM) | Argentina |
| 2505 | Timoshchenko (IM) | U.S.S.R. |
| 2500 | Jul. Bolbochan (IM) | Argentina |
| 2500 | Farago (IGM) | Hungary |
| 2500 | Filip (IGM) | Czechoslovakia |
| 2500 | Knaak (IGM) | East Germany |
| 2500 | Knežević (IGM) | Yugoslavia |
| 2500 | Kotov (IGM) | U.S.S.R. |
| 2500 | Radulov (IGM) | Bulgaria |
| 2495 | Kovacević (IGM) | Yugoslavia |
| 2495 | Rajković (IM) | Yugoslavia |
| 2495 | Tarjan (IGM) | U.S. |
| 2495 | Tringov (IGM) | Bulgaria |
| 2495 | Vadasz (IGM) | Hungary |
| 2495 | Vogt (IGM) | East Germany |
| 2495 | Vukić (IGM) | Yugoslavia |
| 2495 | Zaitsev (IGM) | U.S.S.R. |
| 2490 | Addison (IM) | U.S. |
| 2490 | Bukić (IGM) | Yugoslavia |
| 2490 | Diez del Corral (IGM) | Spain |
| 2490 | Hecht (IGM) | West Germany |
| 2490 | Klovan (IM) | U.S.S.R. |
| 2490 | Kochiev (IM) | U.S.S.R. |
| 2490 | Mariotti (IGM) | Italy |
| 2490 | Osnos (IM) | U.S.S.R. |
| 2490 | Reshevsky (IGM) | U.S. |
| 2490 | Schmidt (IGM) | Poland |
| 2485 | L. Espig (IM) | East Germany |
| 2485 | G. Garcia (IGM) | Colombia |

| Elo Rating | Name and Title | Country |
|---|---|---|
| 2485 | Pachman (IGM) | West Germany |
| 2485 | Pribyl (IM) | Czechoslovakia |
| 2485 | Shamkovich (IGM) | Israel |
| 2485 | Stean (IM) | U.K. |
| 2480 | Bagirov (IM) | U.S.S.R. |
| 2480 | Commons (IM) | U.S. |
| 2480 | Ostojić (IGM) | Yugoslavia |
| 2480 | Padevski (IGM) | Bulgaria |
| 2480 | Y. Sakharov (IM) | U.S.S.R. |
| 2480 | Spassov (IGM) | Bulgaria |
| 2480 | Tatai (IM) | Italy |
| 2475 | Antoshin (IGM) | U.S.S.R. |
| 2475 | W. R. Hartston (IM) | U.K. |
| 2475 | Kraidman (IGM) | Israel |
| 2475 | Marović (IGM) | Yugoslavia |
| 2475 | Nikolac (IM) | Yugoslavia |
| 2475 | Planinc (IGM) | Yugoslavia |
| 2475 | N. Weinstein (IM) | U.S. |
| 2470 | Adamski (IM) | Poland |
| 2470 | Barczay (IGM) | Hungary |
| 2470 | Donner (IGM) | Netherlands |
| 2470 | Marangunic (IM) | Yugoslavia |
| 2470 | Minić (IM) | Yugoslavia |
| 2470 | Raicević (IGM) | Yugoslavia |
| 2470 | Suttles (IGM) | Canada |
| 2470 | Yudovich (IM) | U.S.S.R. |
| 2465 | Calvo (IM) | Spain |
| 2465 | Ciocîltea (IM) | Romania |
| 2465 | Hamann (IM) | Denmark |
| 2465 | Hennings (IM) | East Germany |
| 2460 | Karaklajić (IM) | Yugoslavia |
| 2460 | O'Kelly de Galway (IGM) | Belgium |
| 2460 | Peev (IM) | Bulgaria |
| 2460 | Ree (IM) | Netherlands |
| 2460 | Sahović (IM) | Yugoslavia |
| 2460 | Udović (IGM) | Yugoslavia |
| 2460 | Zhukhovitsky (IM) | U.S.S.R. |
| 2455 | Averkin (IM) | U.S.S.R. |
| 2455 | Benkö (IGM) | U.S. |
| 2455 | Nemet (IM) | Yugoslavia |
| 2455 | Pal Petran (IM) | Hungary |
| 2455 | Plachetka (IM) | Czechoslovakia |
| 2455 | Suba (IM) | Romania |
| 2450 | Antunac (IM) | Yugoslavia |
| 2450 | Barle (IM) | Yugoslavia |
| 2450 | Dueball (IM) | West Germany |
| 2450 | Flesch (IM) | Hungary |
| 2450 | Forintos (IGM) | Hungary |
| 2450 | Jansa (IGM) | Czechoslovakia |
| 2450 | Lilienthal (IGM) | Hungary |
| 2450 | Lukacs (IM) | Hungary |
| 2450 | M. Mukhin (IM) | U.S.S.R. |
| 2450 | Podgaets (IM) | U.S.S.R. |
| 2450 | O. Rodriguez (IM) | Peru |
| 2450 | Soltis (IM) | U.S. |
| 2450 | Spraggett (IM) | Canada |
| 2450 | Szekely (IM) | Hungary |
| 2450 | Zuckerman (IM) | U.S. |
| 2450 | Zuidema (IM) | Netherlands |
| 2450 | Zwaig (IM) | Norway |
| 2445 | Anikayev (IM) | U.S.S.R. |
| 2445 | Augustin (IM) | Czechoslovakia |

| Elo Rating | Name and Title | Country |
|---|---|---|
| 2445 | Böhm (IM) | Netherlands |
| 2445 | Buljovcić (IM) | Yugoslavia |
| 2445 | Ermenkov (IM) | Bulgaria |
| 2445 | Georgadze (IM) | U.S.S.R. |
| 2445 | Hug (IM) | Switzerland |
| 2445 | Kaplan (IM) | U.S. |
| 2445 | Langeweg (IM) | Netherlands |
| 2445 | Schweber (IM) | Argentina |
| 2445 | Toran (IM) | Spain |
| 2445 | B. Vladimirov (IM) | U.S.S.R. |
| 2440 | Bisguier (IGM) | U.S. |
| 2440 | Bleiman (IM) | Israel |
| 2440 | Cuartas (IM) | Colombia |
| 2440 | Dely (IM) | Hungary |
| 2440 | Estrin (IM) | U.S.S.R. |
| 2440 | Ghitescu (IM) | Romania |
| 2440 | K. Honfi (IM) | Hungary |
| 2440 | B. Ivanović (IM) | Yugoslavia |
| 2440 | Kagan (IM) | Israel |
| 2440 | Kestler (IM) | West Germany |
| 2440 | Mohrlok (IM) | West Germany |
| 2440 | Ornstein (IM) | Sweden |
| 2440 | Sergievsky (IM) | U.S.S.R. |
| 2440 | Toth (IM) | Italy |
| 2440 | Velikov (IM) | Bulgaria |
| 2440 | Veresov (IM) | U.S.S.R. |
| 2435 | Barcza (IGM) | Hungary |
| 2435 | Bilek (IGM) | Hungary |
| 2435 | Biyiasas (IM) | Canada |
| 2435 | R. Garcia (IM) | Argentina |
| 2435 | S. Garcia (IGM) | Colombia |
| 2435 | R. Hernandez (IM) | Colombia |
| 2435 | Janosević (IGM) | Yugoslavia |
| 2435 | Kirov (IGM) | Bulgaria |
| 2435 | Krnic (IM) | Yugoslavia |
| 2435 | Liebert (IM) | East Germany |
| 2435 | Mestrović (IM) | Yugoslavia |
| 2435 | Nicevski (IM) | Yugoslavia |
| 2435 | Pilnik (IGM) | Argentina |
| 2435 | Pomar (IGM) | Spain |
| 2435 | Pytel (IM) | Poland |
| 2435 | Radashkovich (IM) | Israel |
| 2435 | Robatsch (IGM) | Austria |
| 2435 | Sofrevski (IM) | Yugoslavia |
| 2435 | Soos (IM) | West Germany |
| 2435 | Szmetan (IM) | Argentina |
| 2430 | Bogdanović (IM) | Yugoslavia |
| 2430 | Damjanović (IGM) | Yugoslavia |
| 2430 | Eliskases (IGM) | Argentina |
| 2430 | Fuchs (IM) | East Germany |
| 2430 | Gaprindashvili (IWG) | U.S.S.R. |
| 2430 | Haag (IM) | Hungary |
| 2430 | R. Jamieson (IM) | Australia |
| 2430 | Kolarov (IM) | Bulgaria |
| 2430 | Matera (IM) | U.S. |
| 2430 | Mednis (IM) | U.S. |
| 2430 | Poutiainen (IM) | Finland |
| 2430 | Radev (IM) | Bulgaria |
| 2430 | Saidy (IM) | U.S. |
| 2430 | Westerinen (IGM) | Finland |
| 2425 | Bertok (IM) | Yugoslavia |
| 2425 | Capelan (IM) | West Germany |

| Elo Rating | Name and Title | Country |
|---|---|---|
| 2425 | Ciric (IGM) | Yugoslavia |
| 2425 | Grefe (IM) | U.S. |
| 2425 | Messing (IM) | Yugoslavia |
| 2425 | Moiseev (IM) | U.S.S.R. |
| 2425 | F. Portisch (IM) | Hungary |
| 2425 | Pritchett (IM) | U.K. |
| 2425 | Sydor (IM) | Poland |
| 2425 | Teschner (IM) | West Germany |
| 2420 | Aronin (IM) | U.S.S.R. |
| 2420 | Balinas (IGM) | Poland |
| 2420 | J. Bolbochan (IM) | Argentina |
| 2420 | Bouwmeester (IM) | Netherlands |
| 2420 | J. Fernandez (IM) | Colombia |
| 2420 | Gerusel (IM) | West Germany |
| 2420 | Jakobsen (IM) | Denmark |
| 2420 | Lehmann (IM) | West Germany |
| 2420 | Marić (IM) | Yugoslavia |
| 2420 | Ogaard (IM) | Norway |
| 2420 | Pietzsch (IGM) | East Germany |
| 2420 | Rubinetti (IM) | Argentina |
| 2420 | Spiridonov (IM) | Bulgaria |
| 2420 | Yanofsky (IGM) | Canada |
| 2415 | Bellon (IM) | Spain |
| 2415 | Boey (IM) | Belgium |
| 2415 | D. Keller (IM) | Switzerland |
| 2415 | Kuijpers (IM) | Netherlands |
| 2415 | Lederman (IM) | Israel |
| 2415 | Lengyel (IGM) | Hungary |
| 2415 | Martinović (IM) | Yugoslavia |
| 2415 | Musil (IM) | Yugoslavia |
| 2415 | Partos (IM) | Romania |
| 2415 | Penrose (IM) | U.K. |
| 2410 | O. Castro (IM) | Colombia |
| 2410 | Ghizdavu (IM) | U.S. |
| 2410 | Guimard (IGM) | Argentina |
| 2410 | Kaldor (IM) | Israel |
| 2410 | Lombard (IM) | Switzerland |
| 2410 | Martz (IM) | U.S. |
| 2410 | Mikenas (IM) | U.S.S.R. |
| 2410 | Minev (IM) | Bulgaria |
| 2410 | Nunn (IM) | U.K. |
| 2410 | L. Popov (IM) | Bulgaria |
| 2410 | Rossetto (IGM) | Argentina |
| 2410 | Rukavina (IM) | Yugoslavia |
| 2410 | Vaisman (IM) | Romania |
| 2405 | Bobotsov (IGM) | Bulgaria |
| 2405 | Cortlever (IM) | Netherlands |
| 2405 | Deze (IM) | Yugoslavia |
| 2405 | Nartoch (IM) | Netherlands |
| 2405 | Johannessen (IM) | Norway |
| 2405 | Johansson (IM) | Iceland |
| 2405 | Möhring (IM) | East Germany |
| 2405 | Nun (IM) | Czechoslovakia |
| 2400 | Bednarski (IM) | Poland |
| 2400 | Duckstein (IM) | Austria |
| 2400 | Ekström (IM) | Sweden |
| 2400 | Enklaar (IM) | Netherlands |
| 2400 | Navarovsky (IM) | Hungary |
| 2400 | Vranesic (IM) | Canada |